ostic, enneth E., 21, awthorne, Nev.	Bouthot, Michael E., 19, Fall River, Mass.	Bowman, Jon E., 21, Dubach, La.	Boyce, Timothy R., 29, North Salt Lake, Utah	Brehm, Dale G.M., 23, Turlock, Calif.	Bridges, James L.D., 22, Buhl, Idaho	Bridges, Michael P., 23, Placentia, Calif.	Bright, Dean R., 32, Roseburg, Ore.
rown, effrey S., 25, rinity Center, alif.	Brown, Kyle W., 22, Newport News, Va.	Brown, Timothy D., 23, Cedar Springs, Mich.	Brown, Timothy W., 21, Sacramento, Calif.	Brozovich, Daniel A., 42, Greenville, Pa.	Bubeck, John T., 25, Collegeville, Pa.	Buckley, Ryan J., 21, Nokomis, Ill.	Bucklin, Brock L., 28, Grand Rapids, Mich.
urkart, rmer N., 26, ockville, Md.	Burke, Timothy R., 24, Hollywood, Fla.	Burnett, Jason K., 20, St. Cloud, Fla.	Burrows, Joshua C., 20, Bossier City, La.	Bustamante, Marlon A., 25, Corona, N.Y.	Butterfield, Anthony E., 19, Clovis, Calif.	Buzzard, Jason J., 31, Ukiah, Calif.	Byler, William J., 23, Ballinger, Tex.
alderon- scencio, oland E., 21, iami, Fla.	Callahan, Bobby T., 22, Jamestown, N.C.	Camilo Matos, Radhames, 24, Carolina, P.R.	Campbell, Jaime L., 25, Ephrata, Wash.	Cann, Adam L., 23, Davie, Fla.	Carbonaro, Alessandro, 28, Bethesda, Md.	Cardelli, Sean T., 20, Downers Grove, Ill.	Cardinal, Anthony O., 20, Muskegon, Mich.
arver, itchell K. Jr., arlotte, N.C.	Cashe, Alwyn C., 35, Oviedo, Fla.	Casica, Kenith, 32, Virginia Beach, Va.	Castner, Stephen W., 27, Cedarburg, Wis.	Castro, Jesse J.J., 22, Chalan Pago, Am. Samoa	Cayer, Geofrey R., 20, Fitchburg, Mass.	Cerrone, Michael A., 24, Clarksville, Tenn.	Chaires, Daniel B., 20, Tallahassee, Fla.
avez, vier Jr., 19, tler, Calif.	Chavis, LeeBernard E., 21, Hampton, Va.	Chisholm, Tyrone L., 27, Savannah, Ga.	Christensen, Ryan D., 22, Spring Lake Heights, N.J.	Christoff, David R., 25, Rossford, Ohio	Ciraso, Kristofer R., 26, Bangor, Me.	Clark, Carlton A., 22, South Royalton, Vt.	Clark, Eric D., 22, Pleasant Prairie, Wis.
ay, rrell P., 34, yetteville, N.C.	Clayton, Hayes, 29, Marietta, Ga.	Cleary, Michael J., 24, Dallas, Pa.	Clemmons, Brad A., 37, Chillicothe, Ohio	Clemons, Thomas W., 37, Leitchfield, Ky.	Cockerham, Benny G. III, 21, Conover, N.C.	Coles, Dominic R., 25, Jesup, Ga.	Collado, Jay T., 31, Columbia, S.C.

THE
PROSECUTION
OF
GEORGE W. BUSH
FOR MURDER

ALSO BY VINCENT BUGLIOSI

Reclaiming History:
The Assassination of President John F. Kennedy

Helter Skelter (with Curt Gentry)

And the Sea Will Tell (with Bruce Henderson)

Till Death Us Do Part (with Ken Hurwitz)

The Phoenix Solution:
Getting Serious about Winning America's Drug War

Outrage: The Five Reasons Why O. J. Simpson Got Away with Murder

No Island of Sanity: Paula Jones v. Bill Clinton:
The Supreme Court on Trial

The Betrayal of America: How the Supreme Court
Undermined the Constitution and Chose Our President
(with forewords by Molly Ivins and Gerry Spence)

THE
PROSECUTION
—— OF ——
GEORGE W. BUSH
FOR MURDER

VINCENT
BUGLIOSI

Vanguard Press
A Member of the Perseus Books Group

Endpapers: Detail from "The Roster of the Dead: The Conflict in Iraq: Fatalities"
from the *New York Times*, National Section, 1/1/2007 Issue, page(s) A23.
Reprinted with permission.

DESIGN BY JANE RAESE
Set in 12-point Dante

Cataloging-in-Publication Data for this book is available from the Library of Congress.

ISBN 978-159315-481-3

Vanguard Press books are available at special discounts for bulk purchases in the U.S.
by corporations, institutions, and other organizations. For more information,
please contact the Special Markets Department at the Perseus Books Group,
11 Cambridge Center, Cambridge, MA 02142, or call (800) 255-1514 or (617) 252-5298,
or email special.markets@perseusbooks.com.

2 4 6 8 10 9 7 5 3 1

To the thousands upon thousands
of men, women, and children
who have lost their precious lives
in the senseless Iraq war
and to all the loved ones they left behind
whose suffering will never end,
with the hope that this book will
help bring those responsible
to justice.

CONTENTS

ACKNOWLEDGMENTS

What is recommended in this book is, as the title says, the prosecution of the president of the United States for murder. Although America is supposedly a free country, with freedom of speech and expression being our most cherished constitutional right, a considerable number of establishment people in this country—including many of the biggest and most powerful publishing houses in America—made it clear that even though they completely agreed with what I was saying in the book and recognized its potential in the marketplace, the book was something they did not want to have their name connected with. (Two law professors, liberal at that, were afraid to even *look* at the book.) In other words, the publishers' fears trumped money. Having *cold* feet, their essential position was that the book, as one publisher put it, was "too *hot* to handle." I understand their position, and I don't criticize them for it. But that doesn't mean I'm impressed with them, either.

Why all the fear? It's because of what this nation has become in the last twenty years, particularly the last eight. A nation whose virulent and dangerous right wing—the most unpatriotic of all Americans, and about whom Barry Goldwater said late in his life, "Don't associate my name with anything you do; you've done more damage to the Republican party than the Democrats have"—has transformed us into a country where many everyday Americans, for the first time ever, do not feel 100 percent comfortable and safe. And most humans yield to fear, even curry favor with those who cause it. When you have a very decent and honorable man like Mario Cuomo being sufficiently intimidated to say, "I respect Rush Limbaugh," an uncommonly loathsome individual (if I may be so presumptuous, Mario

Cuomo does not respect Rush Limbaugh. How would that even be possible?), that one example among countless others reflects the shadow of fear, no matter how small, that has now descended on a once great nation.

Out of this miasma of fear emerged a man, Roger Cooper, the publisher of this book, who loved America enough and had enough courage to step up to the plate and say, in effect, "No matter what, if America is ever to become the nation it once was, this story *has* to be told."

I am deeply appreciative of Cooper, a legendary figure in the book publishing world, for being the American patriot that he is and for giving my book his 100 percent support. He always provided me with whatever I needed to help make it the book I believe it is. It has been a distinct pleasure to work, for the first time in my long writing career, with him and his astute, number one publishing manager, Georgina Levitt, whose delightful British accent could charm a bird out of a tree. The two of them are professionals of the very first order, and I feel fortunate to have found a new literary home with them.

I also want to thank my superlative editor, Betsy Reed, not only for the great job of editing she did on my manuscript, but for the very judicious suggestions she made to change the tone of my writing in several places. Betsy's work ethic, coupled with her being highly intelligent and a trained observer of the American political scene, made her an ideal editor for this book.

And, of course, there is my virtual secretary, Rosemary Newton, who for years has been the person I rely on the most in the writing of my books. Always competent and extraordinarily reliable, she not only has to type hundreds of thousands of words from my less than perfect penmanship, but since I don't have a computer, in the last few years she has saved me many hours in front of the microfilm machine at the library (where I still do much of my research) by finding things for me on the Internet. I don't know what I'd do without Rosemary.

And finally, but certainly not least, I want to thank my wonderful wife of fifty-one years, Gail, who has always brought sunlight to my darkest hours, for the tremendous support and encouragement (and for sacrifices too numerous to mention) she gave me in the writing of this book. Among so many other things, we had been planning a short vacation when I finally, after twenty years, completed my magnum opus, *Reclaiming History: The Assassination of President John F. Kennedy*, in early 2007. But because of the constraints of time and our belief in the importance of this new book, I didn't take one day off from my seven-day-a-week schedule before starting this book. Only my lifetime partner, who has endured so much because of my hectic life throughout the years, would accept something like this. Whatever I have accomplished in life, I owe much of it to her.

Vincent Bugliosi
March 2008

U.S. deaths in Iraq from all corners of the nation

In four years, more than 3,200 U.S. military personnel have died in Operation Iraqi Freedom.

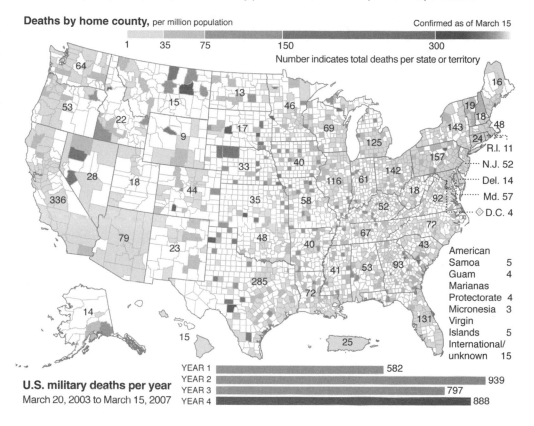

Deaths by home county, per million population

Confirmed as of March 15

| 1 | 35 | 75 | 150 | 300 |

Number indicates total deaths per state or territory

64
16
53
15
13
46
19
22
18
17
69
143
48
9
125
24
R.I. 11
28
33
40
157
N.J. 52
18
44
116
61
142
Del. 14
336
35
58
18
92
Md. 57
52
D.C. 4
79
67
72
23
48
40
43
285
41
53
93
American Samoa 5
72
Guam 4
Marianas Protectorate 4
Micronesia 3
131
Virgin Islands 5
14
International/unknown 15
15
25

U.S. military deaths per year
March 20, 2003 to March 15, 2007

YEAR 1 — 582
YEAR 2 — 939
YEAR 3 — 797
YEAR 4 — 888

SOURCES: AP research; Department of Defense

The preferable venue for the prosecution of George W. Bush for murder and conspiracy to commit murder would be in the nation's capital, with the prosecutor being the Attorney General of the United States acting through his Department of Justice. This book, however, establishes jurisdiction for any state attorney general (or any district attorney in any county of a state) to bring murder and conspiracy charges against Bush for any soldiers from that state or county who lost their lives fighting Bush's war, which as you can see applies to every state in this nation. Since the date of this map, March 15, 2007, hundreds of other United States soldiers have died in the war.

The first casualty when war comes is the truth.
—Senator Hiram Johnson (1917)

THE
PROSECUTION
OF
GEORGE W. BUSH
FOR MURDER

PART ONE

— 1 —

OPENING UP
ONE'S EYES

Introduction

THE BOOK YOU ARE ABOUT TO READ deals with what I believe to be the most serious crime ever committed in American history—the president of this nation, George W. Bush, knowingly and deliberately taking this country to war in Iraq under false pretenses, a war that condemned over 100,000 human beings, including 4,000 young American soldiers, to horrible, violent deaths. That, of course, is the most serious consequence of Bush's monumentally criminal behavior. But let's not forget that, additionally, thousands upon thousands of people have suffered injuries that have disabled them for life; hundreds of thousands of humans have sustained psychic damage from the war, and literally hundreds upon hundreds of thousands of people will involuntarily re-create in their mind's eye, over and over again, what happened to their loved ones. Assuming Bush's guilt for the sake of argument at this point, if what he did is not the greatest crime ever committed by any public official or private citizen in this nation's history, then I ask you, what is?

I am fully aware that the charge I have just made is an extremely serious one. But if there is one thing that I take pride in, it is the fact that I never, ever make a charge without offering a substantial amount of support for it. You may ultimately end up not agreeing with me, but you will have to concede that I offered much evidence in support of my position, something that people frequently do not do. How often, for instance, do you see an assertive, declarative caption or headline in a newspaper or magazine article, but when you read the article you find that either there is no support for the headline, or the evidence is very anemic? I don't do that. That's not my style.

Before I get into the heart of this book, *The Prosecution of George W. Bush for Murder*, I want to discuss some preliminary matters in this and the following two chapters. Without your consideration of these matters, I believe that what I am urging—the prosecution of the president of the United States, yes, the president of the United States, for murder—would be much more of a shock to your sensibilities. That inevitable shock is a burden I know I have to overcome. I am very confident, however, that I will be able to do so, and that open-minded people will agree that in this book I set forth the legal architecture that authorizes Bush's prosecution and, more importantly, I present evidence against Bush that proves, beyond all reasonable doubt, that he is guilty of murder.

If Winston Churchill said something about World War II, and a bum in a Bowery gutter said something quite the opposite, whom would you believe? There's really only one answer to that question, and it's not the one that 99 percent of people would reflexively give—Winston Churchill. The only proper answer to the question is, I'd have to hear what they had to say. This is obviously true since we know that just as a wise man can say something foolish, a fool can say something wise. Now, if neither Churchill nor the bum had weighed in on the issue yet and you were asked, "Who is more likely to say something intelligent about the matter?" the obvious answer would be, "Churchill."

What are we talking about here? We're talking about the fact that most people see what they expect to see, what they want to see, what they've been told to see, what conventional wisdom tells them to see, not what is right in front of them in its pristine condition. The reason I'm going to spend a little time on this phenomenon is that the reader's opening his eyes to reality is a necessary predicate to his accepting the revolutionary conclusions and recommendations I set forth in this book.

I am not, as the *Los Angeles Times* said of me, an "American master of common sense." Indeed, to be perfectly frank with you, I don't even feel I'm a particularly bright person. But at least in my professional life (I go through my private life blindfolded) I seem to naturally—and not as a result, I believe, of any special intelligence at all—see what's in front of me completely uninfluenced by the clothing (reputation, hoopla, conventional wisdom, etc.) put on it by others.

Let me give you a few examples of what I am talking about here. It was reported that Saddam Hussein had been responsible for the deaths of as many as 300,000 Iraqis. But when he was brought to trial in Baghdad on October 19, 2005, for his many crimes against the Iraqi people, and it was reported in the *New York Times* what the first crime was that he was going to be prosecuted for, I literally could not believe what I was reading. Obviously, a prosecutor wants to start his case on a strong note, and purportedly Hussein had been guilty, many times over, of murder on a grand scale—for example, the gassing of the Kurds, the killing of great numbers of Shiites following the Persian Gulf War, the torture and murder of thousands of Iraqis in his prisons, and so on. But instead of starting out on a strong note with one of these crimes, the prosecutor was starting out on no note at all. In fact, he was starting out with no crime at all.

I called my wife over to the breakfast table where I was reading the paper and said to her, "You are *not* going to believe what I'm going to read to you. It is nothing short of unbelievable." I proceeded to read to her the *New York Times* article about what the prosecutor was alleging. The article (and subsequent media and investigative sources) said that on July 8, 1982, in Dujail, Iraq, a largely Shiite Muslim town about thirty-five miles north of Baghdad, twelve to fifteen shots were fired at Hussein in an assassination attempt as his motorcade drove out of town after a visit.

Hussein's security forces later rounded up around 800 residents of Dujail for interrogation. Approximately 400 old people, women, and children were subsequently transferred, in internal exile, for several years to a desert detention center near the Saudi border, and many were released. On May 27, 1984, almost two years later, Hussein signed a document authorizing the prosecution of 148 men (including 20 teenage boys) on the charge of being members of the conspiracy to kill him. He based his decision upon the recommendation of legal advisers who reviewed a 361-page dossier of evidence compiled against the 148. Apparently, 46 of the 148 had already died from physical torture or execution by their interrogators and guards at Abu Ghraib prison, where later, under new and kinder landlords—Americans—we know that many Iraqis continued to be physically abused, some tortured, even killed. The remaining 102 out of the 148 men were eventually convicted and executed for the attempt on Hussein's life.

Note that if Hussein had intended to kill innocent people in retaliation for the attempt on his life, he would have killed many more people, perhaps the whole town. In fact, in a very telling statement by a man whose brothers were among those convicted by Hussein's Revolutionary Court for the attempt on his life and executed, and who rejoiced when Hussein was executed, he acknowledged that several other members of his family, after interrogation for the attempted assassination, were released from custody.

Incredibly, then, Hussein was convicted and put to death for executing those who were members of the conspiracy to murder him!! (He was not convicted of any other crime he is believed to have committed.) To repeat, *Hussein was killed for killing those who had first tried to kill him.*

The bottom line is that it appears Hussein did not commit the crime of murder here, and if this scenario had happened in any other country, including the United States (i.e., there was an attempt on the life of the president or prime minister of a country and the perpetrators were tried, convicted, and sentenced to life or death depending on the law of the country), it wouldn't have raised an eyebrow. Yet, remarkably, I never heard anything on radio or TV, or saw anything in any newspaper or magazine, about what I have just said here. There was total silence in *Time, Newsweek,* the *New York Times, Los Angeles Times,* and everywhere else on this issue. Why? Because although I only saw what I was reading in the newspaper, apparently a great many others did not, seeing only what they expected to see as they read the very same words that I did. Since Hussein was a terrible tyrant who had murdered hundreds of thousands of Iraqi citizens, and people read that Hussein was being brought to trial for "war crimes and crimes against humanity," they just assumed he was being prosecuted for these atrocities, and what the prosecutor was doing, obviously, had to be proper and correct.

Commenting upon the sentence of death Hussein received, the *New York Times* said, "Hussein's horrendous crimes" against the Iraqi people deserved the death sentence. The *Los Angeles Times,* referring to the many atrocities against his people that Hussein had committed in the past, said that Hussein was sentenced to death "for one of the massacres" of his people, "a crime against humanity." The reliably silly Christopher Hitchens said, "Hussein was convicted of massacring the inhabitants of a Shiite village, Dujail, in 1982." (Dujail, in 1982, was a town of some 78,000.)

The trial of Hussein was just another example of people only hearing the music, not the lyrics, of human events.

Another example, this one from the past, concerns the Czech tennis great Ivan Lendl. In the early years of his sterling career, Lendl was a quitter. If things were going well, he'd steamroll over his opponents, but if they weren't, oftentimes he'd give up. In the finals of one U.S. Open years ago, he was facing Jimmy Conners, who doesn't know what the term "give up" even means. At some point in the match,

Lendl stopped running after balls that were any meaningful distance away from him and lost ingloriously to Conners. What Lendl did angered me. How dare Lendl give up? He's in the finals of one of the most important tennis tournaments in the world and he wasn't giving it his all? Even if he didn't personally care, didn't he owe it to the millions of people watching the event on TV? And if he didn't even care about them, didn't he at least owe it to the great game of tennis?

After the match I went to the courts to play. I was still upset and voiced my displeasure with Lendl to no fewer than four or five of the players at the court who had also seen the match, saying that Lendl should be suspended and barred from playing in any sanctioned tennis tournament for at least a year. None of them knew what I was talking about. They hadn't noticed anything unusual about Lendl's performance at all. And the reason, of course, is that these were players who, like me, are willing to crash into a fence to retrieve a ball. And that's where nothing is at stake other than to satisfy our small mind's atavistic desire to win. If we will knock ourselves out in a meaningless practice match, obviously when you're playing Jimmy Conners in the finals of the U.S. Open, you'll kill yourself to win, right?

My tennis colleagues simply didn't see what happened in the Conners-Lendl match. They saw what they expected to see. The next day not one of the accounts of the match I read in the newspapers mentioned Lendl's sorry and inexcusable performance, and there was no mention of his having sustained any injury during the match that would have caused it. I was happy to read, in an edition of *Sports Illustrated* a month or so later, that tennis greats Pancho Segura and Bobby Riggs, who were courtside during the match, were disgusted by Lendl's performance. (It should be mentioned that during the middle and latter parts of Lendl's career, he developed into one of the grittiest, most tenacious and competitive players on the tour, always persevering till the bitter end.)

Just within the past decade or so, this tendency of mine to see what is in front of me in its pristine condition—which certainly is not unique to me—has caused me to hold beliefs at odds with the vast majority of Americans. One example is the criminal trial of O. J. Simpson. Before my book on the case, *Outrage*, came out, the widespread belief was the one set forth by *Newsweek* in its September 30, 1996, issue: "It is *accepted wisdom now* that prosecutors lost the criminal trial virtually the day the predominately African-American jury was sworn in." In other words, as pundit after pundit said or implied, the not guilty verdict was solely the fault of the terrible jury, certainly not that of the prosecution. For example, Jeffrey Toobin, who covered the trial for the *New Yorker*, said, "It is difficult to imagine how else Marcia Clark [who was, per Toobin, "at times brilliant"] might have tried her case. There appears to have been no one thing the prosecution could have done . . . that would have changed the result in this case The result, it now seems, was preordained." Influencing all of this was the implied assumption that since the two lead prosecutors were chosen out of a large staff to try this high-profile case, and since they seemed to be intelligent and articulate, they must have been competent. But the reality, taking place right in front of everyone's eyes, was that they could hardly have been more incompetent.

In my book *Outrage*, I point out with example after example after example that, as bad as the jury was, the prosecution was even worse, their incompetence being almost unprecedented. *Newsday* wrote: "Is everybody in America wrong but Bugliosi? Well, he makes a darned conclusive argument that this is so." The *New York Times* said, "Bugliosi puts the blame where it belongs." The *Los Angeles Times* said, "No one who reads *Outrage* will ever again believe that the most publicized acquittal in the history of American jurisprudence was solely the result of juror prejudice or the machinations of unscrupulous defense attorneys. The D.A. and the prosecutors have been called before the bar of justice."

Consider one more example. When Paula Jones's lawsuit against President Bill Clinton reached the U.S. Supreme Court in 1997 and Clinton asked the court to postpone the civil trial to the end of his term, virtually the entire country, including the major liberal newspapers like the *New York Times* and *Washington Post*, opposed Clinton's request, invoking the mantra "No one is above the law." (But Clinton wasn't asking that he be given immunity from the civil lawsuit. All he asked for was a routine continuance.) And when the court eventually denied Clinton's request and ruled that Clinton had to go to trial *during* his term, again, virtually the entire country agreed with the court's opinion. As an article in the *New Yorker* noted, the Supreme Court opinion "drew wide praise for reflecting the bedrock American principle that no one is above the law." Papers throughout the land applauded the court's decision. Just two among many examples. *Los Angeles Times*: "A unanimous Supreme Court has ruled, correctly, that a president has no constitutional claim to temporary immunity." *New York Daily News*: "When all is said and done, history will remember that the court held that the president is first and foremost a United States citizen, subject to the law like everyone else."

Many papers lamented the decision, saying it was unfortunate and would harm the presidency, but said that the court had nonetheless ruled correctly. This sense that the ruling was unfortunate but the court was nevertheless correct was a view articulated by a great many, including lawyers, law professors, and columnists. Just three examples. An editorial in the *National Law Journal* said that the Supreme Court's decision "holds dangers for the U.S. presidency and for the U.S. political system itself" but concluded that the "court's ruling" in the case "makes legal sense." Walter Shapiro, political columnist for *USA Today*, wrote that what the court's ruling portended for the president "should make us all feel a little embarrassed to be Americans" and "no president deserves the humiliation of this lawsuit." But, he added, "I have no quarrel with the Supreme Court decision. The principle that no one, not even a sitting president, should be above the law is embedded in our legal system." Harvard Law School constitutional law professor Laurence Tribe also bought into this nonsense. In the September 1997 edition of *George* magazine, after "lamenting" the fact that the president might be forced to trial by the court's decision, he added that he nonetheless "agrees with the court's ultimate conclusion. . . . It is a basic axiom of our government that no one is above the law, not even the president, and it follows that no special privileges should attach to whomever holds that august office."

The case I made in my book *No Island of Sanity* (the only book ever written on the Supreme Court decision) for the proposition that the Supreme Court should have granted President Clinton's request to postpone the Jones trial until the end of his term was such that not only did the reviews in the *New York Times* and *Washington Post* agree with *No Island* (in direct conflict with the position others in their paper had taken earlier), but to my knowledge not one conservative scholar who has *read* the book disagreed.* In the Jones case, the Supreme Court, the highest court in the land, displayed *staggering judicial incompetence* that people brighter than I never saw.

The court's unanimous decision in the Paula Jones case (if 50 million people say a foolish thing, it's still a foolish thing) was not only devoid of all common sense, but violated the court's own fundamental legal principles. Whenever the court, *any court in the land*, is confronted with a situation where a valid *private* interest is in conflict with a valid *public* interest—in this case, Paula Jones's interest in having her case brought to trial immediately (i.e., during the president's term), and the right of the nation's citizens to have a full-time president, one that can carry out his duties running the country without the enormous distraction of a private lawsuit—the court *must*, as it had been doing (I cite many cases in *No Island*) for over two centuries, balance the interests to see which interest is the most important and should prevail. For whatever reason, the court strangely, one could almost say mysteriously, *did not balance the interests in the Paula Jones case*. If it had, what conceivable argument under the moon could possibly be made for the proposition that Paula Jones's individual right to proceed to

*The Supreme Court ruling led to the Monica Lewinsky matter (President Clinton's denial, under oath, that he ever had sexual relations with Monica Lewinsky, took place at a deposition in Jones's lawsuit against the president), which grievously wounded the Clinton presidency to Al Gore's substantial detriment, which he compounded by distancing himself from Clinton during his campaign, Gore hardly using Clinton, an excellent vote getter, in the vote-getting effort. Most observers feel that had it not been for the Lewinsky scandal, Gore would have won the extremely close election. And it follows that we would not have had the runaway insanity of the Iraq war.

trial, right in the middle of the president's term, outweighed and was *more* important than the right of 270 million Americans to have their president be undiverted and undistracted in the performance of his duties? Whether we like a particular president or not, he works every day on national and international issues that affect all of our lives.

The reader should know that under the Soldiers and Sailors Civil Relief Act of 1940, even during peacetime, a buck private going through basic training at Fort Benning, Georgia, whose principal challenge is to learn how to assemble and disassemble an M–16 rifle, is legally entitled to a postponement of any civil action against him to the end of his active duty so that he can devote all his energy and attention to his duties. But the president of the United States, who has the most important and demanding job on earth, is not? What previously recognized form of logic would allow this?

I wrote in *No Island* (at a point in time when the case was scheduled to be tried in Little Rock, Arkansas, and before it was settled out of court by Clinton) that "I can easily foresee the trial igniting such a vast and deafening media explosion by the world press, and the situation getting so out of hand because of sensational allegations and *new and damaging revelations* that the president has to respond to, that he might become more than substantially distracted by the lawsuit. Rather, he will be . . . consumed by his political survival." Reviewing *No Island* in *USA Today*, Tony Mauro wrote: "Six days before Monica Lewinsky became a household name, famed Los Angeles lawyer Vincent Bugliosi turned in a book manuscript that foresaw it all." Again, I'm not the brightest person in the world, but a two-year-old should have been able to see the terribly dangerous situation and precedent the court was establishing by its decision in the Jones case, and all lawyers should have seen the court was simply wrong in the ruling, which violated a well-known and universally accepted principle of constitutional law. I view the Supreme Court, in the Jones case, like a driver who causes a massive accident on the freeway, and then drives on, looking at the pileup in the rearview mirror.

In a syndicated column, social historian Gary Wills, in referring to the Supreme Court's decision in *Jones v. Clinton*, wrote: "Vincent

Bugliosi was right." He didn't say, "Those who disagreed at the time with the Supreme Court's decision were right" because there did not appear to be any "those." I say this not to boast, but to make a larger point. In this book, I will be asking the reader to give the lie to Thoreau's dictum that "it is very difficult to see what is right in front of one's eyes." This will be particularly true when I set forth the legal basis and the evidence that support my contention that President Bush should be prosecuted, in an American courtroom, for first degree murder arising out of his war in Iraq.

How the above is all relevant is that if any reader finds it intellectually incongruous, and therefore difficult to accept, that a president of the United States could actually do what I strongly believe George Bush did in leading this nation to war, because, well, one would simply never expect (i.e., seeing what you expect to see) a president of the United States to do such a thing, I say you will be falling into the same unthinking trap that so many humans do. You *have* to disabuse yourself of any preconceived notion you may have that *just because* George Bush is the president of the United States he is simply *incapable* of engaging in conduct that smacks of great criminality. Because if you take that position, a position that has no foundation in logic, you're not going to be receptive to the evidence I set forth in this book, nor to the commonsense inferences I draw from that evidence.

For those who want America to one day be the great nation it once was, it can hardly do this if it doesn't take the first step of bringing those responsible for the war in Iraq to justice.

— 2 —

WHY GEORGE BUSH WENT TO WAR

B EFORE WE BRIEFLY REVIEW in this chapter the reasons George Bush has given for going to war in Iraq, one fact, so easily lost amidst the rubble of the conflict and the trillions of words written about it, should not be forgotten. Although the first Bush administration as well as the Clinton administration viewed Iraq as a troublesome menace, *no one was talking about actually going to war with Iraq before Bush started talking about it*. Indeed, even if someone had come forward (like an Iraqi defector) and said Hussein had plans to attack America or help someone else do so, his words would have been met with immense skepticism and ultimately disregarded, since on their face they would make little sense. *But not even one person told us this*. It all started with Bush and his people creating something out of nothing. To repeat, before Bush, there was nothing. And yet we went to war.

Although Bush *said* he went to war because Hussein was an imminent threat to the security of this country, not everyone believes this was Bush's motivation. Of those who don't, none seem to be too confident about why Bush went to war. The reasons speculated range from oil and politics (getting congressional authorization to go to war to help his party win the 2002 midterm elections; certainly, once the war started, exploiting the war to keep the nation in a constant state of fear to his political advantage) all the way to Bush getting even with Hussein for having, he said, "Tried to kill my dad at one time [1993]." Regarding the latter, in the book *Hubris* by Michael Isikoff and David Corn, the authors write: "That Bush was citing the incident *nine years* later to explain his current policy made some members of Congress uncomfortable. House Majority Leader Dick Armey later said he had 'just cringed' when he read about the president's comment. 'Wow,' he remarked to his wife, 'I hope *that's* [emphasis in original] not what this is all about.'" Some even say the motivation for war was part of a Bush family drama in which Bush was trying to one-up his father by completing the job Bush Sr. failed to do—remove Hussein from power in 1991—at the time of the Persian Gulf War. Whatever Bush's reason was, it was not a good reason. This brief chapter only deals with the main reasons he and his supporters have given for the war.

And as noted, we all know that the principal reason George Bush gave for invading Iraq in 2003 was that Hussein had weapons of mass destruction (WMD), and this posed an imminent threat to the security of this country because he might use these weapons on us, or furnish them to terrorists who would. We also know that Iraq had no such weapons of mass destruction, having disposed of virtually all of them (the extremely small number not being destroyed, if any, being inadvertent) and terminated its effort to build a nuclear bomb in 1991 at the conclusion of the Gulf War. (Whether or not Bush and his people flat-out lied when they said many of the things they did about Hussein's WMD, or simply stretched the truth, or cherry-picked by only furnishing Congress and the American people information that supported their position, not that which undermined it, will be discussed later in this book.)

Although the drumbeat for war because Hussein supposedly had WMD was so loud that it completely dominated the airwaves and the papers, Bush and his people, to gild the lily, did occasionally mention, in more of a parenthetical way, that apart from the issue of whether Hussein was a threat to the security of this country, we should free the Iraqi people from Hussein's despotic rule. That would allow them to have free elections and determine their own destiny. But we all know that America would never have bought Bush's war if that had been given as the main reason for invading Iraq. After all, if that was a sufficient reason for America going to war, during the past seventy-five years alone America would have been fighting in wars in all corners of the globe, every day of every year. We would have been fighting in, among many other places, Russia, China, and Cambodia. And at this very moment in time we'd be fighting in places like Darfur, Iran, North Korea, Cuba, etc. I mean, even Paul Wolfowitz, a chief architect of the Iraq war, acknowledged to *Vanity Fair* that helping the Iraqis achieve freedom from Hussein was "not a reason to put American kids' lives at risk, certainly not on the scale [that] we did it."

To illustrate the virtual insanity of such a policy of our fighting other peoples' wars and sacrificing thousands upon thousands of young American lives to give freedom to the people of other nations, let's say we invaded Russia in 1950 (as we invaded Iraq in 2003) to free the Russian people from Stalin's tyrannical rule. After losing hundreds of thousands of our soldiers in a terribly brutal war, we finally manage to topple Stalin from power, after which we track him down and put him on trial in Moscow for crimes he committed against the Soviet people. After Stalin is convicted and executed, we try to see to it that Russia has free elections, and then we come home (only to next invade China to free the Chinese people from Mao, and so on). If this sounds crazy to you, it's because it is.

In his 2006 Memorial Day column, *New York Times* writer Bob Herbert asked his readers (obviously, mostly those who had always been in favor of the war), "Before you gather up the hot dogs and head out to the barbecue this afternoon, look in a mirror and ask yourself honestly if Iraq [or any other country living under despotic rule] is something you would be willing to die for." The honest answer, of course, is no. And this has to be particularly true where, as with Iraq, most Iraqis quickly came to view us not as liberators but occupiers, and indeed, a January 2006 World Opinion poll showed that close to half of all Iraqis actually approved of deadly attacks on American soldiers.

To remind the reader, after it was determined that Iraq had no WMD, the Bush administration immediately tried to shift this very incidental reason for going to war (liberating the Iraqi people so they could have free elections) into the main justification for the war, and it's surprising how many supposedly very bright Americans, in fine Pavlovian form, went along with this. When the Iraqis had their first national election on January 30, 2005, and long after it was confirmed Iraq had no WMD, political satirist Jon Stewart, although, to his credit, not forgetting at all about the "whole weapons [of mass destruction] thing," said, in reference to the elections as being justification for the invasion, that "Bush [may have] been right about this all along." And looking back, liberal columnist Michael Kinsley wrote that Bush's invasion of Iraq "was worthy in theory: to liberate a country from a dictator, *perhaps** to find and destroy some dangerous weapons." Perhaps? Michael, where were you living in the lead-up to the Iraq war? A bank vault? A Himalayan monastery?

In fact, because it was virtually the sole reason given by Bush in his march to war, the only reason given by Congress in its October 11, 2002, joint resolution authorizing war was national security, nothing else. The resolution read: "The president is authorized to use the armed forces of the United States as he determines to be necessary and appropriate in order to defend the national security of the United States against the continuing threat posed by Iraq . . ." And in Bush's report to Congress on March 19, 2003, the day the war began, he spoke of nothing else but Hussein's weapons of mass destruction and our national security. There wasn't even a hint or mention of any other motive for war.

While all this was going on, it became the conventional wisdom among conservatives everywhere that finding no WMD in Iraq was immaterial because the *real*, unstated reason the Bush administration had for invading Iraq was not just to overthrow Hussein and establish democracy in Iraq—but a democracy that would spread like April

*Unless otherwise indicated, emphasis by italics in quotations in this book has been added by the author.

flowers throughout the Arab world, thereby eliminating the threat of terrorism on our shores by Islamic extremists like those who attacked us on 9/11. And, indeed, this may very well have been the intent of Bush and his batch of neoconservative zanies like Paul Wolfowitz and Richard Perle. There are those who believe that Wolfowitz was suggesting this very thing when he indicated to *Vanity Fair*, in an article published in its May 2003 edition, that WMD, which Wolfowitz said he believed Hussein had and were a real concern, were *not* (repeat, not) the main, overriding reason for invading Iraq. Remarkably, he said, "The truth [the truth? You mean, the American people weren't told the truth?] is that for reasons that have a lot to do with the U.S. government bureaucracy, we settled on [settled on?] the one issue that everyone could agree on, which was weapons of mass destruction, as the core reason [for the invasion]." Wow!!

Assuming, for the sake of argument, that the main, though unstated reason Bush invaded Iraq was to spread democracy throughout the anti-American Arab world (a reason, as indicated, for going to war in Iraq that was *never given* by the Bush administration at the time of its buildup to war), there is a monumentally serious problem with this that I haven't seen mentioned, one that the many Republicans who spout this theory don't seem to be in the least troubled by.

Apart from the wholly unrealistic and fanciful notion of changing the political culture of the Arab world to our liking, if Bush's *real* purpose for invading Iraq was to ignite a restructuring of the Middle East by giving birth to democracy in Iraq, *he obviously would have no right to keep this motivation for such a war a secret from the American people*. It would seem, in a hypothetical situation, that a president might be justified in taking the country to war without the informed consent of the people only if the *immediate* security of this country were at stake (which it wasn't here) and, for whatever reason, it was to the country's benefit that the president not tell the country's citizens his true reason for going to war. But although this justification for war is entertainable in theory, I can't even imagine what that situation would be.

Granted, once a war commences, the necessities and exigencies of war dictate that many secrets be kept from the people for purposes of national security. As Churchill, taking it a step further, observed, "During war, the truth has to be protected by a bodyguard of lies." But *before* the decision is made to go to war, the American people deserve to know and have to be informed why their sons are being asked to shed their blood on foreign soil, and asked if they agree that such a venture is necessary to this nation's security. One shouldn't go so far as to assert that in all cases a *majority* of Americans have to voice their approval for war, but with the exception of the hypothetical situation noted above, in all cases the nation's citizens have to be informed of the reasons for war. Particularly in a nation like America whose roots were at the town hall meeting level, where everyday citizens gave their input on the important decisions of government.

So if, indeed, the reason for the war in Iraq was to spread democracy throughout the Mideast, how is it possible that Bush and his people had the tremendous audacity not to tell the American people this?

Further, *if we assume that the many conservative Republicans who say the real reason behind the Iraqi invasion was to spread democracy in the Middle East are correct, aren't they thereby admitting that Bush lied to the country when he told Americans the principal reason we were invading Iraq was because it had weapons of mass destruction and hence was an imminent threat to the security of this country?*

Returning to the main reason (for virtually all intents and purposes the only reason) Bush and his people gave the American people for going to war in Iraq—that Saddam Hussein had weapons of mass destruction which he might unleash or give to someone else to unleash on America any day—let's look at just some of the many statements from Bush and his people assuring Americans that Hussein did, in fact, have WMD, and if we didn't attack right now, Hussein might attack us first. As you are reading these statements, keep the following things uppermost in your mind:

1. These are statements by the Bush administration that were *directly* responsible for the majority of Americans finally becoming convinced that invading Iraq was the right thing for America to do.

2. Without the approval of this majority of Americans, there is a decent chance that Bush would not have gone to war. Indeed, that was the very reason why Bush and his people made the statements—to get the support of the American people.

3. Because of the war induced by these statements, over 100,000 American soldiers and Iraqi civilians lost their lives, and many thousands of others have been physically or mentally disabled for life.

4. *All of these statements, without exception, have been proven to be completely false.*

PRESIDENT BUSH

September 12, 2002 (Address to United Nations): "Saddam Hussein continues to develop weapons of mass destruction. The first time we may be completely certain he has nuclear weapons is when, God forbid, he uses one . . . [Iraq presents] a grave and gathering danger."

October 7, 2002 (from Cincinnati, Ohio, Bush's first address to the nation on the Iraqi threat. Bush piled it on so heavy that the devil himself, much less an American family sitting in front of the TV set in their living room in Dubuque, Iowa, would have had a hard time fighting back fear): "Hussein is a threat to peace and must disarm. The Iraqi dictator must not be permitted to threaten America and the world with horrible poisons and diseases and gasses and atomic weapons . . . Some ask how urgent this danger is to America and to the world. The danger is already significant . . . If we know Saddam Hussein has dangerous weapons today—and we do—does it make sense for the world to wait to confront him as he grows even stronger and develops even more dangerous weapons? . . . Iraq has a growing fleet of manned and unmanned aerial vehicles that could be used to disperse chemical or biological weapons across broad areas. We're concerned that Iraq is exploring ways of using these UAVs for missions targeting the United States . . . Iraq could decide *on any given day* to provide a biological or chemical weapon to a terrorist group . . . [This] could allow the Iraqi regime to attack America without leaving any fingerprints . . . Saddam Hussein is harboring terrorists and . . . the instruments of mass death and destruction. And he cannot be trusted. The risk is simply too great that he will use them, or provide them to a terror network . . . Facing clear evidence of peril, we cannot wait for the final proof—the smoking gun—that could come in the form of a mushroom cloud . . . Saddam Hussein . . . has chemical and biological weapons and is increasing his capabilities to make more. And he is moving ever closer to developing a nuclear weapon . . . Saddam Hussein must disarm himself, or, for the sake of peace, we will lead a coalition to disarm him . . . [Hussein is] a great danger to our nation . . . We refuse to live in fear . . . We will secure our nation, protect our freedom."

January 28, 2003 (State of the Union address): "The British government has learned that Saddam Hussein recently sought significant quantities of uranium from Africa. Our intelligence sources tell us that he has attempted to purchase high-strength aluminum tubes suitable for nuclear weapons production . . . Year after year, Saddam Hussein has gone to elaborate lengths, spent enormous sums, taken great risks to build and keep weapons of mass destruction . . . Some have said we must not act until the threat is imminent. [Alone, this suggests Bush is saying the threat is not imminent, nothing that has to be dealt with now. But his very next words quickly dispel this inference.] Since when have terrorists and tyrants announced their intentions, politely putting us on notice before they strike? . . ."

March 6, 2003 (National press conference): "Iraqi operatives continue to hide biological and chemical agents to avoid detection by inspectors. In some cases these materials have been moved to different locations every 12 to 24 hours . . . Saddam Hussein and his weapons are a direct threat to this country, to our people, and to all free people . . . I will not leave the American people at the mercy of the Iraqi dictator and his weapons . . . I see a gathering threat. I mean, this is a true, real threat to America."

March 17, 2003 (Bush's address to the nation two days before he invaded Iraq): "Intelligence gathered by this and other governments leaves no doubt that the Iraq regime continues to possess and conceal some of the most lethal weapons ever devised . . . Before the day of horror can come, before it is too late to act, this danger will be removed . . . When evil men plot chemical, biological and nuclear terror, a policy of appeasement could bring destruction of a kind never before seen on this earth . . . Responding to such enemies only after they have struck first is not self-defense, it is suicide. The security of the world requires disarming Saddam Hussein now."

March 19, 2003 (speech to nation announcing that the invasion of Iraq had begun): "The people of the United States and our friends and allies will not live at the mercy of an outlaw regime that threatens the peace with weapons of mass murder . . . We will meet that threat now . . . so we do not have to meet it later with armies of firefighters and police and doctors on the streets of our cities."

VICE PRESIDENT DICK CHENEY

August 26, 2002 (speech to Veterans of Foreign Wars): "Simply stated, there is no doubt that Saddam Hussein now has weapons of mass destruction. There is no doubt he is amassing them to use against our friends, against our allies, and against us . . . We now know that Saddam has resumed his efforts to acquire nuclear weapons . . . Many of us are convinced that Saddam will acquire nuclear weapons fairly soon."

September 8, 2002 (*Meet the Press*): "We do know, with absolute certainty, that Hussein is using his procurement system to acquire the equipment he needs in order to enrich uranium to build a nuclear weapon."*

NATIONAL SECURITY ADVISER
CONDOLEEZZA RICE

September 8, 2002 (CNN): "We do know that [Saddam] is actively pursuing a nuclear weapon . . . We don't want the smoking gun to be a mushroom cloud."

SECRETARY OF STATE
COLIN POWELL

February 5, 2003 (address to UN Security Council): "The gravity of this moment is matched by the gravity of the threat that Iraq's weapons of mass destruction pose to the world . . . There can be no doubt that Saddam Hussein has biological weapons and the capability to rapidly produce more, many more . . . Sad-

---

*And oh yes. Although not quite qualifying for the "Why George Bush Went to War" list of quotes, how can one fail to mention this quote of Cheney, the Old Testament prophet, on NBC's *Meet the Press* on March 16, 2003, just days before the war: "My belief is we will, in fact, be greeted as liberators . . . I think it will go relatively quickly, [in] weeks rather than months." The Iraq war, of course, has already gone on longer than our participation in the Second World War!

dam Hussein has chemical weapons . . . We have more than a decade of proof that Saddam Hussein remains determined to acquire nuclear weapons . . . Saddam Hussein and his regime have made no effort, no effort, to disarm . . . [and] are concealing their efforts to produce more weapons of mass destruction."

SECRETARY OF DEFENSE
DONALD RUMSFELD

September 18, 2002 (House Armed Services Committee): "We do know that the Iraqi regime has chemical and biological weapons."

September 19, 2002 (Senate Armed Services Committee): "No terrorist state poses a greater or more *immediate* threat to the security of our people than the regime of Saddam Hussein and Iraq."

At the time that all of the above false statements were made, there was no credible evidence that Saddam had any more weapons of mass destruction than you or I had in our backyard. What we do know is that at the time, Hussein, pen in hand, was consumed not by the thought of attacking America (after all, he was a hell of a lot more sane than President Bush), but by completing his fourth novel, *Get Out, You Damned One*, a third-rate piece of pulp fiction about "a greedy schemer who plots to overthrow the sheik of a tribe with the help of a powerful enemy aiming to conquer and annihilate all Arabs but is ultimately defeated by the sheik's daughter with the help of an Arab warrior." The first page of the manuscript (later published in book form) was signed by Hussein and dated March 18, 2003, the day before Bush invaded Iraq.

Whether the Iraq war was the second-biggest blunder in American history (behind Vietnam) or the biggest crime ever committed by an American president will be discussed in a succeeding chapter.

PART
TWO

3

PROLOGUE TO THE PROSECUTION OF GEORGE W. BUSH FOR MURDER

A S ADULTS, most of us have learned that there are consequences in life for our misbehavior. If George Bush, as I
believe, took this nation to war in Iraq on a lie, causing catastrophic repercussions on a scale far larger than the attacks of 9/11,
*what should we, as a nation, do about it? As of the publication date of this
book, apparently nothing.* Indeed, and remarkably, there hasn't even
been any investigation of Bush's conduct, nor has one even been seriously proposed.* In the chapter that follows this one, I will make my

---

*Yet the outrageously monstrous Ken Starr (about whom longtime Manhattan dis-
trict attorney Robert Morgenthau said, "He violated every [prosecutorial] rule in the
book") conducted, with federal authorization and funding no less, a seven-year, $70
million investigation of Bill Clinton's involvement in a small and losing real estate
venture (Whitewater) in Arkansas *fifteen years before his presidency,* and finding nothing, decided to investigate Clinton's private and consensual sexual life. In the process,
Starr almost destroyed the Clinton presidency, substantially incapacitated the executive branch of government, and made America a laughingstock around the world.

own small contribution to "doing something about" what has happened. But before I do, I want to talk in this prologue about the thousands of young American men and women who paid for Bush's conduct with their irreplaceable lives, because if these men and women were not in their cold graves, I obviously would not be recommending what I do in the next chapter. I also want to discuss how the author of these deaths, George Bush, has comported himself through the horror of it all.

My anger over the war in Iraq, some will say, is palpable in the pages of this book. If I sound too angry for some, what *should* I be greatly angry about—that a referee gave what I thought was a bad call to my hometown football, basketball, or baseball team, and it may have cost them the game? I don't think so.

Virtually all of us cling desperately to life, either because of our love of life and/or our fear of death. I'm told there is a passage in a novel by Dostoyevsky in which a character in the story exclaims, "If I were condemned to live on a rock, chained to a rock in the lashing sea, and all around me were ice and gales and storm, I would still want to live. Oh God, just to live, live, *live!*"

So nothing is as important in life as life and death. We fear and loathe the thought of our own death, even if it's a peaceful one after we've outlived the normal longevity. We fear not only the loss of our own lives, but the lives of our parents and sisters and brothers, as well as our relatives and close friends. We don't think of our children too much in this regard because our children, in the normal scheme of things, are supposed to outlive us. When they die before us, the already hideous nature of death becomes unbearable. And that's when they die a normal and peaceful death from illness. If the death is from an accident, like a car collision, the death of the child, if possible, is even more unbearable.

So one can hardly imagine the gut-tearing pain and horror when the only child of a couple, a nineteen-year-old son, call him Tim, the center of his parents' lives, whom they showered with their love and lived through vicariously in his triumphs on the athletic field and in the classroom, and who was excited as he looked forward to life, planning to wed his high school sweetheart and go on to become a police officer (or lawyer, doctor, engineer, etc.) dies the most horrible of deaths from a roadside bomb in a far-off country, and comes home in a metal box,* his body so shattered that his parents are cautioned by the military not to open it because what is inside ("our Timmy") is "unviewable." (To make the point hit home more with you, can you imagine if it was *your* son who was killed in Iraq and came home "unviewable" in a box? Yes, your son Scott, or Paul, or Michael, or Ronnie, Todd, Peter, Marty, Sean, or Bobby.)

No words can capture the feelings, the enormous suffering, of Tim's parents. But I think we can say that among a host of other deep agonies, they will have nightmares for the rest of their lives over the horrifying image of their boy the moment he lost his life on a desolate road in Iraq. As a mother of a soldier who died in Iraq wrote in a May 17, 2004, letter to the *New York Times*: "The explosion that killed my son in Baghdad will go on in our lives forever." She went on to say that "seared on" her soul are the "*screams* and despair" of her family over the loss of her son and the "sound of taps above the weeping crowd at the grave site of my son."

Just as Tim's young life ended before he really had a chance to live, so did the lives of thousands of other young men in the Iraq war. Not one of them wanted to die. As one wrote in his diary before he was killed in the battle of Fallouja: "I am not so much scared as I am very afraid of the unknown. If I don't get to write again, I would say I died too early. I haven't done enough in my life. I haven't gotten to experience enough. Though I hope I haven't gone in vain." In letter after letter home by young men who were later killed in combat in Iraq were words to the effect, "I can't wait to get back home and to start my life again."

All of the young men who died horrible and violent deaths in Bush's war had dreams. Bush saw to it that none of them would ever

---

*It is not a casket or coffin, which the survivors of course later put the remains in. The military refers to the aluminum receptacle as a "transfer case," and the case is draped with an American flag.

come true. It is impossible to adequately describe all the emotions and the magnitude of the human suffering that this dreadful war has wrought. But we can at least begin to comprehend the enormity of it by looking briefly at some stories of those young men who paid with their lives for Bush's monumental crime.

As undoubtedly is the case with the reader's local paper, for several years now my hometown paper, the *Los Angeles Times*, every week without fail—sometimes it seems every day, under "Military Deaths"—has an obituary, or two or three, of young American soldiers from Southern and Central California who were killed in Iraq. Many had Hispanic names; almost all were very young and of limited education (only 3.5 percent of the enlisted men in the Iraqi war—the men who, for the most part, do the fighting, the so-called grunts—have a college degree); and virtually all appeared to come from low-income homes. There was a story in each obituary of their abbreviated lives, with reminiscences from their parents, brothers and sisters, wives, as well as girlfriends they were already planning to marry. I wish I had kept all of them, although they would number in the hundreds. A typical caption was "Army Cpl. (name), 20, Rialto; killed by a roadside bomb."

Here are a few random snippets drawn mostly from the *Los Angeles Times*, and a few elsewhere. Though not comprehensive, we can suppose they are representative of the others because they all tell the same story of a young life tragically cut short by the war.

"How long must I wait to go home?" Luis, 21, who was killed by a roadside bomb wrote. "How long must I wait to marry my girlfriend?" Family and friends said the thing they'll always remember about Luis is how easily he made them laugh. He'd recite favorite lines from movies or from comedian Dave Chappelle . . . "He was scared because he was going to Iraq," his younger brother Eric said. "He was telling me he loved me. He was crying. He said he didn't know what to do." His fiancée was planning to surprise him with a scrapbook filled with photographs of themselves. The last page was dedicated to their planned wedding. She included cutouts of a multi-tiered cake, a tuxedo, a wedding dress, and a caption in fancy lettering, "And they lived happily ever after."

"He was just special," said his mother Maria about her son, Michael (20). "He was always there for me and his brothers and sisters. He did a lot for his family." His sister Sasha, 18, said her brother was her best friend, whom she would seek out for advice about boys and other teenage issues. "He would tell me that he would always be there for me," she added.

Guy (23) worked at a Home Depot store and joined the National Guard to help pay for his education. Just before he died, he told his mother that when he returned from Iraq his goal was to return to school and get a degree in computer engineering.

There was something sweetly old-fashioned about Lucente, who was among five Marines killed November 16 in combat in Ubaydi, Iraq. The nineteen-year-old Grace Valley resident went to church regularly, held down a job as a dishwasher, and never failed to tell his family that he loved them. "He was always giving us hugs, always telling us he loved us," his mother said.

Christopher (21) would flash his 1,000-watt smile and remind his sisters how pretty they were as he grew up in Vallejo, California. His parents, Rudy and Margarita, had been surprised in 2004 when their son, who had just turned 18 and completed high school, told them he had joined the Army. "He was afraid we couldn't pay for college," said his mother, who is a clerk at Target. "I said I'll work two jobs. You'll be able to go to college. He wanted to be a policeman someday. He talked about that even when he was younger." "I always thought I was going to be a kid forever," he wrote for his senior class commencement program.

Leon (20) and his fiancée planned to be married in December. He was thinking he might join the Los Angeles Police Department and maybe try for the SWAT squad. When he'd call home to his parents he wanted to know about his family and his neighborhood. He'd say, 'That's the stuff that keeps me grounded, shows me there is something real, something to hold on to,'" his mother said. "He definitely had the heart of a lion and did your family name proud," wrote a Marine buddy to Leon's parents. Army Cpl. Jarred Speller, who was on the roof with Leon, wrote of the frantic moments after Leon was hit by a sniper as medics tried to stop the bleeding to his head. "I held his head in my hands the whole time and kept trying to tell him he was going to be okay."

Tom (23) was killed Monday near Baghdad in a grenade explosion. Like so many young men with dreams but not much money, he saw an opportunity. "The Army flashed dollar signs in their [Tom and his brother's] faces. They jumped at it," said Tom's stepfather. Tom wanted to be a school teacher. He and his wife, Paulette, were married for less than two years and had one child. "Tommy enjoyed life to the fullest," his stepfather said. "He was a good Christian boy. His life was cut short. Tommy won't be able to be anything anymore."

Nineteen-year-old Ryan was remembered by all as a "big kid" with a heart-melting smile. His "easy charm and athletic good looks—he played baseball and football in high school—made for no lonely Saturday nights." He was a "ladies man," said his older brother, Sean, noting the number of grieving young women at his kid brother's funeral. It wasn't just young ladies who were taken with Ryan. "Everybody I ever talked to loved Ryan," his father, a Los Angeles County sheriff's deputy, said. Ryan's job in Iraq was to root out roadside bombs, but one he didn't see killed two of Ryan's buddies near their Humvee in Ramadi, and severely injured Ryan, with third-degree burns over most of his body. He was airlifted to Germany and then Brooks Army Medical Center in San Antonio where he died twelve days later. His father and mother had flown to San Antonio to spend every moment at his side. He was unconscious during most of his hospital stay but had six hours of wakefulness with his family. "I think he fought to get those six hours with us," said his father. "He had a very strong will. He's missed every day" and will be "for the rest of our lives."

In classic Southern California style, Kyle loved heavy-metal rock music and fast cars, perhaps to extremes. He carried a picture of his Camaro in his wallet and had the lyrics of a Pantera song tattooed on his back. Although he was not interested in school, he was exceptionally intelligent, scoring above 150 on an Army IQ test. He taught himself to play his father's guitar at age 11. His relatives said he excelled at it. When his sister Korra Jean was killed in a car accident four years ago, he had her full name tattooed across his chest. Kyle believed in the U.S. mission in the Middle East, relatives said. During a visit home in February, his half-sister found him quieter than usual. She said he told his friends, "If I don't come home, have a raging party for me," and told her to make sure he was buried in his military uniform. Kyle was among four soldiers killed south of Baghdad when mines detonated near the Humvee they were riding in, setting it on fire. He was 23.

[Andres, a 23-year-old Army sergeant,] "turned to the gunner in his Humvee while on patrol in Baghdad on July 15, 2006, and insisted on switching seats. When his commanding officer ordered him to stay put, he said he couldn't explain why but he knew that he needed to be sitting in the gunner's seat. His orders were coming from a higher source, he said. Moments after he made the switch, a roadside bomb exploded and killed him. The other soldier was bruised but alive. That was the story of Andres' life in Iraq, always thinking of his fellow soldiers. This is why his fellow servicemen called him a "soldier's soldier," someone distinguished by his selfless regard for others' welfare above his own. There are no plaques, medals or badges that mark a soldier's soldier. "It's a distinguished phrase you don't just give to anyone," said a peer of Andres. "It's one of those things you earn. He definitely had it." Andres had wanted to return home to become a Los Angeles County deputy sheriff. He left behind a four-year-old daughter, Grace, who lived with his former girlfriend. He doted on her, spending his few weeks at home taking her to Knott's Berry Farm and Disneyland. He would shower her with gifts—lately she favored Winnie the Pooh. Besides his daughter, his survivors were his parents and five younger brothers.

Joseph, 21, was killed near Baghdad on July 25 in an ambush on his convoy. He had married his childhood sweetheart, Cori, 20, shortly before he left for Iraq the previous fall. In the weeks before his death, the soldier had been counting the days until he came home. He was looking forward to settling down with his bride. "We had saved like pack rats to get a house," Cori said. "He was very anxious to get home. We had spent a good part of his military career apart, and it was just time" to start their life together.

Raymond (21) was born six weeks early and weighed a scant three pounds. An accomplished basketball player, he graduated from Anaheim's Western High School, attended Santa Ana College, and dreamed of being a fire fighter. "He came home one day," his mother, Willieta, said, and said to her, "I was talking to a couple of my professors and they said there was a long list for fire fighters. They said the only way I could be a fire fighter without being on the list is joining the military." Willieta begged her only child to talk to her first. "I said, Raymond, I don't object to you going into the military. I object to you going at this time." A few weeks later he signed up. Raymond loved hip-hop music, text messaging, video games and flashy cars. Someday, he said, he would buy a Cadillac Escalade or G.M.C. Yukon with the money he earned fighting in Iraq. Raymond had a big smile, a big heart, a big appetite, a big soul. The best of friends and the sweetest of sons. When he was home on leave, Raymond would buy flowers for his mom. "I want to go on," his mother said, "But I don't know. Do I even have a purpose anymore? It's hard. It's hard. It's hard."

In these obituaries we see, as indicated earlier, that most of these soldiers dying in Iraq come from very modest or low-income roots. That's why they found even the low pay scale of the military so enticing. That these young men from relatively poor families are fighting a war and dying for multimillionaires like Bush and Vice President Dick Cheney, and that companies like Halliburton (Cheney's former company) have made billions, yes billions of dollars off their blood in contracts, is enough to make any decent human being sick to the stomach.

What makes the sickness turn into rage is to know that Bush took these young men to war on a lie, and that when they died they thought they were dying to protect their country against those who were involved in 9/11. The additional fact that these soldiers were sent into a war zone without the equipment necessary to protect them not only increases the rage exponentially but shows exactly how little regard Bush and his administration have for those who have been willing to risk their lives fighting Bush's war. As was clear after the first roadside bombs (known as IEDs, improvised explosive devices) killed U.S. troops in their very vulnerable Humvees in 2003, military vehicles designed to withstand them were desperately needed. Yet the Bush administration was unconscionably slow in replacing the Humvees or in armoring them properly. To date, IEDs have been responsible for almost 70 percent of all American combat deaths in Iraq.

Can anything possibly be more abominable than this very rich nation sending its young men off to war without providing them with the proper equipment? If the young men dying in Iraq in Humvees were the children of wealthy CEOs, wouldn't something have been done immediately in a crash program (special contracts with multiple manufacturers, twenty-four-hour shifts, etc.) to get the necessary protection for them? In reality, a year and a half after the war started, the only Humvee armoring company in America was operating under capacity because of no new orders from the Pentagon (*Newsweek*, December 20, 2004), i.e., although protecting our troops should be a top priority in time of war, the Bush administration was not spending the money necessary to do so, nor insuring that more than one factory was working to get the job done. As was reported many times in the media (e.g., *New York Times*, October 30, 2004), the situation was so bad that American soldiers in Iraq were literally writing home and having their loved ones send requested body and armor parts for the Humvees to them.

When Secretary of Defense Rumsfeld visited Iraq and spoke to a group of soldiers on December 8, 2004, one of them (National Guard Specialist Thomas Wilson) stood up and publicly complained about the lack of protection the Humvees were providing them, saying that troops had to forage for "rusted scrap metal and ballistic glass that's already been shot up, busted, picking the best out of this scrap to put on our vehicles to take into combat." He asked Rumsfeld, to loud cheers from many of his fellow soldiers, why they had "to dig through local landfills" for their armor. Rumsfeld, who himself hid out at Princeton on a student deferment when it was his generation's time to fight in Korea, blithely brushed the soldier off, saying, "You go to war with the Army you have, not the Army you might want or wish to have at a later time." But that terribly arrogant position would only apply if America, for instance, had been invaded by Iraq, in which case we would have to make do with what we had at that particular time. But Bush had all the time in the world to prepare for his war against Iraq. Not only was Iraq never, ever going to attack the United States, or help anyone else do so, but even if it were, it certainly wouldn't be doing so for a long time.

While young American soldiers were scavenging for their "hill-billy" armor to protect themselves in a war that only big corporations, like Halliburton, profited from, a story from the December 10, 2004, *New York Times* (just two days after Specialist Wilson's confrontation with Rumsfeld) was captioned "It's Inauguration Time Again, and Access Still Has Its Price—$250,000 Buys Lunch with President and More." Can you imagine that? A quarter of a million dollars spent by the nation's very wealthy just for lunch, while young Americans, mostly from low-income families, were dying violent deaths on the battlefield in Iraq because of inadequate protection.

Although American soldiers, to this very day, continue to be killed by roadside bombs in Iraq, this, from the August 23, 2007, edition of *USA Today*: "The Pentagon said yesterday that it will fall short of its goal of sending 3,500 armored vehicles to Iraq by the end of the year [2007]. Instead, officials expect to send about 1,500. Pentagon press secretary Geoff Morrell said that while defense officials still believe contractors will build about 3,900 of the mine-resistant, ambush-protected vehicles [MRAPs—these are not armored Humvees] by year's end, it will take longer for the military to fully equip them and ship them to Iraq." This is particularly infuriating because the MRAPs that have been deployed in Iraq thus far have been very effective in withstanding the roadside bombs.

The marines requested the MRAPs (whose V-shaped hull at the bottom deflects a bomb's blast to the sides and away from the crew, as opposed to the Humvees whose flat underside takes the full force of a blast through the floor) way back in December of 2003. Yet because of bureaucratic wrangling and the original unwillingness of the Bush administration to adequately fund the very heavy and expensive MRAPs, which only take four months to manufacture, it wasn't until August of 2007, almost four years later, that a small percentage were available for combat operations in Iraq. As expected, by the end of 2007, only 1,500 of the approximately 14,000 the military requested had been delivered to Iraq.

And there is more. In June of 2004, the army told the Pentagon it needed 2,600 M1117 armored vehicles (again, not armored Humvees) for its military police. Yet the Bush administration only contracted with one company, Textron in New Orleans, and for only 1,250 vehicles. Why no more? "That's all they had the money for," Clay Moise, the Textron vice president, said in January of 2007. And this is from the administration that gave the super rich in America, those who don't need one dime from anyone, a $1.3 *trillion* tax break over ten years.

What about body armor? A Pentagon study in 2006 found that some 80 percent of the marines who were killed in Iraq between 2003 and 2005 from upper body wounds could have survived if they had had extra body armor there. As of late 2005, over two and a half years into the war, less than 10 percent of 28,000 upper armor plates on order had reached our marines in Iraq. That the Bush administration would send young American soldiers to fight its senseless war in Iraq without adequately equipping them for combat is unpardonable and criminal.

As if all of this is not bad enough, consider what the Bush administration has done with our brave young soldiers in Iraq who managed to survive the war but were seriously wounded, many disabled for life. We all know about the subpar performance of this nation's care and treatment of these soldiers as exemplified by the scandal at Walter Reed Hospital. Dr. John H. Chiles, who was chief of anesthesiology at Walter Reed, said that America's military medical system was "*under-funded* [to repeat, this, from a Bush administration that gave a $1.3 trillion tax break to the super rich], understaffed and overwhelmed." To quote from an Ella Fitzgerald tune, isn't that just delovely?

About the $1.3 trillion tax break for the very wealthy in the upper one percent of our society, would you believe it if I told you that the flag-waving, red, white, and blue super patriots in the Bush administration, who want us to believe they love our troops so much more than Democrats do, actually wanted to partially fund the tax giveaway on the backs of these poor soldiers dying for them and their wealthy corporate friends in Iraq? Yes, you heard me right. Although it's unbelievable, it's true. Incredibly, in July of 2003, with the base pay of a private starting at only $1,064 per month, the Bush administration decided to discontinue the $75-a-month bonus that soldiers in combat zones in Iraq were getting. The $75 was called "imminent danger pay," or "combat pay." Bush and his people just felt this was being overly generous with the soldiers at taxpayers' expense, and in the interim budget report sent to Congress by Donald Rumsfeld's Department of Defense, the combat pay was not included.

The *Army Times*, which is distributed widely among army personnel, immediately attacked the White House and Pentagon in editorials for their extremely selfish, callous, and outrageous position. And military families, veterans groups, and Democrats (yes, Democrats) immediately voiced their strong opposition to the Bush administration decision *to cut the combat pay of American soldiers fighting in Iraq.* These are soldiers, mind you, trying to survive—on a virtual second to-second basis in the combat zones—deadly roadside bombs and guerilla-style attacks. Soldiers weighted down with heavy equipment and combat gear fighting sometimes in 120-degree-plus heat. And back in our nation's air-conditioned Capitol, multimillionaire Republicans in the Bush administration, most of whom were draft dodgers in the Vietnam War, wanted to cut their monthly pay by $75.00. Then-Democratic senator Joe Lieberman said that the Bush administration's proposal was "just unconscionable. The government can afford the billions they give in tax cuts to millionaires, but there's not enough to give a little something to men and women who are putting their lives on the line." Democratic representative Mike Thompson, a Vietnam War veteran, wrote a letter to Bush saying, "This is an outrageous and hypocritical affront to our soldiers who are being killed on a daily basis and to their families." Democratic senator John Edwards said, "Our military deserves every dollar they earn and more. The Bush administration should reverse itself immediately," which is exactly what Bush and his people did, withdrawing their call for a cut in combat pay the moment they saw their proposal being met with so much opposition.

But what does Bush and his people *actually wanting to cut the combat* *pay of American soldiers fighting in Iraq* tell you about these people? Is there really anything more to say?*

Visiting the grave site of a relative in May of 2006, I noticed a nearby grave decorated much more than the others. When I walked over, there was a photo of a young soldier in uniform. He was "SPC Sergio"(Hispanic last name) and the headstone said "March 7, 1983–December 25, 2005," so he was twenty-two years old when he died on Christmas day in Iraq. The inscription was "A Beloved Husband, Father, and Everyone's Hero." Then a biblical reference: "I have fought a good fight, I have finished my course, I have kept my faith, II Timothy 4:7." On a large backboard were written the words "1-64 Armor Battalion Desert Rogers Operation Iraq Freedom 111." Many flowers and six American flags surrounded the grave site.

Like all the others, Sergio had a story, and I wondered what that story was. Also like the others, we know he had dreams he never even had a chance to try to make come true. I thought of him in the cold earth beneath me having died, as some liberal commentators have said, "for nothing."

But these liberal commentators are 100 percent wrong. Sergio and all the others didn't die for nothing. They died for nothing worthwhile, yes. But they died for something, make no mistake about that. Although there is an old Turkish proverb that whoever tells the truth is chased out of nine villages, doesn't someone have to tell the truth that

*If more need be said about these absolutely shameless and hypocritical human beings, when Congress, in 2007, passed a bill providing for a 3.5 percent pay raise for U.S. soldiers, the Bush administration, which only was willing to give a 3 percent raise, said it "strongly" opposed the additional .5 percent, calling it "unnecessary" (right, like the $1.3 trillion tax break for the super wealthy), and Bush actually vetoed the bill, though he finally signed it in January of 2008 after Congress made certain changes in the language of the bill. Nothing more has to be said to make the point about George Bush and his people, but in 2007, the base pay per month (after four months) of a private in the U.S. Army fighting in Iraq was $1,301.40. Canada, not nearly as wealthy as we are, was paying its privates fighting in Iraq as part of the coalition $2,366.73 per month. For sergeants it was $1,854 (U.S.) and $4,570.53 (Canada). Isn't that remarkable? And terrible?

Chip Somodevilla/Getty Images

4,000 young Americans decomposing in their graves today died for
the two men shown in the photo above, George Bush and Karl Rove,
and their friend Dick Cheney? We know they didn't die for you and
me. And they certainly didn't die for America. Since Hussein constituted no threat to this country and had nothing to do with 9/11, how
could these young Americans have possibly died to protect this country? Indeed, America has only been greatly harmed by the war. Not
only by the loss of the 4,000 American soldiers who lost their lives in
Iraq, and the 30,000 who have been seriously wounded, but we have
spent over $1 trillion there that could have been used to help fix the

many ills of this country. (Political columnist Nicholas D. Kristof got his calculator out in July of 2007 and computed that "if we take the total eventual cost of the Iraq war, that sum could be used to finance health care for all uninsured Americans for perhaps 30 years." Indeed, Nobel Prize–winning novelist Joseph Stiglitz says that "for a fraction of the cost of this war, we could have put social security on a sound footing for the next half-century or more.")

On top of all that, and to repeat what is well known, we've converted a country that was free of terrorists into one with many terrorists in it, and we've alienated almost the entire civilized world. So please don't say that Sergio and his fellow soldiers died for America.

Since we know that no American interest was being served by the war, and hence, these young men did not die for America or for you and me, whom did they die for? As ugly and grotesque as it is, the fact is that they gave up their lives to further the political interests of Bush, Rove, and Cheney. No political figures in American history ever so shamelessly exploited a war for political advantage as much as these three. Indeed, Rove built Bush's whole successful 2004 reelection campaign around the war in Iraq.

Speaking of the photo of Bush and Rove, do these two "men" look like men of real character, stature, moral strength, and dignity, the type whose word and sterling example could inspire a nation to go to war? I put "men" in quotes, because Bush is obviously not a man of stature. He's a spoiled, callous brat who became president only because of his father's good name. And Rove is a pasty, weak-faced, and mean-spirited political criminal. Neither of them are men of stature, honor, and gravitas, like many of our fine leaders of the past century such as Teddy Roosevelt, Wilson, FDR, Eisenhower, JFK, Ford, and George Bush Sr. These two are human embarrassments, and it's written all over their faces who they are. There's nothing of substance and character on the inside of either of these two "men" for their faces to reflect. These "men" refused to fight for America when it was their time to fight for this country—Bush using his father's influence to get into the National Guard so he wouldn't be sent to Vietnam, and Rove getting a student deferment. Cheney, for his part, got five deferments, later explaining that "I had other priorities" than going to war. Nonetheless, they had no hesitation sending thousands of American soldiers to die violent deaths on foreign soil against a nation that wasn't our enemy (Hussein was only an enemy of George Bush and his father, not America—see discussion in notes) and had nothing to do with 9/11. I repeat, because I don't want anyone to make any mistake about this, *these are the men whom Sergio and other American soldiers died for.*

Isn't that nice, that parents raise their son, whom they love with every fiber of their being, to die for these "men"? That their son's ashes come back in a jar from Iraq or his body is too blown into pieces to be viewed in its metal container, because of George Bush, Dick Cheney, and Karl Rove? If you say our young men didn't die for Bush, Cheney, and Rove, then whom did they die for? Hey, I'm talking to you. If you don't think they died for Bush, Cheney, and Rove, I want you to tell me whom you think they died for?

Indeed, some poor soldiers expressly said they died for Bush. Like young Mariano, who wrote his parents from Iraq a week or so before he was killed by a roadside bomb in Iraq, "I didn't vote for Bush, but I'll take a bullet for him." Can you imagine that? Willing to die for the draft-dodging, arrogant son of privilege from Crawford. The reason Mariano said this, of course, is that because of Bush's lies, as recently as 2006, 90 percent of our soldiers in Iraq still actually believed that Hussein and Iraq were involved in 9/11. As has been said, the epitaph that could be on the gravestone of poor Sergio and other young American soldiers who died in Iraq is "Bush Lied. I Died." Virtually all of the American soldiers who died in Iraq believed they were fighting for their country. The mother of one, Cpl. Sean Kelly, said what we have heard over and over from other parents: "He was proud to be there fighting for our country." Cpl. James L. Moore had told his grandmother in a phone call home from Iraq shortly before he was killed: "Grandma, I'd rather be fighting them here than to have them come there [U.S.] to fight." The mother of Lance Cpl. Robert A. Martinez (one of ten Marines killed in combat in Fallouja in December of 2005—typically, they were very young ["babies" many Americans have called them], two being nineteen, three twenty, and one twenty-one)—said her son "wanted to protect his family. He said he was doing it for us. He was a true patriot who believed in his mission and President Bush."

When Pfc. Thomas Tucker (twenty-five) called home from Iraq in June of 2006 to inform his parents he was going to be gone on a mission for a while, he left a voice mail message that included the following: "Hey, Mama. I love you. I love you too Dad . . . I will be back before you know it . . . I worry about you guys, too. I love you, okay. I'm going to be okay. Everything is going to be okay. *I'm going to defend my country*. Be proud of me." A few days later, the bodies of Tucker and fellow soldier Pfc. Khristian Menchaca (twenty-three) were found, their tattered army uniforms drenched in blood. Both had been brutally tortured and their bodies severely mutilated. One of them had been decapitated, his head sitting next to his body, his chest cut open. A video released by the insurgent group responsible for the killings shows one insurgent picking up the head while another insurgent steps on the face of the other solider. According to his family, Menchaca, who had recently married, believed completely, like Tucker, in the U.S. mission in Iraq. "My little boy," Maria Guadalupe Vasquez, Menchaca's mother, cried out at his funeral.

These words were voiced over and over by the mothers of fallen American soldiers. "Please tell me that I'm going to wake up, and this is just a horrible dream," said Marina Beyer in November 2004 as she stood in the chill outside the San Francisco airport, waiting for the body of her son who was killed in Iraq on his twenty-first birthday to arrive. "In my mind he was still my little boy." When his flag-draped container was pulled on a baggage cart into the cargo area, she broke down as she leaned against it, wailing, "No! No!"

Bush, the man former Mexican president Vicente Fox has called "the cockiest guy I have ever met in my life," insists on thrusting his audacity in our face. Since he ran away when it was his time to fight for his country, one would think, for instance, that when he speaks to audiences about all "the many brave men and women" who have died for "our freedom," he'd simply leave it at that. But he has consistently gone on to use words that one would think, if he had a conscience that served as a harness, he would purposefully avoid since they compel comparisons with his own cowardly conduct during the Vietnam War. He has a fondness for saying that these dead Americans "answered the call" and "stepped forward" to serve. (Could Bush be adding to himself, "I didn't, but hey, so what? I love America. Always have"?)

Bush even has the effrontery to use letters home from innocent young American soldiers who died in Iraq *for him* as evidence they died *for their country*, reading the letters at public events. For instance, on Memorial Day at Arlington National Cemetery in 2005, he read a letter from Sgt. Michael Evans, twenty-two, who was killed in Baghdad, to his family in case of his death: "My death," young Evans wrote, "will mean nothing if you stop now. I know it will be hard, but I gave my life so you could live. Not just live, but live free."

The outrageous nature of what has happened becomes markedly sicker when one considers the fact that many of the parents of soldiers killed in Iraq just love Bush, the man who, unbeknownst to them, was directly responsible for their son's death. When the parents of a young marine from Clovis, California, tried to e-mail their son in Iraq to give him news that Bush had been reelected, the mother said, "Jared, Bush won. Your Dad and I are so happy, but where are you? Where are you?" The parents learned the next day that Jared and his inseparable childhood friend and marine buddy, Jeremiah, were killed by the same hidden bomb near Baghdad. Jared's mother had to locate stitches in the back of her son's head in his coffin to make sure it was really her son lying before her.

Kevin Graves, whose son was killed in Iraq, told Bush in a face-to-face meeting: "It was an honor for my son to serve under you as commander in chief."

And then there are the Jennifer Hartings of the survivors' community. Harting's husband, Jay, was killed in combat in Iraq two days before she gave birth to their son. Responding to the antiwar activism of Cindy Sheehan, who lost her twenty-four-year-old son, Casey, in combat in Iraq, Harting took Sheehan to task: "I sympathize with her pain. But I think Cindy Sheehan doesn't get it," Harting said. "You can't just leave when the going gets tough. Even if tough means that soldiers are going to die." *Time* wrote that "Harting thinks that instead of protesting, Sheehan should take solace in knowing that a soldier's job is to follow the President *no matter what.*"

In talking about the horrors of the Iraq war, one of the problems is that numbers on a page are so lifeless and mean little to most people. Saying that 100,000 people have died in the war in Iraq is just a number to them. But obviously, if they could have seen, up close, the horror and carnage of all 100,000 people dying, the number 100,000 would have a totally different meaning to them. As *New York Times* columnist Bob Herbert put it: "The extent of the suffering caused by the war seldom penetrates the consciousness of most Americans. For the public at large, the dead and the wounded are little more than statistics. They're out of sight, and thus mostly out of mind." That wouldn't be so, he says, if they, for instance, could "imagine a couple of soldiers in flames, screaming, as they attempt to escape the burning wreckage of their vehicle hit by a roadside bomb."

On September 29, 2006, I caught on CNN a young Iraqi man, in bone-deep pain, sobbing into the camera over what had happened to his mother. In the sweep of the civil strife in Iraq caused by Bush's war—in which the Shiites and Sunnis have been slaughtering each other in great numbers—he related that his mother had gone into a nearby grocery store where a gunman from a rival sect had shot her five times, killing her on the spot. Her son cried on TV that "I picked up her brains in my hand."

Is that personal enough? Multiply, if you can, this horror by the thousands upon thousands of Iraqi citizens finding their father, son, sister, husband, or wife dead on the street, their bodies usually mutilated, the victims often beheaded.

These are just some of the captions on the hundreds upon hundreds of articles I read the past several years chronicling the horror of the war in Iraq.

"5 U.S. Troops, 5 Iraqis Killed in Bombings"; "31 American Troops Die as Marine Copter Goes Down in Iraq, 6 Others Also

KILLED"; "BAGHDAD SUICIDE BLAST KILLS 21 AT IRAQI RECRUITING CENTER"; "8 U.S. TROOPS KILLED IN BATTLE"; "BAGHDAD BOMBINGS KILL 43 IRAQIS"; "5 U.S. SOLDIERS, 22 IRAQIS KILLED ON DAY OF VIOLENCE"; "180 IRAQIS KILLED"; "12 AMERICANS ARE SLAIN IN BAGHDAD"; "30 DIE IN CAR BOMB BLAST IN BUSY BAGHDAD MARKET"; "ROADSIDE EXPLOSION KILLS 5 U.S. SOLDIERS"; "AMERICAN FIGHTER JETS KILL 20 IRAQI CIVILIANS"; "6 MARINES SLAIN BY BOMBS IN WESTERN IRAQ OFFENSIVE"; "AT LEAST 19 U.S. TROOPS DIE IN IRAQ"; "SUICIDE ATTACK AT IRAQI MARKET KILLS 20, 3 G.I.s DIE FROM HOMEMADE BOMBS"; "5 U.S. SOLDIERS DIE FROM ROADSIDE BOMB"; "SUICIDE BOMBING KILLS 4 G.I.s IN IRAQ"; "AT LEAST 5 IRAQI CIVILIANS ARE KILLED BY U.S. TROOPS"; "SUICIDE BOMBER KILLS 33 IN IRAQ"; "IRAQI REBELS KILL 5 U.S. TROOPS AND WOUND 11"; "60 IRAQIS, 7 U.S. TROOPS KILLED"; "36 DIE IN SUICIDE FUNERAL BOMBING IN IRAQ"; "U.S. STRIKES IN IRAQ KILL 19 MILITANTS, 15 CIVILIANS, INCLUDING 9 CHILDREN"; "130 KILLED IN IRAQ, 7 AMERICANS INCLUDED"; "ARMY COPTER CRASH IN IRAQ KILLS 12"; "BOMBER HITS BAGHDAD CROWD—AT LEAST 73 DIE"; "4 U.S. SOLDIERS KILLED BY ROADSIDE BOMB"; "BOMB KILLS 10 IN BAGHDAD, 22 FOUND EXECUTED"; "5 MARINES DEAD, 11 INJURED IN AN AMBUSH BY INSURGENTS"; "45 DIE IN IRAQI VIOLENCE"; "IRAQI POLICE SAY U.S.-LED RAID KILLS AT LEAST 17 AT SHIITE MOSQUE"; "ROADSIDE BOMB IN IRAQ KILLS 5 MARINES"; "2 G.I.s, AT LEAST 28 OTHERS KILLED IN SEVERAL ATTACKS"; "9 MARINES DIE AS INSURGENTS MOUNT ATTACKS"; "THREE BOMBS KILL AT LEAST 70 STUDENTS AT UNIVERSITY OF BAGHDAD"; "8 U.S. TROOPS KILLED IN IRAQ"; 5 U.S. SOLDIERS DIE IN BAGHDAD ATTACKS"; "BOMBS IN BAGHDAD KILL 35 IRAQI CHILDREN"; "7 U.S. SOLDIERS DIE IN IRAQ"; "5 G.I.s DIE IN BOMBING"; "INSURGENT VIOLENCE KILLS 4 MARINES, 14 IRAQIS"; "6 U.S. TROOPS KILLED IN IRAQ DURING DAY OF ATTACKS"; "BAGHDAD BLAST KILLS 35 WAITING FOR FUEL"; "ROADSIDE BOMB KILLS 7 U.S. SOLDIERS"; "2 BOMBS AT SOCCER FIELD KILL 12, MOSTLY CHILDREN IN BAGHDAD"; "100 MORE LIVES END VIOLENTLY IN IRAQ, NEARLY 30 BODIES FOUND AROUND BAGHDAD"; "IRAQ VIOLENCE CLAIMS 10 U.S. SERVICEMEN"; "75 IRAQIS KILLED BY INSURGENTS"; "30 IRAQI POLICE, CIVILIANS KILLED"; "NEARLY 90 IRAQIS KILLED IN 2 BAGHDAD MARKETPLACES"; "86 FOUND DEAD IN BAGHDAD STRIFE"; "CAR BOMBINGS KILL 62 IN IRAQ"; "SUICIDE BLAST KILLS 7

MARINES"; "46 IN BAGHDAD FOUND HANDCUFFED, BLINDFOLDED AND SHOT IN HEAD"; "6 MORE GI'S ARE KILLED IN IRAQ"; "25 SLAIN AND 40 WOUNDED IN IRAQ"; "TRIPLE BOMBING KILLS 78 AT SHIITE MOSQUE"; "10 MARINES KILLED IN IRAQ"; "16 POLICE RECRUITS KILLED IN IRAQ, 34 OTHER BODIES FOUND"; "8 AMERICAN TROOPS KILLED"; "BOMB KILLS 10 MARINES AT FALLOUJA"; "SUICIDE BOMBER KILLS 60 IN IRAQ"; "HELICOPTERS COLLIDE, 17 U.S. SOLDIERS DIE"; "68 IRAQIS, INCLUDING 16 CHILDREN DIE IN IRAQ"; "IRAQ SUICIDE BLAST TARGETING U.S. TROOPS KILLS 24 CHILDREN"; "40 STUDENTS, MOSTLY FEMALE, DIE IN SUICIDE BLAST AT UNIVERSITY OF BAGHDAD"; "IRAQ BOMBING KILLS 4 U.S. WOMEN."

I am very convinced (based on conversations with right-wing Republicans and liberal Democrats alike on this) that these almost daily reports in the newspapers of war fatalities in Iraq mean nothing to the overwhelming majority of right-wing Republicans, and even some Democrats, most of them not even bothering to read the short articles. This is the typical response I got, mostly from right-wing Republicans, when I asked them if they became sad or depressed when they read articles in the paper like those above that people were dying horrible deaths in Iraq: "No, not really." "But what if, for instance, you read that a hundred innocent Iraqi citizens, even children and babies, were blown up and killed in a market or mosque in Baghdad. You don't feel anything at all about something like this?" "No, this is what happens during war." But when I learn of such things I am affected by all of them, since I reflexively convert the number of fatalities in my mind into the reality of real human beings—young American soldiers (as well as Iraqi civilians) whose lives were brutally cut short—and imagine the horror of their loved ones when they hear from one of the military representatives at their door the worst and most dreaded news they will ever hear in their lives: "On behalf of the secretary of defense, I regret to inform you . . ."

Some parents don't just scream out in their home upon hearing the news of the death of their son. The Baltimore father of Staff Sgt. Kendall Watersby sobbed in the streets of his neighborhood. Holding up a picture of his marine son, he said, "I want President Bush to get a good look at this, really good look here. This is the only son I had, only son." (Young Watersby, twenty-nine, himself had a ten-year-old son who lost the only father he would ever have.)

Another father in Hollywood, Florida, overcome with grief, anger, and incomprehension, after crying out on the street and calling out, to his twenty-year-old son, "Alexander, Alexander, this is not happening," picked up a hammer and started smashing things in the van that had transported the three marines who brought him the terrible news. He then grabbed a propane torch and a five-gallon can of gasoline and set fire to the van, badly burning himself in the process to the extent of $53,000 in hospital bills. "I miss him every day that goes by," he says of his son. "I wake up and I think of him."

Some survivors can't even bear to hear the news. When the army messenger came to the door of the home in Los Angeles where the wife of army sergeant Evan Ashcroft was staying with her father, to tell her of Evan's death, Evan's wife, Ashley, stayed upstairs. "I was on the floor, screaming," she said. "I didn't want to let them tell me."

And when a soldier dies, it of course isn't only his immediate family that endures great pain and suffering, but also his extended family of cousins, uncles, nephews, nieces, even very close friends.

Then there are the great numbers of American soldiers who don't lose their lives in battle, but their arm or a leg (many times both; some all four limbs), even their eyes and eyesight. Or they come back with injuries that maim and shatter. Or they are severely burned, crippled, or paralyzed—disabled for life.

And there's the much greater number of Iraqi veterans who sustain psychic damage from the war that will torment them for the rest of their lives. Many will probably end up, like many Vietnam veterans, as street people. Though just as real, these are the more hidden wounds of battle that have destroyed everything from marriages to careers. A March 1, 2006, report from the *Journal of the American Medical Association* said that more than a third of the soldiers returning home from the war in Iraq have sought treatment for mental problems including anxiety, depression, and post-traumatic stress disorder. Can you imagine trying to erase from your mind something that, as a soldier said, was "the worst thing I ever saw in my life," the last view of his close buddy who was killed in combat? "My friend didn't have a face," he said. And if you are a sensitive human being, can you actually kill another human being without killing a part of yourself?

The photos in this book attempt to capture, as much as it is possible, the enormity of what Bush has done—and so far has gotten away with. With respect to the photos of American soldiers who have died in Iraq, in looking at them, let me quote a Cleveland mother who lost her son Augie in Iraq: "It's not faceless Marines fighting the war. Augie fought it. We want people to see Augie's picture and say 'Damn, that could have been my kid.'"

How has George Bush reacted to the hell he created in Iraq, to the thousands of lives that have been lost in the war, and to the enormous and endless suffering that the survivors of the victims—their loved ones—have had to endure?

I've always felt that impressions are very important in life, and other than "first impressions," they are usually right. Why? Because impressions, we know, are formed over a period of time. They are the accumulation of many words and incidents, many or most of which one has forgotten, but which are nonetheless assimilated into the observer's subconscious and thus make their mark. In other words, you forgot the incident, but it added to the impression. "How do you feel about David? Do you feel he's an honest person?" "Yeah, I do." "Why do you say that about him? Can you give me any examples that would cause you to say he's honest?" "No, not really, at least not off the top of my head. But I've known David for over ten years, and my sense is that he's an honest person."

I have a very distinct impression that with the exception of a vagrant tear that may have fallen if he was swept up, in the moment, at an emotional public ceremony for American soldiers who have died in the war, George Bush hasn't suffered at all over the monumental suffering, death, and horror he has caused by plunging this nation into the darkness of the Iraq war, probably never losing a wink of sleep over it. Sure, we often hear from Bush administration sources, or his family, or from Bush himself, about how much he suffers over the loss of American lives in Iraq. But that dog won't run. How do we just about know this is nonsense? Not only because the words he has uttered could never have escaped from his lips if he were suffering, but because no matter how many American soldiers have died on a given day in Iraq (averaging well over two every day), he is always seen with a big smile on his face that same day or the next, and is in good spirits. *How would that be possible if he was suffering?* For example, the November 3, 2003, morning *New York Times* front-page headline story was that the previous day in Fallouja, Iraq, insurgents "shot down an American helicopter just outside the city in a bold assault that killed 16 soldiers and wounded 20 others. It was the deadliest attack on American troops since the United States invaded Iraq in March." Yet later in that same day when Bush arrived for a fund-raiser in Birmingham, Alabama, he was smiling broadly, and Mike Allen of the *Washington Post* wrote that "the President appeared to be in a fabulous mood." This is merely one of hundreds of such observations made about Bush while the brutal war continued in Iraq.

And even when Bush is off camera, we have consistently heard from those who have observed him up close how much he seems to be enjoying himself. When Bush gave up his miles of running several times a week because of knee problems, he took up biking. "He's turned into a bike maniac," said Mark McKinnon in March of 2005, right in the middle of the war. McKinnon, a biking friend of Bush's who was Bush's chief media strategist in his 2004 reelection campaign, also told the *New York Times*'s Elisabeth Bumiller about Bush: "He's as calm and relaxed and confident *and happy* as I've ever seen him." Happy? Under the horrible circumstances of the war, where Bush's own soldiers are dying violent deaths, how is that even possible?

In a time of war and suffering, Bush's smiles, joking, and good spirits stand in stark contrast to the demeanor of every one of his predecessors and couldn't possibly be more inappropriate. Michael Moore, in his motion picture documentary *Fahrenheit 9/11*, captured this fact and the superficiality of Bush well with a snippet from a TV interview Bush gave on the golf course following a recent terrorist attack. Bush said, "I call upon all nations to do everything they can to stop these terrorist killers. Thank you." Then, without missing a single beat, he said in reference to a golf shot he was about to hit: "Now watch this drive."

Before I get into specific instances of Bush laughing and having fun throughout the entire period of the inferno he created in Iraq, I want to discuss a number of more indirect but revealing incidents that reflect he could not care less about the human suffering and carnage going on in Iraq, or anywhere.

1. The first inkling I got that Bush didn't care about the suffering of *anyone*, not just those dying in Iraq, was from an article in the September 22, 2001, *New York Times* just eleven days after 9/11. Though 3,000 Americans had been murdered and the nation was in agony and shock, the man who should have been leading the mourning was, behind the scenes, not affected in the tiniest way. The article, by Frank Bruni, said that "Mr. Bush's *nonchalant, jocular demeanor remains the same*. In private, say several Republicans close to the administration, he still slaps backs and uses baseball terminology, at one point promising that the terrorists were not 'going to steal home on me.' He is not staying up all night, or even most of the night. He is taking time to play with his dogs and his cat. He is working out most days." So *right after* several thousand Americans lost their lives in a horrible catastrophe, behind the scenes Bush is his same old backslapping self, and he's not letting the tragedy interfere in the slightest way with the daily regimen of his life that he enjoys.

In fact, he himself admitted to the magazine *Runners World* (August 23, 2002) that after the Afghanistan war began: "I have been running with a little more intensity . . . It helps me to clear my mind." (In other words, Bush likes to clear his mind of the things he's supposed

to be thinking about.) Remarkably finding time in the most important job on earth to run six days a week, Bush added: "It's interesting
that my times have become faster . . . For me, the psychological benefit [in running] is enormous. *You tend to forget everything that's going on
in your mind and just concentrate on the time and distance.*" But even this
obscene indulgence after 9/11 and during wartime by the man with
more responsibility than anyone in the world wasn't enough for
Bush. He told the magazine: "I try to go for longer runs, but it's
tough around here at the White House on the outdoor track. *It's sad
that I can't run longer. It's one of the saddest things about the presidency.*"
Imagine that. Among all the things that the president of the United
States could be sad about during a time of war, not being able to run
longer six days a week is up there near the top of the list.

A *New York Times* article not long after 9/11 (November 5, 2001) reported that Bush had told his friends (obviously with pride) that "his
runs on the Camp David trails through the Maryland woods have produced his fastest time in a decade, three miles in 21 minutes and 6 seconds." *USA Today* (October 29, 2001) reported that Bush used to run 3
miles in 25 minutes and now he was "boasting to friends and staffers"
about his new time, and was "now running 4 miles a day."

So with his approval rating soaring to 90 percent in the wake of
9/11—and with his being the *main* person in America whose job required that he be totally engaged every waking hour in working diligently on this nation's response to 9/11—Bush, remarkably, was
working diligently on improving his time for the mile. I ask you, what
American president in history, Republican or Democrat, would have
conducted himself this way?

2. One thing about Bush. He's so dense that he makes remarks an intelligent person who was as much of a scoundrel as he would never
make. They'd keep their feelings, which they would know to be very
shameful, to themselves. On December 21, 2001, just a few months
after 9/11—a tragedy that shocked the nation and the world in which
3,000 Americans were consumed by fires, some choosing to jump to

their deaths out of windows eighty or more stories high—Bush, who could only have been thinking of himself, told the media: *"All in all, it's been a fabulous year for Laura and me."* He said this because that is exactly the way he felt. What difference does 9/11 make? I'm president. I love it, and Laura and I are having a ball.

Indeed, on January 20, 2005, right in the midst of the hell on earth Bush created in Iraq—when the carnage there was near its worst and American soldiers and Iraqi citizens were dying violent deaths every day—Bush, referring to himself and his wife, told thousands of partying supporters at one of his nine inaugural balls: *"We're having the time of our life."* Can you even begin to imagine Roosevelt in the midst of the Second World War, Truman during the Korean War, or LBJ and Nixon during the Vietnam War, saying something like this?

3. Does it not stand to reason that if Bush were suffering over the daily killings and tragedy in Iraq, he would be working every waking hour to lessen the mounting number of casualties as well as find a way to satisfactorily end the terrible conflict? I mean, as president, that's what you'd expect of him, right? Isn't that his job? Yet we know that although Bush is still in office, he has already spent far more time on vacation than any other president in American history. For instance, by April 11, 2004 (he was inaugurated January 20, 2001), he had visited his cherished ranch in Crawford a mind-boggling thirty-three times and *spent almost eight months of his presidency there.*

Although the office of the presidency follows the president wherever he goes twenty-four hours a day, and at least some part of every day on vacation, no matter how small, was spent by Bush attending to his duties as president, we also know that Bush's main purpose when he goes on vacation, obviously and by definition, is to vacation, not work. CBS News White House correspondent Mark Knoller, who travels with Bush and keeps track of such things, told me that as of January 1, 2008, in Bush's less than seven years as president, he had visited his ranch in Texas an unbelievable 69 times, spending, per Knoller, "all or part of 448 days on vacation there." As amazing as this is, Bush also made, Knoller says, 132 visits to Camp David during this period, spending "all or part of 421 days there," and 10 visits to his family's vacation compound at Kennebunkport, Maine, spending "all or part of 39 days there."

So the bottom line is that of a total of approximately 2,535 days as president, most of them during a time of war, Bush spent all or a part of 908 days, an incredible 36 percent of his time, on vacation or at retreat places. Hard to believe, but true. *Nine hundred and eight days is two and a half years of Bush's presidency.* Two and a half years of the less than seven years of his presidency in which his main goal was to kick back and have fun. You see, the White House digs, with a pool, theater, gymnasium, etc., weren't enjoyable enough for Bush. He wanted a *more* enjoyable place to be during his life as president.*

My position in life is infinitely less important than Bush's, yet during the above same period of Bush's presidency, I not only worked much longer hours every day than Bush, I worked seven days a week, never took one vacation, and only took three days off to go to the desert with my wife to celebrate our fiftieth wedding anniversary. If it had not been for the anniversary, I wouldn't have even taken those three days off. I realize I take working to an extreme, living by the clock each day, always looking up to see how much time I have left, working from morning to morning (retiring usually around two in the morning and starting my day at ten in the morning). Still, it is striking to consider that in seven years, I took 3 days off and Bush, the president of the United States, took 908. Even Americans who lead a more normal life than I, even fat-cat corporate executives, haven't

---

*Remarkably, during his campaign for reelection in 2004 Bush very frequently spoke of the "hard work" he and his administration were engaging in. This was the first time I had ever heard an American president speak of the "hard work" involved in his job. I have heard them speak of the immense "burden" of the office of the presidency in being responsible for the destiny and welfare of millions of people. But you see, for someone like Bush who was born on home plate and thought he had hit a home run, *anything* he does, *any* effort at all, he considers "hard work."

taken anywhere near the time away from their work that Bush has. Indeed, I think we can safely say that even though Bush has the most important and demanding job in this entire land, he has irresponsibly *taken far more time off from his job to have fun during the past seven years than any worker or company executive in America!!!* Is Bush, or is he not, a disgrace of the very first order?

What does this incredible amount of time that Bush spends away from work show? Well, it shows that Bush is a very lazy person, and an irresponsible one. But it also reveals something that has had much more serious consequences for this nation, something I have never heard anyone say before. What I strongly believe (without absolutely knowing) is that this man has no respect or love for this country. I'm not saying he hates it, but he has no particular love for it. Why do I say this? It is obvious that Bush's knowledge of information and events is shockingly low. Even many of those who support him find it very difficult not to acknowledge this reality. For instance, Bush supporter and neoconservative Richard Perle said that the thing that "struck me about George Bush is that he did not know very much." Perle was being kind.

Now let's take you, the reader, and assume for the sake of argument that in terms of knowledge you're like Bush. If you were thrust overnight into the office of the presidency of the United States, the most important job on earth, and you knew your decisions could affect the lives of hundreds of millions of people, what would you do *if you were a responsible person who loved this country?* There's really only one answer to this question. You'd knock yourself out working feverishly to learn as much as you possibly could so you could do as good a job as president as you were capable of doing. You'd do this because you love your country and because your sense of responsibility to it would compel you to do it. Yet Bush, knowing nothing, does the exact opposite, spending, as we've seen, well over one-third of his two terms on vacation or at Camp David or his family's retreat at Kennebunkport, Maine. He prefers to run the most important country on earth not by reading up on what he needs to know, but by lazily relying on what his gut tells him and on what communication he can manage with his God.*

When Condoleezza Rice was Bush's national security adviser, she said her boss operated by "instinct" and it was her job to "intellectualize his instincts." My neighbor has instincts on things, too, Ms. Rice. Shall we make him president and you can do the same thing for him as you did for George?

Bush's determination not to extend himself in any way is so pronounced that even though he apparently has no sense of where major countries of the world are situated on the globe in relation to each other, he did not have enough concern to even bother looking at a

---

*As has been reported often, Bush said he was "called" (obviously by the Lord) to seek the presidency, and said, "I believe that God wants me to be president." And when he was asked whether he was seeking his father's advice on whether to go to war in Iraq, he responded: "You know, he is the wrong father to appeal to in terms of strength. There is a higher father I appeal to."

Isn't it so very reassuring that we have a president who told a *Houston Post* reporter on the day in 1993 that he announced his intention to run for governor of Texas that one "had to accept Christ to go to heaven"? (In other words, Jews, Muslims, and nonbelievers, among others, need not apply.) Who said on Fox News in 2004 that "I am reading Oswald Chambers' *My Utmost to the Highest* . . . on a daily basis to be in the Word." And what is that Word? Delightful gems such as this (that help explain part of the Bush we know): To do what is right, "do not [Chambers, an obscure British Protestant itinerant preacher of the early twentieth century, is telling his pupil Bush] confer with flesh and blood, that is, your own sympathies, your own insight—anything that is not based on your personal relationship with God." And, "Never ask the advice of another about anything God makes you decide before Him. If you ask advice, you will nearly always side with Satan . . . [You] know when a proposition comes from God because of its quiet persistence. When [you] have to weigh pros and cons, and doubt and debate come in, [you] are bringing in an element that is not of God." Chambers tells Bush and his other readers that anytime they are confronted with a pressing problem, they should say "'Speak Lord' and make time to listen."

In other words, don't use your mind (the one that God supposedly gave us to think with) or those of others around you to guide you in your conduct. Do what God personally tells you to do. My God.

map before attending an international summit that Russian president Vladimir Putin was hosting in Strelna, near St. Petersburg, Russia, in July of 2006. While a tape recorder was recording without Bush's knowledge, after saying to Putin that he intended to go back home that afternoon, he asked Chinese president Hu Jintao, seated next to him: "Where are you going? Home? This is your neighborhood. Doesn't take too long to get home?" When Hu said his flight to Beijing was eight hours, Bush said: "Me too."

Bush has so little sense of responsibility to his country that a November 5, 2001, *New York Times* article by a reporter covering the White House beat said that when Bush was elected president, unbelievably, unbelievably, "the plan had been for him to spend nearly every weekend at the Texas ranch, with the White House serving as a kind of Monday to midday Friday pied-à-terre [a term normally used to refer to a small dwelling for temporary use, as an apartment maintained in a foreign city] away from what was *really* home," his ranch house in Crawford, Texas. In other words, the office of the presidency required the inconvenience each week of taking Bush away from where he really wanted to be, but he wasn't going to let the presidency interfere too much with his lifestyle. Again, unbelievable, unbelievable.

I believe that Bush has no strong sense of responsibility to his country because, I maintain, he doesn't love America. His sense of responsibility to his country is so remarkably poor that not only is it well known he doesn't read any reports from those in his administration, so his aides only give him short, one- or two-paragraph summaries of lengthy reports, but he frequently doesn't even read these summaries. In his book about Paul O'Neill, Bush's former Treasury secretary, the journalist Ron Suskind writes: "O'Neill had been made to understand by various colleagues in the White House that the president should not be expected to read reports. In his personal experience, the president didn't even appear to have read the short memos he [O'Neill] sent over." This was compounded by the fact that when O'Neill would meet with Bush, "Bush did not ask any questions."

Bush, the man with the bumper-sticker mentality, had no interest. So little interest, in fact, that he doesn't even read newspapers. "I glance at the headlines just to get kind of a flavor for what's moving," he told *Fox News*. Obviously, America has a president who is a man of considerable substance, depth, maturity, and intellectual curiosity. *Playboy* editor James Kaminsky told *USA Today*: "It's appalling to think that the man who runs the country somehow finds time for a long gym workout each day but can't muster up the intellectual curiosity to peruse the newspaper." And David Kay, the CIA's first chief weapons inspector for the Iraq Survey Group following the defeat of Hussein's regime, said about Bush: "I'm not sure I've ever spoken to anyone at that level who seemed less inquisitive."

I ask you. *Is this the attitude and conduct of someone who feels that as president he has a great responsibility to his country?*

So the flag-waving Bush who wears an American flag pin on his lapel, and patriotism on his sleeve, someone who even John Kerry, his presidential opponent, said loved America, probably has no love for this country at all. Whether I am right or not, I am quite confident that there is enough evidence for the above proposition to be worthy of consideration.

In my work as a trial lawyer and author of nonfiction books, I find that when I start out with a sound premise, as I believe the above to be, subsequent events and other revelations virtually always just fall into place with the premise, fortifying my original assumption. Very briefly, here are a few that support my premise about Bush. Perhaps the clearest way one can show one's love for one's country is by being willing to die for it. The first President Bush, President Kennedy, John McCain, John Kerry, and so many others were willing to do that and became war heroes. But we know that the flag-waving phony, Bush, wanted no part of fighting in any American war, so he joined the Texas National Guard, which was the way in those days to avoid fighting in Vietnam. And it wasn't because he was against the Vietnam War. In fact, he is on record as saying he supported it. But consistent with my premise, Bush was unwilling to show his love for his country

by putting himself in harm's way for it. He chose to flee in the opposite direction for the friendly skies of Texas. But then again, and in all
fairness to Bush, there was always the threat of an invasion from Oklahoma he might have to repel. I mean, Texas and Oklahoma do take
their college football rivalry pretty seriously.

When this issue arose in his run for the presidency in 2000, Bush
and his campaign staff successfully deflected most of America's attention away from the fact that he ran away from the Vietnam War by
lowering the bar so far that an ant would have had difficulty crawling
under it. The only legitimate question, they said, was whether Bush
had "fulfilled his military obligation." And surely enough, well-known
Democratic liberals such as James Carville and Michael Moore actually got suckered into this obvious ploy by accepting it as the main issue, answering that they did not believe Bush had done so, instead of
zeroing in on the *only* fact that was relevant—Bush hid out from the
war. Carville, thinking he was making a point on cable TV with his
conservative sparmate, Tucker Carlson, began reciting the evidence
that Bush hadn't fulfilled his military obligation in the National
Guard. Carlson cut him off midway and said on behalf of his feckless
opponent: "Let's get on to something else. We all know Bush joined
the National Guard to avoid fighting in Vietnam."

Moore, whose film *Fahrenheit 9/11* suffered from a lack of credibility (e.g., in addition to taking things out of context, according to
Moore we went to war in Afghanistan to pave the way for securing an
important natural-gas pipeline; and he even vaguely suggested that
Bush invaded Iraq to destroy it so Bush's wealthy corporate friends
could get richer by rebuilding it), wasn't any better. For example, not
only didn't Moore (who was trying, in his movie, to hurt Bush in the
latter's campaign for the presidency against John Kerry) do the obvious by contrasting Bush with Kerry by noting that Kerry was a genuine war hero, but remarkably, the biggest point he made about Bush
was not that he ran away from the war in Vietnam but, are you ready,
that Bush "failed to take a medical examination" while in the National
Guard in Texas. I couldn't believe Moore's ineptitude. The Republican
Party could say appropriately about Moore (a good man who has his

heart in the right place): "With enemies like Michael Moore, who needs friends?"

On the issue of Bush running away from the Vietnam War, I should add that not one member of the hapless media who covered Bush thought to ask, when questioning him about his National Guard service, the only question that was relevant: "Mr. President, why did you prefer to join the National Guard over regular military duty?" There is no way that Bush could have answered that question without sounding exactly like what he was—a draft dodger who was afraid to fight in the war. Someone who only wanted to wave the flag, not fight for it. Yet this terrible hypocrite urged John McCain in 1992, before the latter was going to speak for George Sr. at the Republican National Convention: "You've gotta hammer Clinton on the draft-dodging."

Another good example showing that Bush has no love or respect for his country is the blatant cronyism he has practiced in his federal appointments. A *Time* magazine inquiry in 2005 found that "at top positions in some vital government agencies," Bush had put "connections [to him] before experience." One of the most well known, of course, was his appointment of his friend Michael Brown to head up FEMA (Federal Emergency Management Agency), the organization that received an F-minus for its handling of Katrina. It turned out that Brown had absolutely no experience to qualify him for such an important job. But hey, he did have experience working on the rules for Arabian horse competition. It's okay to appoint a friend if they are qualified. But Bush couldn't care less if they're qualified. Why? Because I believe he has no respect or love for the country he leads. My God, until there was a storm of protest, Bush even nominated his personal aide and close friend from Texas, Harriet Miers, to sit as a justice on the United States Supreme Court! Not only didn't she have one day of judicial experience (not by itself a disqualifying factor), but she didn't excel in law school or the practice of law. So she had never distinguished herself in any way in the legal profession, being the most ordinary of lawyers. How can you possibly appoint someone like this to the highest court in the land? You can if you have no respect or love for your country.

Another, perhaps even better piece of evidence establishing that Bush has no love for his country is that he places loyalty above everything else. He never fires anyone he likes and is close to, even if they've done a terrible job. There are many examples of this, but the best one is that of former CIA director George Tenet. We have *conclusive* evidence that Tenet's CIA failed the nation on 9/11. By definition, if it hadn't, and had intercepted the foreign conspiracy, 9/11 wouldn't have happened. Inasmuch as Tenet had thereby proved himself to be unable to adequately perform his duties as the CIA director, obviously (that is, if you love your country), Bush should have let Tenet go. And doubly so when Tenet's CIA was 100 percent wrong in assessing Iraq's weapons of mass destruction before the Iraq war. But Bush not only didn't fire Tenet, whom he liked and became good friends with, he never even showed any irritation with him. Instead, Bush vigorously defended Tenet and ended up giving Tenet the *Presidential Medal of Freedom* on December 14, 2004, the highest civil award that can be granted to an American citizen. But you see, Bush was much more interested in what he (Tenet) was doing for him (i.e., the friendship, camaraderie, and loyalty they had for each other) than in what Tenet was doing for America. "George [Tenet] and I have been spending a lot of quality time together," Bush said on September 26, 2001, in giving Tenet a vote of confidence when the CIA director was being urged to resign by critics.

Of course, the ultimate act by Bush showing a lack of respect and love for this country is leading this nation into a deadly war in Iraq for no justifiable reason at all. I said earlier that while Bush may not love America, he never hated it. But Bush's lying to the people of America to lead them into war shows an absolute, utter contempt for the American people. The son of privilege and entitlement has so little respect for the average citizen that he felt they weren't entitled to the truth, even though *he was going to fight his war with the blood of their children.*

Although I went off on a tributary about Bush not loving America, all of the above goes to the issue being addressed here that if Bush cared at all about the enormous suffering and horror in Iraq, he would be devoting his every available moment to stop or lessen it. We know he hasn't done this.

4. Another example of Bush not truly caring about the enormous suffering he has caused is that he went about deciding to go to war in the first place with apparently nary a concern for the consequences. Former lieutenant general Gregory Newbold, a three-star Marine Corps general, was being magnanimous to Bush when he said Bush's decision to invade Iraq "was done with a *casualness and swagger* that are the special province of those who have never had to execute these missions—or bury the results." The first part of what Newbold said is undoubtedly true, but I believe he errs when he attributes Bush's behavior simply to his lack of experiencing war himself. My sense is that the reason for Bush's behavior is much deeper. After all, other presidents, without having experienced war, never acted remotely the way Bush did.

Bush not only went to war with a swagger, he *wanted* war, was looking forward to it. Hearst White House correspondent Helen Thomas, who has been covering the White House since 1960, almost half a century, said of all the presidents she has known, Bush was the only one who "wanted to go to war." Bush was so eager to go to war that according to author Bob Woodward, Bush told him that he never even bothered to ask Colin Powell and Donald Rumsfeld if he should do it. He said he knew Cheney was gung-ho and "I could tell what [Powell and Rumsfeld] thought. I didn't need to ask them their opinion about Saddam Hussein or how to deal with Saddam Hussein." Has it ever happened before in American history that a president has gone to war without seeking the advice of his own secretary of state and secretary of defense as to whether he should do it? "I'm a war president," Bush told TV host Tim Russert on February 8, 2004. "I make decisions here in the Oval Office with war on my mind."

Televangelist Pat Robertson, a friend and supporter of Bush, met with Bush right before the war and expressed some misgivings he had about it. But Bush would have none of it. Robertson said Bush "was just sitting there, like, 'I'm on top of the world,'" which stunned Robertson.

No other American president in the last century (perhaps ever) *wanted* to go to war. In FDR's America, Japan attacked the United States on December 7, 1941, and four days later Germany declared war on the United States. So FDR can't be cited one way or the other on this issue. But no one in their right mind would ever in a thousand years suggest that FDR would have acted like Bush did.

We also know Eisenhower would not have. Recall his saying that "when people speak about a preventive war, *tell them to go and fight it.*" And there's no evidence that Truman was looking forward to and wanted the war in Korea.

We know that before his assassination in 1963, which was before the war escalated in Vietnam in 1965, JFK ordered that 1,000 of our military advisers be sent back to America from Vietnam by the end of that year. Although there is a spirited division of opinion as to whether, if JFK had lived, he would have gone to war in Vietnam (my view is that he would not have), both sides to the debate agree that he did not want to go to war in Vietnam. He was very opposed to it. But that is not the equivalent of saying he wouldn't have gone to war if he felt the situation eventually called for it. What JFK would have ended up doing, of course, is lost to history. But it is a calumny to even mention Bush's name in the same breath as JFK's on this issue.

With respect to LBJ, contrary to popular belief, LBJ was an extremely reluctant warrior in the Vietnam War, only yielding to hawks in his administration a year and a half after JFK's assassination. But the evidence is incontrovertible that he tried, for a long time, to avoid war with Ho Chi Minh. As to whether he cared about U.S. troops dying, the transcript of a May 27, 1964 (before the Vietnam War), White House tape-recorded conversation between LBJ and Senator Richard Russell of Georgia shows LBJ speaking about the "little old Sergeant who works for me . . . He's got six children, and I just put him up as the United States Army and Air Force and Navy every time I think about making this decision [about going to war]. Thinking about sending that father of those six kids in there . . . just makes the chills run up my back." LBJ would later tell his close aide Jack Valenti that reading the casualty reports from Vietnam was "like drinking carbolic acid every morning."

And Nixon ran for president in 1968 on a platform of *ending* the war in Vietnam, promising to bring "peace with honor."

President Clinton, though being urged on by people like John McCain and Colin Powell to put troops on the ground in Kosovo, regurgitating the old military bromide that you can't win a war from the air—foot soldiers have to march forward on terra—didn't want to lose any American lives, which would inevitably have happened on the ground. So the Vietnam draft dodger proved all the military experts wrong by conducting the war against the Serbs entirely from the air and won the war without the loss of one American soldier's life.

Even Bush's own father didn't "want" to go to war in the Persian Gulf. The Reverend Billy Graham says, "I tell the story about being with President Bush the night before the Gulf War began . . . He didn't want to go to war. And I haven't talked to any president yet who wanted to go to war."

Contrast the Reverend Graham's talk with Bush Sr. with the Reverend Pat Robertson's conversation with Bush where he said Bush was "on top of the world" over the upcoming war. Nothing else is needed to distinguish George Bush Sr., a decent man, from his son, but before we move on, one more example is fitting. In a letter to his children a month before the Persian Gulf War, Bush Sr. wrote that ordering American troops into combat "tears at my heart." And on the evening of January 16, 1991, the opening night of the Persian Gulf War, George Bush Sr. expressed his terrible disquietude in his tape-recorded diary before he addressed the nation at 9:00 p.m.: "I have never felt a day like this in my life . . . My lower gut hurts . . . and I take a couple of Mylantas . . . I think of what other presidents went through. The agony of war." Here's how our current president felt about the "agony" of war around 10:00 p.m. on the evening of March

19, 2003, minutes before he would address the nation to inform it the Iraq war had begun. As aides were applying makeup before his televised speech, he pumped his fist and told an aide: "Feel good."

In other words, Bush, "on top of the world," felt just wonderful about launching a high-tech war of destruction and death which his people obscenely titled "shock and awe."

5. British prime minister Tony Blair told members of his Labour Party about receiving letters from those who lost sons in the Iraq war and blaming him for it. He added: "Don't believe anyone who tells you, when they receive letters like that, they don't suffer doubt" about whether the deaths of British soldiers were worth it. When reporter-author Bob Woodward referred Bush to those remarks by Blair, Bush responded, "Yeah, I haven't suffered doubt." Woodward, incredulous, asked Bush: "Is that right? Not at all?" Bush replied: "No."

If Bush cared at all about the enormous human toll and suffering taking place in Iraq, how would it be possible for him to never once say to himself, "God, this is just terrible what's happening over there. I hope I didn't make a mistake," or something like that?

If George Bush really and truly cared about the loss of thousands of young American lives in Iraq, and that of over 100,000 Iraqi civilian lives, and was sensitive in the tiniest degree to the feelings of the victims' survivors, how could he have possibly dismissed all the violence and bloodshed in Iraq by predicting it will someday be viewed as "just a comma" in the history of Iraq's struggle for democracy (*CNN*, September 24, 2006)? Can you imagine how a father and mother who lost their only son in Bush's war, and whose remains came back to them "unviewable" in a box, must have felt to hear the one who sent their son to his death in a foreign land say, in effect, that he was just a part of a comma?

6. For some reason, although the death of Iraqi civilians in the war is always distressing to me, I take the reports in the paper of American soldiers being killed in Iraq harder. But there is no rational reason for this, since the Iraqi people want to live just as much as we do and take

the loss of their loved ones just as hard. All of them, like American soldiers who die, are innocent victims of Bush's war.

In a question and answer session after a speech in Philadelphia on December 12, 2005, Bush was asked how many Iraqis had died so far in the war. "I would say 30,000, more or less," he said. There wasn't the faintest hint in his voice conveying pity, sorrow, pain, regret, or anything. And the reason is that none of these things were inside of him. He was just uttering a number, nothing more, nothing less, like 30,000 barrels of oil, or paint, or oranges. Thirty-thousand human beings in their graves, many of whom were young children and babies, solely because of him, and it couldn't have been more obvious that he couldn't have cared less.

What is the source for a human being like Bush being so, well, inhuman? I don't know, but certainly one's mother cannot be discounted in any search for the source. In an appearance on *Good Morning America* on March 18, 2003, when Bush's mother, Barbara, was asked about the horrible carnage of war that was scheduled to start the next day with her son's invasion of Iraq, Mrs. Bush unbelievably responded: *"Why should we [talk] about body bags, and deaths, . . . I mean, it's not relevant.* So why should I waste my beautiful mind on something like that? And watch him [her son] suffer?" Can you imagine that? Absolutely no concern for young Americans (let alone Iraqis) getting killed. Her only concern was that she didn't want her son to suffer over these deaths. As we've seen, she needn't have worried about that.

Bush has often said he is more like his mother than his father. For a further insight into the soft and very sensitive Mrs. Bush, recall how, following Katrina, she visited the Astrodome in Houston on September 5, 2005, and said that given the fact that the evacuees from the hurricane who were being put up inside the arena were "underprivileged *anyway,*" things were "working out very well" for them. Barbara, apparently, didn't realize (or didn't care) that poor black people didn't want their lives to be totally disrupted, nor to lose forever the warm familiarity of their homes as well as most of their possessions (such as family photos and personal letters) any more than she and her very rich white friends from River Oaks (*the* correct address in Houston) would have.

7. On July 2, 2003, in response to a question about the military situation in Iraq, the reader will probably recall that Bush said, "There are some who feel the conditions are such that they can attack us there. My answer is bring 'em on." Can you imagine that? The media, who can always be counted on to do a minimum of thinking, naturally missed the main point in attacking Bush for the remark, focusing in on how "ill-advised" and "reckless" it was because it could provoke the enemy. But it's just conjecture whether his macho, Joe Six-Pack remark would deter the enemy, or cause them to take Bush up on his invitation. Because it's just conjecture I only gave a moment's thought to it. But two things were not conjecture, and I never saw where the media talked about them. One is that the remark couldn't possibly have been less presidential. I can't even conceive of any other American president talking this way. But what instantly angered me was that this punk who hid out during the Vietnam War, and who is now safe and sound here in America being protected by the Secret Service, dared to issue a challenge to the enemy to attack American soldiers. There's only one translation for his "bring 'em on" remark. "Come on and attack us. *You'll kill some of our soldiers*, but we'll kill more of yours." How dare this wimpish punk invite the enemy to kill American soldiers?

In December of 2005, Bush said, "To all who wear the uniform, I make you this pledge. America will not run in the face of car bombers and assassins as long as I am your commander-in-chief." (Now, I personally would run, as I have, if I were in your shoes. But you and America won't.)

My view from the foregoing is that in Bush we're dealing with an extraordinarily callous, arrogant, self-centered person. The above examples, I believe, demonstrate that Bush does not have much concern at all for the American and Iraqi blood that flows every day in Iraq. For the deaths, burnings, beheadings, screams, and suffering that he has caused. That it is something that probably hasn't caused him a moment of distress. But let's go now to some examples that testify to the fact that he could hardly have cared less by showing he actually had fun and enjoyed himself throughout the hell he gave birth to. That while thousands of young Americans have been blown to pieces by roadside bombs; and thousands upon thousands of Iraqi civilians, including children and babies, have been brutally killed; and thousands of American mothers and fathers have fallen to the floor or couch, screaming and crying out at the news that their son had been killed in Iraq, this small man of privilege has had a smile on his face through it all. He has lived life to the fullest, bicycling, joking with friends, eating hot dogs and blueberry pie, virtually always appearing to be in good spirits.

1. In the photo section of this book are just some of the photos that appeared regularly in the newspapers of Bush smiling broadly throughout the last five years of the war. Not just smiling broadly, but whenever there was a photo of Bush and six or seven other people all smiling, who is seen smiling the most? You guessed it. George Bush. Look at photos of FDR during the Second World War, Truman during the Korean War, and LBJ and Nixon during the Vietnam War. Nearly always the photos of their faces reflected the grimness of the wars. It was a very serious time, not time for fun and laughter. But while the horrors of the war in Iraq continued on a day-to-day basis for the past five years, and the death toll continued to mount in an ocean of blood, Bush laughed and smiled his way through the entire war, right up to the present time. *The very wide smiles on his face, almost by themselves, tell the entire story.*

2. As American soldiers were dying violent deaths in Iraq in August of 2005, Bush was on vacation bicycling with the biggest of smiles on his face at his Crawford ranch in Texas, seemingly without a care in the world. Reporters covering Bush spoke of how much he seemed to be enjoying his bike riding, and he confirmed it. "There's a great sense of exhilaration," he said, "riding a bike up a hill. *It is fun. It brings out the*

child in you. I hope to be biking for a long time. I love the outdoors. Biking provides a sense of freedom." As thousands of humans were dying horrible deaths in Bush's *hell* in Iraq, at the very same time, far away at his ranch in Texas, he told reporters biking with him: "This is a chance for me to show you a little slice of *heaven,* as far as I'm concerned."

So we know that Bush, *right in the midst* of the horror he created, was having a ball. At a time when so many people, including children and babies and American soldiers, were being killed in Iraq, for a president to be playing like a kid on his bicycle sent a very frivolous message. And it showed a total lack of sensitivity and compassion for those American parents who were not going on a vacation themselves because their son was in harm's way in Iraq, or they had already lost him to the war. You think about things like this if you care about the suffering of others, don't you?

3. In April of 2004, four American workers for a security company were ambushed and killed in Fallouja by a mob that burned their bodies and then dragged them through the streets. The mob then hung two of the charred corpses from a bridge over the Euphrates River. Several news crews filmed the horror. (Fifteen miles away, five American soldiers were killed by a roadside bomb.) Just hours after the gruesome pictures were shown in the United States and around the world, Bush, instead of canceling his appearance, showed up at a $2,000-a-plate Republican fund-raiser in an affluent Washington, D.C., neighborhood "all smiles," per the media. One would think that even the coldest heart would be affected by what had just happened, but unbelievably, Bush never said one word about the grisly murders of four Americans earlier in the day. He did, however, crack several jokes to the well-heeled Republican donors, which they laughed heartily at over their elegant lunch.

Back at the White House, presidential spokesman Scott McClelland told reporters that Bush had denounced the acts as "horrific, despicable attacks," cheap, meaningless words that Bush's press department perfunctorily drafted. One thing we most likely do know.

What had happened to the four Americans in Iraq was not horrific enough to have had the slightest effect on Bush, who had much more important things to do—telling jokes, eating a great lunch, and having fun with his wealthy Republican friends. Even if Bush insisted on going to the fund-raiser and telling his jokes, couldn't he have had the decency to at least start out his speech with a concerned, pained look on his face and a brief reference to the tragedy? But there was nothing. Just smiles and jokes and good food.

All this took place while the survivors of the four Americans in North Carolina were crying out in agony over what happened to their loved ones. Bush has taken coldness, vulgarity, crudeness, and self-indulgence by an American president or any high public figure in American history to previously unimaginable heights.

4. Speaking of Scott McClelland, the day in April of 2006 that he resigned from his position, Bush said, "Some day Scott McClelland and I will be in our rocking chairs talking about *the good old days.*" The good old days? A Freudian slip? No, McClelland was with Bush for three years (2003–2006) of the Iraq war, and to Bush, looking back, these *will* be the "good old days" because Bush, by all appearances, enjoyed every day during the war. There was a lot of fun and joking back at the White House through it all.

5. Meanwhile, back at the ranch, though no one would quibble over a few days of vacation time here and there for Bush, when antiwar activists started complaining in 2005 about Bush taking his *five-week* summer vacations right in the midst of the war in Iraq, listen to what Bush had to say: "I think the people want the president to stay healthy." But it's preposterous to believe that without a five-week vacation Bush's health would suffer. At Bush's relatively young age, and with his excellent health, he could easily have taken a much shorter vacation. In fact, if the situation had warranted, he could have worked seven days a week with his advisers on how to satisfactorily end our involvement in the Iraq war, and still have done well healthwise throughout his term in office. I'm seventy-three and have been

working seven days a week for many years, and I'm still able to run around the block. More importantly, I'm not responsible to anyone but my family. Bush is responsible for running the most powerful nation on earth. When you say, Mr. Bush, that you're at the ranch for your health, that is a g—d— lie. You were down there for five weeks because you wanted to have five weeks of fun and enjoyment.

Bush went on to say, *"It's also important for me to go on with my life, to keep a balanced life."* In other words, no sacrifices. (Ask 1,000 politicians if they'd be willing to give up a balanced life if they were given the job of president. At least 998 out of a 1,000 would not only say yes, but "I'll work fifty days a week, if that's possible, and what part of my body do you want me to give you, my left leg or my right arm?")★ Bush continued, "I'm also mindful that I've got a life to live and will do so." Translation: "I'm not going to knock myself out on this job. I want to have fun and enjoy myself, too. You know, you only live once." But Mr. Bush, the teenagers and young men you sent to fight for you in Iraq have *no time* for fun and pleasure, being at risk of being blown up twenty-four hours a day. And those thousands who have died will never have one second of fun ever again.

In a June 28, 2005, speech at Fort Bragg, North Carolina, Bush said what he has said many other times: "Amid all this violence [in Iraq], I know Americans ask the question Is the sacrifice worth it? It *is* worth it." This is easy, of course, for Bush to say, since other people are dying. Although Bush feels that thousands of young American soldiers being killed in Iraq is a worthwhile sacrifice, we've seen that he doesn't believe he himself (or any of his rich friends) should have to

---

★They would say this not only because becoming president of the United States is the greatest honor that can be bestowed on a person, but because, being mature, they would realize that giving up a balanced life would be necessary. For instance, when Barack Obama was asked, before he ran for president, what thoughts ran through his mind when he thought about himself and the presidency, he answered: "That office is so different from any other office on the planet, you have to understand that if you seek that office you have to be prepared to *give your life to it.* How I think about it is that you don't make that decision unless you are prepared to make that trade-off."

sacrifice in any way at all. In fact, remarkably, Bush hasn't asked any-one, anyone at all in America to do so. In every other major war this nation has fought, the whole nation was expected to help in some way, either through the draft, increased taxes (always), rationing of certain products, or what have you. But in the Iraq war, though Bush has invoked the word "sacrifice" over and over in his speeches, the *only* people in America whom he expects to make sacrifices are the soldiers and their families. No one else. This fact hasn't been lost on the soldiers themselves, particularly when they return to America for a short respite from another tour of duty. They see a nation that is *identical* to the way it was before the war. As one Iraqi war veteran put it: "The president can say we're a country at war all he wants. We're not. The military is at war. And the military families are at war. Every-body else is shopping, or watching *American Idol*."

6. This, from Tbilisi in the former Soviet republic of Georgia, on May 9, 2005, a time when the very worst and deadliest fighting in Iraq was taking place. A newspaper article reported that Bush seemed "exuber-ant" upon landing in Georgia, that he was in a "good mood" as he and his wife, Laura, had a long dinner with the Georgian president. Bush loved the fare. "He didn't just eat. He ordered more food," a Georgian official said. "Great food, really good," Bush said. Bush had worked up a healthy appetite before the meal by climbing up on a street stage with Georgian dancers, proceeding to "swivel his hips, Elvis-like, in tune to blasting folk music."

Just think for a moment about Leon, the twenty-year-old Ameri-can marine I mentioned earlier who had dreams of becoming a Los Angeles police officer and died in Iraq when he was shot in the head by a sniper. Recall that while his life blood was flowing out of him his marine buddy cradled Leon's head in his hands telling him he was go-ing to be okay. At the same time that people like Leon and other young American soldiers and Iraqi women and children were dying similar, horrible deaths, a smiling George Bush was dancing on a street stage in Russia, swiveling his hips like Elvis to blaring music, just having a ball. Life is fun. And wonderful. The screams and the blood and the deaths were far, far away from Tbilisi. Bush had learned that in the previous two days eight American soldiers were killed in Iraq. But who cares? Certainly not Bush.

In a similar vein, on April 25, 2007, Bush, giving no indication that he had anything on his mind other than having fun, danced energetically and with obvious gusto and relish alongside the dance director of the West African Dance Company in the White House Rose Garden, his arms flailing in the air and his open mouth bellowing out the heavy, rhythmic African music. The previous day's *New York Times* had reported that nine GIs were blown up in a suicide car bombing on April 23.

Likewise (and these are just some of many examples), on January 15, 2008, with the terrible war in Iraq showing no signs of ending, Bush, on a state visit to Saudi Arabia, took a ninety-minute tour of the Saudi National History Museum. A *Los Angeles Times* reporter wrote that during the welcoming ceremony Bush "held a sword over his shoulder, grinning broadly and swaying to the beat of drummers. When he met with reporters early in the afternoon, he said he was in 'a great mood.'"

I mean, as recently as March 4, 2008, when Bush showed up before John McCain did for a White House press conference in which Bush was scheduled to endorse McCain's candidacy for President, Bush, smiling and having fun, spontaneously started doing a soft shoe tap-dancing routine to entertain the assembled media.

This, I tell you, is a happy man.

Before moving on, we should note that Bush being so insensitive to the suffering and tragedy of others is not surprising. It's his MO. Just one example from the past. Author Frank Bruni, who covered Bush for several years for the *New York Times*, recounts in his not unfriendly biography, *Ambling into History: George Bush*, an incident in September of 1999 when Bush was governor of Texas. It took place at a memorial service at Texas Christian University in Fort Worth for seven people who had been shot to death days earlier by a crazed gunman who entered a nearby church. Bruni writes that the outdoor stadium where the memorial was being held was "a scene of eerie still-ness and quiet, its thousands of occupants sitting or standing with their heads bowed." Bush, Bruni says, was seated up front, and the print reporters, including Bruni, positioned themselves as close to Bush's rear as possible. He writes: "As preachers preached and singers sang and a city prayed, Bush turned around from time to time to shoot us little smiles. He scrunched up his forehead, as if to ask us silently what we were up to back there . . . At one point, when some-one near our seats dropped a case of plastic water bottles and caused a clatter, Bush glanced back at us with a teasing, are-you-guys-behaving-yourselves expression, and he kept his amused face pivoted in our di-rection for an awfully long time."

7. Not finding weapons of mass destruction in Iraq—the reason Bush gave for the Iraqi invasion—was a pretty serious matter. Right? Cer-tainly not something that Bush, of all people, should want to joke about. Wrong. At the Radio and Television Correspondents Associa-tion dinner in Washington, D.C., on March 24, 2004, Bush showed the audience photographic slides on a big screen of himself on his hands and knees in the Oval Office looking under furniture and behind cur-tains for the missing weapons. "Those weapons of mass destruction have got to be somewhere," he cracked to the audience. "Nope, no weapons over there, maybe over here." Here we have Bush having fun about the alleged basis for his war, a war with over 100,000 people dead. And this is funny? It was to Bush. Just another fun-filled evening for Bush as the blood continued to flow in far-off Iraq.

8. After visiting, in January of 2006, the Brooke Army Medical Center in San Antonio where American soldiers who lost their arms and legs in Iraq were being treated, Bush nevertheless was able to find cause to fashion a light-hearted joke. He told reporters: "As you can possibly see, I have an injury myself—not here at the hospital, but in combat with a cedar. I eventually won. The cedar gave me a little scratch. I was able to avoid any major surgical operation here." I mean, Bush

wasn't about to let any soldiers he saw that day with one or more arms or legs missing from fighting his war interfere, not even for one moment, with his right to be funny.

9. August 13, 2005, a Saturday, Bush was enjoying his summer vacation at his ranch in Crawford, Texas. At the start of the week on August 8, the *New York Times* reported that three American soldiers had been killed over the weekend, and thus far, 1,821 American military men and women had died in the war. The next day, August 9, 5 more U.S. soldiers were killed in combat, 4 by insurgent fire near Tikrit, and 22 Iraqi civilians were killed in violence throughout the country. The August 10, 2005, *Los Angeles Times* reported that "At least 43 Americans and 124 Iraqis have been killed by insurgent attacks over the last two weeks." The week commencing on August 15, 2005, was another typical week in Iraq. Through August 19, a period of five days, 9 American soldiers had lost their lives, 4 being killed by a roadside bomb on August 18. Among other civilian deaths during the five-day period, on August 17 three car bombs in and around a crowded bus station in Baghdad killed at least 43 people and injured 88. "The explosions began at 7:50 a.m.," the *New York Times* reported, "sending body parts flying across the bus terminal. Horrified survivors rushed in a wailing frenzy" from the area.

On August 13, 2005, right in the midst of all this violent death, and with hundreds of Iraqis and Americans crying out uncontrollably over the deaths of their children, parents, brothers, and sisters, and in many cases only receiving back the dismembered parts and limbs of their loved ones, and finding no way to cope with the unspeakable horror of it all, Bush, after a hearty breakfast, mapped out for reporters what his schedule was for the rest of the day: "I'm going to have lunch with Secretary of State Rice, talk a little business; we've got a friend from South Texas here named Katherine Armstrong; take a little nap. I'm reading an Elmore Leonard book right now, knock off a little Elmore Leonard this afternoon; go fishing with my man, Barney [Bush's dog]; a light dinner and head to the ball game. I get to bed about 9:30 p.m., wake up about 5:00 a.m. *So it's a perfect day.*"

When I read those last words, I said to myself, "No, you son of a bitch—if I may call you that, Mr. President—you're not going to have a perfect day. Or, I should say, you're not going to have another perfect day as long as you live if I have anything to say about it. Because I'm going to put a thought in your mind that you're going to take with you to your grave. It's the least I can do for the young American boys who came back from your war in a box, or in a jar of ashes, and for the thousands of innocent Iraqi men, women, children, and babies who died horrible deaths because of your war. That's the least I can do."

To fully appreciate the dimensions of Bush's "perfect day" comment, I would ask the reader, if you can for a moment, to think, really think, about how indescribably horrible it would be if your son—the one now on the high school football team, or in college, or married and working—had been blown up and killed in Iraq, his shattered body coming home in a box. It's so horrible a thought you can't even keep it in your mind for more than a few moments. And then imagine reading in the newspaper that the man who caused your son's death, taking him to war under false pretenses, told reporters, smiling, that he was going to have "a perfect day."

I don't know about you, but if I ever killed just one person, even accidentally, like in a car accident, I'd never have another perfect day as long as I lived. And I'm very, very confident that if any other American president had ordered the war in Iraq, and over 100,000 people died in the war, none of them, even if the war was a righteous one, would have a perfect day right in the middle of the hellish conflict. When we add to this the fact that not only was this not a righteous war, but that Bush took this nation to it under false pretenses, and over 100,000 people died directly because of it, for him to be happy and have plans to have "a perfect day" goes so far beyond acceptable human conduct that no moral telescope can discern its shape, form, and nature.

With all the death, horror, and suffering he has caused to hundreds of thousands of people, wouldn't you at least expect just a little remorse, a little depression from Bush? If you're waiting to see it, it's kind of like leaving the front porch light on for Jimmy Hoffa. "I'm feeling pretty spirited," Bush said at a December 4, 2007, White House press conference, "pretty good about life." Can you imagine that? Can you *imagine* that? He's turned almost the entire civilized world against us; he's cost this nation over *$1 trillion* with no end in sight; he's literally destroyed the nation of Iraq; and most important by far, he is directly responsible for over 100,000 precious human beings having died violent, horrible deaths, yet he says he is feeling "pretty good about life." This is simply too unbelievable for words. With all of the death, horror, and suffering he has caused, even if Bush was only guilty of making an innocent mistake in taking this nation to war in Iraq, not murder as I firmly believe, what kind of a human monster is it who could be happy with his life?

Can anything be done to bring George Bush to justice? That is what the next chapter is all about.

4

THE PROSECUTION OF GEORGE W. BUSH FOR MURDER

The Legal Framework for the Prosecution

> That the king can do no wrong is a necessary
> and fundamental principle of the English constitution.
> — Sir William Blackstone,
> *Commentaries on the Laws of England*, 1765

> No living *Homo sapiens* is above the law.
> —(Notwithstanding our good friends and legal ancestors
> across the water, this is a fact that requires no citation.)

WITH RESPECT TO THE POSITION I take in this chapter about the crimes of George Bush, I want to state at the outset that my motivation is not political. Although I've been a longtime Democrat (primarily because, unless there is some very compelling reason to be otherwise, I am always for "the little guy"), my political orientation is not rigid. For instance, I supported John McCain's run for the presidency in 2000. More to the point, whether I'm giving a final summation to the jury or writing one of my true crime books, credibility has always meant everything to me. Therefore, my only master and my only mistress are the facts and objectivity. I have no others. This is why I can give you, the reader, a 100 percent guarantee that if a Democratic president had done what Bush did, I would be writing the same, identical piece you are about to read.

Perhaps the most amazing thing to me about the belief of many that George Bush lied to the American public in starting his war with Iraq is that the liberal columnists who have accused him of doing this merely make this point, and then go on to the next paragraph in their columns. Only very infrequently does a columnist add that because of it Bush should be impeached. If the charges are true, of course Bush should have been impeached, convicted, and removed from office. That's almost too self-evident to state. But he deserves much more than impeachment. I mean, in America, we apparently impeach presidents for having consensual sex outside of marriage and trying to cover it up. If we impeach presidents for that, then if the president takes the country to war on a lie where thousands of American soldiers die horrible, violent deaths and over 100,000 innocent Iraqi civilians, including women and children, even babies are killed, the punishment obviously has to be much, much more severe. That's just common sense. If Bush were impeached, convicted in the Senate, and removed from office, he'd still be a free man, still be able to wake up in the morning with his cup of coffee and freshly squeezed orange juice and read the morning paper, still travel widely and lead a life of privilege, still belong to his country club and get standing ovations whenever he chose to speak to the Republican faithful. This, for being responsible for over *100,000 horrible deaths?**

---

*Even assuming, at this point, that Bush is criminally responsible for the deaths of over 100,000 people in the Iraq war, under federal law he could only be prosecuted for the deaths of the 4,000 American soldiers killed in the war. No American court would have jurisdiction to prosecute him for the one hundred and some thousand Iraqi deaths since these victims not only were not Americans, but they were killed in a foreign nation, Iraq. Despite their nationality, if they had been killed here in the States, there would of course be jurisdiction.

For anyone interested in true justice, impeachment alone would be a joke for what Bush did.

Let's look at the way some of the leading liberal lights (and, of course, the rest of the entire nation with the exception of those few recommending impeachment) have treated the issue of punishment for Bush's cardinal sins. *New York Times* columnist Paul Krugman wrote about "the false selling of the Iraq War. We were railroaded into an unnecessary war." Fine, I agree. Now what? Krugman just goes on to the next paragraph. But if Bush falsely railroaded the nation into a war where over 100,000 people died, including 4,000 American soldiers, how can you go on to the next paragraph as if you had been writing that Bush spent the weekend at Camp David with his wife? For doing what Krugman believes Bush did, doesn't Bush have to be punished commensurately in some way? Are there no consequences for committing a crime of colossal proportions?

Al Franken on the David Letterman show said, "Bush lied to us to take us to war" and quickly went on to another subject, as if he was saying "Bush lied to us in his budget."

Senator Edward Kennedy, condemning Bush, said that "Bush's distortions misled Congress in its war vote" and "No President of the United States should employ distortion of truth to take the nation to war." But, Senator Kennedy, if a president does this, as you believe Bush did, then what? Remember, Clinton was impeached for allegedly trying to cover up a consensual sexual affair. What do you recommend for Bush for being responsible for more than 100,000 deaths? Nothing? He shouldn't be held accountable for his actions? If one were to listen to you talk, that is the only conclusion one could come to. But why, Senator Kennedy, do you, like everyone else, want to give Bush this complete free ride?

The *New York Times*, in a June 17, 2004, editorial, said that in selling this nation on the war in Iraq, "the Bush administration convinced a substantial majority of Americans before the war that Saddam Hussein was somehow linked to 9/11, . . . inexcusably selling the false Iraq-Al Qaeda claim to Americans." But gentlemen, if this is so, then what? The *New York Times* didn't say, just going on, like everyone else, to the next paragraph, talking about something else.

In a November 15, 2005, editorial, the *New York Times* said that "the president and his top advisers . . . did not allow the American people, or even Congress, to have the information necessary to make reasoned judgments of their own. It's obvious that the Bush administration *misled* Americans about Mr. Hussein's weapons *and* his terrorist connections." But if it's "obvious that the Bush administration misled Americans" in taking them to a war that tens of thousands of people have paid for with their lives, now what? No punishment? If not, under what theory? Again, you're just going to go on to the next paragraph?

In this book, I'm not going to go on to the next unrelated paragraph.

In early December of 2005, a *New York Times–CBS* nationwide poll showed that the majority of Americans believed Bush "*intentionally misled*" the nation to promote a war in Iraq. A December 11, 2005, article in the *Los Angeles Times*, after citing this national poll, went on to say that because so many Americans believed this, it might be difficult for Bush to get the continuing support of Americans for the war. In other words, the fact that most Americans believed Bush had deliberately misled them into war was of *no* consequence in and of itself. Its only consequence was that it might hurt his efforts to get support for the war thereafter. So the article was reporting on the effect of the poll findings as if it was reporting on the popularity, or lack thereof, of Bush's position on global warming or immigration. Didn't the author of the article know that Bush taking the nation to war on a lie (if such be the case) is the *equivalent* of saying he is responsible for well over 100,000 deaths? One would never know this by reading the article.

If Bush, in fact, intentionally misled this nation into war, what is the proper punishment for him? Since many Americans routinely want criminal defendants to be executed for murdering only one person, if we weren't speaking of the president of the United States as the defendant here, to discuss anything less than the death penalty for someone responsible for over 100,000 deaths would on its face seem ludicrous.* But we *are* dealing with the president of the United States here.

On the other hand, the intensity of rage against Bush in America has been such (it never came remotely this close with Clinton because, at bottom, there was nothing of any real substance to have any serious rage against him for) that if I heard it once I heard it ten times that "someone should put a bullet in his head." That, fortunately, is just loose talk, and even more fortunately not the way we do things in America. In any event, if an American jury were to find Bush guilty of first degree murder, it would be up to them to decide what the appropriate punishment should be, one of their options being the imposition of the death penalty.

Although I have never heard before what I am suggesting in this book—that Bush be prosecuted for murder in an American courtroom—many have argued that "Bush should be prosecuted for war

---

*Indeed, Bush himself, ironically, would be the last person who would quarrel with the proposition that being guilty of mass murder (even one murder, by his lights) calls for the death penalty as opposed to life imprisonment. As governor of Texas, Bush had the highest execution rate of any governor in American history. He was a very strong proponent of the death penalty who even laughingly mocked a condemned young woman who begged him to spare her life ("Please don't kill me," Bush mimicked her in a magazine interview with journalist Tucker Carlson), and even refused to commute the sentence of death down to life imprisonment for a young man who was mentally retarded (although as president he set aside the entire prison sentence of his friend Lewis "Scooter" Libby), and had a broad smile on his face when he announced in his second presidential debate with Al Gore that his state, Texas, was about to execute three convicted murderers.

In Bush's two terms as Texas governor, he signed death warrants for an incredible 152 out of 153 executions against convicted murderers, the majority of whom only killed one single person. The only death sentence Bush commuted was for one of the many murders that mass murderer Henry Lucas had been convicted of. Bush was informed that Lucas had falsely confessed to this particular murder and was innocent, his conviction being improper. So in 152 out of 152 cases, Bush refused to show mercy even once, finding that not one of the 152 convicted killers should receive life imprisonment instead of the death penalty. Bush's perfect 100 percent execution rate is highly uncommon even for the most conservative law-and-order governors.

crimes" (mostly for the torture of prisoners at Abu Ghraib and Guantanamo) at the International Criminal Court in The Hague, Netherlands. But for all intents and purposes this cannot be done. (For a discussion on this matter, see notes at the end of this book.)

I want to make it very clear that, like the majority of Americans, I feel Bush "intentionally misled" this nation into war, and everything I say in this chapter is predicated on, and flows from, that belief. If my belief (and that of the majority of American people) is wrong, then I of course apologize to Bush and his people for writing this book, and Bush, knowing his innocence, has nothing to worry about. All I can tell you is that as a former prosecutor with twenty-one murder convictions without a loss, seeking and obtaining a death penalty sentence against eight of the murder defendants, I am probably in a better position than the average person to know what type of evidence is necessary to go to trial with and secure a conviction of murder. And in my opinion there certainly is more than enough evidence against Bush to justify bringing him to trial and letting an American jury decide whether or not he is guilty of murder, and if so, what the appropriate punishment should be. I am very confident that, based on the evidence I set forth against Bush on the following pages, a competent prosecutor could convict Bush of murder.

Assuming at this point (see later text for full discussion) that Bush deliberately misled this nation into war, could he be prosecuted for murder and tried by an American jury? I have been unable to find any legal reason why he could not. We all know that no one is above the law, which would, perforce, include presidents. And no federal or state murder statute says that it only applies to certain people, not presidents, or golf pros, or hair stylists, et cetera, and only if the killing is committed in certain places, like a home, or a car, out on the street, and so forth, not a battlefield.

But how, you may ask, could George Bush be prosecuted and convicted of murder when he didn't personally kill anyone? Indeed, the killings took place in Iraq. The reason is that it is not necessary for a criminal defendant to have physically committed a murder to be guilty of it. For example, I convicted Charles Manson of the seven Tate–La

Bianca murders even though he himself did not participate in any of the killings, nor was he even present at the time. I was able to obtain this conviction because of the vicarious liability rule of conspiracy, which provides that each member of a conspiracy is criminally responsible for all crimes committed by his coconspirators or innocent agents of the conspirators to further the object of the conspiracy. If Bush is guilty of the murders I believe him to be, because he took this nation to war under false pretenses, he obviously did not do this all by himself. Necessarily, he conspired with certain members of his inner circle, coconspirators like Dick Cheney and Condoleezza Rice.

But, one might wonder, since even Bush's coconspirators didn't physically kill the victims who would be named in the criminal indictment (the 4,000 American soldiers who were killed in Iraq)—Iraqi soldiers and civilian insurgents did—how could he be guilty of murder under the vicarious liability rule? The reason is that if a conspirator (or anyone for that matter) deliberately sets in motion a chain of events that he knows will *cause* a third-party innocent agent* to commit an act (here, the killing of American soldiers by Iraqis), the conspirator is criminally responsible for that act. In the law, as in its well-known sense, the word "cause" means "to bring about, to bring into existence." Bush, in invading Iraq, certainly brought about the existence of Iraqi opposition, and his act caused Iraqis to kill American soldiers in much the same fashion that a person causes a gun to fire a bullet that kills someone by pulling the trigger. In fact, in the criminal law, third party innocent agents are referred to as "mere instruments" of the principal. To argue that Bush isn't responsible in this case would almost be the equivalent of a conspirator arguing, "My coconspirator never killed the victim, his gun did."

---

*The Iraqi soldiers during the brief war, and the insurgents since then, were "innocent" of Bush's crime of murder because they only killed American soldiers to repel an invader—what the Americans represented to them—or in self-defense, in neither situation possessing the requisite criminal intent to be guilty of murder. They certainly did not kill American soldiers because they were knowingly carrying out the object of a criminal conspiracy in Washington, D.C., hatched by Bush, Cheney, et al.

Here, the object of Bush, Cheney, and Rice was that there be a war in Iraq, which they knew would inevitably result in American casualties. And as the court said in the 1993 case of *Gallimore v. Commonwealth of Virginia*: "The doctrine of innocent agent . . . allows a defendant not present at the commission of the crime [here, the killings in Iraq] to be convicted as a principal in the first degree if the defendant engaged in actions which caused the actual perpetrator to commit the crime as an innocent agent of the defendant." Courts have said that the innocent agent "is not an offender," and the defendant "is guilty as if he had done the act himself," the defendant, under the law, deemed to be "constructively present."

Note that it does not have to be shown that the principal *wanted* the innocent agent to commit the act, only that he *caused* him to.

In many states and federally, the innocent agent doctrine is even codified. Title 18 United States Code, §2(b) provides: "Whoever willfully *causes an act to be done* which if directly performed by him . . . would be an offense against the United States, is punishable as a principal."

In other words, if Bush personally killed an American soldier, he would be guilty of murder. Under the law, he cannot immunize himself from this criminal responsibility by causing a third party to do the killing. He's still responsible. George Bush cannot sit safely in his Oval Office in Washington, D.C., while young American soldiers fighting his war are being blown to pieces by roadside bombs in Iraq, and wash his hands of all culpability. *It's not quite that easy.* He could only do this if he did not take this nation to war under false pretenses. If he did, which the evidence overwhelmingly shows, he is criminally responsible for the thousands of American deaths in Iraq.

Apart from the vicarious liability rule of conspiracy, there is a separate and independent companion legal theory of criminal responsibility that imputes guilt to the nonperpetrator, and prosecutors routinely use it side by side, when the evidence permits, with the vicarious liability rule—the law of "aiding and abetting."

The heart of conspiracy complicity is the *agreement* among the co-conspirators to commit the crime, as distinguished from aiding and abetting, whose heart is participatory in nature. In very general terms, one is guilty of a crime under the theory of aiding and abetting if he *instigates* or encourages the commission of the offense (in the law, to instigate is "to stimulate or goad to action, especially a bad action"), or *assists* the perpetrator in some way in the commission of said offense. Here, Bush clearly instigated the killing of the American soldiers by his invasion of Iraq, which is all that would be necessary, in itself, to make Bush guilty of murder under the theory of aiding and abetting. So Bush would be criminally responsible for the deaths of the 4,000 American soldiers under both the legal theories of vicarious liability and aiding and abetting.

It should be noted that Bush could only be prosecuted *after* he is no longer president. The U.S. Constitution itself is a little ambiguous as to just when a president may be prosecuted for his crimes. In discussing the impeachment of a sitting president, Article I, Section 3, cl. 7, provides: "Judgment in Cases of Impeachment [which is not a criminal prosecution] shall not extend further than to removal from Office, and disqualification to hold and enjoy any Office of Honor, Trust or Profit under the United States: but *the Party convicted* shall nevertheless be liable and subject to Indictment, Trial, Judgment, and Punishment, according to Law." The language "the Party convicted" implies that a conviction of a president by the U.S. Senate in an impeachment trial and his removal from office are a condition precedent to his being prosecuted in an American court of law for his crime or crimes committed while in office. But the language could be more explicit on this point.

However, it has always been accepted by constitutional scholars that a president cannot be prosecuted criminally while he is still in office. To discern the "original intent" of the framers on this question, one must turn to *The Federalist* (commonly referred to as *The Federalist Papers*), a collection of eighty-five essays written by Alexander Hamilton, James Madison, and John Jay under the non de plume "Philo-Publius" between 1787 and 1788 in support of the proposed constitution (which was of course ratified and went into effect in 1789).

In *The Federalist* no. 69 (essay 69), Hamilton writes at page 446: "The President of the United States would be liable to be impeached, tried, and upon conviction of treason, bribery, or other high crimes or misdemeanors, removed from office, and would *afterwards* be liable to prosecution and punishment in the ordinary course of law."

In other words, even if the evidence were clear that a president had committed a crime such as rape or murder, it was the position of Hamilton that he could not be arrested and prosecuted until *after* he was first impeached and removed from office following conviction by the Senate—that is, until his removal he should have temporary immunity from ordinary criminal process. And this, as indicated, has been adopted as virtual law down through the years.

So after the inauguration of a new president on January 20, 2009, unless Bush's successor is outrageous enough to pardon him, he can be prosecuted, like any other citizen, for any crime he committed while president. And here, since we're talking about murder, there is no statute of limitations.

During the Watergate scandal in 1973 and 1974, although impeachment of President Nixon was contemplated, Nixon, we know, resigned in 1974 before he was impeached by the House of Representatives. After his resignation, there were calls by many that he be prosecuted in a court of law for his alleged crimes, as he could have been. President Ford obviated this by granting Nixon a pardon for all crimes he may have committed during Watergate. I was in favor of the Nixon pardon in that Nixon's forced resignation was more than enough punishment for the particular offenses he committed, but I certainly would not be for any Bush pardon, for obvious reasons.

Still, one might say, prosecuting Nixon for conventional crimes like obstruction of justice and illegal wiretapping is one thing. But prosecuting Bush for murder, and where the killings resulted from his taking this nation to war—like those fought through the ages with hundreds of thousands of troops—is quite another. It is because of this expected reaction by many to what I am proposing that I want to make one very important observation off the top. For those skeptics who say that to prosecute for murder a president who takes this country to war—and to do so in a regular American courtroom and in the very same way that, in an adjacent courtroom, a defendant is being

prosecuted for murdering a liquor store proprietor during a robbery—is simply too revolutionary a notion to be viable, I say this.
Since a regular courtroom is the *only* place a president such as Bush
could be prosecuted for murder, if you maintain this position *you
therefore must be willing to say* that if a president takes America to war
under false pretenses (even those as base, hypothetically, as for his
own personal gain), and if thousands of Americans, *even 50 million
Americans*, die as a direct result, other than removing him from office
through the impeachment process, the president should be absolutely
immune from all criminal responsibility and punishment, even one
day in the county jail, and he should be able to go on with his life. Unless you are willing to say this (and if you do, you're going to sound
awfully foolish), then you likewise *must* learn to accept and live with
the revolutionary notion. There is no third alternative.

So although Bush supporters can say that Bush should not be prosecuted for murder because they don't feel he acted improperly, they
cannot possibly say that it is wrong for Bush to be prosecuted for murder if he did what I say he did. To say that is to admit that you have no
respect for our American system of democracy. That you prefer that
presidents have the same rights and protections as tyrannical dictators
like Stalin, Hitler, and Saddam Hussein had. So unless you want to
take this completely untenable position, you should consider the legal
and logical propriety of my proposed prosecution of George Bush for
murder.

As we proceed in this discussion, one has to realize that, as they say
in the law, this is a case of "first impression," meaning a case for which
there is no legal precedent. This is not fatal, per se, since by definition
every legal precedent, on any legal situation, itself had to emanate
from some case of first impression in the past standing for the proposition.

The overriding assumption here *has* to be that if, in fact, Bush lied
to the nation in taking it to war, we all should want to find *some* lawful
way to bring him to justice. That *has* to be the predisposition among
all good men. It cannot be otherwise. I don't like to see anyone get
away with murder, even one. And here we're talking about the need-

less killing and slaughter of over 100,000 human beings for which this man may be criminally responsible. Anyone who is satisfied that Bush lied to the country in taking it to war, but whose predisposition, nonetheless, is to frustrate justice against Bush is, simply put, a very bad human being. So the only proper state of mind is that if the prosecution frequently tries to do whatever it can lawfully do to overcome factual and legal obstacles to bring about justice in even an ordinary criminal case, we should be willing to move hell and high legal water to bring about justice in this case, where so much more is at stake.

Could Bush nip any prosecution of him in the bud by arguing that he could not be prosecuted for murder over the Iraq war for the simple reason that on October 11, 2002, Congress, by a joint congressional resolution, authorized him to use force against Iraq, so how can anyone treat him as a criminal for doing something he was authorized to do by Congress? The answer is that the congressional authorization is no legal defense to a prosecution of Bush for murder. Consent of the victim, though a defense to some crimes (e.g., theft, rape), is not a defense to the crime of murder. And here we're not even talking about the consent of the American soldiers in fighting a war that brought their deaths, and whose only option other than fighting was to be court-martialed. We're talking about congressional consent. But even if the argument were made that Congress, in a democracy, represents all Americans, including these soldiers, again, consent is *not* a defense to the crime of murder. Further, even if it were, it is boilerplate law that fraud vitiates consent. So the consent that Congress gave Bush is nullified by the deliberate misrepresentations he made to Congress in inducing it to give him its consent. I will come back to this issue later in this chapter.

And Bush's criminal conduct can't find sanctuary in the U.S. Constitution either, which, as I have explained, allows for his prosecution after he leaves the presidency. Surely Bush couldn't be heard to argue that a president is incapable of committing a crime under the U.S. Constitution—the Constitution even shielding him from the crime of murder.

Assuming Bush lied to take us to war, and thousands of humans died as a direct result thereof, does his conduct fall within existing legal requirements for a crime and criminal prosecution in an American courtroom? Can a legitimate case for murder be constructed against him whose legal architecture will hold up and withstand judicial scrutiny?

Before I set forth the evidence that proves Bush is guilty of murder, I unfortunately first must talk about the legal elements that comprise the crime of murder, a necessarily dry and sometimes arcane discussion for which I ask your forbearance. Murder is defined as "the unlawful killing of a human being with malice aforethought." All true crimes (as opposed to so-called public welfare offenses like selling alcohol after a certain time of day or hunting during the off-season) require two elements. The first is the prohibited act, referred to in the law as *actus reus*. To be a crime this act has to be accompanied by *mens rea*, criminal intent. The U.S. Supreme Court said in *Morissette v. United States* that criminal intent involves an "evil-meaning mind," variously described with respect to different crimes as "intentional," "knowing," "fraudulent," "malicious," etc. Each crime has a different *mens rea*. The *mens rea* for theft is the intent to steal, for arson the intent to burn down the dwelling of another. The *mens rea* for murder is malice aforethought. For there to be a crime, the commission of the prohibited act and the criminal intent (*mens rea*) have to concur in time.

In this case, the "act" by Bush would be his ordering his military to invade Iraq with American soldiers, 4,000 of whom have already died because of the war. If this act was not accompanied by the required intent on Bush's part, no crime would have been committed. The necessary intent that would have to be shown, as indicated, is malice aforethought, satisfied if Bush either *intended to kill* the soldiers by ordering them to war, or he started the war with *reckless and wanton disregard for the consequences and indifference to human life*. However, neither of these two states of mind would be "criminal" if they occurred under circumstances of legal justification, such as self-defense. Hence, the criminality of an act depends *solely* on the actor's state of

93

mind at the time of the subject act. For example, if X intends to kill Y and does so, but he had a *reasonable* fear (the so-called reasonable man test) that he was in imminent danger of death or great bodily harm at the hands of Y, there would be no criminal intent on his part since he acted in self-defense, and the killing would be called a justifiable homicide. The same act by X of intending to kill Y and doing so would be an unlawful killing, murder, if the killing were not in self-defense.

So we can say that malice aforethought exists (and hence, no self-defense) if there is an intentional killing of another (or indifference to human life) *without any lawful excuse or justification*. Bush's primary defense to any murder charge against him would be, as he argued to the nation, that he was conducting a "preemptive strike" on Saddam Hussein; that is, the self-defense argument—he reasonably believed that Iraq constituted an imminent threat to the security of this country, so Bush struck first. In other words, his mind was pure. He had no criminal or evil state of mind. In a trial of Bush, the prosecution would have to show that he *did* have a criminal state of mind. The evidence would be the many lies he told that Hussein's alleged weapons of mass destruction made him an imminent threat to the security of this country, and his attempt to deceive the nation into believing that Hussein was involved with Al Qaeda in 9/11. Therefore, Bush did not act in self-defense and hence, did have a criminal state of mind. Since he had criminal intent, every killing of an American soldier that took place during Bush's war was an "unlawful killing" and murder.

Before we get into the seminal issue of whether Bush acted in self-defense, let's return, to examine in more depth, the requirement for murder of malice aforethought.

You should know that the term "malice aforethought" is a legal anachronism that everyone continues to use, while ignoring the conventional meaning of the words. "Malice" means a hatred, an ill-will for another. Though that frequently is the situation in a murder case, all legal authorities agree that no malice in the traditional sense has to be shown to secure a murder conviction, and many murders are committed without the slightest presence of hatred by the killer against the victim, e.g., a contract killing. So hatred or ill-will toward those American soldiers who died in the war, which Bush obviously never had, does not have to be shown. And the word "aforethought" is an ancient appendage to the word "malice" that has no relevance in the current criminal law. Although the word literally means the thought must precede the criminal act, in the term "malice aforethought," aforethought doesn't mean this. It only means that the malice exists at the time of the killing, that it is not an *after*thought. So what does malice aforethought mean today in the criminal law? It means simply a specific intent to kill (express malice) or an intent to commit a highly dangerous act with reckless and wanton disregard for the consequences and indifference to human life (implied malice).

In most states, in order to have *first* (as opposed to second) degree murder there has to be not only a specific intent to kill (express malice) but this intent to kill has to be premeditated. The courts have consistently held that although a spontaneous intent to kill does not constitute premeditation, premeditation does not have to be long at all. There are cases where a period of time as short as several seconds sufficed. In a prosecution of George Bush, we're dealing with a premeditation to go to war that took place over months, so there is no question that there was premeditation in this case.

Implied malice (no intent to kill) will only give you *second* degree murder. However, some states, like Texas, do not have degrees of murder. Even a killing where there was only implied malice *and no specific intent to kill* can not only result in a conviction of murder (which it could in any state), but a sentence of death, which in most states can only be imposed *after* one has already been convicted of *first* degree murder.

The most common malice aforethought is a specific intent to kill. Any Bush apologist who is unfamiliar with the criminal law will undoubtedly say that even assuming for the sake of argument that Bush lied to the country to take it to war, and the war was not in self-defense, it is ridiculous to think he could be prosecuted for murder because he obviously never intended to kill anyone (other than enemy soldiers). But the criminal law dealing with murder is, unfortunately for them and particularly Bush, not that simplistic. Not only is there implied malice, which does not require an intent to kill, but in Bush's case a very credible argument could be made that in a real sense he did intend to have American soldiers killed in his war.

In a typical intent to kill (express malice) case, A picks up a gun and fires a bullet into B's head, intending to kill him. A typical implied malice situation would be where there's no intent to kill, but the act the defendant committed, which resulted in a death, involved a high degree of danger to others and the defendant's state of mind was that he was willing to take that risk—he acted with reckless and wanton disregard for the consequences, showing an indifference to human life. For instance, a defendant killing someone while driving 100 mph in a school zone; or blowing up a building without legal cause, even though he is unaware that someone was in the building. In these two situations, and others like them, not only didn't the defendant intend to kill, but *he had no way of knowing whether someone would die or not.* As opposed to the implied malice situation, while Bush never specifically intended to kill any American soldier, he absolutely *knew* American soldiers would necessarily die in his war. Therefore, a case could be made that unless Bush intended to have a war without any casualties, which is nonsensical on its face (and an argument that would make Bush sound absurd), *he did, in fact, specifically intend to have American soldiers killed.*

Am I just engaging in a play on words here? I don't think so. As the court said in a 1963 Illinois case, *People v. Coolidge*: "Since every sane man is presumed to intend all the natural and probable consequences flowing from his own deliberate act, it follows that if one willfully does an act, *the natural tendency of which* is to destroy another's life, the irresistible conclusion . . . is that the destruction of such other person's life *was intended.*"

But assuming, just for the sake of argument, that a court would not accept the position that Bush did, in fact, have an intent to kill, then we are left with Bush's conduct being somewhere in between express malice (intent to kill) and implied malice (no intent to kill, but not caring if someone is killed). Courts create new law all the time, and I can easily see a court ruling that when a defendant engages in conduct that not only creates a situation where someone *might* die, but which he *knows* will result in their deaths, this would satisfy the intent to kill requirement of first degree murder. I mean, what difference does it make if someone intends to kill B, or doesn't intend to kill B but intends to do an act that he *knows* will kill B? As the expression goes, it's a distinction without substance. It would be elevating technical words ("intent to kill") over the substance and spirit of the law of murder to say there was no intent to kill in the Bush type of situation, and hence, no first degree murder. For the monumentally horrendous act that Bush committed—taking a nation to war where there's not just one victim, but thousands—all fair and true men have to say that whether or not Bush is guilty of first degree murder should be left up to an American jury to decide, and if they say yes, left to an appellate court to rule on the legal propriety of its verdict.

I was saying that courts (judges) create new law all the time. I can give you a perfect example dealing with first degree murder itself that will be a surprise to many lay readers. The classic type of first degree murder is where there was a premeditated intent to kill. But there's one other type of murder in all the courts of the land, both federal and state, for which many defendants have been convicted and paid the ultimate penalty of death—the felony-murder rule. Since the law took cognizance of the fact that certain felonies were so inherently dangerous, in and of themselves, that the risk of death was high, to discourage this conduct they came up with the felony-murder rule. The rule provides that if a "killing takes place during the perpetration or attempted perpetration of" certain felonies, the killing is automatically first degree murder, even though there was *no* malice, setting the definition of murder as the "unlawful killing of a human *with* malice aforethought" on its head. The main underlying felonies that are usually mentioned in statutes throughout the land are robbery (where the felony murder rule has been applied far more than in any other crime), burglary, kidnapping, arson, and rape. All that has to be shown is that the defendant had the requisite intent to commit the underlying felony. Once that is shown, and a death occurs, the ordinary requirements for first degree murder that there be malice afore-thought and premeditation are dispensed with, and the robber, for instance, is guilty of first degree murder. (Many legal scholars have said that the intent to commit the underlying felony is transferred into an intent to kill; a legal fiction, of course.)

Under the felony murder rule many robbers (and other felons) have been convicted of first degree murder throughout the years not only where there was no malice aforethought, but even where the killing was accidental. A robber, for instance, was convicted of first degree murder under the felony-murder rule where, as he was leaving the store in which he had robbed the owner, he told the owner not to say a word or he'd be harmed, and fired into the ceiling to scare the owner. The shot, after two or three ricochets, pierced the head of the owner, killing him. In fact, the felony-murder rule applies even where the defendant is not the killer! There have been cases where the proprietor of the store fired at a robber, missed him and hit and killed a customer. And the robber was convicted of first degree murder of the customer.

In any event, if the law can find an intent to kill when the defendant never had such an intent, even where the defendant specifically did *not* want to kill, surely, in a case of first impression, a court should have little difficulty finding an intent to kill in those situations where the defendant intentionally commits an act that he *knows* will kill people.

As indicated, in most states, to obtain a conviction of first degree murder, a prosecutor must prove a premeditated intent to kill. However, in the federal courts, the best place to prosecute Bush, there is authority for the proposition that the premeditation necessary to constitute first degree murder does not have to be an intent to kill. It can also be a premeditated intent to do an act "without regard for the life and safety of others," which is *implied* malice. In the 1983 case of *United States v. Shaw*, the premeditation was in the form of "lying in wait," but not specifically to kill, only to fire at a passing car, the defendant thereby doing an act exceedingly dangerous with reckless and wanton disregard for the consequences, though no specific intent to kill was shown. So current law would seem to authorize the first degree murder prosecution of Bush in the federal courts without the prosecution even having to prove an intent to kill.

In any event, at an absolute minimum, in the absence of a legal justification such as self-defense, *Bush's taking the nation to war would constitute implied malice, that is, an intent to do a highly dangerous act with reckless disregard and indifference to human life, and hence, at least second degree murder in every state, as well as under federal law.* Ironically, the case relied on in the federal courts for the best definition of implied malice in a second degree murder prosecution is *United States of America v. Bush*, where the court, in its words, describes the present Bush's conduct to a T. It said, "Malice does not necessarily imply ill-will, spite, hatred or hostility by the defendant toward the person killed. Malice is a state of mind showing a heart [not regardful] of the life and safety of others . . . Malice can also be defined as the condition of mind which prompts a person to do willfully, that is, on purpose, without adequate justification or excuse, a wrongful act whose foreseeable consequence is death or serious bodily injury to another."

Who would argue that under the language in *United States of America v. Bush* we should regard as criminal someone who, knowing he is too drunk to drive, nevertheless gets in a car and drives it at night, killing someone, but not a president who deliberately lies to a country to take it to war where thousands are killed, dying violent deaths? What reason could you have for arguing this other than that you are a conservative Republican, and Bush is a conservative Republican, and therefore *anything* he does, even murder, is just fine with you?

As I have said, under state or federal law Bush could at least be prosecuted for second degree murder and sentenced to life imprisonment (only a conviction of first degree murder can carry a possible sentence of death), and that would be better than nothing. But this should only be a fallback position. Bush's alleged crime is so prodigious and on such a grand scale that it would greatly dishonor those in their graves who paid the ultimate price because of it if he were not to pay the ultimate penalty. This is why all attempts should be made to prosecute him for first degree murder.

THE FIRST LIE GEORGE BUSH TOLD
THE AMERICAN PEOPLE

Getting on to the most important question by far of whether Bush has a viable defense to his killings in that he acted in self-defense, as noted previously, if Bush either lied when he said Hussein's alleged weapons of mass destruction made him an *imminent* threat to the security of this country, or lied when he led Americans to believe that Hussein was involved in 9/11—both of which justified in the minds of Americans our going to war—this clearly wouldn't be the conduct of a person acting in self-defense. Therefore, such a legal defense would necessarily fail at his trial.

In attempting to answer whether Bush lied about either of these two matters, we obviously have to make reference to and examine Bush's conduct and statements before, during, even after he went to war—circumstantial evidence—to determine what his state of mind was at the time he went to war. For those who feel a case based on circumstantial evidence is, by definition, not a strong one, let me correct a common misperception. Circumstantial evidence has erroneously come to be associated in the public mind and vernacular with an anemic case. ("Oh, that's just circumstantial evidence.") But nothing could be further from the truth. In fact, most first degree murder cases are based on circumstantial evidence. This is so because other than eye-witness testimony (and in some jurisdictions, a confession), which is direct evidence, *all* other evidence, even fingerprints and DNA, is circumstantial evidence.

We can't open up the top of a defendant's head, peek in, and say, "So that's what was on your mind at the time you engaged in the subject conduct." (Recall that a defendant's criminal intent or state of mind has to concur in time with his criminal act.) Obviously, we have to look at his conduct and his statements to infer what was on his mind. I've convicted many defendants of first degree murder based solely on circumstantial evidence by putting one speck of evidence on top of another until ultimately there was a strong mosaic of guilt. You can analogize circumstantial evidence to the spelling of a word. One letter by itself could be the first of thousands of words. But with the addition of each letter, you narrow the number of words those letters can belong to. Pretty soon there's just one word you can be spelling, and that word is *guilty*.

Let's first briefly look at some of the evidence (there undoubtedly is more I don't even know about which could be uncovered by a prosecutor with the power of subpoena if this matter proceeded forward legally) showing that Bush and his people lied to the country on the issue of whether Hussein was an *imminent* threat to the security of this country. (Keep in mind that if no imminent threat is shown, then Bush's defense of self-defense would be defeated. The threat *has* to be imminent.) I think you will see that Bush did not honorably *lead* this nation, but deliberately *misled* it into a war he wanted.

1. One of the strongest pieces of evidence that Bush lied to Congress and the American people when he said Hussein was an imminent threat to the security of this country so he could get their support for the war, is the preposterous nature of the allegation itself. Hussein, an imminent threat to America? As humorist Will Rogers would say, "That's the most unheard of thing I ever heard of." Almost a high-water mark in folly. At the time of the Persian Gulf War in 1991, Hussein's Iraq, after a devastating eight-year war with Iran that had concluded just three years earlier in 1988, was proven to be extremely weak. And since then, as everyone, including Bush's father, agreed, Iraq had even become much weaker because of the economic sanctions against it resulting from the Gulf War, as well as the great number of U.S. inspections that forced Iraq to destroy most of its weapons and all nuclear facilities. Back on October 15, 2001, which is before he knowingly decided to become a pitiable water-carrier for the Bush administration, Secretary of State Colin Powell told the press: "Iraq is Iraq, a wasted society for 10 years. *They're sad*. They're contained . . ."

The conclusive proof of the military weakness of Hussein's Iraq at the time of the war in Iraq was that it fell to Coalition forces in only three weeks, with only 128 Americans dying, and 44 of these by accident or friendly fire. Thousands upon thousands of Iraqi soldiers died in the very short conflict. Army major Kevin Dunlop said in the midst of it, "It's not a fair fight. We're slaughtering them." When we couple this with the fact that we know Hussein wanted to live—and no person who was not insane (as Hussein was not) and wanted to live would even dream of attacking the United States or helping anyone else to do it—the absurdity of Bush's contention that Hussein was an imminent threat to the security of this country is apparent. That alone is circumstantial evidence of the strong likelihood that he himself had to know the notion was absurd, and therefore he was lying.

Wait a minute, Bush apologists might say. True, it turned out that Hussein never had any weapons of mass destruction, but not only did virtually the entire country think he did (including many prominent Democrats in Congress), but that having them, he constituted a threat to this country. So if almost the whole country felt this way, why is it preposterous that Bush would have, too? Translation: maybe Bush and his people were as stupid as everyone else. In other words, he may have acted in self-defense, and his act was a reasonable one. At first blush, this sounds like it may have a little merit. But there's one very big difference between Bush and his people on the one hand and the rest of the nation on the other. *Bush and his people were the ones who came up with this entire preposterous notion.* The rest of the nation's people (more appropriately, *sheeple*) merely went along with it as an accepted truth. The fact that the whole argument that Hussein was an imminent threat to this country, and that we should invade Iraq, *originated* with Bush and his people substantially weakens the contention that they were as stupid as everyone else in buying into this absurdity. They didn't buy into anything. They invented it, and then proceeded to dress up their invention with one lie and distortion after another. (We'll examine these in detail later.)

The Bush administration has said that Bush never used the word "imminent" in describing the threat of Hussein. He didn't have to. From the context of everything he said, no other inference could be drawn but that Bush was asserting that America was in imminent danger of harm from Hussein. This is why analyst after analyst said that Bush claimed Hussein was an imminent threat. Moreover, Bush used words that meant imminent. Just a few examples: he said Iraq could act "on any given day"; that "before the day of horror can come, before it is too late to act, this danger must be removed"; "Some ask how urgent this danger is to America. The danger is already significant, and it only grows worse with time"; "Each passing day could be the one on which the Iraqi regime" gives weapons of mass destruction "to a terrorist ally"; Iraq constituted "a threat of unique urgency"; "Iraq could launch a biological or chemical attack in as little as forty-five minutes." And when Bush said at a press conference on March 6, 2003: "Saddam Hussein *is* a threat" to our nation no less than six times (he also said: "Saddam and his weapons *are* a direct threat to this country"), that, by definition, meant he was an imminent threat. The word "is" means *now*, not in the future. If Bush intended to convey the latter, the only proper words to have used would have been "Saddam Hussein will be (or might be) a threat to America" or "in the future" or "near future." Indeed, in Bush's statement to the nation on the evening of March 17, 2003, two days before he invaded Iraq, he said, after talking about the impending war with Hussein and Iraq: "When evil men plot chemical, biological and nuclear terror, a policy of appeasement could bring destruction of a kind never before seen on this earth. Terrorists and terror states do not reveal these threats with fair notice in formal declarations. And responding to such enemies only after they have struck first is not self-defense. It is suicide. The security of the world requires disarming Saddam Hussein *now*."

It should be pointed out that the very fact Bush never used the word "imminent," though certainly not conclusive, is itself circumstantial evidence of his criminal state of mind. Let me explain. Bush and his people had to know that the word everyone uses, legally and otherwise, in any discussion of self-defense is "imminent." Since the evidence is very clear that the threat from Hussein was not imminent, it is a safe assumption that they thought it would be dangerous for them to use the word because by doing so they would be *more apt* to be asked what evidence they had that Hussein was about to strike any day, a question they could not answer. And if they failed to answer it, it would be so much more difficult for them to later claim they were acting in self-defense. So they stayed away from the word "imminent" the way the devil stays away from holy water. They chose instead to use other comparable words (like "now," "any given day," "urgent," etc.) to convey the same thought. If they truly thought they were acting in self-defense, how is it possible that not once in the many months of the buildup to war did any of them, in all their speeches and interviews, use the one word that was associated with self-defense more than any other? The one word that was the most natural and obvious one for them to use? I firmly believe it was because of a conscious effort on their part to not use the word. And this deliberate effort is just one more nugget of circumstantial evidence, which, though small, is totally compatible with all the other evidence pointing irresistibly to their guilt.

2. The fact that Bush stopped pursuing, for all intents and purposes, the person responsible for 9/11, Osama Bin Laden, by diverting most of this country's resources and military personnel to his pursuit of Hussein, who was not involved in 9/11, is circumstantial evidence that it was always Hussein whom he really wanted to go after, and 9/11 was just a convenient pretext enabling him to do so. Indeed, it has since emerged from many sources that the neoconservatives in the Bush administration had been dreaming about invading Iraq for years before 9/11. Since Bush sent ten times as many troops to Iraq as he did to Afghanistan, doesn't that suggest that Hussein was much more important to Bush than Bin Laden? But how could that possibly be? The fact that Bush was willing to shirk his constitutional duty to "take care that the laws [of this nation] be faithfully executed" by all but abandoning pursuit of the person (Bin Laden) responsible for 3,000 American murders—the one he promised to bring back "dead or alive"—is circumstantial evidence that his passion for invading Iraq and removing Hussein from power was so strong that he would be much more likely to lie to the American people about Hussein being an imminent threat to this country.

3. It clearly appears that Bush deliberately lied to the nation in his first nationally televised address on the Iraqi crisis on the evening of Octo-

ber 7, 2002, when he spoke from Cincinnati, Ohio, at the Museum Center. As noted earlier, Bush told the nation that Hussein was "a great danger to our nation," either by Hussein himself using "unmanned aerial vehicles" with "chemical or biological" payloads "for missions targeting the United States" or by providing these biological or chemical weapons to a "terrorist group or individual terrorists" to attack us. Bush framed the threat as being imminent when he said this could happen "on any given day."

On October 8, the day after Bush's Cincinnati speech, and only after the Senate's Select Committee on Intelligence exerted considerable pressure on him, CIA director George Tenet declassified a letter he had sent to Senator Bob Graham, chairman of the Senate committee. The letter from Tenet—which was signed for him by John McLaughlin, the deputy director of the CIA who was Tenet's number one deputy—was read that day to a joint hearing of the House and Senate Intelligence Committees. It stated that the CIA had concluded that "Baghdad *for now* appears to be drawing a line short of conducting terrorist attacks with conventional or CBW (chemical or biological weapons) against the United States. Should Hussein conclude that a U.S. led attack [against him] could no longer be deterred, he probably would become much less constrained in adopting terrorist actions." Clear translation: Saddam Hussein was *not* an imminent threat to the security of this country, and would not use any of his chemical and biological weapons against us unless we attacked him first; that is, he would only use these weapons in self-defense.

The media reported (very cursorily) on the matter, most noting only that the letter was declassified on October 8, 2002. It could conceivably have been written a couple of months earlier. But a source at CIA headquarters in Langley, Virginia, told me (in a telephone conversation on March 10, 2003) that the date of the letter was October 7, 2002, and the physical letter itself was couriered to Graham that same day, October 7, *before* Bush's speech that night. Senator Graham's press office told me that the letter was also faxed to Graham's office at 4:27 p.m. on October 7.

Though the letter was not addressed to Bush, there can be little question that Bush received a copy of it, and even if he didn't, he certainly knew of its contents. The CIA is an agency of the executive branch of government, and the CIA director is responsible and answerable *only* to the president. As Thomas Powers wrote in his book *The Man Who Kept the Secrets: Richard Helms and the CIA*: "The President is the sun in the CIA's solar system. The Central Intelligence Agency and its Director serve the President *alone*." The Senate Intelligence Committee isn't even in the executive branch of the government, and it is inconceivable that Tenet would confide something to them that he would not to the president. *No one* would believe this. Also, since Tenet, who had become a close friend of the president, briefed the president every morning in the Oval Office, it is equally inconceivable that on the morning of October 7, 2002, Tenet would tell Bush that Hussein *was* an imminent threat to this country, and later in the day tell the U.S. Senate Intelligence Committee that he was not. (By the way, the White House press office confirmed to me that Tenet did brief Bush in the Oval Office on the morning of October 7. Bush left Washington on Air Force One at 5:50 p.m. that day and started his speech to the nation in Cincinnati at 8:01 p.m.)

Bush had said that with respect to going to war with Iraq: "I'll be making up my mind based upon the *latest* intelligence." Facts are stubborn little devils, and whatever other CIA document or documents the Bush administration might come up with to support Bush's statement to the American people on the evening of October 7, 2002, it cannot get around the fact that at the time of his speech, the *very latest* intelligence of the CIA about Hussein was that he was *not* an imminent threat to this country. And just as obviously, this CIA assessment on October 7 would not have been made overnight. It almost certainly preceded October 7 by weeks, maybe months, throughout all of which time Tenet would have been informing Bush of essentially the same conclusion he expressed in his October 7 letter.

In fact, we *know* it preceded October 7 by at least one week. The classified 2002 National Intelligence Estimate issued by the CIA to the Bush administration and Senate Select Committee on Intelligence on October 1, 2002, sets forth the same conclusion as the October 7 letter in slightly different words. (See later text). It should be noted that this October 1 CIA report, then, *also* gave Bush notice, *prior* to his speech in Cincinnati, that the CIA did *not* consider Hussein an imminent threat to this nation.

So *when Bush told the nation on the evening of October 7 that Hussein was an imminent threat to the security of this country, he was telling millions of Americans the exact opposite of what his own CIA was telling him.* In other words, to further his own personal agenda, Bush lied to the country, and on the very gravest of matters concerning war and peace. And there was no way he could invoke national security as a defense for his lie. As it turned out, he didn't have to offer any defense at all. When the aforementioned memo surfaced on October 8, 2002, a few papers briefly mentioned the apparent contradiction between Tenet's letter and Bush's speech to the nation and then the matter was immediately forgotten. None of the books or articles or newspaper columns on the case since then that I am aware of focused on this matter. In other words, the media gave Bush a pass and let him get away with his monumental lie to the nation.

To summarize this all-important point, since we know, by the Bush administration's own admission, that it was *relying on* U.S. intelligence to form its conclusion on whether Hussein was a threat to the security of this country, and since we know that U.S. intelligence (in the form of the sixteen U.S. intelligence agencies that gave their input into the CIA's 2002 National Intelligence Estimate) *told* the Bush administration that Hussein was not an imminent threat, by definition Bush and his people could not have been acting in self-defense when they went to war in Iraq. That is, not if they were relying on U.S. intelligence as opposed to some Washington, D.C., fortune-teller. In other words, Bush and his gang can't have it both ways.

4. Bush, at a trial, would never, of course, admit that he took the country to war under false pretenses, not in self-defense. But as I have indicated, this can be shown by circumstantial evidence. However, we also have *direct evidence* of Bush and his people lying in several statements on an extremely important document, which is circumstantial

evidence of their state of mind that they *wanted, intended*, to lie, and that was their modus operandi.

The most important prewar intelligence report that the Bush administration relied upon to justify its going to war in Iraq was the aforementioned *October 1, 2002*, National Intelligence Estimate (NIE), a CIA report that utilized the input of every intelligence agency in the federal government, such as the Defense Department's DIA (Defense Intelligence Agency), the National Security Agency, etc., and was classified "Top Secret." The NIE report (titled "Iraq's Continuing Programs for Weapons of Mass Destruction"), which was sent to the Senate Select Committee on Intelligence, was of course kept under lock and key in a secure room. But although any member of Congress could have read the report, as set forth in *Hubris, the Inside Story of Spin, Scandal, and the Selling of the Iraqi War* by Michael Isikoff and David Corn, "Senate aides would calculate that no more than a half dozen or so members actually went to the secure room" to read it. One might ask why? One reason is incompetence, another reason is sloth. Yet another reason is that members of Congress are very busy people with many other matters to tend to, though none more important than becoming as knowledgeable as possible before voting on whether to go to war.

But one thing has to be said in defense of the many Democratic members of Congress who didn't read the report yet voted for the war, mouthing almost the same dire warnings of the Iraqi threat as Bush and his team did. (In the House of Representatives, 81 Democrats voted for the war, 126 against it; no Republican voted against it. In the Senate, 29 Democrats voted for the war, 21 against it, and only one Republican voted against it.) The Bush administration conducted many briefing sessions for congressional members in which the briefers grossly overstated and distorted the existing evidence, just as they did to the American public. How could these senators and representatives who were present at these briefings have been expected not to accept what they were being told, and say to themselves, "I'm going to try to check all this out myself"? How could these members of Congress have imagined that a presidential administration consisted of a bunch of people who were deliberately lying to them and the American public about a matter of war and peace? Since there is no prior record of such criminal conduct in American history, why would they have any reason to be skeptical about what they were being told?

As former Democratic senator Bob Graham, who was a member of the Senate at the time, said, "Yes, more than 100 Democrats voted to authorize him [President Bush] to take the nation to war. Most of them, though, like their Republican colleagues, did so in the legitimate belief that the president and his administration were truthful in their statements that Saddam Hussein was a gathering menace—that if Hussein was not disarmed, the smoking gun would become a mushroom cloud." Democratic senator Tom Daschle, the senate majority leader at the time, said, "Bush was telling me that Iraq had WMD and we had to move."

But perhaps most importantly, even if more members of Congress had bothered to read the classified NIE report, it would have been unavailing because we know that all of the CIA conclusions in the report that Iraq had weapons of mass destruction were wrong. But the senators and representatives would have had no way of knowing this at the time. It was the responsibility of the Bush administration, not individual members of Congress, to vet all CIA documents and information for accuracy.

The 2004 report on prewar intelligence of the Senate Select Committee on Intelligence* said that the CIA's conclusions in its October 2002 NIE classified report on Iraq's illicit weapons were "either overstated, or were not supported by, the underlying intelligence reporting." (The committee gave, as examples, the CIA saying it was its belief that Iraq was "reconstituting its nuclear program," had "chemical and biological weapons," and was developing an unmanned aerial vehicle "probably intended to deliver biological warfare agents.")

---

*The report was released on July 9, 2004. After a twelve-month inquiry, the committee concluded what the 9/11 Commission had; namely, that there was no evidence that Hussein and Iraq had any relationship with Al Qaeda, and there was no evidence that Hussein and Iraq had anything to do with 9/11.

Now, why would CIA professionals do something like this? The most reasonable inference, and many independent observers agree, is that the Bush administration, seeking to secure the support of Congress in using force in Iraq, was putting relentless pressure on the CIA to state as strong a case for war as they could. In preparing the NIE report, people at the agency like CIA director George Tenet, whose very job depended on the pleasure of the president, must have felt like a rope in a tug-of-war between their conscience on one side and the lying, immoral Bush administration on the other side.

But even the CIA's bloated and inaccurate conclusions in its classified NIE report weren't good enough for the Bush administration. Additionally, the classified version contained some vigorous dissents to these conclusions. When, on October 1, 2002, Democratic senator Bob Graham, the chairman of the Senate Select Committee on Intelligence (commonly referred to as the Senate Intelligence Committee), requested of the CIA that it provide an unclassified, public version of the NIE report Graham and his committee had just received, so the American people could see these dissents and reservations, the Bush administration reportedly had its chief water-carrier, Condoleezza Rice, contact George Tenet at the CIA and tell Tenet what the American people really should see. Who won out? Graham or the water-carrier? The twenty-five-page unclassified version of the classified NIE report, titled "Iraq's Weapons of Mass Destruction Programs" and issued by the CIA on October 4, 2002, clearly showed that the water-carrier carried more weight with the CIA than Senator Graham.

As Senator Graham told me in a conversation on November 29, 2007: "The unclassified version the CIA sent over [which became known as the 'White Paper'] not only didn't give me what I requested, they gave me a document that was nothing more than propaganda, a full-throated cry for war with no tempering information." The White Paper, issued by the Bush administration to Congress and the public to persuade them to support its rush to war, deleted the very dissenting opinions Graham wanted the public to hear. Moreover, the CIA literally changed its conclusions in a way that made them more frightening to the American public. There can be little question at all that by unstated words, or more, Rice communicated to Tenet that the Bush administration (of which the CIA, in the executive branch, is a part) wanted a stronger report, which would be the Bush administration's version of the original classified NIE report. It is inconceivable that without the intercession of Rice or some other Bush administration representative, the CIA would decide, on its own and in print, to contradict a report it had just issued three days earlier. This new version, then, was the Bush administration's version of the original classified NIE report.*

Let's now look at the NIE's October 1, 2002, classified report and then the Bush administration's October 4, 2002, unclassified version, the White Paper, which was presented to Congress and the American people just one week before the congressional vote authorizing the Bush administration to invade Iraq. We'll see how the Bush administration lied to the American public to make the case for war much stronger. Like typical criminals, Bush and his people left their incriminating fingerprints everywhere, showing an unmistakable conscious-

---

*What we will be examining in this book—how the Bush administration *used* (misused) the intelligence it came to possess—was not examined by the Senate Intelligence Committee in 2004, because the Republican majority on the committee overruled the effort by the Democratic minority to do so. As this book went to press, the Senate Select Committee on Intelligence was scheduled to finally release its report on whether the Bush administration misused its intelligence in the lead-up to war. (The report will be classified and will not be immediately released to the American public.) But we can already just about know certain things. The report will be a mixed one because of intense quarreling by Republicans and Democrats on the Committee, particularly since there's a presidential election in the coming months. And the hedges in the report will do the most plush Long Island estate proud. Further, when it comes to assigning personal culpability (never criminal) to individuals, nothing ever comes out of these congressional committees but pablum, thinned and pasteurized at that.

My guess is that, for the most part, the report will say that when members of the Bush administration made certain assertions, there was or was not evidence that allowed them to do so. In any event, since virtually all the inferences I have drawn in this book are based on established facts, no Senate report can change these facts.

ness of guilt on their part. But they never did so as openly and audaciously as they did with the NIE report and White Paper. Bush and his people's selective use of intelligence information and outright distortion of facts to justify going to war with Iraq would have caused even Machiavelli's jaw to drop.

Here's the evidence. When the 2002 NIE report (the original top-secret CIA classified report which the Bush administration publicly promoted as its gold standard, its main evidence for going to war) was declassified in part in July 2003 and April 2004, we learned that it said, for instance: "*We judge that* Iraq has continued its weapons of mass destruction programs in defiance of UN resolutions . . ." Bush's White Paper, shown to the American public and Congress, deleted the words "We judge that" (words that clearly signified this was merely a CIA opinion) and started with the words "Iraq *has continued* its weapons of mass destruction programs . . ." So essentially *opinion* was turned into *fact* by a compliant CIA operating under the heel of the gang of thugs in the White House. For those Bush apologists who say this change was not an important one, and that I'm nitpicking, I would respond— then why did Bush and his people bother to make the change? By definition, by their doing it they revealed that they believed their change *did* make a difference, that it *was* substantive and important. There would have been no other valid reason to make the change.

Going on, the CIA's classified NIE report says, "*We assess that* Baghdad has begun renewed production of mustard, sarin, GF (cyclosarin) and VX." In the White Paper issued by the Bush administration to the American public and Congress, the words "We assess that" are deleted and it reads "Baghdad has begun . . ."

In the classified NIE report, the words are "although we have little specific information on Iraq's CW [chemical weapons] stockpile [they had *no* information], Saddam probably has stocked at least 100 metric tons (MT) and possibly as much as 500 MT of CW agents—much of it added in the last year." The White Paper issued to the American public and Congress deleted the words "although we have little specific information on Iraq's CW stockpile." It simply reads, "Saddam probably has . . ."

The classified NIE report says, *"We judge that* Iraq has some lethal and incapacitating BW [biological weapons] and is capable of producing and weaponizing a variety of such agents, including anthrax, for delivery by bombs, missiles, aerial sprayers and covert operatives." In the White Paper, the honorable and moral and ethical and patriotic and very religious people in the White House deleted the words "We judge that" and started with the words "Iraq *has* some lethal . . ." Then, incredibly, after the words "for delivery by bombs, missiles, aerial sprayers and covert operatives" in the original NIE report, the White Paper actually inserted these words that were not even in the report: "including potentially against the U.S. homeland." We're in the majors, now, folks. This is big-time deception.

How, you may ask at this point, would these thugs have the guts to change the language of an official document that they had to know at some point would become declassified? I guess for several reasons. First, by the time the NIE document was declassified, it would be long after the start of the war the Bush administration wanted so badly. Secondly, they know how completely out of it the American public (the Walking Dead) is and how they only focus, if at all, on what's happening today, their memory lasting as long as a breath upon a mirror. And finally, they know from experience that with the very weak "liberal media" and pathetic liberal TV personalities like Charlie Rose, Ted Koppel, and George Stephanopoulos—physiological marvels who are somehow able to sit erect in front of a camera without a spine—they can literally get by with murder. After all, this is 2008, and I'm just a former prosecutor working out of a converted stall of my garage in far-off LA. Yet before this book, who has really hit these despicable human beings the way they deserve to be hit?

Continuing, the classified NIE report stated that Iraq was developing unmanned aerial vehicles called UAVs, "probably intended to deliver biological warfare agents." But in the White Paper, our friends in the Bush administration *left out* a footnote to this in the original NIE report that stated that the U.S. Air Force director for Intelligence, Surveillance and Reconnaissance did not agree. The Senate Select Committee said that by eliminating that footnote from the unclassified version, the White Paper given to Congress and the American public "is missing the fact that [the] agency with primary responsibility for technological analysis on UAV programs did not agree with the [CIA] assessment."

The White Paper said that *"all* intelligence experts agree that Iraq is seeking nuclear weapons." But this was a lie. The White Paper deleted the dissent of the Intelligence and Research bureau of the State Department that "the activities we have detected do *not*, however, add up to a compelling case that Iraq is currently pursuing . . . an integrated and comprehensive approach to acquire nuclear weapons."

Was anything else deleted from the classified report? Yes. The White Paper said that Baghdad, which, prior to the Gulf War in 1991 was attempting to develop a nuclear weapon, was "vigorously trying" to buy uranium from Niger to reconstitute its nuclear program. But Congress and the American people weren't told that the classified NIE report contained a dissent to this conclusion from the U.S. State Department's Bureau of Intelligence and Research, which said that such claims were "highly dubious."

Likewise, the White Paper said that Hussein was purchasing high-strength aluminum tubes, which were believed to be intended for use as "centrifuge rotors" in the production of nuclear weapons. But Congress and the American people were not told that the classified NIE report contained dissents from the U.S. Department of Energy as well as the State Department's Bureau of Intelligence and Research, which said that they believed the tubes were "not intended" for and "not part of" any alleged Iraqi nuclear program.

By far the most serious and inexcusable change the Bush administration made in its White Paper is that the classified NIE report said that Hussein would only use the weapons of mass destruction he was believed to have if he were first attacked; that is, in self-defense. It read: "Baghdad for now appears to be drawing a line short of conducting terrorist attacks with conventional or CBW against the United States, fearing that exposure of Iraqi involvement would provide Washington a stronger case for making war. Iraq probably would attempt clandestine attacks against the US Homeland *if* Baghdad feared [that] an attack that threatened the survival of the regime were imminent or unavoidable . . ." With Bush and his people desperately trying to frighten the American people into war by making them believe Hussein was an imminent threat to the security of this nation, these were the very last words in the world they would want the American people to hear. So they simply omitted every one of these all-important words from the White Paper.*

So Bush and his gang of criminals were constantly telling Americans that Hussein constituted an imminent threat to the security of this country, but they kept the truth from the American people that their CIA was telling them the exact opposite, that Hussein and Iraq were not an imminent threat to this country. Indeed, that Iraq would only attack us if *they*, Iraq, were in fear of an imminent attack on them by *us*. How evil, how perverse, how sick, how criminal can Bush and his people be? Yet unbelievably, they got away with *all* of this.

I have a question for Condoleezza Rice, Bush's national security adviser, who has said, "I read the National Intelligence Estimate *cover to cover* a couple of times." Since it was the consensus of sixteen U.S. intelligence agencies that Hussein was not an imminent threat to this country unless he feared we were about to attack him, wasn't keeping this all-important conclusion out of the White Paper so egregiously wrong that even you should have said to your gang: "You know, guys, these other distortions are bad enough. But this is going too far." What I'm saying is—was there no level of deception beyond which you were unwilling to go in helping your boss take America to war under false pretenses? Of course, certain questions answer themselves by being asked.

---

*And when Bush, just six days later, told the American people in his speech from Cincinnati that Hussein was an imminent threat to the security of this country, the opposite of what the CIA and fifteen other U.S. intelligence agencies had told him six days earlier, this alone, and all by itself (though there is so much more), is virtually conclusive evidence that Bush took this nation to war under false pretenses. It also destroys his expected defense to any murder charge brought against him that in going to war in Iraq he acted in self-defense.

Although the truth is often an elusive fugitive, what do all of the above deliberate deletions and distortions in the White Paper—every one of which went in the same direction, to exaggerate the threat posed by Hussein and Iraq—show very, very, very clearly? They show, unmistakably, the state of mind of Bush and his people to deliberately lie and distort the truth to further their objective of persuading the American public and Congress that it was the right thing, in self-defense, to go to war with Iraq *now*. With that state of mind, which we know (not think) they had, all of the many other allegations about the Bush administration's lies and distortions *necessarily* become more believable.

What the above also shows is that the CIA's George Tenet, Bush's personal friend, entered into a Faustian bargain and sold his agency and America out. As six former CIA officials wrote to Tenet at the time Tenet published his memoirs in April of 2007: "You helped build the case for war. You betrayed the C.I.A. officers who collected the intelligence that made it clear that Saddam did not pose an imminent threat. You betrayed the analysts who tried to withstand the pressure applied by Cheney and Rumsfeld . . . Although [the] C.I.A. learned in late September 2002 . . . that Iraq had no past or present contact with Osama Bin Laden and that the Iraqi leader considered Bin Laden an enemy . . . you still went before Congress in February 2003 and testified that Iraq did indeed have links to Al Qaeda . . . Your tenure as head of the C.I.A. has helped create a world that is more dangerous. It is doubly sad that you seem still to lack an adequate appreciation of the enormous amount of death and carnage you have facilitated."

Before we continue, let's briefly discuss a matter that infuses all of these points—whether the Bush administration put undue pressure on U.S. intelligence agencies to provide it with conclusions that would help them in their quest for war. The Senate Intelligence Committee was split on the issue. While Republicans on the committee claimed the administration did not exert such pressure, the Democrats,

though agreeing with the report's conclusion that the Bush administration never tried to *coerce* an intelligence agency to "change" a finding the agency had already reached in a report, did not agree with the
Republicans that no political pressure had been placed on U.S. intelligence analysts by the Bush administration. Senator John Rockefeller
said that the Senate committee's report "fails to fully explain the environment of intense pressure in which the intelligence community officials were asked to render judgments on matters relating to Iraq
when the most senior officials in the Bush administration had already
forcefully and repeatedly stated their conclusions publicly. It was clear
to all of us in this room . . . and to many others that they had made up
their mind that they were going to go to war."

Indeed, the evidence is clear that the Bush administration did put
pressure on the intelligence community. Before I present just some of
the evidence, consider this. If a man told you that while he was walking down the street he saw orange trees on the block, and another
said he did not, whom would you believe? Assuming neither man was
crazy or lying, obviously you'd believe the man who saw the orange
trees. The one who didn't could have had all sorts of reasons for not
seeing the orange trees, such as not looking, or being distracted with
other thoughts. But how can you refute the statement of the man
who saw the orange trees?

Here, there is much, much evidence—the witnesses who saw the
orange trees—that the Bush administration pressured the CIA and
others. This is just some of the evidence.

In an interview with *Good Morning America* in 2004, Bush's former
counterterrorism chief, Richard Clarke, said that on September 12,
just one day after 9/11: "The President in a very intimidating way left
us— me and my staff—with the clear indication that he *wanted* us to
come back with the word that there was an Iraqi hand behind 9/11."
Clark explained in his book *Against All Enemies: Inside America's War on
Terror* that when he told Bush the day after 9/11 that the CIA was already explicit that only Al Qaeda was guilty of the attacks, Bush
wasn't satisfied with this answer and insisted that he and his people
look again for an Iraqi connection. "Absolutely, we will look again," he

told Bush. "But you know, we have looked several times for state sponsorship of Al Qaeda and not found any real linkages to Iraq. Iran plays a little [with Al Qaeda], as does Pakistan, and Saudi Arabia, Yemen." "Look into Iraq, Saddam," the president said "testily," according to Clarke.

At a meeting in August 2002 of the Pentagon's Defense Intelligence Agency on the proposed war in Iraq, Douglas J. Feith, the Pentagon's under secretary of Defense for Policy, showed up at the meeting (which several DIA analysts said was very unusual) and proceeded to criticize the CIA's failure to turn up any link between Bin Laden and Hussein. The obvious message was that he didn't want them to do likewise. (Feith at the time was running a rogue intelligence operation out of his office for the Bush administration that was dedicated to finding any real or imagined link between Hussein and Al Qaeda—regardless of how poor the source—to help make its case for war. A favorite source of Feith's shadow intelligence unit was the Iraqi National Congress, an Iraqi exile group headed by Ahmed Chalabi, a sworn enemy of Hussein whom the Bush administration at one time was grooming to replace Hussein when he fell, and whose "information" was sometimes flat-out fabricated.)

Robin Raphel, a twenty-eight-year veteran of the U.S. State Department's Foreign Service, said that in the buildup to war, key decisions were "ideologically based. They were not based on analytical, historical understanding." She said the invasion's timing was driven by "clear political pressure" and the atmosphere was one of apprehension, in which the Bush administration people kept close watch on others. "There were political people round and about. One had to be careful."

David J. Dunford, a Middle East specialist for the State Department who was put in charge of the Iraq Foreign Ministry right after the invasion, said that prewar in the Bush administration, "you could feel there was a drive to go to war *no matter what the facts.*"

Richard Kerr, a former deputy director of the CIA, said that in 2003 there was significant pressure on the intelligence community to find evidence that supported a connection between Iraq and Al

Qaeda. He told the Senate Intelligence Committee that the [Bush] administration's "hammering" on Iraq intelligence was harder than any he had seen in his thirty-two years at the agency.

Kenneth Pollack was a Clinton administration National Security official who strongly and outspokenly supported the invasion of Iraq. Nonetheless, in an op-ed piece in the *New York Times* on June 20, 2003, which was after the war started, he said he had heard "many complaints from friends still in government that some Bush officials were mounting a ruthless campaign over intelligence estimates. I was told that when government analysts wrote cautious assessments of Iraq's capabilities, they were grilled and forced to go to unusual lengths to defend their judgments, and some were chastised for failing to come to more alarming conclusions."

In an article in the journal *Foreign Affairs* on February 10, 2006, retired CIA agent Paul Pillar, who oversaw CIA intelligence assessments about Iraq from 2000 to 2005, accused the Bush administration of "cherry-picking" intelligence on Iraq. "Intelligence was misused publicly [i.e., to the American public] to justify decisions that had already been made." He wrote that as a result of political pressure, CIA analysts began to "sugarcoat" their conclusions regarding the threat posed by Iraqi weapons and about ties between Hussein and Al Qaeda.

Larry Johnson, a registered Republican and former CIA official who voted for and contributed to Bush's 2000 campaign for the presidency and thereafter became the deputy director of the U.S. State Department's Office of Counterterrorism, said that in "April of last year [2003], I was beginning to pick up grumblings from friends inside the intelligence community that there had been pressure applied to analysts to come up with certain conclusions. Specifically, I was told that analysts were pressured to find an operational link between Osama Bin Laden and Saddam Hussein. One analyst in particular told me they were repeatedly pressured by the most senior officials in the Department of State."

5. Continuing on with the pieces of evidence showing that the Bush administration lied to the country when it claimed that Hussein was

an imminent threat to the security of this country, though we obviously have no admission from Bush or his people that they cooked the books and distorted the truth to take us to war, the closest thing to an admission from an insider is contained in the famous "Downing Street Memo" from Bush's staunch ally in the war, Britain. The July 23, 2002, memo, written by Matthew Rycroft, a foreign policy aide of British prime minister Tony Blair, was not really a memo but the minutes of a meeting between Blair and members of his war cabinet on the impending Iraq war. The minutes (memo) said that Sir Richard Dearlove, the chief of Britain's Secret Intelligence Service (the equivalent of our CIA), told Blair at the war cabinet meeting that, from his meetings in Washington with Bush administration officials, it was obvious that "Bush wanted to remove Saddam, through military action, justified by the conjunction of terrorism and WMD. But the intelligence and facts *were being fixed around the policy.*" In other words, Bush and his gang had decided to go to war with Iraq, "so now let's fix the facts to warrant what we've already decided we want to do." This is criminal, folks, and the source for this information couldn't be more credible and reliable—a high-level official from Bush's biggest ally in the war, the British. The Bush administration consistently twisted and distorted the truth by omitting, exaggerating, or trivializing the facts to fit its purpose.

Vincent Cannistraro, the former head of the CIA's counterterrorism unit, said during the Bush administration's relentless buildup for war: "Basically, cooked information is working its way into high-level [Bush administration] pronouncements, and there is a lot of unhappiness about it in intelligence, especially among analysts at the CIA."

6. The evidence of "cherry-picking" by the Bush administration in taking the nation to war, only giving the American public information that supported the Bush administration's position, never anything that refuted it or threw it open to question, could be the subject matter of an entire book.

A March 6, 2004, *New York Times* article, quoting several U.S. government officials, said, "U.S. Intelligence agencies and the Bush administration cited only reports from informants who supported the view that Iraq possessed so-called weapons of mass destruction. Other government officials said they knew of several occasions from 2001 to 2003 when Iraqi scientists, defectors and others had told American intelligence officers that Iraq did not possess illicit weapons." But these reports were "dismissed" because "they did not conform" to the Bush administration position. "It appears," one government official put it, "that human intelligence wasn't deemed interesting and useful if it was exculpatory of Iraq."

Here is an extremely important example of cherry-picking, and even then, the cherry was a rotten one that should never have been swallowed. The main source the Bush administration relied upon to claim that Iraq had a fleet of mobile labs (or "factories") producing biological poisons (proven by UN inspectors to be false information *before* the war) was an informant aptly code-named "Curveball" by his German handlers. Curveball claimed that he had actually been a part of the team that built the labs. Although Bush used "information" from "Curveball" in several prewar speeches, including his 2003 State of the Union address, and Secretary of State Powell used the same information in his address before the United Nations on February 5, 2003, and everyone agrees that Curveball's information was one of the most important pillars Bush and his administration used to justify going to war, the CIA itself never even personally interviewed Curveball, a Baghdad-born chemical engineer who sought political asylum in Germany in 1999 after earlier being fired from his job and jailed for theft.

But the biggest problem is that "Curveball" was a completely unreliable informant. Curveball's German handlers in the BND (German intelligence service), who knew him well, said that Curveball was "not a psychologically stable guy. He's not a completely normal person." Indeed, when Tyler Drumheller, in 2002 the head of clandestine services in the CIA's European division, met with the BND station chief at the German embassy in Washington, the German officer told Drumheller that Curveball, a heavy drinker, had had a mental breakdown and was "crazy. Principally, we think he's probably a fabricator." Just one example of a Curveball fabrication: In Colin Powell's presentation to the United Nations he said that "an eyewitness, an Iraqi chemical engineer [Curveball] actually was present during biological agent production runs. He was also at the site when an accident occurred in 1998. Twelve technicians died from exposure to biological agents." But the Presidential Commission on Illegal Weapons noted in its 2005 report that when the alleged 1998 accident happened, Curveball "was not even in Iraq at that time, according to information supplied by family members and later confirmed by travel records."

Indeed, almost everything about Curveball seemed to be a lie. Even the name he used, Ahmed Hussein Mohammed, was a false name (true name: Rafid Ahmed Alwan). He said he graduated number one in his chemical engineering class at the University of Baghdad. But a later check of the school records revealed he finished at the bottom of his class. His childhood friends called him a "great liar" and a "con artist."

The *Los Angeles Times*, which interviewed five senior officials from BND, reported in its November 20, 2005, edition: "The senior BND officer who supervised Curveball's case said he was aghast" when he heard Powell use Curveball's information in his speech before the United Nations as "justification for war."* The official told the *Times*: "We were shocked. *Mein Gott*. We had always told them [U.S.] it [what Curveball said] was not proven . . . It was not hard intelligence." It was simply a report on what Curveball told them which they forwarded on to U.S. intelligence agencies (specifically the CIA and DIA), never saying the information contained in the report was verified. Another German official told the *Times*: "This was not substantial evidence. We made clear [to the U.S.] we could not verify the things he said."

In a speech at Georgetown University on February 5, 2004, CIA director George Tenet confirmed what this German official had told the *Times*. In the process he inadvertently all but confirmed that the CIA,

---

*Curveball and his fabrications were sufficiently important to the Bush administration in its argument for war to warrant having an entire book written about him by *Los Angeles Times* reporter Bob Drogin titled *Curveball: Spies, Lies, and the Con Man Who Caused a War.*

at the Bush administration's stated or implied behest, was knowingly distorting intelligence information. Speaking of Curveball, Tenet said his CIA had "missed the notice [obviously from the Germans] that identified" him "as providing information that in some cases was *unreliable* and in other cases *fabricated*. We have acknowledged this mistake." But how in the world could trained CIA analysts look at correspondence and other information from German intelligence and see what Curveball is alleging but not see where the Germans are saying this source is not reliable and is a fabricator? I mean, I guess anything is possible. But how believable is this? Not at all.

In fact, in 2005 Drumheller told the Presidential Commission on Illegal Weapons that everyone in the CIA's chain of command knew about the severe problems with Curveball's credibility, and documentation on his unreliability was circulated widely within the agency. (The *Times* reported that Drumheller had told it the same thing.) James L. Pavitt, the CIA's deputy director of operations at the time, told the *Times* that "there was yelling and screaming about this guy" at the agency.

"CIA officials," the *Times* wrote, "now concede that the Iraqi [Curveball] fused fact, research he gleaned on the internet, and what his former co-workers [in Iraq] called 'water cooler gossip' into a nightmarish fantasy that played on U.S. fears after the September 11 attacks." Never mind. What Curveball was saying sure as hell sounded good to Bush and his people, who were gunning for war, and ready to use any information, confirmed or not, from an unreliable source or not, that could help them in their immoral and I say highly criminal marketing campaign to sell America on the Iraqi war.

The Bush administration never once shared what they knew about Curveball's lack of credibility with Congress or the American people. Indeed, there is no evidence that either Congress or the public even knew of Curveball's existence. All they knew was that the CIA said it was its belief that Iraq had biological weapons of mass destruction.

7. One of the most notorious instances of the Bush administration using thoroughly discredited information to frighten the American

public into war was the famous Niger incident. Briefly, in Bush's January 28, 2003, State of the Union speech he declared that "the British Government has learned that Saddam Hussein recently sought significant quantities of uranium from Africa," sixteen now infamous words that have come back to haunt the Bush administration. Uranium, once enriched, can be used for nuclear weapons fuel. The country in Africa was alleged to be the former French colony of Niger, a very poor country in northern Africa. One of Niger's resources is uranium. And, indeed, the 2002 NIE said that Baghdad had been vigorously seeking to buy uranium from Niger.

The only problem was that the Niger allegation was not true. In fact, Joseph C. Wilson IV, the former ambassador to Iraq, was sent to Niger by the CIA in February of 2002 because Vice President Cheney's office wanted to know if there was anything to an intelligence report that referred to a memorandum of agreement that documented the sale of uranium yellowcake (a form of lightly processed ore) to Iraq by Niger in the late 1990s. After spending eight days investigating the matter in Niger, where he had been a U.S. diplomat in the mid-1970s, Wilson reported back to the CIA that it was "highly doubtful" such a transaction had ever taken place, and in an op-ed piece in the *New York Times* on July 6, 2003, he attacked the Bush administration for claiming there was any truth to the story.

Further, the *Los Angeles Times* reported in its December 11, 2005, edition that Alain Chouet, the former chief of the counterintelligence division of France's national spy service (*Direction Générale de la Sécurité Extérieure*), had told the paper that nearly a year *before* Bush declared in his 2003 State of the Union address that Hussein was trying to buy uranium in Niger, his group, per the CIA's request, conducted an extensive investigation in Niger, where the uranium mines are owned and operated by French companies, and found that there was absolutely no evidence to support the claim. Chouet said his spy service furnished the CIA with this information, and when the allegation continued to surface, his unit repeatedly warned the CIA that there was no truth to it. A former CIA official confirmed to the *Times* that the French had, indeed, given the agency this information. The *Times* reported further that another French government official informed the paper that when Bush said in his 2003 address he was basing his information on a British report, French intelligence viewed the British report as "totally crazy because there was no backup for this." Nevertheless, he said, the French once again conducted an investigation, turning things "upside down" to see if there was any basis for the story, but again, they found nothing.

No wonder. The original documents making the claim that the country of Niger had agreed to sell Hussein uranium were crude forgeries. The story first surfaced in Rome, after the documents were taken (along with many other documents and items like a wristwatch, stamps, perfume, etc.) in a purported January 1, 2001, burglary at the Republic of Niger's embassy there. In late September of 2001, the documents came into the hands of Italy's military intelligence agency, SISMI, which in mid-October sent a report on the entire incident to the CIA.

There were several indications that the documents were forged. For instance, although the main document (dated July 6, 2000) said its contents were "top secret," it was only stamped "confidential." And it bore the signature of a Niger foreign minister who hadn't served in that capacity for several years. Even the representation of Niger's national emblem was incorrect. Also, an accompanying document had the heading of an organization that had ceased to exist five months prior to the date of the document. And so on.

On March 7, 2003, Mohamed ElBaradei, the director of the International Atomic Energy Agency, told the UN Security Council that "based on thorough analysis" his agency concluded that the "documents which formed the basis for the report of recent uranium transactions between Iraq and Niger are in fact not authentic." Indeed, author Craig Unger conducted extensive research into the Niger incident for a 2006 article in *Vanity Fair* and interviewed many former CIA and DIA officials who worked for these agencies at the time, such as Melvin Goodman, a former senior analyst at the CIA and State Department; Vincent Cannistraro, former chief of operations of counterterrorism at the CIA; and Larry Wilkerson, Colin Powell's former chief of staff. Unger uncovered at least fourteen instances *prior* to the 2003 State of the Union address by Bush in which analysts at the CIA, the State Department, or other government agencies that had examined the Niger documents "raised serious doubts about their legitimacy—only to be rebuffed by Bush administration officials who wanted to use them."

The Niger documents, even though they were thoroughly discredited by U.S. intelligence, were seen by Bush and his people as providing them with the opportunity to frighten and deceive the American public. The water-carrier, Condi Rice, started the propaganda campaign on September 8, 2002, when she told CNN: "There will always be some uncertainty about how quickly [Saddam] can acquire nuclear weapons. But we don't want the smoking gun to be a mushroom cloud." Bush, Cheney, and Rumsfeld were apparently quite taken with the mushroom cloud allusion and began using it, or variations of it, in many of their speeches to the country.

Several days before Bush's speech to the nation in Cincinnati on October 7, 2002, in which he alleged that Hussein posed an imminent threat to the country, his National Security Council sent a draft of the proposed speech, which asserted that Hussein "has been caught attempting to purchase up to 500 metric tons of uranium oxide from Africa—an essential ingredient in the [nuclear] enrichment process," to the CIA. The CIA faxed a reply back telling the White House to delete the uranium reference, but the White House was persistent, sending another draft deleting only the 500 metric ton reference. George Tenet, the CIA director at the time, testified before the Senate Intelligence Committee that this time he personally called Deputy National Security Adviser Stephen Hadley (the current National Security adviser) on October 7 and told him that the president "should not be a fact witness on this issue" because the "reporting was weak." The attempt to purchase uranium was removed from the draft, but as noted earlier, Bush still stuck in his speech that night in Cincinnati that Hussein "could have a nuclear weapon in less than a year." And in subsequent speeches by Bush and his administration, they used the Niger reference.

Finally, the Department of Defense asked the CIA's National Intelligence Council, which oversees all federal agencies that deal with intelligence, to look into the Niger matter. On January 24, 2003, four days before the president's State of the Union address on January 28, the council sent a memo (drafted by national intelligence officer Robert G. Houdek) to the White House stating that "the Niger story is baseless and should be laid to rest."

So how did the sixteen words get into Bush's address to the nation on January 28? Everyone claims ignorance, including Condoleezza Rice. Rice—whose very job it was as national security adviser to coordinate all intelligence from the intelligence community and present it, with advice, to the president in a cohesive manner—while acknowledging that the Niger information was "not credible," claimed, unbelievably, that no one in the White House was aware of this until *after* Bush gave his address. "No one knew at the time in our circles that there were doubts and suspicions" about the Niger information, she said. "We wouldn't have put it in the speech if we had known what we know now." She says she never saw the January 2003 memo and even says, "I don't remember reading [an October 6, 2002] memo" from CIA director George Tenet which she admits was addressed directly to her that said the Niger-uranium claim was without merit. Why didn't she read it? "Because," she said, "when George Tenet says, 'Take it out,' we simply take it out. We don't need a rationale from George Tenet as to why to take it out." But Condoleezza, how would you even know what to take out if you didn't read the memo?

CIA director George Tenet did Rice one better. Although on January 27, 2003, the day before Bush's State of the Union address, he was given a draft of it at a National Security Council meeting, he claims he never read it, so did not know the sixteen words about Hussein trying to buy uranium from Niger were in it. Tenet later acknowledged in July of 2003 that his CIA, however, had "vetted" the speech, and apologized for himself and his agency. "These sixteen words should never have been included" in Bush's speech, he said.

Also in July, there was another *mea culpa*, this one by Stephen Hadley, Rice's number one deputy, who fell on his sword for the Bush administration. He admitted to reporters that he had read two memos the CIA sent to his office at the National Security Council on October 5 and 6 (the one on October 5 addressed to him and the one on the 6th addressed directly to Rice, a copy being sent to the White House Situation Room) before Bush's speech on October 7. Bush's chief speechwriter, Michael Gerson, received copies of both memos, Hadley said. The memos, Hadley acknowledged, stated that the Niger information was no good and the reference to it should be removed. However, Hadley claimed that by the time of Bush's State of the Union address less than four months later he had forgotten about what he had read, and he took full blame for the incident. "I should have asked that the 16 words be taken out" of Bush's address, he said. Note that Hadley's admission proves the falsity (and almost assuredly the lie) of Rice's statement that prior to Bush's State of the Union speech, "no one in our circles" knew about the problems with the Niger reference. I mean, if Hadley, Rice's chief deputy at the National Security Council, and the White House Situation Room were not in Rice's circle, who was?

If you believe that Rice never read the CIA's October memo sent directly to her, and never learned, from her chief deputy Hadley or anyone else, that doubt had been cast on the Niger claim (if, during their workday, Rice and Hadley didn't discuss extremely important things like this, then what *did* they talk about?), and you believe that Tenet never bothered to read a draft of Bush's State of the Union address which was given him to read, and Hadley (a man known for his attention to detail), just a few months after reading about the CIA's challenging the validity of the Niger claim, had completely forgotten about it, and Bush, after seeing the Niger reference deleted from his Cincinnati speech, never asked and was told why, then you are probably the type who would believe someone who told you he had seen a man jumping away from his own shadow, that Frenchmen were no longer drinking wine.

The truth was that the Bush administration, desperately trying to find a way to include the Niger reference in Bush's January 28, 2003,

State of the Union address, finally found it by simply quoting and embracing a British intelligence report on September 24, 2002, that Hussein was trying to buy uranium from Niger, a report that the CIA warned the British should not be given credence. In closed-door testimony before the Senate Intelligence Committee in July of 2003, Alan Foley, a CIA expert on weapons of mass destruction, testified that Robert G. Joseph, a senior adviser to Rice, faxed a draft of the president's State of the Union speech with the Niger reference in it to the CIA days before the speech. Foley told Joseph that the Niger reference should be taken out. Joseph then suggested alternative language be used attributing the Niger reference not to U.S. intelligence but to the British report, and Foley assented.

Of course, you have to know (I'm being sarcastic here) that although Joseph was a chief adviser to Rice, he was running off completely on his own on this, and his superiors, Hadley and Rice, had no idea what he was up to. That is why when the entire Bush administration was later embarrassed by the erroneous Niger reference in Bush's State of the Union address, and they learned it was all Joseph's fault, he was reprimanded and fired. Right. He was not, of course, since he was only a spear-carrier for Bush, Cheney, Rice, and Hadley. And if you fire an emissary spear-carrier, you have to worry, don't you, about his spilling the beans in an exposé book.

As Colonel Wilkerson, Powell's chief of staff, said about Bush, Cheney, Rice, et al., "They were just relentless. You would take language out" of a speech and they would find some way to "stick it back in. That was their favorite bureaucratic technique."

"All of these things," Senator Harry Reid (D-Nevada) said, referring to the Niger nuclear threat issue, "simply were not true. The [Bush] administration knew that, but they did not share that with me or anyone else in Congress that I know of."

Because of what Bush said in his State of the Union address, America could only think that there was a strong possibility that Hussein was planning a nuclear attack on us, exactly what Bush and his people wanted them to believe to build up their claim of self-defense (a preemptive attack) in going to war. The information was phony and the Bush administration had been told it was phony, but Bush and his people decided to lie to the American public to drag them into a horrendous war, one in which over 100,000 people have died horrible deaths.

Has any American president, ever, engaged in such monumentally criminal and deadly activity? No. Indeed, I don't believe any other president would even have dreamed of doing such a thing.

If all of the above, enough to enrage a saint, doesn't make your blood boil, it's only because you are a bloodless wonder, and belong as a feature exhibit at the Smithsonian.

Before I move on to a discussion of the second lie Bush foisted upon the American people (that Hussein was connected with Al Qaeda and 9/11), I want to discuss another point that fortifies the conclusion that Bush's war in Iraq had nothing to do with self-defense. The question that presents itself is, *Why was Bush in such an incredible rush to go to war?* The UN inspectors were making substantial progress and Hussein was giving them unlimited access. So why the rush? Surely he and his advisers couldn't possibly have truly believed that Hussein would launch a nuclear attack on us any day. Everyone knew that even assuming the worst—that Hussein was working on developing a nuclear capability—he wasn't even remotely close to having nuclear weapons yet. As former general Anthony Zinni pointed out, if indeed Hussein was a threat, "containment [of him by inspections] was working remarkably well." So again, why was Bush acting like a child who just had to get his hands on that piece of candy?

It would be difficult to come up with better evidence than the following that Bush wanted to go to war at all costs, that he was not acting in self-defense, and he was lying to the country when he said Hussein had weapons of mass destruction that made him an imminent threat to this country. In self-defense one kills because he *has* to in order to survive, not because he wants to kill his assailant and is searching for an opportunity to do so. Yet it clearly appears Bush was doing the latter.

With over 100 UN inspectors swarming all over Iraq from November 27, 2002, up to March of 2003 to ascertain if Hussein had any WMD* and reporting that after 731 inspections they had not found anything, surely Bush had to know that Hussein wouldn't try, right under the inspectors' noses, to develop any nuclear capacity or other weapons of mass destruction to use against us, and he couldn't do so even if he wanted to since he'd be discovered. Bush also had to know that if the United Nations' inspectors ultimately confirmed that Hussein had no such deadly weapons, *and* the inspectors *stayed* in Iraq to make sure Hussein never rearmed, he (Bush) could achieve his supposed objective of eliminating Iraq as a threat to the security of this country without the draconian resort to war. Wouldn't that have been better than having thousands of Americans and Iraqis die? Yes, if your objective truly was only to insure that Iraq no longer posed a threat to this country. But no, if Hussein's alleged weapons of mass destruction were just a pretext used by Bush to go to war.

On March 7, 2003, less than three weeks before Bush invaded Iraq, Hans Blix, the UN's chief weapons inspector in Iraq, addressed the UN Security Council. He said that since Hussein, in a letter to Blix, had invited UN weapons instructors back into his country in late November of 2002 (almost undoubtedly because just the previous month in Bush's speech to the nation from Cincinnati, it was obvious to Hussein that Bush wanted to go to war with Iraq and he was justifying it on the allegation that Hussein had weapons of mass destruction), his inspection teams had faced "relatively few difficulties," the most notable of which was that Iraq, as it had since 1991 after the Gulf War, objected to U.S. helicopters and aerial surveillance planes flying over Iraq in the "no-fly" zones. However, Blix said, Iraq's objections to this "were overcome." He said that "at this juncture [March 7, 2003] *we are*

---

*After seven years of UN inspections, Hussein threw all UN inspectors out of Iraq in 1998.

able to perform professional, no-notice inspections all over Iraq and to increase [our] aerial surveillance."

The only remaining problem was that Iraq was unable to provide documentation on all the illicit weapons it claimed it had destroyed. Still, when it directed the UN inspectors to some of the destruction sites, many destroyed bombs were found by the inspectors upon excavation and, Blix said, "samples have been taken." Also, Blix said, "The Iraqi side seems to have encouraged interviewees not to request the presence of Iraqi officials" to help ensure the "absence of undue influence." On a related matter, Blix said that Iraq contended its Al-Samoud 2 missiles were within the permissible range set by the UN Security Council. When Blix and his people disagreed, Iraq agreed to start destroying all these missiles, and Blix said that as of March 7, the date of his address to the UN, "34 Al Samoud 2 missiles, including four training missiles, two combat warheads, one launcher, and five engines" had been destroyed.*

Blix, a taciturn and methodical Swedish constitutional lawyer, said that "after a period of somewhat reluctant cooperation there's been an acceleration of initiatives from the Iraqi side" to resolve all disarmament issues, and that these initiatives "can be seen as active, even proactive." Blix added that "no evidence of proscribed activities have so far been found" by his inspectors and "no underground facilities for chemical or biological production or storage were found so far." How much time would it take to resolve the key remaining disarmament tasks? He said that for his inspectors to absolutely confirm that Iraq had no WMD "will not take years, nor weeks, but months." He noted

---

*During those months before the war, which started on March 19, 2003, Bush and his people were so eager for war that they almost seemed offended by Iraqi efforts to avoid it. To take just one example, when, in early March 2003, Iraq started to destroy the above-referenced conventional missiles of theirs that the UN had ruled to be illegal, unbelievably, the Bush White House called the destruction of these missiles by Iraq "the mother of all distractions," i.e., "We want to go to war. Quit distracting us by proving the war is unnecessary." In other words, that which should have been viewed as good news was looked upon as bad news by Bush and his gang in their rush to war.

that even after there had been "verified disarmament" in accordance with UN resolutions, "a sustained inspection and monitoring system is to remain in place . . . to give confidence and to strike an alarm if signs were seen of the revival of any proscribed weapons programs."

And Mohamed ElBaradei, the chief UN nuclear inspector in Iraq who was the head of the International Atomic Energy Agency, told the UN Security Council that "we have to date found no evidence or plausible indication of the revival of a nuclear weapon program in Iraq."

To anyone who did not want to go to war in Iraq unless necessary, this report from Blix and ElBaradei could not have been better news. Nine hundred and ninety-nine out of one thousand people who wanted, if possible, to avoid the horror and bloodshed of a terrible war in Iraq would have been extremely encouraged by the Blix and ElBaradei reports and wouldn't have dreamed of invading Iraq in a few weeks. Instead, Bush ordered Blix, ElBaradei, and their inspectors out of Iraq, refusing to grant them the requested time they needed to confirm the absence of WMD.

You see, when Blix and his UN inspectors reported that they were unable to find any weapons of mass destruction anywhere in Iraq, and that within months the inspectors would probably announce they were certain no such weapons existed, in a very real sense the United Nations inspectors paradoxically became Bush's greatest adversaries, the biggest obstacle to his desire, his passion, to go to war. In other words, if the UN inspectors confirmed that Iraq had no weapons of mass destruction, this would have robbed Bush of his main argument for war, a war he wanted to fight at all costs. Yet when George Bush told the nation on the evening of March 19, 2003, that the war in Iraq had started, he had the breath-stealing audacity to say that "our nation enters this conflict *reluctantly.*" He paved the way for this obvious lie by using the following identical words in speeches on January 28, February 10, and February 20, "If war is *forced* upon us . . ." At this point, right and wrong had as much chance of surviving as a cow in a Chicago stockyard.

As Hans Blix would later say (on the *Today Show*, March 15, 2004) about the Bush administration: "I think they had a set mind. They *wanted* to come to the conclusion that there were weapons of mass destruction . . . They were wrong. There wasn't anything." Earlier, on February 24, 2004, Blix told *People's Daily*: "The Americans and British *created* facts where there were no facts at all. The Americans needed [Iraq to have] weapons of mass destruction to justify war."

Obviously, even before Blix presented his findings to the United Nations on March 7, 2003, Bush and his people were already completely aware, as everyone else was, that Blix and his inspectors were not finding any WMD. So Bush and his gang came up with a new demand, one that was not only beyond the power of the UN inspectors to satisfy, but one they virtually knew Hussein would never comply with, thus guaranteeing the war Bush wanted so desperately. Since Hussein was complying with UN orders to allow UN inspectors total access, and the inspectors were carrying out their mission effectively and finding nothing, on February 28, 2003, just three weeks before the war started, Bush suddenly *raised the bar* for avoiding war. Although the term "regime change" normally suggests a change of leadership, new leaders, Bush had said back on October 21, 2002, that "regime change" in Iraq could result if Hussein merely gave up all his weapons of mass destruction. "If he [Hussein] were to meet all the conditions of the United Nations," Bush said, *"that in itself* will signal that the regime has changed." Earlier, on October 7, 2002, Bush said, "By taking these steps to disarm, the Iraqi regime has an opportunity to avoid conflict . . . Taking these steps would change the nature of the Iraqi regime itself. His [Hussein's] only choice is full compliance [with the UN resolution to disarm]." In other words, if Hussein complied with the UN resolution (1441) to disarm (something it has been confirmed he had already done way back in 1991 following the Persian Gulf War), he himself could survive since, as Bush said, a regime change would have taken place through Hussein's "change." It was, per Bush, Hussein's "only choice."

But on February 28, seeing that Hussein had apparently already complied with the UN resolution, Bush suddenly said that he would only not go to war if Hussein himself departed from Iraq for good, the condition the White House war-mongers just about knew Hussein would be unwilling to comply with.

To summarize, when it became clear that *the whole purpose* of Bush's prewar campaign—to get Hussein to disarm—was being (or already had been) met, the despicable man from Crawford and his people, to save their war, came up with a demand *they had never once made before*—that Hussein resign and leave Iraq.

In a speech to the nation on the Monday evening of March 17, 2003, Bush said that "Saddam Hussein and his sons must leave Iraq within 48 hours. Their refusal to do so will result in military conflict." Hussein stayed put, and U.S. planes started dropping bombs on Baghdad on March 20, 2003, at 5:30 a.m. Baghdad time (9:30 p.m. EST, March 19). Bush had his war, and over 100,000 people would pay for it with their blood and lives.

I would like to raise one other matter—the effort of France to take this nation back from the brink of a catastrophic war—before getting to a discussion of Bush's second lie.

When France (as well as Germany, Russia, China, and most other nations that were members of the UN) refused to go along with Bush's rush to war, many insipid Americans started viciously attacking France verbally, even going so far as to boycott French food and restaurants. And even after it was discovered that Hussein had no WMD and was not involved in 9/11, these meathead Americans continued their denunciation of France. *But the reality is that France never opposed the notion of war with Iraq.* Responsibly seeking to avoid, if possible, the inevitable horror of armed conflict, it only opposed Bush's mad and irresponsible rush to war in Iraq. Such a war, French president Jacques Chirac feared, would outrage Arab and Islamic public opinion and "create a large number of little Bin Ladens." In a joint interview with CBS and CNN in Paris on March 16, 2003, three days before Bush invaded Iraq, Chirac said, "France is not pacifist. We are not anti-American either. But we just feel there is another option, another more normal way, a less dramatic way than war. And we should pursue it *until* we've come to a dead end, but that isn't the case."*

In other words, if we did come to a dead end after exhausting all nonviolent options, then he would not oppose war as a last resort. (Earlier, on February 5, 2003, Dominique de Villepin, the silver-haired French foreign minister, told the UN, "For now, the inspection process has not been completely explored. The use of force can only be a final recourse.") What other "more normal way" did Chirac have in mind? He spelled out the obvious: "The UN inspectors have said on several occasions that it [confirming whether or not Iraq had WMD] was not a matter of years, but not a matter of days either—that it was a question of months. Is it one month, two months? I am ready for any agreement on this point that would have the backing of the inspectors."

Literally hundreds of thousands of Americans and Iraqis (now in their graves or otherwise disabled for life and suffering incalculably) were alive and leading normal lives at the time Chirac made this appeal to reason. But reason only visits those who welcome it. What was the Bush administration's response to Chirac's proposal for a deadline of possibly one or two months before going to war? Vice President Dick Cheney told CBS's *Face the Nation* on March 16, 2003, that "these are just further delaying tactics." You know, let's get on with the show, though Cheney was a no-show during the Vietnam War when it was his generation's time to fight.

---

*One has every reason to believe Chirac—that his position was not the result of France being pacifist or anti-American. After all, when it was clear to France and the world that Al Qaeda was responsible for 9/11, and Afghanistan was protecting Bin Laden, Americans seem to forget that France sent thousands of soldiers to Afghanistan to help us in our war against Al Qaeda and the Taliban. But obviously, Iraq, for all the reasons already alluded to in this book, was an entirely different matter. Most Americans, unable to see the difference, didn't agree, and an April 2003 national poll showed only a 12 percent approval rating for Chirac.

THE SECOND LIE GEORGE BUSH
TOLD THE AMERICAN PEOPLE

With respect to the second lie that Bush told the American public in the run-up to war—his unmistakable innuendo and implication* that Hussein was involved with Al Qaeda in 9/11—the evidence against him is overwhelming. And very unfortunately for Bush, unlike his first lie, he doesn't even have the Ken Lay, Jeffrey Skilling Enron defense (unsuccessful) that everything was carried out by people in his administration, and he had no idea what was going on. You know, like the guy at the bordello who says, "I only play the piano here. I have no idea what goes on upstairs." Bush can't make this argument on his second lie because we have proof from Bush himself that when he strongly suggested that Hussein was involved in 9/11, he knew he was lying. On the evening of September 20, 2001, just nine days after 9/11 and long before he started implying that Hussein was involved in 9/11, he told Congress and the American people: "Americans are asking: 'Who attacked our country?' The evidence we have gathered *all* points to a collection of loosely affiliated terrorist organizations known as Al Qaeda." *Not one word about Hussein and Iraq.*

As reported in the March 14, 2003, edition of the *Christian Science Monitor*: "Polling data show that right after September 11, 2001, when Americans were asked open-ended questions about who was behind the attacks, only 3 percent mentioned Iraq or Hussein." Yet we know that it wasn't long before the majority of Americans (eventually, as high as around 70% in an August 7–11 *Washington Post* poll—62% of Democrats, 80% of Republicans, and 67% of Independents) believed that Hussein was involved in 9/11. If it wasn't Bush and his people

---

*I said earlier that Bush took this nation to war under false pretenses, which were the lies he told the American public about Hussein being an imminent threat and being involved in 9/11. For those who believe that there is no lie or false pretense unless the defendant states it expressly, this is not the law. Indeed, even conduct will suffice. As the courts have consistently held, "A false pretense may consist in any act, word, or symbol calculated and intended to deceive. It may be made either expressly, or by implication."

who were responsible for this suddenly widespread misconception, then who was it? You? Me? Danny DeVito?

Indeed, Bush and his people made their message that Hussein was involved so unambiguously clear, and did such a good job of convincing the American public of their lies, that *after five years* of revelations and the findings of the 9/11 Commission as well as the Senate Select Committee on Intelligence that Hussein was not involved, and not the tiniest speck of evidence surfaced showing any umbilical cord between Hussein and 9/11; in fact, after Bush himself finally admitted on September 17, 2003, that there was "no evidence" of Hussein being involved, and said at a news conference on August 21, 2006, that Hussein had "nothing" to do with 9/11, a September 2006 national CNN poll showed, unbelievably, that 43% of Americans *still* believed that Hussein was involved! And as previously indicated, a June 2006 poll of American soldiers in Iraq showed that an astonishing 90% of them thought Hussein was involved in 9/11, that they were fighting to bring about justice and to protect our country from further attacks.

"Dad," a young soldier said to his father in a phone conversation before he was killed in Iraq, "if we don't fight them here, we will fight them on the streets of America. *They proved that on 9/11.* We don't want IEDs [roadside bombs] and suicide bombers on the streets of America."

So we have the grotesque spectacle of young Americans fighting bravely and dying in Iraq thinking they are fighting the people responsible for 9/11, and Bush, knowing there is "no evidence" at all that Hussein or Iraq was involved in 9/11, seeing to it that the soldiers fighting and dying in Iraq were never informed of this fact.

If in fact Bush lied to this country in taking us to war, these young American soldiers, from their graves, cry out for justice. And their surviving loved ones, who will suffer unimaginably the rest of their lives over what happened to their son, father, or brother, cry out for justice. If they don't, it can only be because they are unaware of Bush's monumental crime, unaware that Bush's lies led directly to the death of their loved ones.

Stephen Kull, director of the Program on International Policy Attitudes at the University of Maryland, said before the war that "the [Bush] administration has succeeded in creating a sense that there is some connection between September 11 and Saddam Hussein." Deborah Tannen, a professor of linguistics at Georgetown University, studied Bush's speeches and concluded: "Clearly, he's using language to imply a connection between Saddam Hussein and September 11th. There is specific manipulation of language here to imply a connection," and that in Iraq "we have gone to war with the terrorists who attacked us." And Senator John D. Rockefeller IV (D-West Virginia), the ranking Democrat on the Senate Intelligence Committee, said that the White House "led the American public into believing there was a connection between Iraq and 9/11 in order to build support for the war in Iraq."

Let me just give you one representative example of how much most Americans were deceived by Bush. Wilson Sekzer, a retired New York City cop, lost his son Jason, who was working on the 105th story of Tower One on 9/11. He told *Parade* magazine in 2006: "After 9/11, I thought, I gotta do something. Somebody has to pay for 9/11. I want the enemy dead. I want to see their bodies stacked up for taking my son. That's when President Bush said 'Iraq.' [Obviously, he couldn't remember precisely what Bush said, but Bush's message was clear and that's why Sekzer formed the impression he did.] On the basis of that, I thought we should go in there and kick Iraq's ass. And I wanted Jason to have a part in it. And that's when I said, 'Put his name on a bomb.'" (On April 1, 2003, a 2,000-pound bomb inscribed with the words "in loving memory of Jason Sekzer" was dropped on Iraq by a marine aircraft.) Later, when Sekzer was watching TV and saw Bush, in response to a reporter's question, saying, "No, we've had no evidence that Saddam Hussein was involved with September the 11th," he recalled saying, "'What did he just say?' I mean, I almost jumped out of my chair. I said, 'What is he talking about? If Saddam didn't have anything to do with 9/11, then why did we go in there?' I'm from the old school. Certain people walk on water. The President of the United States is one of them. It's a terrible thing if someone like me can't trust the President."

Bush had a mandate from the Wilson Sekzers of America to go after the terrorists responsible for 9/11. Instead, he decided to go after those who were not responsible, essentially abandoning the war on terrorism to go after Saddam Hussein, and over 100,000 people have died because of it. Yet up to this point, no one has brought Bush to justice. Or even tried to.

Note that Bush knew he couldn't ever say straight out that Hussein *was* involved in 9/11 because not only did he know he wasn't (as we have seen, Bush's own counterterrorism expert, Richard Clarke, told him the day after 9/11 that U.S. intelligence knew that only Al Qaeda was involved in 9/11, not Hussein), but he knew if he said this, even the mostly mindless media would automatically ask, "What evidence do you have, Mr. President, that Hussein was involved?" and he wouldn't be able to say anything. So Bush and his people got around the media and gave the American public the same, identical message by innuendo, and they succeeded.

But the subtle effort to make this same point by innuendo is itself circumstantial evidence of the Bush administration's intent to deceive the American people into war. In other words, this isn't a case of a bunch of monkeys in a room with typewriters, and they just happened to accidentally come up with these words. It took thought, calculation, and a conscious effort to deceive (all of which would have been unnecessary if Bush and his people were being honest and straightforward with the American people) on the part of Bush, Cheney, and Rice to use words that never directly stated their position, but got across the very same identical message linking Hussein to 9/11 that they wanted to convey.

Is there any evidence, other than by inference, of what I am saying here? Yes. On March 20, 2006, after a speech in Cleveland, Ohio, a questioner in the audience asked Bush how he could maintain his credibility with the American public when, among other assertions he made before the war that turned out to be false, he had claimed "that Iraq was sponsoring the terrorists who had attacked us on 9/11"?

Bush was quick to say that he had never made a "direct" connection between Hussein and 9/11, then added, as he blatantly reframed the question to make it far more narrow: "I was *very careful* never to say that Saddam Hussein *ordered* the attack on America." So this was all a matter of careful calculation on the part of Bush and his people.

Remarkably, *even after* Bush admitted, but only in response to the reporter's question on September 17, 2003, that he had "no evidence" that Saddam Hussein was involved with 9/11, he audaciously *continued*, in the months and years that followed, to clearly suggest, without stating it outright, that Hussein was involved in 9/11. Not that we needed it, but *Bush's admission that there was no evidence connecting Hussein with 9/11 proves beyond all doubt that every time he suggested thereafter that Hussein was involved, he was deliberately lying to the American people to gain their support for continuing the war.*

If Bush is intelligent, he hides it very well. However, he is bright enough to think that giving a message by innuendo instead of flatly declaring it might afford him more protection for his lie. After the 9/11 Commission found that there was no connection between Hussein and 9/11, Bush told the media on June 17, 2004: "This administration *never said* that the 9/11 attacks were orchestrated between Saddam and Al Qaeda." Mr. Bush, I'd like to see how far you would get with this position if you were being prosecuted for murder before a jury by a competent prosecutor.

These are just a few examples among many of Bush unequivocally suggesting that Hussein was involved in 9/11 when he knew this to be untrue. Consider, for instance, what he said when he was declaring victory over Iraq in his "Mission Accomplished" speech aboard the aircraft carrier USS *Abraham Lincoln* on May 1, 2003. Dressed in a green flight suit and, like a war pilot, holding his helmet under his left arm, Bush emerged strutting from a Viking military jet. He was surrounded by adulating servicemen and women who cheered lustily for him during his speech on the deck of the aircraft carrier. (When you're a draft dodger like Bush was in the Vietnam War, how do you muster the guts to be a part of the heroic imagery that Karl Rove put together for Bush that day?) Addressing the 9/11 attacks on American soil, Bush said, "*With those attacks*, the terrorists and their supporters declared war on the United States. And war is what they got." In other words, Hussein helped Al Qaeda take down the Twin Towers so we went after Hussein and Iraq.

The following year, in Bush's January 20, 2004, State of the Union address he said, "After the chaos and carnage of September the 11th, it is not enough to serve our enemies with legal papers. The terrorists and their supporters declared war on the United States, and war is what they got." In an Independence Day speech in West Virginia on July 4, 2005, Bush said, "The war we are fighting [in Iraq and Afghanistan] came to our shores on September the 11, 2001. After that day, I made a pledge to the American people . . . We will bring our enemies to justice." On February 24, 2006, in talking to the American Legion in Washington, D.C., about the war in Iraq and Afghanistan, Bush expressly said, "*We're taking the fight to those that attacked us.*" There is only one way to interpret this: Iraq was involved in 9/11. What other interpretation can you possibly put on these words?

Anyone with an ounce of brains would know that Hussein would never have attacked or participated in any attack on the United States. Despite Bush and Cheney lying through their teeth when they led the American people to believe this,* something happened in December of 2003 and June of 2004 that conclusively proves, all by itself, that the Bush administration never believed for a moment that Hussein was involved in 9/11 and it was all a lie when they strongly implied that he was. As you recall, on December 13, 2003, Hussein was captured by American soldiers in Iraq. Two days later, Bush all but said that it would be the Iraqi people, not America, who would mete out justice to Hussein. And on June 15, 2004, the Bush administration formally

---

*An example, for instance, of Cheney lying just as terribly as Bush: In an appearance on *Meet the Press* on September 14, 2003, which was long before Al Qaeda jihadists started going to Iraq to fight the "American infidels," Cheney said, "If we're successful in Iraq, then we will have struck a major blow right at the heart of the . . . geographical base of the terrorists who had us under assault now for many years, *but most especially on 9/11.*"

THE
PROSECUTION
OF
GEORGE W. BUSH
FOR MURDER

A Photographic Brief

USAF /Landov

AP Photo/Murad Sezer

Nina Berman/Redux

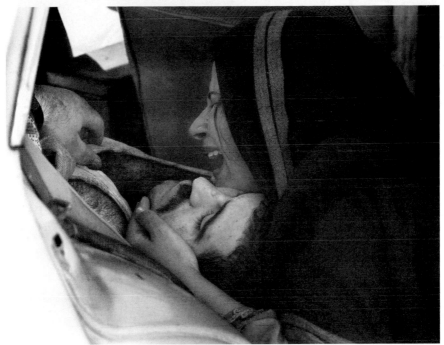

Ruth Fremson/*The New York Times*/Redux

AP Photo/Khalid Mohammed

A NOTE FROM VINCENT BUGLIOSI

In looking at the photos in this section, which are intended to bring life to the bare words in Chapter 3, the "Prologue to the Prosecution of George W. Bush for Murder," let me share with you some thoughts beyond the obvious you may or may not have had.

One is that the photographs in the section do not even remotely begin to do justice to what cannot be shown or captured under any circumstance—the unspeakable horror of what has happened in Iraq. Indeed, even if there were 10,000 photos, they would fall far short in this regard. They do not and cannot convey the fact that each victim was once a vibrant human being with hopes and dreams. And because of one man, the man in the title of this book, they are no more.

Likewise, the photos of the survivors catch but a fleeting moment in a lifetime of nightmares they will have over the horrible, violent deaths of their loved ones. So while it is true that a picture is worth a thousand words, I am suffused with the sense of stark inadequacy in looking at these photos, which provide but a mere glimpse of the torment, devastation, and anguish caused by this president and *his* war in Iraq.

As for the photos of Bush himself, the prologue proves beyond all *reasonable* doubt that throughout the sea of blood and the screams and cries of men, women, and children, even babies, coming out of the hell on earth he created in Iraq, unbelievably, he laughed and joked, had fun, and enjoyed every day of his presidency. I mean, he told us this. I'm going to have "a perfect day," he said. Laura and I had "a fabulous year" and we're "having the time of our life." Bush, in addition to his transcendent criminality, has added a snapshot view of extreme grossness and vulgarian audacity to this otherwise sacred selection of photos.

announced that it was turning Hussein over to the legal custody of Iraq to be prosecuted for crimes against the Iraqi people.

No one on radio or TV that I know of, not even liberal newspaper columnists who routinely savaged Bush, said to the Bush administration, either in December or June, "What? Something's wrong here. You've been leading us to believe [because people understandably took what Bush said as the equivalent of his having said this] for over two years that Hussein was involved in 9/11. Aren't you going to bring him back to America to be tried on charges of murdering 3,000 Americans?" *Turning Hussein over to the Iraqis for crimes he committed in Iraq, not bringing him to the United States for crimes he committed in the United States, was an unequivocal admission that the Bush administration knew (not just that, at the moment, they hadn't found any evidence) he had nothing to do with 9/11.* I kept waiting to hear someone say this, but not a peep, from anyone.

Actually, Bush didn't really have to say one single word suggesting that Hussein was involved in 9/11 to convince the American public that he was. Why? Because his *entire* buildup to the war in Iraq was predicated on 9/11. If there had been no 9/11 there would have been no war in Iraq, certainly not one the American people would have approved of. So when Bush kept telling the American people that Hussein was a threat to this nation's security, and in the very same speech juxtaposed his words with constant references to 9/11, it couldn't have been more normal and understandable for the American people to infer from the subliminal message that Hussein must have been involved in 9/11.

For instance, Linda Feldman, staff writer for the *Christian Science Monitor*, in writing about Bush's prime-time national press conference on March 6, 2003, said, "President Bush mentioned September 11 eight times, and referred to Saddam Hussein many more times than that, often in the same breath with September 11." Since Bush, then, in his bully pulpit, was connecting the war he was so fervently urging with 9/11 and terrorism, and since any rational person would assume that you only go to war with those terrorists who were responsible for 9/11, how many American people in the pews would be apt to parse

Bush's words and reach a different conclusion—that Bush was up to no good?

Bush had an additional and very effective way to convince the American people that Hussein was involved in 9/11, and that was simply to lie to them by alleging Hussein had a close relationship with Al Qaeda. "You can't distinguish between Al Qaeda and Saddam when you talk about the war on terror. They're equally as bad. *They work in concert*," Bush said on September 25, 2002. "We know that Iraq and the Al Qaeda terrorist network share a common enemy—the United States of America. We know that Iraq and Al Qaeda have had high-level contacts that go back a decade," and that "Iraq has trained Al Qaeda members in bomb-making and poisons and deadly gases," he said in his speech to the nation on October 7, 2002. "We know he's got ties with Al Qaeda," Bush said about Hussein on November 1, 2002. The Bush people correctly reasoned that if one believed these assertions, it would not take an Olympian leap of logic to conclude that Hussein most likely joined with Al Qaeda on 9/11. Particularly when most Americans already viewed Hussein as a villainous figure capable of nefarious deeds.

And again, to make its point of a connection between Iraq and Al Qaeda, the Bush administration's modus operandi was to either flat-out lie, or present as true, evidence that they knew was highly questionable. An example was the report that surfaced soon after 9/11 that Czech security officials had been told by an informant that Mohammed Atta, an Al Qaeda terrorist who flew one of the highjacked planes into one of the Twin Towers on September 11, met in Prague on April 9, 2001, with Ahmad Khalil Ibrahim al-Ani, an Iraqi intelligence agent stationed in Prague. The bipartisan 9/11 Commission investigated the matter and concluded that the meeting never took place. They learned that Czech officials were unable to confirm the story, and that the sole source for the story made his report to them *after* it had been reported in the Czech media that Atta had been in Prague a year earlier. What's more, they learned that the FBI had a photograph of Atta taken by a bank surveillance camera showing him inside a bank in Virginia on April 4, 2001, and his cell phone records showed his phone was used in Florida on April 6, 9 (the day he was supposed to be in Prague), 10, and 11.

The Bush administration ignored all of this evidence and continued to cite the original, unconfirmed "I saw Elvis and he is still alive" report to Czech officials to lead Americans to believe before the war that Hussein was involved with Al Qaeda in 9/11.

Another example concerns Shaykh al Libi, a top member of Al Qaeda's leadership who was captured in Pakistan in 2001. Libi told U.S. intelligence debriefers that Iraq was training members of Al Qaeda in the use of chemical and biological weapons. But the Department of Defense's DIA wrote in a February 2002 report that Libi's claims lacked details and information as to the Iraqis involved, the specific weapons used, and the location where the training took place. The DIA report went on to say it was probable that Libi was "intentionally misleading the debriefers . . . Ibn al-Shaykh has been undergoing debriefs for several weeks and may be describing scenarios that he knows will retain their interest." (The 9/11 Commission in 2004 concluded that Iraq had not been training Al Qaeda in the use of illicit weapons.)

But even though the Bush administration had been warned that Libi's story was very questionable, they went ahead and presented it as a fact to the American people. As we've seen, Bush did so in his October 7, 2002, speech in Cincinnati. And in Powell's speech to the United Nations he cited Libi's information as being "credible" evidence that Iraq was training Al Qaeda in the use of illicit weapons. Dick Cheney, Condoleezza Rice, and other members of the Bush administration continued to cite Libi's claims in speeches and appearances all over America, helping the Bush administration to convince Americans that Hussein was involved with Al Qaeda in the 9/11 attacks.

Indeed, even after the 9/11 Commission said in June of 2004 that their investigation found "no credible evidence that Iraq and Al Qaeda cooperated on attacks against the United States" and there did not appear to be any "collaborative relationship" between Iraq and Al Qaeda, Bush and Cheney continued to declare the opposite, Bush saying categorically that Iraq and Al Qaeda had "terrorist connections" and Cheney saying that "the evidence is overwhelming" of an Iraq–Al

Qaeda relationship. Bush, being as lazy and as unknowledgeable as he is, probably couldn't have even picked out where Iraq was on an unmarked map before he decided to invade the country. Yet he apparently knew more about what was going on between Iraq and Al Qaeda than the bipartisan 9/11 Commission, which based its conclusion on months of investigation and interviews with U.S. intelligence agents (including agents from the FBI and CIA) as well as on examination of the classified reports of these agencies.

Though all of official Washington already knew there was no connection between Hussein and Al Qaeda, on September 8, 2006, the Senate Select Committee on Intelligence issued its long-awaited report in which it said that it had found no evidence that Hussein had ties to Al Qaeda or that he had provided safe harbor to the terrorist Abu Musab al-Zarqawi, which again directly contradicted claims made by the Bush administration in its lead-up to the war. To the contrary, the committee concluded that "Saddam did not trust Al Qaeda or any other radical Islamist group and did not want to cooperate with them, . . . refusing all requests from Al Qaeda to provide material or operational support."

Indeed, a document written by Hussein (and in his possession at the time of his capture) directed his Baathist Party supporters not to join forces with foreign Arab fighters entering Iraq to battle U.S. troops. He believed the latter were only eager for a holy war against the West, which was totally different from the agenda of his Baathist Party to recapture power in Iraq. And Bin Laden had the same opposition to working with Hussein. According to a CIA classified report, several years before 9/11 Al Qaeda leaders had broached the possibility to Bin Laden of working with Iraq, but Bin Laden immediately rejected the proposal.

The reason why neither Hussein nor Bin Laden wanted to have anything to do with each other is that they were as incompatible as a mouse and a hungry cat. Hussein, whose governance in Iraq was secular and subjugated his people, and who worshiped vulgarian opulence, was the antithesis of Bin Laden, a religious fanatic who is violently opposed to all Mideastern autocracies (believing, he said, that they have "enslaved" their people) and lives like a Bedouin shepherd. Yet the Bush administration shamelessly tried to convince Americans that Hussein and Bin Laden were working closely together to destroy America.

Despite the Bush administration's claim of repeated contacts between Iraq and Al Qaeda, the Senate Select Committee said that U.S. intelligence had been able to confirm only one single meeting—in 1995 in Sudan between Bin Laden and an Iraqi intelligence officer—but nothing had come of it. The report also said the committee learned that at one point before the war Hussein was warned by his intelligence chief "that U.S. intelligence was attempting to fabricate connections between Iraq and Al Qaeda" to justify the invasion.

As for Zarqawi, the committee found that although he was in Baghdad for seven months in 2002, Hussein was unaware of his presence in the country, and when he later became aware of it, ordered his intelligence services to capture Zarqawi. The committee quoted a classified CIA report that concluded that Iraq "did not have a relationship, harbor, or turn a blind eye toward Zarqawi and his associates." (In Colin Powell's speech to the United Nations on February 5, 2003, he mentioned Zarqawi no fewer than twenty times, and said Iraq "today harbors a deadly terrorist network" headed by Zarqawi.)

Did this Senate report, which came out on September 8, 2006, stop the lies of the Bush administration? Not in the least. Condoleezza Rice, *just two days later*, said on Fox News that "there were ties between Iraq and Al Qaeda" before the war. One almost gets the impression that the mantra adopted by Bush and his inner circle was "Never admit anything, ever." You know, like the guy who is caught by his wife in *flagrante delicto* with another woman, and says to her, quoting the late comedian Richard Pryor: "Who are you going to believe, me or your lying eyes?"

If Bush and Cheney have any evidence of an Iraqi–Al Qaeda connection that hasn't already been thoroughly discredited, what is it? Are they too busy (Bush, too busy?) to provide the evidence? How dare they continue to lie to the American public when they have no support for their position from either the 9/11 Commission, the U.S. Senate Intelligence Committee, or even their own FBI and CIA? Yet because of their persistent lies to the nation, as late as July of 2006, a national Harris poll found that an astonishing 64 percent of Americans believed that Hussein had had a strong connection with Al Qaeda prior to 9/11.

I'll say this about Bush and Cheney. Although they are both unusually small men in every sense of the word other than physical size, they have the gonads of 10,000 elephants. They are also, in my estimation, criminals who should be prosecuted for murder. *New York Times* columnist Bob Herbert says that what Bush and his people have done is "one of the great deceptions in the history of American government." I'd modify that to say it *is* the greatest, not one of the greatest. I mean, what even comes remotely close?

It couldn't be any clearer that although Bush may have believed (like nearly all Americans did) that Hussein had at least some WMD, he knew that Hussein did not constitute an imminent threat to the security of this country, and not being able to make his case for the war with the truth, he and his people decided to manipulate the facts and tell one lie and distortion after another to the American people to get their support for the war.

How successful were Bush and his band of criminals in convincing Americans that America should invade Iraq? Despite the fact that we know Hussein had no weapons of mass destruction, and no connection with 9/11 or Al Qaeda, a national Gallup poll on March 14–15, 2003, just days before Bush invaded Iraq on March 19, showed that an incredible 78 percent of Americans were in favor of the invasion. Bush's lies were so successful that the majority of Americans (54 percent) were in favor of invading Iraq as soon as militarily possible even if the United Nations Security Council specifically rejected a resolution (still being sought at the time by the Bush administration, and never given) authorizing the invasion. That's how effective Bush had been in scaring the living daylights out of the American people with his lies that Hussein was about to attack us, or help someone else attack us, with deadly force.

When we're talking about national security and matters of war and peace, American citizens have every right to expect and demand from their president the very highest standard of truthfulness. Instead, Bush and his people, like the lowest of common criminals, gave the American people one fabrication and distortion after another. For Bush to argue, under these circumstances, that he acted in self-defense would be an extremely weak and specious argument that no intelligent jury would ever buy. But as weak as the self-defense argument is here, unfortunately for him it would be the only substantive argument he could even make to the charges against him. What other legal defense would be available to him? Not guilty by reason of insanity? Or since Bush has suggested that he believes he is following God's will, the God defense?

If there is any reader who still has a small question in his or her mind whether Bush acted in self-defense, what I am about to tell you should dispel this small doubt of yours. On January 31, 2003, less than two months before Bush ordered the invasion of Iraq, he had a two-hour meeting in the Oval Office with British prime minister Tony Blair and six of Bush's and Blair's top aides. Bush's aides who attended the meeting were National Security Adviser Condoleezza Rice, Dan Fried, a senior aide to Ms. Rice, and Andrew Card Jr., the White House chief of staff. Blair's aides were Jonathan Powell, his chief of staff, Matthew Rycroft, a foreign policy aide, and David Manning, Blair's chief foreign policy adviser.

In a five-page memo stamped "extremely sensitive" dated January 31, 2003, that summarized the discussion at the meeting (a summary the Bush administration has never challenged), Manning wrote that Bush and Blair expressed their doubts that any chemical, biological, or nuclear weapons would ever be found in Iraq, and that there was tension between Bush and Blair over finding some justification for the war that would be acceptable to other nations. Bush was so worried about the failure of the UN inspectors to find hard evidence against Hussein that, unbelievably, he talked about three possible ways, Manning wrote, to "*provoke* a confrontation" with Hussein, one of which, Bush said, was to fly "U2 reconnaissance aircraft with fighter cover over Iraq, [falsely] painted in U.N. colours. If Saddam fired on them, he would be in breach" of UN resolutions and that would justify war.

Can you imagine that? Can you *imagine* that? Bush is telling the American people that this nation is in imminent danger of a deadly attack from Hussein so we have to strike first; that we are being forced into war. But behind closed doors, this morally small and characterless man was talking about how to *provoke* Hussein *into* a war. The very essence of self-defense is that someone is about to kill you and you strike first only to save your life. The last person in the world whom someone acting in self-defense would try to provoke is the person he's in deathly fear of, someone who is about to kill him. If Bush actually felt America was in imminent danger of great harm from Hussein or those he was associated with, the thought of provoking Hussein into doing something that would justify going to war against him would *never* have entered Bush's mind.

Bush's argument of self-defense would easily fail in any murder prosecution against him. Indeed, Lord Goldsmith, the British attorney general, said at the famous July 23, 2002 (before the war), meeting of British prime minister Tony Blair's war cabinet (which was reported on in the aforementioned Downing Street memo) that with respect to a war in Iraq, "self-defense was not a legal basis for military action." So going in, Bush and Blair were aware that the war had nothing at all to do with the "preemptive strike" (self-defense) they were selling to the people of their respective countries, the majority of Americans buying the absurd notion, the majority of British citizens rejecting the obvious fraud out of hand.

Bush could only come to the conclusion that Iraq was an imminent threat to the security of this country if his lead intelligence agency, the CIA, told him so. But we know that not only didn't any CIA document say this, the CIA's 2002 NIE report said the exact opposite. In fact, CIA director George Tenet himself said that *at no time* before the war did the CIA say that Iraq was an imminent threat to this nation. We "*never* said," Tenet asserted on February 5, 2004, that "there was an imminent threat" from Iraq. Moreover, the notion is so preposterous on its face that, get this, Bush and his people *never even bothered to talk about it.* Tenet, in his memoir *At the Center of the Storm*, acknowledged that "there was never a serious debate that I know of within the [Bush] administration about the imminence of the Iraqi threat." But if the whole purpose of the war was to preempt Hussein, beat him to the punch, wouldn't Bush and Cheney automatically talk with their people about the fear that Hussein might strike America within the near future? Since that is all they talked about to the American people to scare them into supporting the war, why didn't they talk about it amongst themselves? Because they knew there was no threat. It was all b—s—, moonshine, a lie.

Let's never lose sight of the fact that in the circumstances existing from 9/11 up to Bush's invasion of Iraq on March 19, 2003, President Clinton—or Al Gore and John Kerry if they had become president— would never have invaded Iraq. Civilized people don't do uncivilized things.

For example, we know Bush's father would never have invaded Iraq. When, after the Persian Gulf War in 1991, he had a much better opportunity to invade Iraq than Bush had in 2003, he said no. And on March 14, 2003, just five days before Bush invaded Iraq, former president Clinton said, "I'm for regime change too, but . . . we don't invade everybody whose regime we want to change." Only these moral mongrels in the Bush administration could have done what they did, and thousands upon thousands of human beings have died horrible deaths because of it.

What George Bush and his accomplices did is so monumentally base, so extraordinarily wrong, dishonorable, and criminal, that I'm not gifted enough as a writer to describe it. In view of the ghastly, incalculable consequences of their act and the greatness of their sin, it would take a Tolstoy, a Shakespeare, a Hemingway to give people an illuminating glimpse into the darkness of their souls.

But I suspect that a great writer would be trying to give verbal flesh to the fact that Bush and his group had absolutely no regard, no respect for the millions of Americans they knowingly deceived into war. That Bush had no appreciation for, nor sense of responsibility to, the exalted and towering office he occupied, no concern at all about a betrayal of trust unparalleled in the recorded annals of American history.

As indicated, Bush's expected main defense to the murder charge would be that he acted in self-defense. Bush would have to use this argument at his trial since this defense (the Bush doctrine of preemption) was the main argument he used to convince Americans to support his war. "We must do everything we can to disarm this man before he hurts one single American," Bush said at a campaign rally on October 5, 2002. Indeed, in his report to Congress on the first day of the war, March 19, 2003, Bush said the United States was invading Iraq "in the exercise of its inherent right of self-defense." How could he then, at his trial, take the position that he was not speaking the truth when he told the American people and Congress he was acting in self-defense? That the truth was that he was not acting in self-defense? Such a position at his trial would be tantamount to a confession of guilt.

Would that mean that Bush would have the legal burden of proving he acted in self-defense? No. The burden of proof in a criminal trial always remains with the prosecution, and therefore, Bush's prosecutor would have the burden of proving that Bush did *not* act in self-defense. But the prosecution's burden of proof would only be to prove this beyond a *reasonable* doubt, not beyond *all* doubt. I am very confident that a competent prosecutor could do this in a prosecution of Bush for murder, any rational jury concluding that Iraq was a war of choice, not self-defense.

Although self-defense would be the heart of Bush's defense, I can just about guarantee you that among his secondary defenses would be what is called in the criminal law the "character defense," not a defense that normally carries much weight at a criminal trial. Bush, Cheney, Rice, et al. would call "character witnesses" to the stand to testify to their good character. The witnesses would say they knew the defendants well and the defendants did not have the traits of character inherent in the murder charge brought against them, i.e., that of being partial to violence (taking us to war), which the prosecutor, I assume, would not allege, and that of being deceptive and dishonest (taking us to war on a lie). I imagine the prosecutor could and would call a number of witnesses to challenge the defense's character witnesses on this latter point.

The essence of the character defense, then, would be that the defendants Bush, Cheney, and Rice simply did not possess the defect and absence of character that would have allowed them to do what the prosecutor alleged they did. Concomitantly, the defense lawyers would undoubtedly also argue, "We're talking about the president of the United States here, the highest constitutional and elected officer in this great land of ours, as well as the vice president of the United States, and the president's national security adviser. On its face, it makes no sense that people of this enormous stature in our society would have done the horrendous things that Mr. [prosecutor's last name] is claiming they did." And if I were the prosecutor in a situation like this, I would say, "Fine. *Now let's look at the evidence.* And when we look at the evidence, not just some or most of it, but all of it points irresistibly to the conclusion that these three defendants did, indeed, deliberately take this nation into a terrible, terrible war under false pretenses."

THE MATTER OF JURISDICTION AND
BUSH AT TRIAL

On the issue of jurisdiction to prosecute Bush, the best venue would be the District of Columbia in Washington, D.C., with the prosecutor being the attorney general of the United States through his Department of Justice. The statutory authority for prosecuting Bush for conspiracy to commit murder and for first (or second) degree murder would be 18 U.S.C. §§'s1117 (Conspiracy) and 1111 (Murder).

I can just about tell you what Bush's advisers will tell him if the position I am taking in this book reaches him, if in no other way than by a reporter asking if he has any thoughts about what my book is urging. They will tell him what they *have* to tell him: that there is no legal merit to my position at all. (Indeed, this is probably what partisan conservative lawyers will tell the media.) And that he should not give it another thought. But I can also almost assure you that in the moments when Bush is alone and not surrounded by his coterie of assistants, he *will* give it another thought. "This guy who is saying this," he'll think. "He's not some nut off the street. I think he's a fairly well-known former prosecutor. What *if* there is something to what he is saying? If there is, I couldn't expect my people to tell me there was." It will be a disquieting thought, and Bush, though not a knowledgeable person, probably knows about the statute of limitations for crimes, and somewhere down the line he'll ask about the statute of limitations on the case I am proposing, and he'll be told there is no statute of limitations for murder.

What I am saying is that if Bush is guilty of what I believe him to be guilty of, he will never have a future free of the thought entering his mind that some federal prosecutor in the future might decide to prosecute him for murder. For instance, in Chile, murder and kidnapping charges were brought against eighty-nine-year-old former Chilean dictator Augusto Pinochet in December of 2004. The crimes the formerly untouchable general was accused of being responsible for went as far back as 1973, thirty-one years earlier. "Finally, justice," the survivors of the victims exclaimed. Pinochet has since died, ending the prosecution process against him.

Although a federal prosecution (by the U.S. attorney general in Washington, D.C., or any of the ninety-three U.S. attorneys in the ninety-three federal districts throughout the land) against Bush would be the easiest procedure, I also believe that any state attorney general in the fifty states (or any district attorney—called the state's attorney in cities like Chicago and Miami—in any county of any state) could bring a murder charge against Bush for any soldiers from that state or county who lost their lives fighting Bush's war. Although the jurisdiction would not be quite as natural, I believe it definitely would exist. Yes, Bush sent his soldiers to war while he was residing at the White House, and he conspired to commit his grand crime there with Cheney, et al. But a *necessary element* of the corpus delicti of the federal crime of conspiracy is that at least one overt act be committed by one or more members of the conspiracy to further the object of the conspiracy. It is well accepted in the criminal law that any act at all qualifies as an overt act. For example, if A and B conspire to rob a bank, buying gasoline for the getaway car is enough. If any overt act, then, was committed by Bush, et al. in any of the fifty states, *part of Bush's conspiracy to commit murder is deemed to have taken place in that state*, and hence, the subject state would have jurisdiction to prosecute Bush for conspiracy to commit murder, as well as for all murders that resulted from that conspiracy.

Here, the main overt act by Bush (as well as his coconspirators) that would convey jurisdiction to the states would be all the lies and misrepresentations that have been discussed on these pages which he used to take this nation to war. Although most of the lies (overt acts) were made by Bush in Washington, D.C., because of the media, these lies (overt acts) were often contemporaneously carried into the homes of Americans throughout the fifty states. So, for example, it was Bush's face and voice on television, or his voice over radio, that a resident of Fargo, North Dakota, heard in his home in Fargo. And if what Bush said in Washington, D.C., was the basis for a federal prosecution in the nation's capital, obviously it would likewise be a basis for a state prosecution in North Dakota.

Another overt act by Bush in the fifty states that would give each of them jurisdiction to prosecute him for conspiring to commit murder would be the recruiting of the soldiers in the fifty states by military personnel under his ultimate direction. (The May 1, 2007, map in the front matter of this book is a visual reminder of the loss of life in the Iraq war by soldiers from all fifty states. Today, over one year later, hundreds of other U.S. soldiers have died in the war.) To repeat, the attorney general in each of these fifty states would have jurisdiction to prosecute Bush for conspiracy to commit murder and murder.

It has to be pointed out that even if we were to assume that Bush, for whatever legal reason, could not be prosecuted and convicted in the states for the murders of any of the American soldiers under the law of conspiracy, he nevertheless *could* be prosecuted and convicted of the separate crime of conspiracy to commit murder since, as we've seen, an integral part of Bush's conspiracy to commit murder was the overt acts committed in the subject states. And unfortunately for Bush, the punishment would be identical in most states to what it would have been if he had been convicted of the murders themselves. For example, in California, if one is convicted of two or more murders, under Sections 190 and 190.2 (3) of the California Penal Code the punishment that the jury can impose is either life imprisonment without the possibility of parole or the death penalty. And §182 of the code provides that when two or more people *conspire* to commit any felony [here, the felony of murder], "they shall be punishable in the same manner and to the same extent as is provided for the punishment of that felony." Only if there were a federal prosecution of Bush *and* the court ruled he could only be prosecuted for conspiracy to commit murder, not murder itself, would he not receive the same punishment. Although under §1111 of the U.S. Code the punishment for murder is life imprisonment or the death penalty, under §1117, the punishment for conspiracy to commit murder carries a maximum sentence of life imprisonment.

So Bush will have to live, for the rest of his life, while he is enjoying the good life at his ranch in Crawford, with the thought that an aide might tell him that some state attorney general in, say, Illinois, has indicted him for the murder of, for instance, 157 American soldiers from Illinois who died in Bush's war, or that some attorney general in Louisiana has indicted him for the murder of, let's say, 22 soldiers from that state who died fighting Bush's war. If thousands of American people will have nightmares for the rest of their lives over the horrible deaths suffered by their young son (or father, husband, etc.), as I indicated earlier, the least I can do in return is to put the thought in Bush's mind for the rest of his life that he may someday be held accountable in a criminal courtroom for all the murders he alone is responsible for.

I say he alone is responsible for all the murders. By that I mean only he had the authority to order the invasion, and he alone had the power to stop the commission of this grand crime. But if he is guilty, there can be no question that he conspired with others to commit this monstrous crime. And the existence of the conspiracy "can be inferred if the evidence reveals that the alleged participants shared 'a common aim or purpose' and 'mutual dependence and assistance existed.'" It is obvious that such a common aim or purpose with mutual dependence and assistance existed between and among Bush and his top aides in taking the nation to war.

Who in Bush's inner circle should be prosecuted for murder with him? Two who definitely should be are Cheney and Rice, coconspirators and aiders and abettors in the murders. I don't know enough about Rumsfeld's culpability, but with the prosecutor's office subpoenaing documents and getting statements and grand jury testimony from key people, that should not be hard to determine. The same holds true for Rove. But since we know he is a person without political morals and was, by Bush's own words, his "architect," the likelihood is that he is deeply implicated in the intentional deception of the American people. This could be confirmed, if it be the case, by an indepth investigation. James C. Moore, the author of *Bush's Brain: How Karl Rove Made George W. Bush Presidential*, opined that Rove was "probably the most powerful unelected person in American history," and said that Rove "sat in on all the big meetings leading up to the Iraq war and signed off on all major decisions."

And we know that Rove was a member of the White House Iraq Group, a group of White House officials including, among others, National Security Adviser Condoleezza Rice, Cheney's chief of staff Scooter Libby, and chief presidential speech writer Michael Gerson. The group's mission was to come up with the best way to sell Congress and the American people on the war. We know that virtually all that came out of that group, formed in the summer of 2002, was lies, half-truths, and distortions.

I don't know about Powell, but my sense is that he is innocent, his only sin being weakness.

Although it is my firm belief that the jury would convict Bush, Cheney, and Rice of first degree murder,* it could turn out during the pretrial phase that the prosecutor makes a determination that, although he believes he can convince the jury of Bush's, Cheney's, and Rice's guilt, he is not sure he can convince them of it *beyond a reasonable doubt*, the requirement for a conviction. If so, and if he is seeking the death penalty in one of the thirty-eight states that provide for such penalty, he could be expected to offer life imprisonment to Cheney and Rice (and Rove if the evidence warrants his prosecution) to testify against Bush.

Not only would someone in their shoes be likely to accept this plea bargain under any circumstances, but it should be particularly easy with these people. Rice, completely complicit with Bush in helping him take this nation to war on a lie, has already sold her soul to George Bush and his administration, so I can't conceive that someone of her character would have the loyalty to risk death for Bush. And

---

*In all states, it would then be up to the jury to decide what the appropriate punishment should be for the convicted defendants. Depending on the state, the punishment would range from life imprisonment with the possibility of parole, to life without the possibility of parole and the death penalty.

Cheney is a sniveling coward who did everything possible to keep out of harm's way in the Vietnam War, so certainly he's not going to risk death for Bush. Rove would probably drop to his knees and start crying like a baby, begging for mercy. What I'm saying is that even people of character aren't usually loyal to each other when their own life is on the line. But these moral weaklings will all probably sing like canaries against each other, since they all appear to be almost amoral individuals who are devoid of any character. If they were willing to lie to the American public about a matter of war and peace that resulted in the deaths of over 100,000 people, certainly they'd be willing to tell the truth to save their worthless hides from the gas chamber or electric chair. Indeed, I suspect that the prosecutor's biggest problem won't be to get them to talk to save their lives, but to make sure they don't embroider the truth and start telling lies in an effort to get a better deal from the prosecutor.

Though Bush himself could be expected to sing any aria the prosecutor would ask him to sing against the others, unfortunately for the small man from Crawford, the prosecutor wouldn't be interested in his songs, only those of the other three. You don't give a plea bargain to the stickup man (Bush) in a bank robbery to testify against the driver of the getaway car (Cheney, Rice, Rove). It's the other way around.

Like rodents scurrying away from a sinking ship, I would be very confident that Cheney, Rice, and Rove would make the case against Bush, already very strong, air-tight. They probably could tell us things about Bush that would make our hair curl.

In view of what I've presented on these pages, and with a national poll already showing that the majority of Americans believe that Bush "intentionally misled" the nation into war, I can see no reason, legal or otherwise, why some state or federal prosecutor now or in the future should not bring murder charges against Bush. If justice means anything in America, and if we're not going to forget the thousands of young American soldiers in their graves whom Bush deceived into thinking they were fighting for America against an enemy that had attacked us, and if we want to deter any future president as monstrous as Bush from doing the same horrendous thing, I say we have no choice but to bring murder charges against the son of privilege from Crawford, Texas.

My guess is that Bush, at his trial, would no more want to take the witness stand and be cross-examined than he would want to stare into the noonday sun. But unfortunately for him, if he elected not to take the stand and defend himself against the murder charges against him, despite any instructions given to the jury by the judge, he'd look as guilty as sin to the jury. No sound in any courtroom is as loud as a defendant's silence when he has been accused by the prosecutor and witnesses of murder (or any serious crime), and he doesn't bother to walk those few steps to the witness stand to deny his guilt. The members of the jury know that if they were being charged with murder and they were innocent, it would take a team of wild horses to keep them from shouting their innocence from the highest rooftops.

If Bush did take the witness stand, the cross-examination of him should consume hundreds of transcript pages. One among many areas of inquiry would certainly be Bush's statement to the nation from Cincinnati on the evening of October 7, 2002, that Hussein and Iraq constituted an imminent threat to the security of this country. We know that on this very same day in a letter to the Senate Intelligence Committee by CIA director George Tenet (signed for him by the CIA's John McLaughlin, the number two man at the CIA), the CIA said Hussein was not an imminent threat. Bush should obviously be asked if he was aware of this letter. If he said no, he could be asked if the CIA, in its daily morning briefings of him up to that point, had given him this same position of theirs. If he said yes, then he could be asked why he told the nation on October 7 the exact opposite of what he had been told by the CIA. If he said no, he'd look like an even bigger liar, because he'd be telling the jury that even though he was the CIA's boss, the CIA was telling the Senate Intelligence Committee (which isn't even in Bush's executive branch of government) something extremely important on a matter of war and peace they weren't telling him. No one would believe this.

If he nonetheless stuck to that transparently false line, Tenet and McLaughlin could be called to the stand. Unless they both wanted to commit perjury for the former president who was no longer their boss, they would tell the truth; that they had been advising Bush that Hussein was not an imminent threat to the security of this country. If they denied doing this, and testified they had been telling him that Hussein *was* an imminent threat, then they would be admitting that they lied to Congress in their October 7, 2002, letter, a felony under 18 USC §371.

If Bush decided to lie all the way through and deny that the CIA had informed him that Hussein was not an imminent threat, he could be asked, "Then upon what U.S. intelligence agency were you relying in your speech to the nation on October 7, 2002, when you suggested to everyone that Hussein *was* an imminent threat?" He, of course, couldn't come up with any such agency (or member thereof) that had said or suggested this. Nor could he come up with any document that said or suggested this. (We know this because if there were such a document, the Bush administration would have made sure that all of us had seen it by now). And this would make him look terrible on the witness stand. "In other words, Mr. Bush, you made this whole thing up yourself about Hussein being an imminent threat?" "No, I didn't make it up. I believed it." "So even though no U.S. intelligence agency told you this, and even though no document said this, you still formed the opinion it was true?" "Correct." "Did you tell the American people on the evening of October 7, 2002, that it was merely *your* opinion that Hussein constituted an imminent threat to the security of this country, and no U.S. intelligence agency agreed with you?" Since Bush didn't tell the nation's people this he would have no choice but to answer, "No." "Why not, sir?" Whatever answer he gave he could be asked, "Since it was going to be the blood of their sons that was going to be shed in far-off Iraq, not your blood or the blood of your children, don't you feel the people of this country, in deciding whether to give their support to you for this war, were entitled to know this?" And so on.

In the additional way of establishing, on cross-examination, that Bush not only lied to the nation on October 7, 2002 (as well as the many times thereafter that he told the nation Hussein was an imminent threat to the security of this country), but that he had no sense at all that he was acting in self-defense when he invaded Iraq, he could be asked, "Mr. Bush, you have said, and I quote you, that in deciding whether or not to go to war in Iraq, 'I'll be making up my mind based upon the latest intelligence.' Was that a true statement?" Bush would have no choice but to say, "Yes." "Just for purposes of clarification, when you said 'intelligence' you were referring to U.S. Intelligence agencies, like the CIA, whose job it was to furnish you with the best and latest intelligence they had gathered on the issue of whether Hussein was a threat to the security of this country, is that correct?" "Yes, of course." "Now, you have a reputation for not liking to read long reports, including intelligence reports. Is that a reputation you feel you have earned?" Bush could be expected to say words to the effect, "Well, it's partially true. The job of president is a busy one, you know, and I like to get to the heart of a problem as quickly as I can." "So as I've read, you prefer to read summaries of these long reports, is that true?" "Yes, but if the report is important enough, I'll read the whole report." "Would you agree that the war in Iraq, for good or for bad, has defined your presidency more than any other single issue?" (Bush would have to say yes to this, unless he wanted to sound foolish and say his position on stem cell research or global warming or immigration was more important.) "With this in mind, would you agree that the National Intelligence Estimate report of 2002 that was delivered to your office on October 1, 2002, just ten days before Congress voted on the resolution authorizing you to go to war in Iraq, and that set forth the consensus of all sixteen U.S. intelligence agencies on the issues of Iraq's weapons of mass destruction and whether Iraq was an imminent threat to the security of this country, *would* be important enough for you to read?" Bush would be compelled to say yes. How could he say no? "Did you, in fact, read this ninety-one-page report?" If he said yes, as you will soon see, he would be committing legal suicide. My guess is that Bush, trying to walk between raindrops throughout the cross-examination, would smell a rat and say no. "But I take it you at least read the five-page summary of this report?" If he said no, he'd sound like a terrible liar to the jury, or like the most irresponsible American president in history.

There is no way to know for sure the precise direction the cross-examination on this point would go. However, just as not even Houdini could pull a rabbit out of a hat when there was no rabbit in the hat, a witness cannot go somewhere when he has nowhere to go. And in this case, I can conceive of no answers by Bush that would extricate him from the most incriminating of inferences by the jury. And whatever his answers were, at some point (either to reemphasize or in the first instance) the prosecutor would approach Bush and say, "Mr. Bush, I show you People's exhibit number ——, the ninety-one-page report sent to your office on October 1, 2002, which represents the conclusions of sixteen U.S. Intelligence agencies on Iraq's alleged weapons of mass destruction, and the danger, if any, that Hussein posed to America. Pages 5 through 9 contain the summary of the report, called 'Key Judgments.' Turning to page 8, I want to read to you the most important of the Key Judgments. (The prosecutor reads the report's judgment that Hussein would only attack the United States if he feared we were about to attack his country first, i.e., that he was only a danger to us in self-defense.) Mr. Bush, would you tell this jury if you read these same words when the report was sent to you, or had someone else read them to you or summarize their essence for you?" If Bush said no to all these questions he could be asked: "So even though you were the president of the United States, you never bothered to read even a summary of this extremely important report, were not informed of it by your national security adviser Condoleezza Rice* or anyone else, and had absolutely no idea that the six-

---

*At this point, people like Rice might be testifying for the prosecution as part of a plea bargain, and if so, she could be expected to testify (if Bush maintained that he personally did not read the summary) that she informed Bush fully of the highlights of the report. As indicated earlier, Rice has said, "I read the National Intelligence Estimate cover to cover a couple of times."

teen U.S. intelligence agencies under your command all agreed that Iraq did not pose an imminent threat to this country, is that correct, sir?" If Bush answered yes, no one would believe him.

If he said that he did read the key judgment on page 8, the next question would be, "Mr. Bush, the report clearly and explicitly says that Hussein would not attempt an attack upon the United States unless he 'feared an attack' by us on his country that 'threatened the survival' of his regime and he thought the attack by us was 'imminent.' I ask you, sir. Being in possession of this information from sixteen U.S. intelligence agencies, the very people you admit you relied upon in making your decision on whether to go to war, how could you possibly tell the American people just six days later in Cincinnati the exact opposite—that unless we stopped Hussein first, he constituted a great and urgent danger to our nation? How could you *do* this, sir? Please tell the jury."

In a similar vein on the issue of Hussein being an alleged imminent threat to the security of this country, the prosecutor could jump ahead from Bush's Cincinnati speech in October of 2002 to the invasion in March of 2003. "Mr. Bush, at the time you ordered this nation's military forces to invade Iraq on March 19, 2003, did you believe that Saddam Hussein constituted an imminent threat to the security of this country?" If he said yes, again he could be asked what U.S. intelligence agency or member thereof or document did he rely on that said or suggested this. And he of course could not name any such agency, member thereof, or document. (The line of questioning from that point would establish that this "belief" of Bush that Hussein was an imminent threat only came from him and his coconspirators.) *If he said no to this question, this would be tantamount to his pleading guilty to the 4,000 murders, since if a defendant kills another without being in imminent fear of imminent death or great bodily harm, the legal defense of self-defense necessarily falls. And self-defense is the only real, substantive defense Bush could possibly raise to the murder charges against him.*

If Bush, as part of his "no" answer, said, "I never said Hussein was an 'imminent' threat," he could be asked if he thought the words he *did* use (e.g., Hussein constituted "a threat of unique urgency," he could act "on any given day," "Iraq could launch a biological or chemical attack in as little as forty-five minutes," etc.) were the equivalent of imminent. If he said no, his ludicrous position would make him look like a terrible liar to the jury.

Bush could also be asked, "Mr. Bush, you have always said that you didn't want to go to war, that war was a last resort, is that correct?" "Yes." "If this is so, when Hans Blix, the UN's chief weapons inspector, testified before the United Nations on March 7, 2003, that he and his inspectors were being given complete cooperation by Hussein and they were "able to perform professional no-notice inspections all over Iraq," and thus far they couldn't find any weapons of mass destruction in Iraq but requested a few more months to confirm their tentative findings, why, sir, did you proceed to refuse this request, boot Blix and his people out of Iraq, and proceed to war in less than two weeks?"

Another line of inquiry: "Mr. Bush, since, on September the 17th, 2003, you acknowledged, but only in response to a lawyer's questions, that there was 'no evidence' that Saddam Hussein was involved in the September 11, 2001, attacks, why did you thereafter continue to strongly suggest that he was?" Bush would have no choice but to say he did not, whereupon he and the jury could have their attention directed to the screen (or a chart) in the courtroom where all of such statements were set forth. "For instance, Mr. Bush, on February 24, 2006, in a speech you gave to the American Legion, you said, while talking about the war in Iraq and Afghanistan, 'We're taking the fight to those that attacked us.' If you weren't suggesting by these words that Iraq was involved in 9/11, then what were you talking about?" Whatever answer he gave, he could be asked, "But don't you agree that millions of Americans hearing these words of yours could naturally believe that you were saying that Hussein was involved in 9/11?"

Also, "Mr. Bush, you have already testified that you believed Hussein constituted an imminent threat to the security of this country, and that's why you invaded Iraq. In other words, you wanted to strike him before he attacked, or helped someone else attack America, is that correct?" "Yes." "But if you actually believed this, sir, and had this fear, why in the world did you propose, at your January 31, 2003, meeting with Prime Minister Tony Blair in the Oval Office that America and Britain should try to *provoke* Hussein *into* a war?" Bush couldn't admit doing his because if he did that would be tantamount to his admitting that he did not believe that Hussein was an imminent threat to the security of this country. But if he denied making any such proposal, Blair and his three aides who attended the meeting, including David Manning who wrote the memo quoting Bush on provoking Hussein, could be called to the witness stand. What is the likelihood that they would be willing to commit perjury and say Bush never proposed any such thing? Not only don't I believe they would, but if Manning did, he could be asked why he wrote his false memo saying that Bush did.

Also, "Mr. Bush, you're aware that as late as 2006, polls showed that 90 percent of our soldiers in Iraq mistakenly believed that Hussein and Iraq *were* involved in 9/11. Since, as you yourself have said, these young American soldiers were bravely giving up their lives in combat to fight for America and the security of their loved ones back home, don't you think it would have been the decent thing for you to do to make sure these young Americans were informed that Hussein was not involved in 9/11?" If he said no, jurors would be fighting over who got to pull the switch on him in the electric chair. If he said yes, he would then obviously be asked, "Did you, then, see to it that American soldiers in Iraq were informed that Hussein was not involved in 9/11?" Bush's answer would have to be no. "Would you tell this jury why you did not do so, sir?"

I would be more than happy, if requested, to consult with any prosecutor who decides to prosecute Bush in the preparation of additional cross-examination questions for him to face on the witness stand. I believe the cross-examination would be such that they'd have to carry the arrogant son of privilege off the stand on a stretcher.

If, in the unlikely event that some court, for whatever reason, held that a president could not be prosecuted for murder for taking his country to war on a lie, then, for the future, Congress should enact legislation making it a crime punishable by death or life imprisonment without the possibility of parole for a president to do so. There could even be a provision that if the lie could be shown to be "reasonably necessary" to protect the immediate safety of this country, then the law would not apply.

What about the inevitable argument that such a law would be bad because it would inhibit our future presidents in the performance of their duties, making them fearful to act? Horse feathers. This argument is not a sound one. (If it were, I guess we should also amend the U.S. Constitution and never impeach a president again either, since, to avoid being impeached for his misconduct, convicted, and removed from office, he would be inhibited in the performance of his daily duties as president.) Such a law would only be inhibiting to those who intended to lie to take us to war. But what American president would want to do such an extremely immoral and criminal thing? Bush is a grotesque anomaly and aberration. No president has ever done what he did and it is not likely this nation will see a president do what Bush did for centuries to come, if ever. At least we know that in the previous three centuries there was no one like this monstrous individual. And if one were to come along in the future, yes, we do want to inhibit him.

Moreover, no president acting in good faith, who acts in error, would have to worry. In the first place, it would be obvious to everyone in the know that he had acted in good faith, whereas with Bush, it is so very obvious that he did not. Therefore, there would never be a prosecution of such a well-intentioned president in the first place. But even if, perchance, there were, not only would he be likely to prove his innocence (which would not even be his legal burden but one he would be happy to assume), but how in the world would the prosecution be able to prove to a jury beyond all reasonable doubt that this president lied to take us to war when he did not?

All good Americans should want to deter any future president from doing what Bush did. To not be in favor of this is the equivalent of saying that *whatever* a president does in matters of war and peace—

even if he tells a monstrous lie to take us to war, a lie that only serves his self-interest, and even if 10 million Americans die because of it—nothing should be done to him or about it. This is not a position that any self-respecting person would want to utter in public.

I hope that at some time in the near future a courageous U.S. attorney general, U.S. attorney, state attorney general, or district attorney in America who is committed to the rule of law and who has dedicated his career to enforcing the law fairly against all who, big or small, violate it, will hear the cries for justice from the graves of the thousands upon thousands of men, women, and children who had their lives violently cut short because of the lies of a man who smiled through it all. And that, with a sense of uncompromising righteousness, he will take the ample case I have laid out in this book before an American jury to let them decide whether George W. Bush is guilty or not guilty of murder, and if so, what his punishment should be.

Even if this doesn't happen and what I have said in this book receives all the attention of a new fly in the forest, I do know that someone had to say what is written on the pages of this book.

PART THREE

5

BUSH
"COULDN'T POSSIBLY"
HAVE BEEN ANY WORSE
IN HANDLING THE
WAR ON TERRORISM

LTHOUGH THE HEART OF THIS BOOK lies in the two Prosecution of George Bush for Murder chapters, I feel I cannot possibly leave the subject of George Bush without offering an indictment of his conduct of the war on terrorism. This is an easy transition because the two subjects, after all, are closely linked. And Bush's conduct in the war on terrorism has been not only completely consistent with that which is set forth in the two prosecution chapters, but it fortifies all the conclusions I have drawn about Bush in these two chapters.

The only American who has even come close to George Bush in profiting from and exploiting 9/11 is former New York City mayor Rudy Giuliani. But Bush exceeds even Giuliani. After all, Bush made 9/11 and his response to it the "centerpiece" of his campaign for reelection in 2004, and most people seem to agree he won reelection because of 9/11 and his supposedly great response to it. (The theme made over and over by Bush and his surrogates during the campaign, one that most Americans accepted, is that Democrats are soft on terrorism and weak on national security, and therefore, it would have been dangerous for America to turn the nation over to a Democratic president.) *Indeed, after all that has gone wrong, Bush and his administration to this very day talk as if they are speaking from a position of strength when they talk about fighting the war on terrorism.*

As *Time* magazine said before the 2004 election, Bush's handling of the war against terrorism was a *"fortress* that so far has protected Bush's presidential advantage in this campaign season." *Time* pointed out that it was the belief of Americans that "Bush has done everything he could to keep the country safe, and managed the war on terrorism well." Indeed, *Time* said, *"Any* fair-minded person" would have to give Bush good grades in foreign policy, i.e., the war on terrorism. The *New York Times* said that Bush's "anti-terrorism record" was his "key strength." The *Los Angeles Times* averred on its front page before the election that although Americans were becoming more unhappy with the economy, "the President's *strongest asset* in the 2004 campaign has been the unwavering sense among most Americans that he is providing resolute leadership against terrorism." In March 2006, CNN spoke of "President Bush's strong suit," the war on terrorism. As late as July of 2006, the *Los Angeles Times* said that Bush and his party's "uncompromising stance against terrorism . . . helped the GOP to take control of the Senate in 2002 and Bush to win reelection in 2004." Knowingly not going after Osama Bin Laden at Tora Bora, thereby allowing him to escape, and instead going to war against Iraq, a nonterrorist nation that had nothing to do with 9/11, is an "uncompromising stance against terrorism"? How could a paper like the *Los Angeles Times* permit incredibly silly words like these, written by two reporters, to survive editing and appear on page 1 of their July 2, 2006, edition in their main headline story?

The reality—and I'm confident that no one has *quite* told you what I'm about to tell you—is that short of being in cahoots with Bin

Laden, Bush *could not possibly have been any worse fighting the war against terrorism, from the very beginning of his administration up until now*, almost seven years later. That is not an opinion. That is a fact. His conduct has been so extremely bad that if it had never happened and someone told a rational person it had, the latter would be compelled to say, "That can't be. I don't believe it." Giving Bush an F minus would be being generous, since his conduct has been so horrendously bad it goes beyond the grading system. So bad that virtually no sensible American in this vast country would have acted the same way. John Kerry, who lost the 2004 election for several reasons, one of which is that Bush was perceived as being much more capable to fight the war on terrorism than he, would have done much, much better than Bush in fighting this war. So would Al Gore and Bill Clinton, which isn't really saying anything. Who wouldn't have done better?

As I cite one monumental failure after another of Bush's in his "war" against terrorism, the thought should enter your mind that even without looking at them in the aggregate, nearly every one of them, all by themselves, would be enough to cause any prudent person to say, "This is terrible, inexcusable behavior. This man does not deserve to be president." Each one of these failures should lead you, if you are a rational person, to have the most extremely negative impression of Bush imaginable. But the majority of Americans, while most of these things were happening, did not. Why not? In large part it's because most people love to rest their minds, being much more fond of talking than thinking. In fact, the majority of Americans don't even read the daily newspaper, and of those who do, many only read sections like sports, cartoons, and crossword puzzles, not the news pages. Indeed, only one percent of Americans, I am told, read the editorial section of the paper.

Because of this ignorance, as well as general stupidity, instead of provoking a universal denunciation of Bush, his antiterrorism persona remained popular among the American people for several years after 9/11, and as late as August of 2006 a national poll showed the majority of Americans gave Bush a positive rating in his war on terrorism. Indeed, right up to the present, most pundits, including

Democrats who deeply dislike Bush and have attacked him on the Iraq war, still declare that the "war on terrorism" and national security are Bush's "strong suit," his "strength. " But again, it virtually could *not* have been possible for him to have been any worse.

As you read on these pages about Bush's colossal malfeasance in his war on terrorism, keep in mind that, unbelievably, in the eyes of the nation and media, 9/11, *which happened on Bush's watch,* was nevertheless viewed by virtually everyone to be a *huge plus* for George Bush. I mean, he even used footage of 9/11 in his reelection campaign! Listen to Jonathan Alter, a liberal Democrat who writes a weekly column for *Newsweek.* Alter is smart and fairly consistently writes anti-Bush articles. I cite Alter to show you that if he can write such lunacy, you know it is downhill from there. As late as February 6, 2006, Alter wrote that 9/11 was Bush's emotional "trump-card." Now, why was Alter calling 9/11 Bush's trump card? Because Alter knows, being a major political writer for *Newsweek* and at the center of things, that 9/11 is perceived by virtually everyone as Bush's trump card. If it were not, or there was some question about it, Alter would have had no reason to say this. And Alter gave no indication whatsoever that he disagreed.

Before we get into setting forth Bush's incredibly bad blunders and malfeasance bordering on criminal negligence, here is a brief history. The focus on tracking down and destroying Bin Laden and his Al Qaeda network of terrorists dates back to the CIA under President Clinton. (Very predictably, the right-wing print and radio and TV pundits—e.g., *National Review, Washington Times,* Rush Limbaugh—blamed Clinton for 9/11 and gave Bush a complete pass on his eight months in office before 9/11.) In late 1995, Clinton signed Presidential Decision Directive 39 that instructed the CIA to capture foreign terrorists "by force," even "without the cooperation of the host government." It was widely accepted that killing Bin Laden in the process of attempting to capture him was not to be discouraged. Pursuant to this directive, in January of 1996 the CIA created a unit (code-named "Alec Station") whose sole function was to capture Bin Laden. In 1998, Clinton created the office of national coordinator for counterterrorism, and Richard Clarke filled the position. Several efforts were launched by the Clinton administration to capture or *kill* Bin Laden, but most were aborted for various reasons, such as lack of confidence by the CIA in the intelligence it had, or in the ability of those the CIA intended to use to get the job done—Afghan tribal leaders and their fighters.

But it wasn't because of any hesitation on Clinton's part. In fact, Clarke said that "President Clinton authorized two U.S. cruise missile attack submarines to sit off the Pakistani coast for months on end waiting for word that we might have sighted Bin Laden."

On August 20, 1998, Clinton's CIA did launch sixty Tomahawk cruise missiles on an Afghan camp where Bin Laden was believed to be, but he apparently had left an hour or so earlier.

Throughout the period between 1996 and September 11, 2001, U.S. intelligence agencies picked up signs from many sources, including electronic, of Al Qaeda plans to commit acts of terrorism throughout the world against U.S. interests, but only on *foreign* soil. Among the acts of terrorism against the United States believed to be ordered by Bin Laden were car bombings of American embassies in Kenya and Tanzania on August 7, 1998, in which 224 people, including 12 Americans, were killed. And suicide bombers who attacked the American destroyer USS *Cole* at anchor in the Yemeni port of Aden on October 12, 2000, killing 17 American sailors, were believed to have had links to Al Qaeda.

So Bin Laden and Al Qaeda were on America's national security radar screen. But the summer of 2001 preceding September 11, 2001, *with George Bush as president*, was different than ever before in terms of the number of Al Qaeda threats to commit terrorist acts against the United States or its interests. Indeed, the stepped-up activity was so pronounced that the National Commission on Terrorist Attacks Upon the United States (hereinafter the 9/11 Commission), in its 2004 report, captioned its chapter on this period "The System Was Blinking Red." Threat reports from U.S. intelligence agencies "surged in June and July," reaching an unprecedented "peak of urgency," the commission report said. A terrorist threat advisory from the State Department in late June indicated a high probability of "spectacular" terrorist attacks in the near future, one as soon as two weeks hence. On June 25, Bush's counterterrorism expert, Richard Clarke, warned National Security Adviser Condoleezza Rice that there were six separate U.S. intelligence reports showing that Al Qaeda was preparing for a pending attack.

The 9/11 Commission report said that "the intelligence reporting consistently described the upcoming attacks as occurring on a *calamitous* level, indicating that they would cause the world to be in turmoil." On June 28, Clarke wrote Rice that Al Qaeda activity suggesting an imminent attack "had reached a crescendo . . . A series of new reports continue to convince me and [intelligence] analysts at [the Department of] State, CIA, D.I.A. [Defense Intelligence Agency] and NSA [National Security Agency] that a *major* terrorist attack or series of attacks is likely in July." One Al Qaeda intelligence report, he said, warned that something "very, very, very, very" big was about to happen. A CIA report on June 30 was captioned "Bin Laden Planning High-Profile Attacks," and said they were expected in the near term and to have "dramatic consequences of catastrophic proportions." The CIA director, George Tenet, although a Bush friend and apologist, nevertheless acknowledged to the 9/11 Commission that "the system was blinking red" and could not "get any worse." Also, throughout this whole period, Tenet met daily with Bush in the morning at the Oval Office whenever Bush was in Washington. According to the commission's 9/11 report, the PDB (President's Daily Brief) turned over by Tenet showed that "there were more than forty" reports "related to Bin Laden" furnished to Bush by Tenet or one of his deputies during these morning briefings from Bush's first day in office, January 20, 2001, to September 10, 2001, the day before 9/11.

Now for the staggering blunders and incompetence of Bush and his people:

1. On August 6, 2001, a little over one month before 9/11, Bush, on a five-week-long summer vacation at his Crawford, Texas, ranch, was briefed by a CIA official on a one-and-a-half page top secret memo

titled "Bin Laden Determined to Strike in U.S." The memo referred to U.S. intelligence on Al Qaeda back to 1997, cited evidence of active Al Qaeda cells in the United States, and said with respect to them that the FBI had observed "patterns of suspicious activity in this country *consistent with preparations for hijacking [of planes] or other types of attacks, including recent surveillance of federal buildings in New York* . . . Bin Laden implied in U.S. television interviews in 1997 and 1998 that his followers would follow the example of *World Trade Center* bomber Ramzi Yousef and 'bring the fighting to America.' The FBI is conducting approximately 70 full field investigations throughout the U.S. that it considers Bin Laden-related."

The significance of the August 6 memo (included in the thirty-sixth of forty PDBs) was that it was the very first one that dealt with a terrorist attack *in the United States.* Also, what was striking was the memo's specificity—the reference to Al Qaeda preparing to possibly *hijack* a plane or planes, *their surveillance of federal buildings in New York City,* even the reference, in an indirect context, to the *World Trade Center.*

Obviously, there was only one thing for Bush to have done. What *any* normal president would have done. Cut short his precious five-week vacation, fly back to Washington, and immediately call a meeting of all his intelligence and military advisers to ascertain what specifically was being done by the CIA, FBI, and Department of Defense on the Al Qaeda threat, discuss the hijacking issue in detail, and map out a *stepped-up strategy* to meet the threat, including, automatically, the increasing of airport security. And perhaps also call a meeting of his cabinet to get every top official and his department involved at least to the extent of offering immediate advice and suggestions. The point is not that if Bush had responded immediately the disaster would have been averted. There is no way to know this. We can only know that he should have made an effort to respond instead of just ignoring these warnings of 9/11.

With the terrorist warnings "blinking red," not just every other president would have done something, you and I would have also. But what if I were to tell you that Bush did absolutely nothing—he stayed on his vacation, intent on continuing to have as much fun as he could, not returning to Washington until August 30. Did you get what I just said? Should I repeat it? I said Bush did nothing. Nothing at all. How do I know that he did nothing? Not only because there's absolutely no evidence that he did, but because Bush and Condoleezza Rice have never said they did, even when they were trying to defend themselves in 2004 before the 9/11 Commission. All Rice would tell the commission in her testimony on April 8, 2004, was that throughout the summer in question, federal agencies like the CIA and FBI continued to send out "warnings" to their people about a possible terrorist attack by Al Qaeda. But she did not mention a single thing that Bush, or she, at Bush's direction, did to ensure that *new additional steps* were taken to meet the imminent threat posed in the August 6 memo.

The essence of her testimony (though she never used these precise words) was that the Bush administration left it up to the federal bureaucracy to deal with the escalating threat. In other words, under existing protocol, federal agencies and departments like the FBI, the CIA, and Department of Defense were assigned the job of protecting the country, and she assumed they were doing their jobs. "The president knew that the FBI was pursuing this issue," Rice testified. "The president knew that the Director of Central Intelligence was pursuing the issue." Rice added: "My view . . . is that, first of all, the Director of Central Intelligence and the director of the FBI, given the level of threat, were doing what they thought they could do to deal with the threat that we faced." But she never went on to say what *she* did in *her* job as national *security* adviser, and what *leadership* Bush was providing. The reason she didn't, of course, was that she did nothing, and, more importantly, Bush did not provide any leadership at all that she could point to.

By the way, Rice, although she was Bush's national security adviser, was pathetically ill-informed about what was even going on. For instance, when she was asked in her 9/11 testimony whether she knew that "numerous young Arab males were in flight training" in the United States that summer, she said: "I was not." Question: "Were you told that the U.S. Marshal Program had been changed to drop any

U.S. Marshals on domestic flights?" Answer: "I was not told that." When she was asked if she knew that FAA inspection teams had found "that the U.S. airport security system never got higher than twenty percent effective and was usually down around ten percent for ten straight years," she responded: "To the best of my recollection I was not told that." Bush, everyone knows, knows very little, and has such a mature and advanced case of incuriosity that he will never change. *But this is Bush's national security adviser!*

Although Ms. Rice spoke very vaguely about the Bush administration having worked prior to 9/11 on a "comprehensive strategy" to destroy the Al Qaeda network, resulting in "a national security principals meeting" on Al Qeada on September 4, *just one week before 9/11,* and a presidential directive of the same date that made the elimination of Al Qaeda a high priority, she inconsistently acknowledged that while she and other national security officials had thirty-three meetings between the time Bush took office on January 20, 2001, and the meeting on September 4, which was almost eight months later, *not one of them dealt with the Al Qaeda threat.* Three of the 33 meetings, she said, "dealt at least partially with issues of terrorism *not related to Al Qaeda.*" Despite this, Rice told the 9/11 Commission that she definitely was very aware of the Al Qaeda threat before 9/11 and she and the Bush administration were definitely focused on Al Qaeda, making it a high priority. But she was unable to come up with one single, solitary thing the administration did in response to the August 6 report.

And the 9/11 Commission Report said that between the time of the August 6 memo or report and 9/11, unbelievably, "no . . . meeting was held to discuss the possible threat of a strike in the United States as a result of this report." (The September 4 meeting, a week before 9/11, dealt with how to combat Al Qaeda generally, not about the Al Qaeda threat to hijack planes and strike inside the United States as set forth in the August 6 report.) Not only wasn't any *meeting* called to discuss the threat of an internal attack in the United States by Al Qaeda before 9/11, but the 9/11 Commission Report said it "found no indication of any further *discussion* before September 11 among the president and his top advisers of the possibility of a threat of an Al Qaeda attack in the United States." In other words, not only didn't the Bush administration *do* anything pursuant to the August 6 memo, they didn't even want to *talk* about it. It was that bad.

Indeed, it was so bad that although Bush received the August memo near the beginning of the month (August 6), per the testimony of George Tenet, Bush's CIA director, before the 9/11 Commission on April 14, 2004 (see discussion in notes for Tenet's later version), Bush didn't meet with Tenet, his main intelligence adviser, during the rest of the entire month of August. He didn't even bother to talk to him over the phone. In Tenet's testimony, when he was asked, "When did you see [President Bush] in August?" Tenet answered, "I don't believe I did." When the questioner asked, incredulously, "You didn't see the president of the United States *once* in the month of August?" Tenet responded, "He's in Texas, and I'm either here [Washington, D.C.] or on leave for some of that time. So I'm not here." "But you never got on the phone or in any kind of conference with him to talk at this [time] of high chatter and huge warnings?" "In this time period, I'm not talking to him, no."

With respect to the critical August 6 report or memo, which was actually requested by Bush, Rice first told the 9/11 Commission that it "did not warn of attacks *inside* the United States," despite the fact that the very title of the memo was "Bin Laden Determined to Strike *in* U.S." She then tried to explain what she meant by saying that the August 6 memo "was not a threat report" because "there was nothing in this memo as to the time, place, how or where" of the attack. "No specifics," she said. In other words, folks, unless the Bush administration knew the exact day and time of day that Al Qaeda was going to attack, and the exact city, and the exact building or buildings in that city, there was nothing the Bush administration could or even should have done. Further translation: "If Al Qaeda didn't announce that they were going to hijack four planes on 9/11, two of which would fly into the north and south World Trade Center towers in New York City at 8:46 and 9:03 a.m. on September 11, 2001, we can't be criticized for doing nothing at all to prevent 9/11."

Bush told reporters on April 11, 2004, essentially the same thing. "Of course we knew that America was hated by Osama Bin Laden. The question was *who* was going to attack us, *when*, and *where* and with *what*." (Bush would later say, "Had I known there was going to be an attack on America, I would have moved mountains to stop the attack." But other than some nuts on the far left who were loony enough to actually believe that Bush was complicit in 9/11, shouldn't this go without saying?) Bush told *Washington Post* reporter Bob Woodward that before 9/11, "I didn't feel that sense of urgency . . . I was not on point." Even if we went no further, isn't it hard to see how it can get any worse?

It should be noted that President Clinton warned Bush during the presidential transition period in 2000 that Al Qaeda was the nation's number one security risk, and his secretary of state, Madeleine Albright, warned her successor, Powell, of the same thing. Likewise, Clinton's national security adviser, Sandy Berger, remembers telling his successor, Condoleezza Rice (and she never has denied this), during the transition that "the number one issue you're going to be dealing with is terrorism generally and Al Qaeda specifically."

One of the biggest blows to the incredibly inept Bush administration came when Richard Clarke, the former counterterrorism chief for the Bush administration (who previously served as Clinton's counterterrorism chief and also served in the administration of Bush's father) came out with his book *Against All Enemies* in 2004. In it, and in his testimony before the 9/11 Commission, as well as in remarks he made to the media, Clarke attested to how the Bush administration was not as focused on Al Qaeda and the terrorist threat as the Clinton administration had been.

Clarke said that on January 25, 2001, in the very first week of the Bush administration, he asked "urgently" for a high-level meeting on the Al Qaeda threat. However, as noted, it wasn't until September 4, nearly eight months later and just one week before September 11, that the Bush administration finally had a meeting on terrorism and approved of a plan to eliminate the Al Qaeda threat. And it wasn't until September 10, *the day before 9/11*, that the Bush administration forwarded the plan and directive to George Tenet, the CIA director, to start implementing it, a process that was to take two to three years. Clarke said that Bush "ignored terrorism for months, when maybe he could have done something to stop 9/11." Terrorism, he said, should have been the first item on the Bush administration's agenda. Instead "it was pushed back and back and back for months."

Virtually every charge Clarke made has been substantiated by independent evidence. The White House itself has never denied that Clarke made his request for a meeting on Al Qaeda way back in January 2001, and the meeting didn't take place until September 4. But the Bush administration made a concerted effort to attack Clarke's very serious allegations not by disputing them directly but by attacking him personally, even though on Clarke's retirement the previous year, Bush, in a handwritten letter to him, said that Clarke had served with "distinction and honor." Among other things, Bush's surrogates said, very predictably, that Clarke was making his allegations to sell his book. They also said he was a "disgruntled" former employee who was angry with Bush because, under Clinton, Clarke had briefed cabinet-level officers, but in the hierarchy set up by Rice he was demoted and only briefed deputies on counterterrorism. But, unwittingly, Bush's people were confirming Clarke's central allegation that the Bush administration wasn't focused at all on Al Qaeda and terrorism. If they were, why was Clarke reporting now only to deputies, not cabinet-level officers, on counterterrorism? In a similar vein, Cheney attacked Clarke by saying that he was "out of the loop." But since Clarke headed up the counterterrorism unit in the Bush White House, if the Bush administration was focused on terrorism, why wouldn't its head counterterrorism guy be *in* the loop?

Let's look at a few other pieces of evidence supporting Clarke's claim that Bush did a terrible job on counterterrorism. Right at the beginning of the Bush administration, incoming Defense secretary Donald Rumsfeld decided not to relaunch a Predator drone being used by the CIA under Clinton's authorization to track the movements of Bin Laden. And Deputy Defense Secretary Paul Wolfowitz shut down a disinformation program created by the Clinton administration to create dissent within the Taliban, which was giving a sanctuary to Bin Laden and his Al Qaeda in Afghanistan. These, you might say, are small points, but small points are snapshot glimpses of larger realities. In a May 10, 2001, letter to his department heads, Attorney General John Ashcroft set forth seven "strategic goals" of his Department of Justice, and fighting terrorism was not one of them. As a member of Bush's cabinet, Ashcroft knew where the emphasis was. It was not on combating terrorism.

Most tellingly, on September 10, 2001, just one day before 9/11, Ashcroft submitted his first budget. He asked for increased funds for sixty-eight programs in his Department of Justice, not one of which directly involved counterterrorism. Even worse, he rejected a request by the FBI for $58 million for 149 new counterterrorism field agents. He also proposed a $65 million cut (from $109 million to $44 million) in grants to the states and local authorities to increase their counter-terrorism preparedness.

On May 9, 2001, Ashcroft testified before Congress that "the Department of Justice has no higher priority" than fighting terrorism. But if the old injunction "Put your money where your mouth is" means anything, which I believe it does, it is impossible to reconcile these words of Ashcroft's with the budget he submitted. One of my favorite expressions is "Your conduct speaks so loudly I can't hear a word you are saying." Under the Clinton administration, Ashcroft's predecessor, Janet Reno, increased the counterterrorism budget by 13.6% in fiscal year 1999, 7.1% in 2000, and 22.7% in 2001. Ashcroft's 2002 budget cut counterintelligence spending by $476 million, a whopping 23% drop from the previous year. This fact alone shows that the Clinton administration placed more emphasis on counterter-rorism than the Bush administration prior to 9/11.

All of the aforementioned actions of the Bush administration are clearly very revealing ones, showing its intent to deemphasize the war on terrorism. And note that Rumsfeld, Wolfowitz, and Ashcroft were not only very high up in the Bush administration, but spokes of the same wheel. Though the Bush administration has proven to be in-competent overall, one thing it prizes and demands above all else is loyalty, and everyone is always on the same page. So these points I have mentioned reflect the policy of Bush and his administration to almost look the other way when it came to fighting terrorism. Yet, let's not forget as we read on that Bush's approval rating among Americans shot up to 90 percent as a result of 9/11.

General Henry H. Shelton, the chairman of the Joint Chiefs of Staff at the time of 9/11, said that the Bush administration had moved counterterrorism "farther to the back burner" than the preceding administration of President Clinton. Three-star General Don Kerrick spent the final four months of his military career in the White House. In a memo to Rice's National Security Council on "things you need to pay attention to," he warned (about Al Qaeda), "We are going to be struck," but he said he never heard back. "I don't think it was above [their] waterline. They were gambling nothing would happen," he later observed. The likes of Clarke, Shelton, and Kerrick were simply voices in the wilderness to a Bush administration that clearly had its mind on other things.

Indeed, Rice's own words (actually, the lack of them) prove this. A search conducted by Peter Bergen, a fellow of the New America Foundation, of all of Rice's public statements and writings from the moment she became national security adviser in January of 2001 to September 11, revealed, astonishingly, that she only mentioned Osama Bin Laden's name one time and "never mentioned Al Qaeda at all as a threat to the United States before 9/11."

So there can be little question that Rice, Bush's obedient national security adviser, lied under oath to the 9/11 Commission when she said the Bush administration "understood that the Al Qaeda network posed a serious threat to the United States . . . We worked hard [yes, the CIA and FBI did, but what about you and Bush, Condoleezza?] on multiple fronts to detect, protect against, and disrupt any terrorist plans or operations that might lead to an attack." Do you know what my sense of Rice's fidelity to the truth is? I trust her as far as I could throw the Empire State Building.

Former president Bill Clinton summarized the difference between his administration and that of George Bush well in an interview on the Fox News channel in September of 2006. Referring to the Bush administration he said, "They had eight months to try" to get Bin Laden and put Al Qaeda out of business. "They did not try. I tried and failed. At least I tried."

2. Knowing what you now know, in looking back to the moment when Al Qaeda–hijacked planes toppled the Twin Towers on 9/11, you should have an extremely low estimation of Bush's competence in the war against terrorism, and you ought to wonder whether, if he and his people had been competent and responsible public officials, 9/11 could have been averted. Immediately following 9/11, Bush deserved the harshest criticism and denunciation there is for his pre–9/11 conduct. Instead, as indicated, he became more popular than ever, which you have to agree was 100 percent insanity.

In fact, even if Bush and his people had acted properly and responsibly, he'd still have to be condemned for 9/11. Why? Because of something that Americans and the nitwit media have apparently forgotten. Nine-eleven happened on Bush's watch, and in life, when something happens on your watch that is bad, you automatically get the blame for it. We all know that's simply the way it is—even, as I say, when you've acted responsibly. An army loses a battle. The general is canned. The grade level at a university goes down. The president of the university is either fired or told he will be if things don't improve. Joe Paterno, the ageless football coach at Penn State, knocks himself out every year, seven days a week, trying to make Penn State a winner. But when he had some losing seasons a few years ago, everyone and their grandmother wanted to get rid of poor Joe. Because he is so much of an integral part of Penn State, they kept him on against a tide of criticism, and he's had better seasons the last few years. But basketball, football, and baseball coaches are routinely fired when their team doesn't do well, no matter how hard and diligently they work. As Harry Truman said, referring to the Oval Office: "The buck stops here."

But unbelievably, with the draft-dodger from Crawford, no one was blaming him for 9/11. I've saved the newspapers from around that time. Day after day the CIA and FBI took a beating, but the press, which influences public opinion, refused (in stark contrast to its savage treatment of Clinton) to criticize Bush. They gave him a free ride, not even mentioning him in their news articles dealing with the issue of culpability, and totally forgetting the rule of life that the guy in charge is the one who gets the blame. And that's true, as I indicated, even if he has been working diligently. Here, it wouldn't have been possible for Bush to have been more remiss, negligent, lazy, and irresponsible. Not possible.

All that the media would say was that 9/11 "was the biggest failure by U.S. intelligence agencies in U.S. history," not adding that both the CIA and FBI are in the executive branch of government—Bush's branch—and he, obviously and naturally and automatically, is ultimately responsible for their performance. In fact, as indicated, most of the right-wing and their political hacks and scribes were making a great deal of noise that 9/11 should be blamed on President Clinton for not already having gotten Osama Bin Laden. The fact that 9/11 happened on their guy's watch, and he did absolutely nothing for eight months to combat Bin Laden's Al Qaeda, was ignored by these people who specialize in being obnoxious.

Bush, of course, if he had a molecule of manly leadership in his body—particularly since he knew very well how culpable he was for doing absolutely nothing before and even after he received his briefing on the August 6 memo—would not have allowed his CIA (who warned him of the threat) and FBI to take the fall. True, both the CIA and FBI could hardly have been more incompetent in their own right in their antiterrorism effort, but they were Bush's incompetents, and he alone was responsible for their performance. Bush should have apologized to the nation for the terrible event that happened on his watch, assuring the public that his administration would do everything in its power to never let them down again. But you see, with Bush the buck stopped below him. Indeed, Bush elevated unaccountability to a fine art.

Other presidents in recent memory, in analogous situations, have done the right thing and accepted blame as a part of leadership. When 241 American servicemen (220 marines, 18 navy personnel, and 3 army soldiers) were killed by a terrorist bomb at their compound in Beirut, Lebanon, on October 23, 1983, the State Department prepared a release severely criticizing the military for its failure in not protecting the troops. The release was sent to President Reagan for his approval. An aide of Reagan's, David Gergen, said that Reagan read the release, and with virtually no discussion went to the White House pressroom and announced to the media: "If there is to be blame, it properly rests here in this office, and with this president. And I accept responsibility for the bad as well as the good." When the CIA-organized Bay of Pigs invasion in April of 1961 turned into a disaster, an invasion that President Kennedy had inherited from the Eisenhower administration, but had signed on to, John F. Kennedy, just three months into his presidency, told the nation that "victory has a hundred fathers and defeat is an orphan. I'm the responsible officer of the government." His press secretary, Pierre Salinger, said that Kennedy wanted everyone to know that he was solely responsible.

But not the small man from Crawford. Just as he ran away from his generation's war, Vietnam, he ran away from all responsibility for the biggest failure in our national defense ever, only stepping forward to attempt to become, unbelievably, a hero of 9/11. And again, unbelievably, he succeeded.

We've talked about the media giving Bush a free ride. What about the American public? Although *everyone* knows it's a negative when something bad happens on one's watch,* *there never was a moment when the American public blamed Bush for his administration's failure to prevent 9/11.* And the moment he said that he was going to go after the perpetrators, virtually the whole nation fell hopelessly in love with him. The fact that 9/11 happened on his watch was treated as

---

*All humans, even the duke of duplicity, Vice President Dick Cheney, knows this is so. Stung by accusations by Bush's former counterterrorism chief, Richard Clarke, that the Bush administration had essentially ignored the Al Qaeda threat before 9/11, Cheney, in an interview with his favorite radio host, Rush Limbaugh, countered that terrorist attacks on the USS *Cole* and U.S. embassies in Kenya and Tanzania had taken place "on Mr. Clarke's watch."

something completely irrelevant. Worse yet, the public, untouched by common sense, apparently never even considered the issue. It wasn't just the media and the American public that gave Bush a pass on 9/11. When a joint panel of the House and Senate intelligence committees later issued its close-to-900-page report on July 24, 2007, it was a damning indictment of the CIA and FBI for their failure to prevent 9/11. But not one negative word about George Bush.

3. How did Bush respond to this moment of great crisis, the first deadly attack by foreigners on American soil in our history? If we didn't know what he did, no one could possibly believe it. It is so incredible that I am certain one would be extremely hard-pressed to find one other person out of a million—but certainly no public official of any rank, much less another president of the United States—who would have responded the way he did. At 8:55 on the morning of September 11, 2001, Condoleezza Rice, the president's national security adviser, informed Bush over the telephone that a plane had hit one of the Twin Towers of the World Trade Center. He was then told this in person by his chief of staff, Andrew Card, before he walked into the Emma E. Booker Elementary School in Sarasota, Florida, at 9:04 a.m. He would have had no way of knowing at this point that it was a terrorist attack, and could have reasonably assumed it had been an accident. Eighteen second-graders rose to their feet as the president entered the classroom, and he proceeded to sit down next to the teacher (Sandra Kay Daniels) at the front of the class and listen to the students as they read aloud a children's story about a girl's pet goat. A small battery of news reporters and camera crews in the back of the room recorded the event.

At 9:07 a.m., Card entered the classroom and whispered into the president's ear: "Mr. President, a second plane has struck the second tower. *The nation is under attack.*" Unbelievably (why can't there be more powerful words in our lexicon to describe special, yes, unique situations like this other than this tired, terribly overused adverb), Bush did not instantly apologize to the students and excuse himself to immediately respond, as the president of the country and the commander-in-chief of our armed forces, to this attack on the nation's soil. While inside the two towers were scenes of horror and death that Hollywood would not even try to capture on celluloid, Bush, after a momentary show of concern upon hearing the news, "grew cheerful," per the *Orlando Sentinel*, as the seven-year-olds continued to show off their reading skills to the beat of Miss Daniels's tapping pen. "Reading more than they watch TV?" the president asked, smiling. "Anybody do that?" The children's hands shot up. "Really good readers—whew. This must be the sixth grade," Bush joked, remaining in the classroom.

You, I, or anyone else in Bush's shoes would have instantly excused ourselves from the children's classroom and demanded to be briefed immediately by our national security adviser and secretary of defense on exactly what happened, asking if they had any idea who was behind the attacks. Was there any fear that this was just the opening salvo of a much greater attack on the entire nation? What steps should be taken to protect the nation? What emergency measures were being taken at the Twin Towers site? Have our military forces been placed on national alert—and a host of other questions. What Bush did before 9/11 was bad enough, by itself, to be thrown out of office. It was grossly irresponsible conduct; conduct that was inexcusable. But that type of behavior was at least "imaginable" and has happened before in different contexts. But I maintain that what Bush did in that classroom could *not* have been imagined.

Bush continued to sit in the classroom to the very end of the reading session, leaving the room at 9:12 a.m., *five minutes* after learning the nation was under attack! God knows how long he would have stayed in the classroom if the reading session had been longer. Indeed, he showed no indication at all that he wanted to leave. When that part of the reading session scheduled specifically for him came to an end, and the children closed with the phrase "more to come," Bush asked, "What does that mean, more to come?" The president was told by Miss Daniels that they didn't intend to take up any more of his time, at which point he finally left the classroom.

Bush later told *Newsweek* that when Card said to him that America was under attack—"I'm trying to absorb that knowledge. *I have nobody to talk to.* I'm sitting in the midst of a classroom with little kids, listening to a children's story, and I realize I'm the commander-in-chief and the country has just come under attack." In other words, Bush, a very small man, was in a state of paralysis because he knew he was so far beneath the situation.

In his interview with the 9/11 Commission, Bush tried to improve on what he told *Newsweek* by not only telling a transparent lie, but a remarkably bad one at that. The 9/11 Commission reported that Bush said he stayed in the classroom because he "felt he should project strength and calm until he could better understand what was happening." But how could he better understand what had happened by remaining inside the classroom rather than leaving the classroom and being informed by his advisers? And to whom did he want to project strength and calm? The seven-year-old children? Even if that were his demented goal, how could he project strength and calm to them when they didn't even know the attacks had taken place? Or was he trying to project strength and calm to the American public? But how could he do this when the public couldn't see him inside the classroom?

To call Bush's conduct a dereliction of duty would be to minimize it a thousandfold by employing a term used to routinely describe commonplace, garden variety types of negligence and failure in public office. No. What Bush did here was not only unprecedented, but most assuredly will never happen again, no matter how long this crazed little planet of ours revolves around the sun. When I told a right-wing acquaintance of mine about what the president had done, I already knew he would defend it. You see, you have to understand that because Bush is a conservative Republican, he could be caught sodomizing a goat on the front lawn of the White House and they'd say this only showed his love for animals. My right-wing acquaintance told me: "The president didn't leave because he probably didn't want to upset the children." Even if his leaving would have left a scar on the psyches of the children for the rest of their lives (which, of course, is ridiculous and impossible to believe), Bush still had absolutely no choice but to immediately excuse himself from the classroom to attend to the security of 280 million Americans. (Indeed, even if the two planes that struck the Twin Towers did so as a result of an accident, what happened was still catastrophic enough for Bush to have excused himself.) But the reality is that it wouldn't have hurt the children a bit, since seven-year-olds are old enough to understand emergencies. If they were hurt at all, it was when they heard the president speaking at the school minutes later on television about the attack on the towers. There would be a full-scale investigation, he said, to track down "the folks" who were responsible.

Let me add that in view of Bush's mind-boggling, extremely bizarre, and utterly incredible malfeasance in the way he responded to learning that the nation was under attack, the whole nation should have been terrified down to the marrow of its bones that someone like George Bush was our president. Yet unbelievably, far from being lambasted as he should have been for his severely aberrational behavior, Bush was treated with kid gloves by the nation's press at the time, and the incident was mostly ignored.

The first time Bush started receiving some serious ridicule for what he did was when Michael Moore came out with his movie *Fahrenheit 9/11* in 2004. Though Bush, of course, came off badly in the movie, I didn't think there was any possible way for anyone to even partially redeem or explain Bush's otherworldly conduct in the Florida classroom until Moore did so. As I have suggested, I believe there was only one true reason for Bush's behavior—he was in way, way over his head, and no one was immediately nearby to coach and mother him in this moment of crisis. Not so, says Moore, determined to throw out a rope to a fellow human in an unforgiving sea and pull him from the other world aboard our planet earth. Moore, inadvertently moonlighting for Bush, came up with a possible explanation for Bush's behavior, which, though still depicting Bush in a negative light, brought his conduct within the margins of imaginable human behavior. Moore told his audience that Bush may have stayed in the classroom because he was immobilized by the thought that one of his friends (like a Saudi billionaire) might have been behind the attack. Moore asked, "Was he thinking, 'I've been hanging out with the wrong crowd. Which one of them screwed me?'"

The sultans of silliness over at the editorial board of the *New York Times* (the nation's paper of record) went far beyond Moore in defending Bush. They actually wrote (I'm not making this up—you can't make up stuff like this—September 2, 2004, edition, page A22) that in "judging Bush's leadership" abilities, his staying in the classroom after being informed the nation was under attack is "irrelevant." Can you imagine that?

In any event, Bush's conduct in remaining in that classroom for five minutes after being told the nation was under attack is nothing short of unbelievable. And this is the "war" president who was re-elected because he was perceived as being a strong and effective leader against terrorism.

4. Let's continue the litany of Bush's egregious failures, one after another. What else did he do this day of 9/11 that caused Rudy Giuliani to say, "I do think that there was some divine guidance in the President being elected. I remember saying it on the street [on 9/11], 'Thank God he's there.' [Where, Rudy? In the classroom?] President Bush's *leadership on that day* is central to his record, and his continued leadership is critical for our ultimate success against world terrorism." I agree, Rudy. If I had been the president and I had been in the classroom, I would have stayed much longer than five minutes. In fact, I might have never come out. And the fact that Bush did after only five minutes stamps him as a great leader.

We've all heard so many times that the real president is Dick Cheney, not George Bush. My guess, without having any inside knowledge about the situation, is that Bush gets his way on whatever he wants. But he is smart enough to know he doesn't know anything and Cheney does, and lazy enough to not want to work to acquire this knowledge, so he defers to Cheney's judgment almost out of necessity, making Cheney close to the de facto president. Indeed, jokes have been made about this, and Bush has made no ostensible public effort to disabuse people of this perception. The incident I'm about to relate to you is illuminating as a corollary of the above—that the members of Bush's inner circle realize he is hopelessly ill-suited for his job, and whenever necessary, they act accordingly.

Following is the finding, from testimony and interviews, of the bipartisan (five Republicans and five Democrats) 9/11 Commission that investigated the 9/11 catastrophe. After Bush emerged from the classroom and spoke briefly to the press, Cheney urged him, understandably, not to return to Washington, while Cheney proceeded to the shelter conference room in the bowels of the White House. Cheney told the 9/11 Commission that he called Bush (now aboard Air Force One flying west away from the East Coast with no particular destination) right after entering the conference room around 10 a.m. to discuss the so-called rules of engagement for American fighter jets in the sky. Cheney recommended that they be allowed to shoot down any plane in the sky that would not follow their orders to divert. He said that Bush signed off on this, meaning that Bush authorized the shooting down of any additional hijacked aircraft with Americans aboard, an order that Cheney knew only the president of the United States was supposed to give. And because he knew this, it may have been the reason why, we shall see, it appears he lied to the 9/11 Commission and said he called Bush for authorization when he in fact did not. For Americans, as numb as they are, to hear that within minutes of 9/11 Dick Cheney was deliberately ignoring Bush and running the country would have been very harmful to Bush's image.

Did Cheney in fact call Bush and get authorization? Though not 100 percent conclusive, the weight of the evidence is that he did not. The only two people who support Cheney's assertion that he called Bush to secure authorization are Bush himself (who had an even greater motive to lie than Cheney, in that if he didn't lie and say Cheney called him, he would be acknowledging his irrelevance) and the old (though young) reliable Condoleezza Rice. With her history of lying before the 9/11 Commission, Rice would certainly not be considered the best of witnesses on this point. (Cheney's military aide said he *believed* that Cheney called Bush upon entering the conference room, but did not know what they talked about.)

The evidence that Cheney did not call Bush is much more persuasive. Cheney's chief of staff, Scooter Libby, was sitting right next to Cheney when Cheney allegedly made the call, and was taking notes. Libby told the commission that he was unaware that Cheney had called Bush upon entering the room to secure shoot-down orders. Mrs. Cheney, also taking notes, was also unaware of any such call. The 9/11 Commission's report reads that at some point between 10:10 and 10:15 a.m., "a military aide told the Vice President . . . that [an] aircraft [United 93, which eventually crashed in Pennsylvania] was eighty miles out . . . The Vice President authorized fighter aircraft to engage the inbound plane. [Cheney] told us he based this authorization on his earlier conversation with the president." The commission said that Joshua Bolton (the White House deputy chief of staff who was present throughout this whole period) told them he thereafter "suggested that the Vice-President get in touch with the president and confirm the [alleged] engage order . . . He said he had not heard any prior discussion on the subject with the president." Pursuant to Bolten's suggestion, "the Vice-President was logged calling the president at 10:18 for a two minute conversation that obtained the confirmation." And on Air Force One, the president's press secretary, Ari Fleischer, was taking notes. The commission report said that "Fleischer recorded that at 10:20 the president told him that he had authorized a shoot-down of aircraft if necessary." Fleischer had no record of any previous phone call between Cheney and Bush in which the president gave a shoot-down order.

The above alone strongly suggests that Cheney only called Bush for a shoot-down authorization per Bolten's suggestion, and no such call was made by Cheney to Bush earlier, as Cheney and Bush would later claim. What virtually proves that no such call was made is the fact that, as the 9/11 Commission report said, "There's no documentary evidence for this call" allegedly made around 10 a.m. In other words, there was no official log (which, as I learned in writing my book on the assassination of President John F. Kennedy, is automatic for all calls to and from the president) confirming this call, as there was a log for the 10:18–10:20 call. Lee H. Hamilton, cochairman of the 9/11 Commission, told reporters that "the only evidence" that

Cheney got earlier approval for the shoot-down orders "is the statement of the president and the vice-president."

I think we can be satisfied beyond a *reasonable* doubt (if not beyond all doubt) that Cheney, accustomed to calling the shots, simply ignored Junior and issued a shoot-down order, only calling Bush later upon the suggestion of Bolten.

5. There really was only one essential message for Bush to deliver after the 9/11 attacks, and that was that he intended to bring the perpetrators to justice. Instead, he also told the nation he not only was going to go after terrorism wherever it existed on the globe, but he suggested he'd also go after any nation that protected the terrorists, making, he said on the evening of September 11, 2001, "no distinction between the terrorists and those who harbor them." Not knowing Bush well at this point, nor knowing of his intentions in Iraq, I nonetheless immediately said to myself, you're not going to go after anyone but Bin Laden and Al Qaeda, so why sound like such a fool to the world? And we now know Bush never went after terrorists anywhere except Al Qaeda in Afghanistan and the terrorists he personally created in Iraq, virtually ignoring (except by words) the Israeli-Palestinian terrorists, those in Northern Ireland, Lebanon, Sudan, Uganda, Myanmar, Colombia, Liberia, Sri Lanka, or wherever else they may exist in the world. So why did he sound like such a fool to anyone with an ounce of sense? Because he is a fool and has no business leading a nation such as the United States of America.

About Bush's unqualified assertion that he would go after any country that protected terrorists, I said to myself, right. If China or Russia winds up giving Bin Laden asylum, we're going to invade Russia or China. With both sides having nuclear weapons, it would be a golden opportunity to blow up the globe. I just don't see any leader of a European nation making such rash, idiotic remarks. But I don't recall anyone in the media taking Bush to task for them.

Continuing his idiocy, Bush said in his speech to Congress and the nation on the evening of September 20, 2001, that those behind the World Trade Center destruction did what they did because "they hate our freedoms, our freedom of religion, our freedom of speech, our freedom to vote and assemble and disagree with each other." Any sensible person would have to know this is preposterous. People don't do what Bin Laden did because they don't like our freedoms and lifestyle, which would be a motivation for an act like this that would not take residence in an adult mind.

Bin Laden eventually spoke up on November 24, 2002, and gave his reasons, none of them dealing with Bush's childlike thoughts. They had everything to do with our foreign policy. The very first reason he gave for the attack was our support of Israel in the ongoing Israeli-Palestinian conflict (something that almost the entire Arab world hates us for). Two other reasons were our having American troops stationed in (and hence defiling, in his mind) certain areas of Saudi Arabia considered to be sacred places by Muslims, and our stealing the oil of Muslims at paltry prices because of our international influence and military threats. He also blamed us for what he said was the death of 1.5 million Iraqi children from starvation because of our sanctions following the Gulf War.

Focusing on "the political roots of the terrorist atrocity of September 11," Zbigniew Brzezinski, President Carter's national security adviser, said, "American involvement in the Middle East [which he said was our "support of Israel and Israel's treatment of the Palestinians, as well as the direct injection of American power into the region"] is clearly the main impulse of the hatred that has been directed at America." Yet we had a president who was using a sandlot, playground mentality to address the issue, and no one was criticizing him for it.

I must digress for a moment here to make an observation about a phenomenon that is terribly vapid and irrational, one that is almost solely responsible for the great favor with which the American people viewed Bush, giving him the Oval Office a second time. Bush's approval rating at the time of 9/11 was around 50 percent. Since 9/11 happened on his watch it should have dropped to 10 percent overnight. That is, if we're talking logic and common sense. After 9/11, Bush and his people, figuratively speaking, should have been hiding behind the curtain, peeking out every now and then to see how much lower he was dropping on the American stage, at some point whispering to each other about whether they would be able to survive in office.

But a different reality took over that I've seen over and over again. You see, most everyday Americans don't seem to know, the media doesn't know, even the *New York Times* editorial board doesn't know that *credit necessarily implies a choice.* You don't give anyone any credit for something he had no choice but to do. But apparently not too many people have enough common sense to realize this. Even though Bush should have been "stoned (for 9/11 as well as his terrible malfeasance leading up to it) by the entire American community" like the man in the Book of Leviticus was for using the Lord's name in vain, all Bush had to say was that he intended to go after those responsible for 9/11, bring them to justice, and get Bin Laden "dead or alive," and almost the entire nation swooned, and his approval rating soared to an astronomical 90 percent almost overnight. (In fact, in the Gallup poll's annual survey of Americans in 2001, 39 percent chose Bush as the man they admired most in the entire world, the highest ranking any man had ever received since Gallup started asking the question over a half-century earlier in 1948.) But what else could he have said—that he was *not* going to go after these people? That it was fine with him what they did? Or that he was going to seek justice for 9/11 by going after whale hunters in Alaska? Obviously, he said the *only* thing he could say, the *only* thing that you, I, or anyone else would have said. Yet virtually the entire American public, Republicans and Democrats alike, thought Bush was the greatest thing since sliced bread.

Nelson Warfield, a Republican political consultant, said, "I think *everyone* agrees that an asset for Bush is his performance in the aftermath of the terrorist attacks." Warfield was right. *Everyone* did seem to agree on this. But why? What had he done to deserve any credit at all? What other option did he have? It is remarkable that both Republicans and Democrats were singing Bush's praises. Indeed, Republicans were saying to Democrats, referring back to the 2000 national election the Democrats thought Bush stole from Gore: "Aren't you glad *now* that Bush won?" and remarkably, it appeared the majority of Democrats were agreeing.

Newsweek's Jonathan Alter said that Bush's remarks about pursuing those responsible for 9/11 were "a defining moment for his presidency," and he lauded Bush for the "moral clarity" of his words. Moral clarity? Are you actually suggesting, Jonathan, that there could have been some moral ambiguity here? That others in Bush's shoes may have wondered whether or not to go after Al Qaeda? Alter went on in another article: "After September 11, we trusted Bush not to let us down, and he didn't." Jonathan, you actually thought that maybe Bush, like many people you know, may have decided *not* to go after the perpetrators of 9/11? Jonathan, you may be a sadist, but I'm not a masochist, and I'm going to have to wear some heavy armor the next time I'm exposed to your words about Bush's words vis-à-vis 9/11.

The *New York Times* editorial board, again demonstrating its sweet tooth for silliness, wrote in a lead editorial that Bush's conduct "right after 9/11 . . . was the high point of the Bush presidency. We [the nation] hung on every word [not knowing, the *Times* implies, if Bush might say he intended to let Al Qaeda get by with it] when Mr. Bush denounced Al Qaeda [you see, he might have praised them] and made the emotional . . . vow to track down Osama Bin Laden." And this, again, is the editorial board of the *New York Times*, writing stuff like this, totally unaware that giving credit implies someone had a choice.

Ronald Brownstein, a liberal columnist for the *Los Angeles Times*, wrote that "many, perhaps most Americans appeared to take a snapshot of Bush in the frenzied, frightening days after the attacks and concluded that he *passed* as wrenching a test as any president had faced in decades." He passed a wrenching test? Was there any conceivable way for him to fail? If so, how? By going back to the Florida classroom and moving in? Not giving a speech saying he was going to go after the terrorists?

Pollster Frank Luntz, in an op-ed piece in the *Los Angeles Times*, sounded just like Alter, only slightly crazier, if that's possible. He wrote: "The *moral clarity* that Bush espoused and acted upon immediately following September 11 was articulated at *perfect pitch*. Black and white language to a grieving nation was exactly what was called for and why his credibility surged even among those who had cast votes for his opponent just ten months earlier. This was a president," Luntz went on to say, who said, "I know what I believe and I know what I believe is right. My job isn't to nuance.'" But Frank, are you saying there's reason to believe that others would have had an ambiguous response to 9/11? Who, Frank? Who? Are you suggesting that there are many people out there who did not feel it was right to bring the perpetrators to justice?

When, in early August of 2006, the British foiled a terrorist plot to put liquid bombs on commercial planes bound for the United States, Greg Valliere, a member of the Stanford Washington Research Group, told CNN that the British terrorist plot "is Christmas in August for Karl Rove" because this meant "we are still in a war." Translation: If the terrorists are still out there, obviously, only the Republicans can stop them, not the Democrats. And Valliere said this even though the Republican administration of George Bush had already failed miserably in the war on terror. Moreover, the Bush administration didn't even have anything to do with the foiling of the plot. And Valliere, as I say, is employed by a prominent research group. My God, what level of common sense IQ is good enough to work for these think tanks? Can you imagine that? "Christmas in August for Karl Rove."

And Gary Jacobson, a political scientist from the University of California in San Diego, told *USA Today* that the British incident "reminded people that terrorists were out there, and *this is [George Bush's] strong suit.*" Can you imagine that? This is in 2006, close to three long years after Bush started his war, when *all* the evidence, every single piece of it, without exception, clearly showed that Bush couldn't possibly have performed any worse in the war against terrorism. And people in think tanks and political scientists can talk like this.

Al Neuharth is the usually reliable founder of *USA Today*, a fine paper that is a lot better than many people think who haven't bothered to take a really good look at it. Though not of the quality of some of the major papers of America, it has less silliness in it, indicating that *USA Today* has a splendid editor. But Al decided to be silly about Bush and added a new twist to the insanity. "Bush," Al said, "*bravely* took on a necessary fight against terrorists who attacked us." Al, Bush was personally *brave* to have his military go after Bin Laden? In what possible conceivable way? Since I like your paper, particularly the front-page feature stories, which usually are better than in any other paper in the land, and you usually talk sense, if you want to take that word "brave" back, I'll let you. You couldn't possibly have been thinking clearly when you wrote it.

Al, I'll tell you what I'll do if you don't want to take the word back. If you can tell me how Bush was "brave" to command his military to invade Afghanistan and bring back Bin Laden dead or alive, I'll get up every morning at six (or whenever I have to) to deliver *USA Today* papers for six months free. Is that a deal? The reason I'm making such a big deal of this, Al, is that you know how words influence people. We have enough idiots in America without a few more who are on the fence voting for people like Bush because of some loose but powerful words some member of the media used. Remember Al, stupidity is not benign. There are over 100,000 people in their graves today from the war in Iraq because of it.

Professor and political scientist Richard Sylves wasn't just observing a fact, but clearly seemed to be embracing it himself when he said that when Bush walked into the rubble of the World Trade Center on September 14 and vowed that the perpetrators of the attack would hear from the United States, it was "a major symbolic statement for the president and created a tremendous confidence" in him by the American people. I don't blame the American people. If I had been president, I wouldn't have gone to the World Trade Center site. If I had been in town, I would have gone to a Mets game at Shea Stadium. And if the media caught up with me, I would have told them I had no intent to go after the perpetrators, because next time they might come after me.

What was the message of all this extreme praise for Bush, including the popular slogan "Aren't you glad *now* that Bush won?" There is only one interpretation of this. That if Al Gore had been in the White House at the time of 9/11, he would not have strongly vowed to go after the perpetrators. But a moment's reflection—not even that—will tell you that no thought could be more irrational than this. Any president, you, I, or any other rational person would automatically do the same thing Bush did. If he didn't, as incredibly spaced out as the majority of Americans are, they'd be dumbfounded and undoubtedly be screaming for his head. But that would never happen. Ever. It's out of the question. And that is the precise reason why to sing Bush's praises for doing something he had no choice but to do can only be categorized as a very serious type of stupidity.

Although the lauding of Bush—with his approval rating rocketing from 50 percent to 90 percent and people everywhere saying, "Aren't you glad now that Bush won?"—necessarily conveyed the message that Gore would not have vowed to go after, and gone after, those behind the murder of 3,000 Americans, *those words were never uttered*. They didn't have to be. It was understood. (Indeed, one could say that the official party line of right-wing Republicans is that if Democrats had been in power at the time of 9/11, they would have hidden in a corner in a fetal position and hoped the terrorists wouldn't strike again. And if they ever came out of their corner they wouldn't fight the terrorists but instead coddle them.) It also wasn't expressly uttered because if anyone for a moment thought of doing so, they would know how crazy and ridiculous they would sound.

So *saying* that Gore and the Democrats wouldn't have responded to 9/11 would sound absurd and no public figure or columnist I know of said it, at least publicly, until the debate over the war in Iraq, at which time one prominent person I know of said it. And it was a big surprise since he has demonstrated himself to possess a very fine and facile mind in the area of social satire. I'm referring to Dennis Miller, a previously fairly liberal guy by his own admission, who fell madly in love with the Republican Party, he says, at the time of 9/11. "Nine-eleven changed me," he said. Why? Dennis mentioned the unmentionable, that which people who have far less gray matter than he knew enough not to mention. Listen to this. (And I hate to come down on Dennis. He invited me to be a guest on his former show several times; publicly called me "brilliant"; invited me and my wife to have dinner with him and his wife; and when he was on *Monday Night Football*, even worked me into one of his social allusions that he's so famous for—something on the field caused him to opine: "That's like being cross-examined by Vince Bugliosi." So I don't eagerly relish verbally assaulting Dennis, but just as Bush never had any choice to do what he did, Dennis has given me no choice. I'll be as nice to Dennis as I possibly can be under the circumstances.)

Here is what Dennis told *Time* magazine for its September 22, 2003, edition: "September 11 was a big thing for me. I was saying to liberal America, 'Well, what are you offering?' And they said, 'Well, *we're not going to protect you.*'" Dennis, please. What in the world happened to you? Should someone be taking your temperature? *Anyone,* Dennis, anyone holding the office of the presidency would protect you by going after Bin Laden. Not only that—which is a given and beyond discussion—but Dennis, since these liberals you said wouldn't protect you *also* live in America, even if they didn't want to protect you, why wouldn't they want to protect themselves? You see, Dennis, if they're not going to protect you, then necessarily they wouldn't be interested in protecting themselves either. But Dennis, last time I heard, liberals wanted to live just as much as conservative Republicans.* Dennis, you know how, when you're in the audience and someone is making a fool out of themselves on stage, you almost reflexively avert your glance because you're embarrassed for them? When I read those words by you, I was embarrassed for you.

Circumstantially, it couldn't be more obvious that in the context of what he was saying, Dennis forgot about *Afghanistan.* He uttered those words at a time when the majority of Democrats were opposed to going to war in *Iraq,* and the Republican Party made a lot of yardage arguing that not wanting to go to war in Iraq meant the Democrats didn't want to fight terrorism, a stunning non sequitur if I ever heard one. The hapless and pathetic Democratic leaders are apparently too thickpated to say, when the Republicans continue to make that charge: "Wait a second. Have you forgotten *Afghanistan*? No one in our party was against invading Afghanistan, and *all* the national polls showed that

---

*Rudy Giuliani said what Miller said, in a slightly different way, almost four years later. In April of 2007, Giuliani actually said that any Democrat who became president would endanger the nation because he would "go on defense" in the war on terrorism and "wave the white flag." Can you imagine that?

Democrats were in favor of militarily pursuing Bin Laden as much as Republicans were.* Again, have you forgotten that there were no demonstrations out on the streets of America by hundreds of thousands of people urging no invasion of Afghanistan, as there was before the war in Iraq? Democrats are just as much against terrorists as Republicans. But in a war on terrorism, aren't you supposed to go after the terrorists? That's why so many Democrats were against the war in Iraq. There were no terrorists in Iraq. They were in Afghanistan. That's where Bin Laden was. You know, the guy who murdered 3,000 Americans." Instead, Democrats keep taking it on the chin and virtually *never cite the conclusive evidence, Afghanistan*, to rebut the Republicans' outrageous charge that they are against, or very weak on, fighting terrorism.

Dennis Miller, there would seem to be little question, had to be confusing Iraq with Afghanistan. There simply was nothing taking place around 9/11 or when we went to war in Afghanistan in October of 2001 that would have ever been fertile soil for such a deranged thought by him to emerge. Dennis, you're a bright guy, but a word you might not possibly be overly familiar with is the word "conflation." It can be used in more than one way, but colloquially it implies a confusion resulting from combining events that don't match in time. "Yes, you saw Joe yelling his head off a year ago about the Red Sox game, but he didn't do this where you say he did." It happens to all of us, Dennis, and you had to be conflating the Democrats' position at the time of the Iraq war with what was happening around the time of 9/11.

Dennis, not satisfied with saying that the Democrats, if they were in office at the time of 9/11, would have, you know, cried, and begged Bin Laden not to do it again, decided to join Al Neurath, actually (I'm not kidding) calling Bush "ballsy" for going after Bin Laden and the

---

*A January 7–9, 2002, national Gallup poll showed that only 6 percent of Americans were opposed to our going to war with Afghanistan. Ninety-four percent approved, with virtually equal support among Republicans and Democrats. And the support was worldwide. For instance, eighty-nine nations joined the United States in the Afghanistan conflict by providing troops, including those from every major European country. Only thirty-two countries joined the United States in Bush's war in Iraq, among which was only one major power, Britain.

terrorists. Dennis, Bush has balls? Really? Pardon the pun, Dennis, but that's really a low blow. That's really hitting below the belt. Dennis, the wimp from Crawford only has balls with the lives of other people's children. People don't change. The prophet Mohammed said, "Tell me you can move a mountain, but don't tell me people change." And when it was Bush's time to fight during the Vietnam War, he ran like hell in the opposite direction. Dennis, if Bush has balls for what he did, I live in Sweden, I'm Elvis Presley's brother, I just broke the record in the 100 meters.

Dennis, you don't have a newspaper, so I can't deliver papers for you, but let me put myself on record by saying that if you can tell me how Bush had balls to order the U.S. military to bomb Afghanistan and try to capture Bin Laden, I'll send you a certified check for $10,000. And if you can't do it, you don't have to pay me a dime. Is that a fair deal? For old times' sake, Dennis, I hope you don't hurt yourself more than you already have and try to explain how Bush had balls after 9/11. I hope you come to your senses and return, from your political apostasy, to where you used to be on the political spectrum. Anyone can make a mistake.

In brief summary here, it's hard to see how Bush could possibly have been more negligent and irresponsible in defending this nation against terrorism prior to 9/11. So when 9/11 happened, the nation should have been thoroughly disgusted with him, and the House Judiciary Committee should have been preparing articles of impeachment. Instead, all Bush had to do (not one, single thing more) was vow to get the perpetrators of 9/11, something he had to say, and his approval rating soared to stratospheric heights, Bush miraculously becoming a hero of 9/11. So much of a hero, in fact, that when he ran for reelection, as I indicated earlier, he showed footage of 9/11 as part of his television ads for reelection. *Unbelievably, Bush was advertising his biggest failure.* This is impossible, right? But it happened. Indeed, the distortion of reality was so severe that Cheney felt confident and comfortable saying (actually, it was the main thrust for Bush's reelection) close to the 2004 election: "If we make the wrong choice, then the danger is we'll get hit *again*" by the terrorists. Cheney was subliminally saying, "Hit *again* by the terrorists like we were the last time the Democrats were in office. When *we* were in office you never had to worry about something like this." Right on.

Bush was so successful in using 9/11 to his advantage that former *Los Angeles Times* columnist Robert Scheer, who disapproves of every breath of air Bush breathes, could only criticize Bush for "exploiting 9/11," which necessarily implies that Scheer felt Bush had something to exploit, Scheer not adding words to the effect, "How does Bush have the gall to advertise his biggest failure?"

Indeed, an article in the *Los Angeles Times* said that "privately, some Democratic strategists agree that Bush should be able to invoke the disaster, as long as he doesn't overplay the theme." Can you imagine that? One Democratic mental paraplegic told the *Times* that 9/11 "is a big part of their record and they should be allowed to talk about it." When this candidate for the mental poverty program said that 9/11 "is a big part of their record," he could only have meant that 9/11 was something that Bush and his people had a right to be proud of. Said another Democrat: "If the shoe were on the other foot, there would be 9/11 ads coming out of the Kerry White House." This incredible Democrat was saying that "if 9/11 happened on our watch, we'd be bragging about it in our campaigns, too." Unbelievable. Isn't this logic turned completely on its head, a topsy-turvy world, like the one Alice found on the other side of the looking glass? Or maybe it's like a farce or a cartoon, where one angry combatant says to the other, "If you don't shut up, I'm going to hit your fist with my nose."

So although the Republican Party should have been hiding from 9/11, and the only party that should have been able to exploit it was the Democratic Party since the tragedy happened on Bush's watch (remarkably, I know of no Democratic columnist who made this point), the situation was the exact reverse. In other words, defeat is victory. White is black. Up is down. Night is day. Where can one hide to escape from all this madness?

6. If anyone reading what I've written so far is not thoroughly disgusted with Bush, it gets worse, much worse. Obviously, when a

catastrophe like 9/11 happens, as a direct result, by definition, of a failure of U.S. intelligence (for which the president is ultimately responsible), the automatic response is to conduct a congressional investigation, and/or one appointed by Congress, to find out why this catastrophe was able to take place beneath our radar, and to identify what prophylactic measures this nation has to take to ensure it never happens again. And that's precisely what Democrats in Congress, everyday Americans, and survivors of the victims of 9/11 proposed. But g—d— unbelievably, George Bush, the person who should have been spearheading the movement for an investigation, actually resisted the investigation and made a big effort to block Congress's proposal to have an independent commission investigate the 9/11 terrorist attacks.* Hey, *stupido* (Italian-American slang for a stupid person; here I'm talking to any reader to whom what I just said did not sink in), did you hear what I just said? If you didn't, I'll repeat it one more time: *9/11 was the first attack on American soil in American history and 3,000 Americans were murdered. George Bush never wanted (and did everything he could to stop) any investigation of how and why the tragedy happened, and what could be done to prevent it from happening again!!*

On October 11, 2002, two prominent senators from opposite sides of the aisle (Republican senator John McCain and Democratic senator Joseph Lieberman) openly accused the Bush administration of deliberately sabotaging their efforts to create an independent commission appointed by Congress to investigate 9/11, suggesting the administration was afraid the investigation might turn up government failure. McCain said, "Every bureaucracy in this town is scared to death of an investigation. [McCain, of course, could only be referring to Bush and his executive branch of the government, since *everyone* in the Demo-

---

*Right after Pearl Harbor on December 7, 1941, and the assassination of President John F. Kennedy on November 22, 1963, President Franklin Delano Roosevelt and President Lyndon B. Johnson, respectively, pushed for a federal, nonpartisan investigation of the tragedies, which were thereafter conducted. What other conceivable position could they have taken? *Only* a George Bush would have tried to sabotage an investigation of 9/11.

cratic Party supported the creation of the commission.] No one has really been held accountable [by Bush]. No one has lost their job [i.e., Bush hadn't fired anyone], no one has even been reprimanded [by Bush], nothing has happened as a result of September 11. Unless responsibility is assigned, then we can't cure the problem." Lieberman said, "The question we pose to the White House today is, 'Do you really want to allow this commission to be created? And if you don't, why not?'"

The incredible story that George Bush did not want an independent commission to look into 9/11 should have been a major, front-page headline in all the newspapers of the country, a cover story in all national magazines, and the lead story on all TV and radio shows, with all of the above expressing absolute astonishment and outrage. Everyone in American should have been talking about it. People should have been calling their friends on the phone, saying, "Did you hear what I just heard? You're not going to believe it but President Bush is trying to block an investigation of 9/11. This is unbelievable. Why isn't he being thrown out of office?"

Instead, nothing like this took place. The struggle went on in Congress between Democrats who wanted the investigation and Republicans who did not (Republicans obviously knew that an investigation would reveal that the Bush administration had been grossly derelict in trying to prevent 9/11). What seemed to tip the scales toward the appointment of a commission was a group of four widows of the victims coming to Washington and prodding Congress, as well as pleading over radio and television that there be an investigation. "We simply wanted to know why our husbands were killed, why they went to work one day and didn't come back," they said.

Conducting rallies with signs made from wood they bought at Home Depot; entering and cajoling senators in elevators marked "Senators Only"; and doing whatever else was necessary, including crying, the widows made headway. Although Bush had no interest in knowing why their husbands died, these widows wanted to know why. They kicked up such a storm that a recalcitrant Congress, pressured by Bush and his people to say no, finally yielded and the 9/11

Commission, a bipartisan commission chosen by Congress, was created on November 27, 2002. Their mission was, in the concise language they would later use in their report, to answer the questions, "How did this happen, and how can we avoid such tragedy again?" The chairman of the 9/11 Commission, the former Republican governor of New Jersey, Thomas H. Kean, would later say about the widows: "I doubt very much if we would be in existence without them."

How can it possibly get any worse than for the president of the United States to resist an investigation as to why 3,000 Americans were not protected by the U.S. government and hence had to die? This fact alone should cause any American who loves this country, and has a sense of right and wrong, to have the greatest disgust and contempt for Bush imaginable.

Jumping ahead to the work of the 9/11 Commission, Bush and his people did everything they could to sabotage it. Their main tactic was to deny the commission access to the critical documents the commission sought. It had nothing to do with national security. If it did, the Bush administration would have claimed this and gone to court to resist turning over the documents on that ground, which they did not do. The Bush administration's only purpose in not turning over the documents to the commission, of course, was to prevent the nation's people from learning how much the administration knew about the Al Qaeda threat before 9/11, and how very little it did about it. Remarkably, this stonewalling by the White House itself, as well as Bush's Pentagon, Justice Department, and other federal agencies acting under his direction, was done at the very same time the Bush administration was soaking up and exploiting the credit everyone was giving Bush for his handling of the entire 9/11 crisis. Bush got away with it because other than the editorial pages of the major newspapers, which the vast majority of the public doesn't read, Bush's inexcusable lack of cooperation with the commission was not a major story anywhere in the news.

The obstructionism took different forms, one of which was the Bush administration's insistence that when any member of any federal agency testified before the 9/11 Commission, at least one or more other members of that agency be present. At a July 8, 2003, news conference, 9/11 Commission chairman Thomas Kean openly complained that it was a form of "intimidation" to have "somebody sitting behind you all the time who you either work for or works for your agency. You might get less testimony than you would . . . without [these] minders."

The lack of cooperation got so bad that on October 25, 2003, Kean said that if the White House continued to withhold documents the commission requested, he would issue a subpoena for the documents. "I will not stand for it," Kean said, referring to the Bush administration's deliberate obstructionism. Lieberman said the Bush White House had "resisted this inquiry at every turn. After claiming they wanted to find the truth about September 11, the Bush administration has resorted to secrecy, stonewalling and foot-dragging. President Bush may want to withhold the truth about September 11, but the American people—and especially the victims' families—demand and deserve it." On NBC's *Meet the Press*, Republican senator Charles Hagel urged Bush to cooperate.

The White House backed down, but only a little. Just enough to avoid a subpoena. Bush's lack of cooperation, supported by most Republicans in Congress, was so pronounced that in February of 2004 the commission said it actually could not complete its work by the May 27, 2004, deadline because it did not have access to many crucial documents the Bush administration was withholding, and requested more time to complete its task. Bush and his people said no, vigorously opposing any extension of time. But eventually, and after much pressure, Bush reluctantly agreed to a short two-month extension. However, congressional Republicans, implicitly carrying out Bush's obvious wishes, refused to agree to the extension. Once again, the 9/11 widows kicked up a big storm, demanding an extension, and once again, they succeeded, Congress granting a sixty-day extension. John Feehery, spokesperson for Republican House Speaker representative J. Dennis Hastert, told the media that "public pressure by the 9/11 families" was responsible for Hastert's reversing his position. "There's no doubt about that," Feehery said.

The failure by Bush to cooperate with the commission created to investigate the tragedy extended to his only grudgingly agreeing to meet with the commission and answer questions after months of resistance on his part. But he had strict conditions that he insisted upon, and there were several. He would meet with the full, ten-member commission (originally he said he'd only meet with the chairman and cochairman), but only in private and not under oath (not unreasonable, and consistent with tradition). Also, the session could not be recorded, nor could there be any transcript. What? Also, his appearance had to be limited to one hour, and he refused to appear alone, demanding that Cheney appear with him at his side. (This merely lends credence to late-night comedy routines that Bush is but a puppet of the ventriloquist Cheney.)

Other than meeting in private and not under oath, Bush's requests were out of line, but the commission caved in to each of them and agreed. Condoleezza Rice, knowing full well how preternaturally lazy her boss, Bush, is (and that he has spent more time at his ranch and away from the White House than any other president in history) had the guts and gall to say on NBC's *Meet the Press* about Bush's demand for a limitation of one hour: "I would hope that the Commission would recognize that he's President, and people would be judicious in the use of his time." She said this the same week that Bush found enough time to attend a rodeo in Houston, Texas, and with his well-known daily exercise regimen, spending at a very minimum ten hours exercising. But he was only willing to spend one hour, and no more, with the bipartisan commission investigating the 9/11 tragedy.

One poignant moment during testimony before the 9/11 Commission occurred when Bush's former counterterrorism chief, Richard A. Clarke, began his testimony by telling families of the 9/11 victims, many of whom were in the spectator section of a hushed Senate hearing room, something that it was Bush's job to have done: "Your government failed you. Those entrusted with protecting you failed you. And I failed you . . . I would ask, once all the facts are out, for your understanding and your forgiveness." Relatives of the victims in the room applauded Clarke. It was Bush, of course, who should have apologized to the nation, but if I were to wager, I'd say that the thought never even entered the mind of the terribly arrogant son of privilege. Actually, why would it, when terminally idiotic Americans were giving Bush high approval ratings and making a hero out of him?

It should be noted that although the 9/11 bipartisan commission consisted of distinguished people, they were all political insiders and seemed reluctant or incapable of asking the necessary, tough questions. As Ross Baker, a political scientist at Rutgers University, puts it, the 9/11 Commission members were "very much people who are at the heart of the establishment." Describing their questions as "probing" but not "aggressive," he said, "I think there's a very, very strong disposition to avoid finger pointing. It's very clear that they [didn't] want to single out people for incompetence or not being vigilant."

Indeed, when the 9/11 Commission issued its report on July 22, 2004, Chairman Thomas Kean said, "It is not our purpose to assign blame . . . Our goal is to prevent future attacks." That's just polite politics, though the report was specifically hard on the CIA for its failures. In other words, even if the members of the commission were aghast at Bush's gross irresponsibility and behavior, they never would say this publicly.

Nevertheless, and given the above realities, the conduct of the Bush administration prior to 9/11 was so extremely inept and irresponsible that the commission, in its report, felt compelled to say that before 9/11 the U.S. government (i.e., Bush administration) was hobbled by "failures of imagination, policy, capabilities, and *management*."

When the 9/11 report was issued in July of 2004, the totally shameless Bush, who had done everything he could to make sure the independent bipartisan commission was never formed, said the commission had "done a really good job of learning about what went wrong prior to September 11" and that it had "identified steps we can take to better defend America [in the future]," both of which, Mr. Bush, you did your best to prevent them from doing.

With respect to the forty-one recommendations made by the commission to improve our nation's security, on December 5, 2005, almost a year and a half later, the 9/11 Public Discourse Project, a watchdog group established by the commission when it went out of business to monitor the Bush administration and grade it on its efforts to comply with their recommendations, gave the administration seventeen F's and D's. They gave the administration only one A, an A minus at that, for efforts to stem the financing of terrorist networks. Commission chairman Thomas Kean said, "Many obvious steps that the American people assume have been completed have not been. Our leadership is distracted," a euphemistic way of saying that Bush, who did nothing to prevent 9/11, was doing very, very little to ensure that it never happened again.

Before we move on, it should be reiterated that the 9/11 Commission, after a twenty-month investigation, said they could find no "collaborative relationship" between Iraq and Al Qaeda, and no evidence that Iraq was involved in 9/11.

7. At this point, you should be beyond shock at the terrible performance of Bush, but there is so much more. Let me give you a little background on this next matter. The words used to describe Bush's stance on terrorism by those who love him as well as the simpleton media are "steadfast" and "resolute" and "unflagging." Even most of those who don't like Bush, like Jonathan Alter, use words like this, conceding this point. *But it would hardly be humanly possible for him to be less steadfast*. Other than going after the terrorists whom he himself gave birth to in his invasion of Iraq, which obviously cannot count since the war in Iraq continues, Bush has only pursued (and then, extremely poorly) one group of terrorists in this whole world—Bin Laden and his Al Qaeda. No one else.

And before I enumerate just how "steadfast" he has been in his pursuit of Bin Laden, let me remind you of something you might not be thinking about. How often do you read a fairly long personal interest story in your daily newspaper about a detective in the police department of your city who has very nearly dedicated his life to finding the murderer of someone who was killed many years ago, often, twenty, twenty-five, thirty years ago? Frequently, he continues the pursuit even after he retires. He feels he won't be able to rest in peace until he finds, for instance, the killer of the young woman he found dead, lying in a pool of blood on the floor of her home, her throat slashed, and her baby sitting next to her crying loudly. Usually, at the time you read the story you have long forgotten about the murder, and just as frequently, if you live in a big city, the murder may have only been reported in a small article on an inside, back page of the paper when it happened, or not at all. And nearly always, as you well know, you read in the paper (maybe in the same article about the detective) that the killer has been apprehended in some far-off state living under an assumed name, and he is returning to the city to be prosecuted for a murder he committed several decades earlier. This happens all the time. Major homicide bureaus in big cities even have what they call "cold case" files that remain open, and the bureau pursues the killer for years and years, sometimes as many as fifty to sixty years.

That's life, real life in the big city, and with real human beings who care, care about bringing about justice for the victims of terrible murders. Yes, even though they are dead, they are entitled to justice. (Certainly their surviving loved ones are.) Near the end of my final summation in the Charles Manson murder trial in 1971, I gave what the newspapers would come to call my "roll call of the dead," the seven Tate–La Bianca victims. After each name I paused, so the jurors could stop and think, really think about the fact that the name wasn't just a name, but one that belonged to a human being who at one time lived and breathed just as they were now. Too often, in the heat of battle at a trial, and with all the legal procedures, issues, and complexities being wrangled over by lawyers on both sides, people tend to forget about the victims, whose death is the only reason for the trial. "Ladies and gentlemen of the jury," I quietly began, "Sharon Tate . . . Abigail Folger . . . Voytek Frykowski . . . Jay Sebring . . . Steven Parent . . . Leno La Bianca . . . Rosemary La Bianca . . . are not here with us now in this courtroom, *but from their graves*," I said in an increasingly loud crescendo, *"they cry out for justice.* Justice can only be served by coming back into this courtroom with a verdict of guilty."

So we know how unheralded detectives, quietly and tenaciously and steadfastly pursue, for several decades, the killer of just one human being, and almost desperately want to find him and bring him back to face justice. Let's see now what Bush did with his pursuit of Bin Laden, the murderer of not one, but 3,000 Americans.

In December of 2001, just a few months after 9/11, the American military learned that Bin Laden was hiding in Tora Bora, a dense mountain range in southeastern Afghanistan. By the way, not only was Bin Laden there, but for the Bush lovers who say we don't know for sure that he was, that is irrelevant. I personally saw on television Secretary of Defense Rumsfeld say at a TV press conference that they had located Bin Laden in Tora Bora and he was trapped there. So even if he wasn't there (and subsequent evidence has confirmed that he was), the Bush administration cannot use this as an excuse for their absolutely incredible conduct. That conduct has to be viewed from the state of mind we know they had, which was the belief that Bin Laden was at Tora Bora. And what was that conduct? Instead of sending thousands of American soldiers to go into the mountain range to capture or kill Bin Laden, *Bush did not send one single American soldier.* He only dispatched forty American Special Forces soldiers there to coordinate the bombing, by U.S. B-52 bombers, of caves and areas in the mountain where Bin Laden, the world's most wanted man, was believed to be.

The job of capturing Bin Laden was given to three anti-Taliban Afghan warlords and their men. Haji Mohammed Zaman, one of the warlords, in disbelief and frustration told the assembled press who had converged on Tora Bora: "If America wants to capture Osama, why aren't they trying?" A top aide to Zaman said: "I don't think the United States wants to capture Osama. We know where he is, we tell them and they do nothing. So they are not as serious as they say they are." Also, knowing Bin Laden's most likely route of escape (to cross the southeastern border of Afghanistan into Pakistan), instead of massing thousands of American soldiers along that border, the United States decided (I also heard Rumsfeld say this on television) that they were going to rely on the Pakistani military (with no help from us) to prevent Bin Laden from escaping. Unbelievably, then, Bush, that ballsy, steadfast, great fighter of terrorism, decided to rely on Afghan warlords and the Pakistan military to capture the most important terrorist of all, Bin Laden, who was responsible for the murder of 3,000 Americans on September 11, 2001. To repeat, *Bush did not use one American soldier*. It almost seemed like Bush was more interested in Bin Laden and what he had done as a pretext to invade Iraq than he was in capturing him.

This is 2008, seven long years after Bin Laden murdered over 3,000 American citizens, and Bush promised to bring him back "dead or alive." Where is the outrage in America that this mass murderer is still a free man, free to make threatening videotapes and plan further attacks upon us? The lack of outrage in America over the fact that Bin Laden has not been brought to justice is nothing short of astonishing.

The Bush administration, embarrassed by its having allowed Bin Laden to escape, came up with the preposterous excuse that they didn't pursue Bin Laden at Tora Bora because they wanted to minimize American casualties and they also wanted to prevent the war in Afghanistan from being viewed by the world as an "American war." But why shouldn't it be an American war? Weren't Americans the only victims of 9/11? So the ballsy, brave Bush didn't feel that going after someone who had murdered 3,000 Americans was really, after all, a good idea (and he got a 90 percent approval rating and was re-elected precisely because he said he would). Instead, we should let the Afghan warlords and Pakistani military (mostly Muslims, who at least religiously and culturally were not antagonistic to Bin Laden), whose people were *not* murdered by Bin Laden, go after him. Yet the outrageous Bush was willing to send 150,000 American soldiers to risk their lives in Iraq to get Saddam Hussein, who we know was as innocent of complicity in 9/11 as a newborn baby.

Lutfullah Mashal, a senior spokesperson for the Afghanistan Interior Ministry, confirmed in 2005 what everyone already assumed, that Bin Laden had paid for his escape from Tora Bora into Pakistan. But the recipients of the money were not the Pakistani military, as some had assumed, but Afghan commanders loyal to Maulvi Yunus Khalis.

Khalis was a top mujahedin leader during the Afghan-Soviet War whose family compound Bin Laden, with his four wives and many children, moved into for a while. Mashal said, "The help was provided because of monetary aid [provided] by Al Qaeda and also partly because of ideological issues" (among which, naturally, was the fact that everyone on both sides was Muslim).

In 2005, August Hanning, the head of German intelligence, confirmed this, saying his agency had learned that Bin Laden had been able to elude capture at Tora Bora by paying "a lot of money" to the very same militias of the Afghan warlords to whom the United States had delegated (outsourced) the task of capturing him, and they allowed his safe passage into Pakistan.

And listen to this. As reported in *USA Today* and never denied by the Bush administration: "In 2002, troops from the Fifth Special Forces Group who specialize in the Middle East were pulled out of the hunt for Osama Bin Laden to prepare for their next assignment, Iraq." So way back in 2002, going after Hussein, who had nothing to do with 9/11, was more important than going after Bin Laden, who was responsible for the catastrophe. And Bush is the one whom the morons in the media, with graduate degrees in nitwitolgy, continued to praise for his "tough," "steadfast," and "resolute" stand against terrorism. It's enough to make the cat cry.

It has to be added that the incomprehensible and virtually psychotic posture of the Bush administration to let Bin Laden, who was responsible for 9/11, go free, yet engage in a terribly costly and long war against Iraq, which had no connection with 9/11, continues, believe it or not, to this very day. While the Bush administration persists in carrying on the bloody fight in Iraq, it has pledged to Pakistan that it will honor Pakistan's territorial sovereignty and not cross the border of Afghanistan to pursue Bin Laden into Pakistan, where we know he is presently headquartered. So we wouldn't pursue the mastermind of 9/11 at Tora Bora, nor will we do so in Pakistan, even though no invasion would be involved since Pakistan is our ally. But we were very willing to invade Iraq and fight a monstrous war there. And remember, this was all over 9/11, and not only was Iraq completely innocent of 9/11, but *like the United States*, it was a sworn enemy of the very group, Al Qaeda, that *was* responsible for 9/11, which made Iraq a natural ally of ours against Al Qaeda. How can the conduct of Bush make any sense to a rational person?

Before we continue, one very important observation has to be made that I can assure you most Americans have completely forgotten—if they were ever aware of it. When I was talking earlier about Bush never sending one American soldier after Bin Laden at Tora Bora, relying on Afghan warlord allies to do so, this actually was no shock at all to anyone following the Afghan war. I say this because up until and through December of 2001, when Bin Laden was at Tora Bora, Bush had decided he did not want America to "fight" *anyone* in Afghanistan. Yes, you heard me right. When I said previously, in talking about Dennis Miller, that there was no justification for Miller and everyone else heaping praise on Bush for "going after" those who attacked America on 9/11, because *"anyone* holding the office of the presidency" would likewise have done so, I was speaking very loosely (to Bush's benefit) because *Bush never even did this!!!* You see, the evidence is clear that Bush decided that America was not going to go after Bin Laden and Al Qaeda and the Taliban in Afghanistan. Instead, he was going to have someone else do it for America—Afghan allies of America called the Northern Alliance, a U.S.-backed resistance movement formally known as the United Islamic Front for the Salvation of Afghanistan.

Although eventually U.S. soldiers fought in Afghanistan, from the day of the invasion (commenced by air strikes) in Afghanistan on October 7, 2001, through December 7, when the Taliban regime collapsed, *not one single American soldier died in combat.** Why? Because the real fighting in the Afghan war was being done almost exclusively by the Northern Alliance. Our military was only there in an advisory and support capacity to the Northern Alliance, and our air force, from its safe position high in the clouds beyond the range of the very limited

---

*The first American combat casualty in Afghanistan was Sgt. 1st Class Nathan Ross Chapman, who was killed on January 4, 2002, *three months after the war commenced.*

Taliban antiaircraft artillery, dropped bombs on the almost medieval country. If you want to call this "fighting" a war, then you have a different view than I do of what this word means.

So all Bush did was *vow* to go after those responsible for 9/11, and those who harbored them (the Taliban). *He didn't actually do it*, though a mentally anesthetized nation gave him immense credit for doing so. Even if he had, as I indicated earlier, he would have been entitled to no credit at all, since anyone in his shoes would have done the same thing. *But he didn't even do this*, deciding to fight a war by proxy, achieving victory on the cheap *by having others fight for America*.

As Major General Frank L. Hagenbeck told reporters in a briefing in Bagram, Afghanistan, on February 26, 2002: *"We want the Afghans to go after these guys. It's their country."* (Yes, but it was 3,000 Americans who were killed by Bin Laden and his Al Qaeda on 9/11, not 3,000 Afghans.) You have to know, of course, that General Hagenbeck did not make this decision. He was only carrying out the orders of George Bush and his administration.

A man is seated with his wife at a restaurant table. An armed killer enters the restaurant, shoots and kills the wife, then flees. The man, who everyone would automatically assume would pursue the killer since it was his wife who was killed, and since, it turns out, he was fully armed to do so, decides not to. He tells a stranger at a nearby table that he would appreciate it if he would pursue the killer, which the third party does. That's *exactly* what Bush did in the Afghanistan war. Three thousand Americans were murdered, Bush *vowed* to go after the perpetrators, but instead asked the Northern Alliance, which never lost one of its members during 9/11, to in effect "get even" with the 9/11 killers *for* us. Shocking? Unbelievable? Yes, but 100 percent true. And through all of this, Bush's approval rating remained extremely high (84 percent in a January 2002 Gallup poll), and we learned from the likes of Al Neurath and Dennis Miller how very brave and ballsy Bush was.

With respect to Bush not wanting to use one American soldier to fight the Afghan war, it wasn't until March 4, 2002, *five months after the war commenced*, that American soldiers started fighting in a normal, military way. This, from the March 5, 2002, edition of the *New York Times*: "In some of the fiercest fighting of the five-month war in Afghanistan, American ground forces took the lead in a large-scale combat operation *for the first time*, American officials said."

And even then, our military involvement in the war was still taking a backseat to the Northern Alliance. A March 10, 2002, headline in the *New York Times* read: "Afghans' Retreat *Forced* Americans to Lead a Battle." The article read, in part: "American troops were unexpectedly *forced* to do the fiercest fighting in Afghanistan this week after an allied Afghan general retreated under withering fire from . . . Al Qaeda. Soldiers from the Army's 10th Mountain and 101st Airborne Division moved quickly to fill the breach left by their bloodied Afghan allies."

Bottom line: Although 3,000 Americans were murdered by Bin Laden's Al Qaeda on 9/11, and we knew the Taliban was harboring Bin Laden and his Al Qaeda—and although Bush was receiving towering praise in America from Republicans as well as Democrats for his supposedly tough stance against terrorism and his vow to bring back Bin Laden "dead or alive" and to "make no distinction between the terrorists who committed these acts and those who harbored them"—Bush's original intent was to not send one American soldier to go after Bin Laden, Al Qaeda, and the Taliban,* all of whom were responsible for 9/11. But Bush was very, very eager, to the point of lying to the American public to get his way, to put over 150,000 American soldiers in harm's way to go after Saddam Hussein, who he knew had nothing to do with 9/11.

For the next thing I'm going to tell you, which actually is completely consistent with what you have just read, I suggest you strap yourself in your seat because it could affect your physical equilibrium if you are standing. I'm going to tell you something that is going to

---

*One might say it's wonderful that we could bring about the collapse of the Taliban without the loss of one American life by having someone else fight *our* war for us. And I would agree. But just because it's wonderful doesn't mean it's anything to be proud of, which it certainly is not. Also, probably because of this approach, we never did capture Bin Laden and bring him to justice.

cause you to say, "Impossible. I don't believe Bush said this." But he said it all right. It's just that if you're like ninety-nine out of a hundred people, you weren't listening.

Recall that many detectives throughout the land frequently pursue relentlessly the killer of just one murder victim for fifteen, twenty, twenty-five years. Now let's just look at the state of mind of George Bush on his feelings about the killer of 3,000 American victims *just six months* after the murders of 9/11. In a March 13, 2002, press conference, a reporter said to Bush: "Mr. President, in your speeches now you rarely talk about or mention Osama Bin Laden. Why is that?" The man who vowed to get Bin Laden "dead or alive" answered: "This is a fellow [since Bush is now unscripted, Bin Laden has become a "fellow," language that is remindful of his use of "folks" outside of the Florida classroom to describe those responsible for 9/11] who is willing to commit youngsters to their death and he, himself, tries to hide." (Bush could well have been describing himself as he committed young American soldiers to their death in fighting his war, yet he himself hid out during the Vietnam War.) Then the "steadfast" and "resolute" fighter of terrorism, George Bush, proceeded to say, unbelievably, the following, which is, again, *just six months* after 9/11: "So I don't know where he is. You know, *I just don't spend that much time on him, to be honest with you . . . I truly am not that concerned about him.* I *was* concerned about him when he had taken over a country [Afghanistan]." So while detectives think about the killer of one person for years and years, *Bush had apparently stopped thinking about Bin Laden just six months after Bin Laden murdered 3,000 Americans!!** Bin Laden has been routinely described as "the world's most wanted man." But

---

*The above is in keeping with what former U.S. senator Bob Graham, who was chairman of the Senate Select Committee on Intelligence in 2002, wrote in an op-ed piece in the *Washington Post* on November 20, 2005: "In February 2002 [one month before Bush's remarks about Bin Laden at the press conference], after a briefing on the status of the war in Afghanistan, the commanding officer, General Tommy Franks, told me the war was being compromised as specialized personnel and equipment were being shifted from Afghanistan to prepare for the war in Iraq—a war more than a year away."

not, apparently, to Bush, who decided that the world's most wanted man was Hussein, someone who had nothing to do with 9/11.

By the way, at the aforementioned press conference Bush said, in an apparent attempt to justify his state of mind about Bin Laden, that "terror is bigger than one person." While terror is bigger than one person, what does that have to do with the price of tea in China? So what? To capture or kill the main person who was responsible for 9/11, the founder as well as the active and spiritual leader of the world's main terrorist organization, would have to be *a* principal objective of *any* sensible leader, just like we tried to kill Hitler during the Second World War. During my prosecution of Manson and three female members of his "family" for the Tate–La Bianca murders, I told the media that "if I convict Manson's co-defendants, and he walks out of court, it will be an unsuccessful prosecution."

Furthermore, even if we were to assume, just for the sake of argument, a situation we know doesn't exist—that Bin Laden no longer had any control or influence over Al Qaeda, perhaps that he even retired, and was no longer a threat to the security of this country—what about this thing called justice? What about the 3,000 murders Bin Laden committed? Don't we absolutely *have* to capture him, bring him back to this country, and after a trial and conviction, put him to death for what he did? Take the situation we spoke about earlier. A killer gets away, changes his name, and for twenty to thirty years is living elsewhere, never repeating his crime again, and is no longer a threat to any other human, much less a nation. Yet a lone detective, wanting to bring about justice for a single homicide, pursues the killer to the ends of the earth for years and years. If a lone detective can seek justice for one murder, how is it possible that Bush had already apparently lost interest in seeking justice for 3,000 murders?

Remarkably, *in the very same press conference* in which Bush said, in effect, that he wasn't thinking about Bin Laden anymore, he said, "The *more firm* we are and the *more determined* we are to take care of Al Qaeda," the better chance we have "of solving some difficult problems . . . But it's going to require a *resolve and firmness* from the United States of America. If the United States were to waver, some in the world would take a nap when it comes to the war of terrorism. And we're just not going to let them do that. [This is] why I'm *so determined* to remain *firm* in my *resolve.*" That Bush would use these words to describe himself, after just admitting that he had already lost interest in pursuing Bin Laden, the architect of 9/11, and no one blinked an eye, is simply incredible.

One footnote to the above. The July 4, 2006, *New York Times* reported that "the Central Intelligence Agency has closed the unit that for a decade had the mission of hunting Osama Bin Laden and his top lieutenants, intelligence officials confirmed Monday. The unit, known as Alec Station, was disbanded late last year and its analysts reassigned within the CIA to a Counterterrorist Center, the official said. The decision is a milestone for the agency, which formed the unit before Osama Bin Laden became a household name, and bolstered its ranks after the September 11 attacks when President Bush pledged to bring Bin Laden to justice 'dead or alive.'" Isn't that something?

8. The most unbelievable thing Bush did in his so-called war on terrorism has already been alluded to in this chapter. Instead of making an all-out effort to capture Bin Laden and destroy his Al Qaeda, Bush all but stopped the pursuit of Bin Laden and hence, the *real* war against terrorism, and diverted most of the American military's strength to going after Saddam Hussein and invading Iraq, a nation that was not our enemy, had no terrorists, was not involved in any way in 9/11, and represented absolutely no threat to this country. (A report published in January 2004 by the U.S. Army War College strongly criticized the Bush administration for its "war on terrorism" as being "unfocused," pointing out that the war in Iraq was "unnecessary" and a "detour" that had diverted attention and resources away from the real threat posed by Bin Laden and Al Qaeda.) It would be difficult to imagine a more colossal and incomprehensible failure by the leader of any nation.

As indicated previously in this book, to this day we don't know for sure why Bush started his war in far-off Iraq. But going after Hussein in Iraq when Bin Laden was in Afghanistan or Pakistan recalls the vaudevillian skit where a man is on his knees searching for something at night beneath a lamppost. When a passerby asks him what he's looking for, he tells him it's his car keys. "When did you lose them?" the passerby asks. "About five minutes ago when I was walking down the block," he says, pointing some distance away to the darkness. "So why are you looking for them here?" the passerby asks. "Because there's better lighting here," the man says. So instead of Bush giving Bin Laden a bullet or noose for killing 3,000 Americans, he gave Bin Laden the best birthday present imaginable by invading Iraq, fulfilling Bin Laden's wildest dream that there be an abundant supply of virulently anti-American terrorists for years to come.

As noted, the Taliban regime in Afghanistan fell on December 7, 2001. However, by diverting most of our military forces from Afghanistan to Iraq shortly thereafter, we squandered our opportunity to truly finish off the Taliban. We know this is so because the Taliban has reemerged as a much stronger force than it was during the brief Afghan war, inflicting hundreds of casualties on American forces in an ongoing war, whereas prior to December 7, 2001, as indicated earlier, they had inflicted none. We never, under any of the existing circumstances, should have invaded Iraq. But to do so before we completed our mission in Afghanistan of capturing Bin Laden and destroying Al Qaeda and the Taliban makes Bush's conduct all the more incomprehensible and egregiously wrong.

If we were living in a normal country, what happened on September 17, 2003, should have been the biggest story of the year, with the entire nation talking about it. Saddam Hussein had as much to do with 9/11 as you or I. But that's not the point. There can be no question that Bush, by his very strong innuendo, led Americans to believe that he did. And the majority of Americans believed it at the time. In fact, as we know, as late as 2006, five years after 9/11, 90 percent of the soldiers in Iraq said they thought Hussein was involved in 9/11. So that's the important point—what people thought. As indicated earlier, on

September 17, 2003, six months *after we invaded Iraq* under the belief, by most Americans, that Hussein was involved in 9/11, Bush, only in response to a reporter's question, said, *"No, we've had no evidence that Saddam Hussein was involved with September 11th."* (Say what?!?!) This should have been a screaming headline all over America, and everyone, on radio, TV, and on the streets should have been talking about it. One reason they didn't is that the press virtually ignored it. Conservatives always speak of the "liberal press" and believe the *New York Times* represents the citadel of American liberalism. Do you know where the story in the *New York Times* about Bush's admission was? Page 16 of the next day's paper. So either that paper is not liberal (no paper savaged Clinton more during the Monica Lewinsky affair than the *New York Times*), or liberals simply don't know how to fight. If this had happened to Clinton, the right-wing, who are natural (and mostly dirty) fighters, would have seized on this in an extraordinarily major way.

And when the 9/11 Commission said on June 16, 2004, that they could find no evidence that Hussein had anything to do with 9/11 or Al Qaeda, the story didn't get anywhere near the attention it should have, although several papers in the country did at least make a headline out of it. However, they used words from which an inference had to be drawn (far too much for most Americans, who have to have a bib put on them and be spoon-fed) that Hussein had no connection with 9/11. For example, the June 17, 2004, *New York Times* headline read: "Panel Finds No Qaeda-Iraq Tie."

When the 9/11 Commission found that Hussein had nothing to do with Al Qaeda or 9/11, the story should have swept the country like wildfire. Very angry and outraged Americans, feeling Bush had either deliberately misled them into war, or was terribly and dangerously incompetent in taking this nation into an ill-advised war, should have been calling for Bush's scalp. His defeat at the polls should have been automatic, Kerry winning in an overwhelming landslide. But as we know, no such thing happened.

Everything I've mentioned thus far on the pages of this book about Bush's mind-boggling failures fighting terrorism had *already* taken place when American voters went to the ballot box in the 2004 presidential election on November 2, 2004. Yet *Time* magazine reported that of those voters who said terrorism was their leading concern, an astonishing 85 percent voted for Bush. (Only 15 percent had confidence in the genuine war hero, Kerry.) Knowing that stupidity is not benign, if you don't find this scary, what *is* scary to you?

Although the things that follow are well known, they are so important on the issues of Bush's extreme failure in his war against terrorism, and the incalculable damage and harm he has done, that they bear repeating. Everyone knows what a disaster the war in Iraq has become—that no weapons of mass destruction were found; that apart from Kurdish territory, Bush literally physically destroyed and set aflame an entire nation, one that before the war was a stable nation; that Bush, against the counsel of his own military, never sent anywhere near the number of troops into Iraq that would have been necessary to not only defeat Saddam Hussein's military but to also secure the peace by not allowing the insurgency to even get off the ground; that, remarkably, Bush and his people engaged in virtually no postwar planning at all, something that is automatic when a nation, intending to win a war, is preparing for that war.

We also all know that Iraq had no terrorists before Bush invaded it. The only one we know of who was in Iraq was Abu Mousab al Zarqawi. But not only were his ties to Bin Laden shaky and tenuous, if they existed at all, more importantly, he had no ties or relationship with Hussein. Moreover, he operated in Kurdish territory, which was outside the control of Hussein.

Bush's war, then, has turned a completely nonterrorist nation into a nation with many terrorists in it, Iraq serving as a magnet for Islamic terrorists from other nations to join the native Iraqi insurgents in a fight against an America they both hate. *So Bush created terrorism in Iraq*, with thousands upon thousands of innocent, everyday Iraqis targeted by suicide bombers paying the ultimate price by losing their lives in markets, restaurants, mosques, etc. Bush's invasion of Iraq, we all know, thrust Iraq into a bloody, rudderless chaos, a civil war between Sunnis and Shiites where American soldiers, caught in the middle of the carnage and crossfire, are being killed by members of both groups, the very people, ironically, Bush said he wanted to liberate.

We also know that before Bush invaded Iraq, the majority of Iraqi people led safe, productive lives as long as they did not oppose Hussein, were free to pursue any lifestyle or religion they wanted—Muslim, Christian, gay, etc.—and walk the streets of Baghdad or any other city at two in the morning without any fear. Since the invasion they are afraid to go anywhere outside their homes, a great many even being murdered there. And children, on their way to school, routinely see dead bodies and decapitated heads out on the street, even bodies hanging from lampposts, a virtual nightmare the likes of which hasn't ever been depicted in any Hollywood horror film.

Before Bush, Baghdad was a relatively modern city with perhaps the finest university in the Mideast. Women had virtually full equality with men. They were free to become doctors, lawyers, etc. and enjoyed personal freedoms, the *Los Angeles Times* noted, "undreamed of by women in neighboring [Muslim] nations"—a far cry from what their lives will be like if Iraq becomes a Shiite theocracy.

On March 14, 2003, just days before Bush's invasion, although the people of Iraq were worried about what was going to happen if the invasion actually took place, the *New York Times* found them to be going on with their regular lifestyles. A featured article in the paper started with a reporter's visit to the Amiriya racetrack and his interviews with jockeys, racetrack employees, and bettors. The reporter observed that life among the Iraqi people—other than the omnipresent photos and paintings of Hussein and the realization that no Iraqi was free to challenge his rule, those that did being brutally murdered—mirrored life in the United States. "Perhaps 5,000 people turned up at the track to watch the eight-race card, about average for a Friday meeting. In the city, pool halls and Ottoman-era coffee shops and pinball arcades were busy as usual. The expressways that crisscross the Dallas [Texas] that Saddam Hussein's bulldozers have made of one of the oldest cities in the Arab world . . . were busy carrying families out to stroll in the park, or to linger over kebab lunches in restaurants, or to visit friends."

One pre-invasion image of Iraq that sticks in my mind was on the television news a few nights before the war started: two young Iraqi adults, speaking surprisingly good English, talked on the sidewalk with an American newsman while eating ice cream cones.

We know that before the war, Iraq, although poor because of UN-imposed sanctions following the Persian Gulf War, was a fully functioning country with a very low unemployment rate. Since the war, unemployment has skyrocketed, at one point reaching a staggering 50 percent. And while Baghdad and most of Iraq's cities had regular electricity for lighting, heat, and air conditioning, only a few hours a day are now available to the nation's citizens, and sanitation services are almost nonexistent.

We know that before Bush invaded Iraq, the Shiites and Sunnis lived peacefully with each other, and now members of both sects have viciously killed one another in great numbers. Also, that almost 5 million Iraqis (in a nation of only twenty-four million) have been driven from their homes. Two million have actually fled the country, leaving virtually all of their belongings behind. The remaining 3 million are living with friends or relatives or in makeshift shelters. Of those who fled the country, a disproportionately large percentage are from the nation's professional class of doctors, lawyers, scientists, engineers, and educators, the very people the country needs to rebuild Iraq into a functioning society. A Sunni Iraqi pathologist said, "it will take a decade just to train new physicians," almost half of whom have been part of the exodus. He said the war "has turned the country into an empty vessel, drained of talent." Two *Los Angeles Times* staff writers, reporting from Baghdad on January 6, 2008, said, "Hundreds of thousands of skilled professionals have left the country. Businesses have closed. Insurgents and thugs have targeted professors, doctors and businesspeople, killing them, abducting them or driving them out of their jobs and out of Iraq." This, from a nation that was almost free of crime before the war.

And it has to be noted that a September 2006 poll showed that about six out of ten Iraqi citizens actually approved of attacks on U.S. forces. Slightly more than that do not even want us in their country, viewing us not as liberators but as invaders and occupiers.

We also know that the invasion of Iraq was opposed and clearly denounced by the overwhelming majority of people throughout the civilized world, even in countries like Britain, Spain, and Italy whose weak leaders went along with Bush's suicidal (and homicidal) mission.* We know that Bush and his war have caused our traditional allies and people throughout the world not only to lose substantial respect for us, but for the first time ever, to disrespect the once great United States of America. Indeed, polls now consistently show that although the United States, before Bush, was the most widely respected nation in the world, the majority of people in the world today now have a negative feeling about the United States. This is particularly true, of course, in the vast Muslim world, where we were never popular, but which now abhors us for invading, without any justification at all, a sovereign and fellow-Muslim nation. Out of the blood and debris of the Iraq war, how many young Bin Ladens will we eventually have to deal with down the line, whom Bush created when their mother, father, brother, sister, wife, or child was killed (and in some instances murdered) by Bush's soldiers fighting for George Bush in George Bush's war?

Indeed, the CIA's 2006 National Intelligence Estimate (to repeat, the consensus view of all sixteen federal agencies that comprise the U.S. intelligence community), released on September 26, 2006, confirmed that Bush's crazy war against terrorism (going after nonterrorist Iraq) has not only been unsuccessful but counterproductive, making America *less* safe than before. The report said that although the U.S. effort had seriously damaged the leadership of Al Qaeda and

---

*It is estimated that an incredible 36 million people took to the streets in six hundred cities throughout the world to demonstrate against Bush's threat to invade Iraq. In Rome, 3 million people participated in the largest antiwar protest ever. In Barcelona, 1.3 million protested; in London, 1 million, and in Melbourne and Sydney, Australia, 500,000.

disrupted its operations, "a large body of all-source reporting [from around the world] indicates that activists identifying themselves as jihadists . . . are *increasing in both number and geographic dispersion*. If this trend continues, threats to U.S. interests at home and abroad will become more diverse, leading to increasing attacks." The CIA's 2007 National Intelligence Estimate, released on July 17, 2007, was no more reassuring. The report said, "We judge that the United States currently is in a heightened threat environment."

We also know, of course, that over 100,000 people have died horrible, violent deaths in the war, including 4,000 young American soldiers and thousands upon thousands of innocent Iraqi civilians, including women and children, even babies. And untold thousands of Americans and Iraqis have suffered devastating psychic damage and disabling physical injuries. Also, the war has been a prodigious drain on the American economy, costing us $250 million per day and more than $1 trillion thus far, with no light at the end of the tunnel.

Remarkably, with the worst track record in the war on terrorism conceivable, in the past year or two Bush and his people have come up with new disparaging terms to describe the Democratic Party's position on Iraq, calling Democrats "quitters" and people who want to "cut and run" because they want to end our disastrous war in Iraq by bringing our young soldiers home as soon as possible.

When you see Bush and Cheney (and their right-wing supporters) *still*, after seven years, with all we have seen and all that we know happened, shamelessly continuing to use their 9/11 failure and their insane and disastrous war against Iraq not only as assets and weapons for political victory, but to depict innocent Democrats as dangerously weak traitors to America, the thought that comes into one's mind, even a civilized and timid one, is that only a figurative stake through the heart could ever stop these diabolically monstrous charlatans.

I cannot leave this section without at least a brief reference to a very predictable but nauseating phenomenon that was under way at the time this book went to press in mid-March of 2008. I'm talking about some of the painfully brainless members of the media buying into the Bush administration's propaganda that we finally are "winning" the war in Iraq. And when you have the stupid (media) influencing the ignorant (masses), well, that's a toxic combination. Let's look at this dynamic at play. In a front-page *New York Times* story on November 25, 2007, the reporter said that since violence was declining in Iraq,* Democrats would have to acknowledge "that *success.*" He then went on with his self-fulfilling prophecy for the masses to live up to by saying that "the changing situation suggests for the first time that the politics of the war *could shift* in the general election next year (in other words, favor the Republican Party whose president gave us the horrible war), *particularly if the gains continue.*"

This terrible nonsense—that the only thing that is important is what is happening at the moment—has been echoed many times in the past several months, despite the fact that the situation in Iraq remains terrible, with thousands of Iraqi civilians and hundreds of American soldiers continuing to die violent deaths. The horrors and monstrous crimes of the past not only are forgiven and forgotten, *they never even happened.* You know, 100,000 people haven't already died in the Iraq war. No, really. They're still alive, leading normal, regular lives with their families. You didn't know that? And the country of Iraq was never decimated. Look around and see. It looks just like it did before the war. And people of the world don't look down on America. Really. Just ask them. And the more than $1 trillion that people claim have been spent by America on the Iraq war was never spent. It's still in the U.S. Treasury.

Just like the expression "What have you done recently?" the past doesn't count. All that counts is now, and violence is down, which means that we should not only celebrate, but declare that we're on

---

*Wouldn't it have to be after five years? I mean, there are only so many adversaries to kill. As columnist Rosa Brooks observed: "The process of 'sectarian cleansing' is nearing completion: Sunnis have been driven out of Shiite neighborhoods [by mass murders], and Shiites out of Sunni neighborhoods."

the road to victory. "Victory is within our grasp," conservative columnist Max Boot exclaimed on January 28, 2008. But *what* victory? That
Hussein was an imminent threat to the security of our country and
we eliminated him and destroyed his weapons of mass destruction?
That there is real democracy in Iraq, and this democracy is spreading
throughout the Middle East? That Bin Laden has been captured and
executed and his Al Qaeda destroyed and they are no longer a threat
to this nation?

With no end in sight for the war, and the worst atrocities imaginable still being routinely perpetrated, and the once bustling, safe and
open metropolis of Baghdad being reduced to a city of high concrete
walls and military checkpoints to help keep the Sunni and Shiite death
squads out and the murders down, America is not only starting to
show signs, with the help of the mindless media, of settling for fewer
dead bodies, but of pronouncing the whole disastrous adventure a success. In other words, instead of the absolutely horrible and intolerable
situation in today's Iraq being viewed as *terrible* but better than it once
was, it is viewed as *good* because it's not as bad as it once was.

Terrible is good, black is white, up is down. The insanity continues, and the bodies keep being buried, and Bush keeps smiling.

6

AMERICA,
UP OR DOWN?

I SHOULD TELL YOU that I don't think too much of modern-
day America. It's not the America I grew up in, one I had always
assumed was the greatest nation in the world. In fact, I do not
believe that America is a great nation anymore. If the only criterion
for being a great nation is military power and wealth, then of course
America is still a great nation. But I suspect that when, during most of
the twentieth century, people throughout the world said America was
a "great nation" or "great country," they weren't just referring to our
military strength and wealth, but to the type of nation we were, what
America stood for. Today, polls show that people around the world no
longer look up to America as a great nation. In fact, the majority of
the world's people have a negative feeling about America, and a great
many regard it with contempt. These are the very same people, or
their parents, who used to look way up to this country.

Although every single one of the following nations had a very positive opinion about the United States in the past half century, less than
three years of Bush being president had passed when 67% of the people in France already had a negative feeling about America (and 87%
were opposed to Bush's war). Other figures were 71% (and 85%

against war) in Germany; 40% (and 60%) in Britain; 59% (and 76%) in Italy; 74% (and 79%) in Spain; and 68% (and 83%) in Russia. Andrew Kohut, director of the Pew Research Center, which conducted the international poll between March 10 and 17, 2003, said, "This is the most negative international public opinion about America and an American president that I've ever seen."

How can a nation be considered great if it invades another country (Iraq) in violation of international law—a country not its enemy and not a threat to its own security—something unprecedented in America history? And perhaps worse yet, after America did this its people cheered its leader, Bush, on, the vast majority thinking it was just fine when we did this. And this support continued *even after*, mind you, we learned there were no weapons of mass destruction in Iraq (the main, stated purpose for the invasion) and *even after* Bush acknowledged there was no evidence connecting Hussein and Iraq with 9/11, which had started the whole movement toward war in the first place.

In the midterm elections in 2006, the Democrats, just barely, gained control of the Senate and House of Representatives. Immediately, liberal columnists, even particularly bright ones like Paul Krugman of the *New York Times*, declared that the nation had finally, finally turned on the administration of George Bush because they were fed up with the excesses of right-wing politics, and more importantly, they finally realized that going to war in Iraq was wrong. But it is these columnists who were wrong. America turning against the Bush administration had very little to do with right-wing politics and believing that the war in Iraq was wrong. *It had virtually everything to do with the fact that we had lost the war in Iraq, with no end in sight.* Do you really think that if Bush had completely succeeded in Iraq that the very same polls that today show our invading Iraq was wrong would still say that? No. Definitely no. Bush would still have an approval rating far in excess of 50 percent instead of being where he is, in the low thirties.

The *only* reason why a great number of Americans turned against Bush was that his war against Iraq turned out to be such an abysmal failure and disaster. Before that outcome had become clear, polls showed that most Americans could hardly have cared less that we invaded Iraq, a broken-down country that had no weapons of mass destruction, and was not involved in 9/11. (For instance, at a time when we had the upper hand in Iraq, when things hadn't yet spun out of control, a January 12–15, 2004, *New York Times–CBS News* national poll showed almost 70 percent of Americans, including majorities in both the Republican and Democratic parties, gave Bush high marks in his war against terrorism.) In fact, they could hardly have cared less that thousands of lives had been lost, including those of young Americans, and billions of dollars had been spent in the war. Why didn't they care that much? Because, they would tell you, these are the things that happen during a war.

But hey, we want to win. I mean, that's the American way, right? There was an April 16, 2007, article in the *Los Angeles Times* about the little hamlet of McCook, Nebraska, located in an area of America's heartland that is overwhelmingly conservative, and where God and the flag are supreme. The piece captured the hints, for the first time, that some of the residents of the prairie town were having second thoughts about the war in Iraq, primarily because one of its young men, age twenty, was killed by a roadside bomb there, and the small town, which heretofore would not have questioned Bush if he wanted to invade New Zealand, was taking the death of the young man very hard.

Why were there some heretical thoughts in McCook about the war? It wasn't really because of the twenty-year-old who was killed. I mean, they sincerely mourned his loss, but again, that's what happens in war. No. As the McCook mayor, Dennis G. Berry, said about the war: "Nebraskans like to win, whether it's on the football field or the battlefield. But there's this feeling of where is this going, and will this ever end?" So I hate to break it to you, Paul (Krugman), but the Democrats' midterm victory had very little to do with America becoming disenchanted with the politics of the right, as you and many other columnists have suggested. It had virtually everything to do with the way the war is going in Iraq.

Is it a great America when a monstrous, grotesque, obscene figure like Ken Starr can literally set up shop in Washington, D.C., to find anything he could, anything at all, to destroy the president of the

United States, mostly over his private, consensual sex life—with our federal government not only funding his entire effort, but the majority of this nation's media, liberal (most notably the *New York Times*) as well as conservative, actually aiding and abetting and encouraging him in this criminal and immoral conduct?

What kind of America is it (again, is it a great America?) where, in the 2000 presidential election, the highest court in the land, the United States Supreme Court, stopped the recount in Florida that was authorized under Florida law, took the election away from the American people, and openly *appointed* George Bush president? It unquestionably was one of the biggest crimes in American history, yet the nation quickly put this epic crime behind it, going on to other things as if nothing really serious had taken place. For example, five days after the court's high crime, the caption of an article in the *Los Angeles Times* read: "The Supreme Court Should Weather This Storm." The following day an Associated Press story noted that Justice Sandra Day O'Connor had fired a hole-in-one at a Phoenix golf course.

I do not believe any of the above things (invading Iraq, Ken Starr almost destroying the Clinton presidency over nothing at all, the theft of the presidential election), each of which represented conduct that was unprecedented in U.S. history, would have happened during nearly all of the twentieth century in America. Nor do I believe any of these things would happen *today* in any of the major European nations. Indeed, can you think of even one (much less, all three) of these things, or something similar to them, happening in even one of these countries in the past half century? With the exception of banana republics and dictatorships in third-world countries, things like this just aren't done. But here in America, not just one but all three of these things happened.

And the most frightening thing of all, by far, is that this nation let Starr, the U.S. Supreme Court, and Bush get away with it, doing absolutely nothing to any of them. Bush, Starr, and the five Supreme Court justices in *Bush v. Gore*, as horribly immoral as their respective conduct was, are, after all, just individuals. And we will always have monstrous people in our society. But it's quite another thing when this nation and its institutions, by not punishing these individuals in any way whatsoever, in effect tells them that their conduct, though not commendable, was permissible, tolerable. If the United States of America can actually overlook the horrendous conduct of Bush, Starr, and the five justices, what does that say about this country? What does it say about what we've become? And in these circumstances, under what theory do we remain a great nation?

Can we still be a great nation when, in running for the presidency, it is considered to be politically unwise for a presidential nominee to talk about "helping the poor"? Fritz Mondale certainly learned that reality in spades. Challenging Ronald Reagan in 1984 on the issue of "compassion" and "fairness" and speaking often of "the poor," he won only one out of the fifty states. When John Kerry ran against Bush in 2004, not only, of course, didn't Bush talk about helping the poor, but I am unaware that Kerry ever once allowed the word "poor" to come out of his mouth, only speaking, over and over again, of his concern for "the middle class." The closest I ever heard him get to the poor was when he once referred to those "aspiring to the middle class."

When America was still a great nation, FDR and Truman spoke often of the plight of the poor and helping them. For instance, FDR said that "the test of our progress is not whether we add more to the abundance of those who have much; it is whether we provide enough for those who have too little." JFK, among other references, said in his inaugural speech on January 20, 1961: "If a free society cannot help the many who are poor, it cannot save the few who are rich." On November 8, 1963, just fourteen days before he was assassinated, he told the Protestant Council in New York City that our nation could not "long endure the growing gulf between the rich and the poor." Why would such political rhetoric sound foreign and completely out of place in modern-day America? And LBJ had his "war on poverty." He said, "The richest nation on earth can afford to win the war on poverty." What happened to the soul of America that it is now a political negative to speak of helping the poor?

Indeed, as early as 1991, a U.S.-European poll published in the *Los Angeles Times* showed that America had already lost the compassionate state of mind it was once so well known for. Very tellingly, although the poll found that "most everyone [in the civilized world] feels that the state has a responsibility to take care of poor people who can't take care of themselves," *only 23% of Americans did*. In Britain and France, the figure was 62%. In Spain, 71%; Italy, 66%; Russia, 70%. The closest to the United States was Germany, but it was still at 50%, over 100% more than the United States.

How can we still be a great nation when, though we are the richest nation in the world, almost 40 million Americans, nearly 15 million of whom are children, exist below the poverty line ($19,000 annual income for a family of four)? How can we be viewed as a great nation when, among the eighteen leading industrial nations in the world, we rank number one in the percentage of our population living in poverty?

How can we be considered a great nation when the United States is the only major industrialized country in the world that does not provide health care for all of its citizens? Indeed, though we are, again, the richest of all nations, *close to 50 million Americans have no health insurance*. A typical horrible consequence? *USA Today* reported in July of 2006 that among those in America without health insurance who have cancer, "nearly 70 percent have missed or delayed care for the cancer, and 43 percent went without vital prescriptions."* This, of course, is inexcusable for the richest nation in the world. For those uninsured cancer patients who are paying for the treatment they need, their life savings are being depleted, giving rise to this type of terrible dilemma that no American citizen should have to face: A father (or mother) with advanced cancer and young children has to ask himself if he should go through his children's education and limited inheritance money to delay his death. His family naturally tells him yes, he should. But he has to wonder, doesn't he?

---

*When Bush was asked about the fact that millions of Americans have no health insurance, he replied that "people have access to health care in America. After all, you just go to an emergency room." Can you imagine that? Among many other illnesses, how does one treat cancer in an emergency room?

While we're talking about health insurance, what kind of nation are we that can't find the money to provide health care for almost 9 million of its children, but can find all the money in the world—over $1 trillion thus far—to finance a war against a nation not our enemy and no threat to us?

What kind of a nation do we have when millions of Americans are homeless on the streets, yet Cuba, one of the poorest of countries, provides health care for all its citizens and does not have homeless people on the streets? One might say, "Yeah, but we have freedom here, and Cubans don't. Which is more important?" Not only won't that argument get you a cup of coffee, it won't even entitle you to a sip of water at a public water fountain. What about the fact that England, France, Sweden, etc., also have medical care for all their citizens and no significant homeless problem—and the people in these nations have the same freedoms we do?

How can we still be considered a great nation when, although throughout most of the twentieth century we ranked number one in giving (as a percentage of our gross national income) to the poor nations of the world, today we rank number twenty-one, second to last among industrialized nations?

A 2005 CNN Gallup poll showed that 95 percent of Americans were "proud" to be Americans. (Only 1 percent was not.) But under what theory? The willy-nilly theory?

How can we be a great nation when justice is so wildly disproportionate in America? When the super rich defraud investors out of hundreds of millions of dollars, they usually don't spend one day in jail for it. This is so because normally either nothing is done about their fraud, or only a *civil* action (not a criminal one, as should be the case) is brought against them by the likes of an Eliot Spitzer, and they have the corporations they run pay civil fines for their criminal conduct out of the corporate treasury. And yet, average citizens who steal as little as $500 are *always* prosecuted and, upon conviction, routinely serve jail time, sometimes state prison time. On those very rare occasions when corporate executives are prosecuted and convicted, they virtually always get very short sentences that bear no relation to their crime, and they serve their sentences not in real prisons but detention institutions that resemble college campuses with barbed wire around them. Is that how a great nation, committed to equality, treats its citizens?

Speaking of corporate executives, what kind of an America have we become when, although millions of Americans struggle for a crumb, corporate greed in today's America has gone far, far beyond what anyone could have ever imagined in the America of yesteryear? We know that many workers today are being laid off by big corporations, or their health care coverage is being reduced or terminated, or they are losing their 401K retirement plans. Yet we hear and read every day how corporate executives are pillaging millions upon millions of dollars from the corporate troughs (to the direct detriment of the stockholders) in wildly excessive salaries, bonuses, stock options, perks, and severance packages, often at the very same time their corporation is going under. I'm not talking here about the great number who receive obscene yearly compensation of $20–25 million. That's small potatoes to these CEOs, for whom too much is not enough. While the minimum wage in America is around $6 per hour, and while the president of the United States is paid only a yearly salary of $400,000, many of these corporate predators—already leading a highly luxurious lifestyle of multiple mansions, private jets, and servants—are making, are you ready, *$100 million, $200 million, even $500 and $600 million a year*!! And even this is not enough for them. Last year, for the first time, three corporate executives were paid from $1 to $3 *billion* for the year, thousands of times the salary of the president of the United States.

I know that greed is a condition that most people unfortunately are afflicted with. But America seems to be taking greed to vertiginous heights. The above corporate greed is an example. I think we can all agree that Marx notwithstanding, it is not only wise but fair to pay a CEO of a company much more than the average employee, because he is far more important to the economic health of the company than one single worker, and has much, much more responsibility. The question is how much more. J. P. Morgan, one of the leading industrialists of the twentieth century, and someone whom no one would consider to be an enemy of wealth or capitalism, said that a reasonable ratio of executive pay to that of the average worker would be twenty to one. And, indeed, that's what it was in 1968. Do you know what it is today? The last figures I saw were in 2003, but *the ratio was an incredible 531 to one!!!* Can you imagine that? What was it in some other major countries of the world? Japan's CEO pay as a multiple of employee pay was 10:1. Germany's was 11:1; France, 16:1; Britain, 25:1. The country next to the United States in CEO pay was Brazil at 57:1.

I guess we can't put a cap on corporate pay, since that would be un-American, and with all the inherent sins and vices of capitalism, it has proven to be better than any other socioeconomic system man has devised. But when the average CEO in today's America makes 531 times as much as the employee with the lunch pail, what does that say about the country this nation has become, one that, more than any other nation in the world, seems to be losing the ability to distinguish between its needs and its greeds.

America, for better or worse, has been the leader of pop and cultural change throughout the world for many years. Other nations take their cue from us. What type of a nation do we still have whose movies are routinely laden with profanity of the worst kind and gratuitous, unrelated-to-the-plot grunting sessions of sex in bed or against the wall; whose movies are now actually starting to show people sitting on a toilet going to the bathroom; even, unbelievably, wiping themselves—something, of course, we all want to see very badly. A nation with a very rich heritage of great music whose past Academy Awards for best song in a movie went to songs like "Over the Rainbow," "The Last Time I Saw Paris," "White Christmas," "It Might as Well Be Spring," "Love Is a Many Splendored Thing," "Secret Love," "The Way We Were," and many more such songs, yet whose 2005 Academy Award for best "song" in a movie, believe it or not, was a rap song (meaning, not even a song or music at all since rap has no melody), "It's Hard Out Here for a Pimp," about a pimp and his black and white whores? Whose teenagers, polls show today, treat oral sex as almost the equivalent of mere kissing?

America has changed, hasn't it? And is there any question it's for the worse? Deploring, for instance, the Bush administration's decision not to follow international law in the area of torture and the rights of terrorist defendants at their trial, retired general Wesley K. Clark, formerly the supreme commander of the North Atlantic Treaty Organization, said, "It was America that led the creation of the Geneva Convention, and now we're walking away from it, from the very values we espoused."

I may be wrong in what I'm about to suggest here, but are many of the American soldiers Bush sent to war in Iraq reflective of a coarser and more cruel America than we once knew? I always thought that soldiers went to war because they felt it was their duty as American citizens to do so. I can't recall hearing or reading in the newspaper coverage of the Korean or Vietnam wars (or in any of the literature or movies about these wars and World Wars I and II) that American soldiers were *having fun* killing the enemy, not just doing their job. Yet, in a number of articles on Bush's war in newspapers as well as magazines, there is reporting of just that.

In an article in the *Los Angeles Times* about a marine sniper's unit in the battle of Fallouja in 2004, the two reporters wrote that "on the roof of a U.S. military compound, Marine snipers cranked up the volume on their CD player so they could listen to the music of Metallica as they fired at their foes." Can you imagine that? One sniper (snipers, we all know, kill the enemy with just one shot from a distance far away), a corporal, referred to his job in Fallouja killing Iraqis by saying, "It's a sniper's dream. I couldn't ask to be in a better place. I just got lucky." In other words, this soldier was just having the time of his life killing young Iraqi men. It apparently didn't have anything to do with any *duty* he had. In another article about Fallouja, a private said, "None of us have ever actually fired a shot before. We're all itching to do that." In other words, actually eager to start killing people.* As

---

*But I believe (or I should say I certainly hope) that the majority of our fighting men in Iraq are not this way; that they have the frame of mind exemplified by a young soldier who, when a brainless American television reporter asked him, "Are you eager for combat?" responded. "I'm ready." "But are you eager?" the reporter persisted. "I said I'm ready," the sensible soldier answered.

USA Today reported about American soldiers on the first day of the Iraq war: *"Impatient for action,* troops welcomed news that air strikes had begun. 'OK, we're finally at war,' said Pfc. Todd Carter [not real name], 19, of Chattanooga, Tennessee. 'It's time to get serious and light some people up.'"

And who can forget the photo taken during the battle of Nasiriya—in March of 2003, before Hussein's army fell in the "war" that lasted but twenty-one days—when young Iraqi neighborhood civilians in T-shirts and tennis shoes (not the later insurgents) picked up rifles and tried to repel the irresistible advance of American forces (supported by the precision bombing of jets and the gunships of tanks) whose objective was to conquer their homeland. Virtually defenseless, their few grenades bouncing off the monstrous Abrams tanks like plastic toys, they were slaughtered. The photo showed young marines standing over a stack of Iraqi corpses, taking photos of each other, and with their thumbs up, smiling broadly for the camera. What part of America did these marines come from? What families did they come from?

But maybe it was always this way. Maybe, further, some British soldiers fighting in Iraq are the same way. But why do I have the sense that this type of attitude among many young U.S. soldiers is new and very "American"?

Charles Wilson, the president of General Motors in the 1940s and early 1950s, coined the phrase "As General Motors goes, so goes America." And this was true for most of the twentieth century, GM being the biggest corporation in America—in fact, the world. But today, not only isn't General Motors the biggest corporation in the world, it's not even the biggest auto manufacturer. In 2006, and for the first time ever, Japan's Toyota overtook GM in auto sales.

As far as science is concerned, in an October 13, 2005, *New York Times* article it was reported that "last year, more than 600,000 engineers graduated from institutions of higher education in China, compared to 350,000 in India and 70,000 in the United States. Recently, American 12th graders performed below the international average for 21 countries on general knowledge in math and science. Chemical companies last year shut 70 facilities in the United States and marked 40 for closure. Of 120 large chemical plants under construction globally, one is in the United States and 50 are in China."

General Clark notes that although we are presently the world's only superpower, it is just an illusion that this can never change. He points to the tremendous economic development in China and India, countries that have "four or five times America's population," and says this could result in these nations attaining superpower status in the foreseeable future. "Scale is one of the most important laws of economics, and they've got scale over us."

In some other signs of national decline, America now ranks number 9 in the world on the Adult Literacy Scale (survey by Organization for Economic Cooperation and Development); number 12 on student reading ability (OECD); number 37 (France is number 1, Italy 2) on the Healthcare Quality Index (World Health Organization); number 17 on women's rights (World Economic Forum Report); number 29 on life expectancy (UN Human Development Report); in a real surprise, number 48 (Norway and Iceland are tied at number 1) on the Journalistic Press Freedom Index (Reporters Without Borders); number 13 on the quality of life survey (*Economist* magazine); number 45 on the Environmental Sustainability Index (Yale Center for Environmental Law and Policy; Center for International Earth Science Information Network of Columbia University); number 3 (the UK pound sterling is number 1 and the fifteen-nation European Union euro number 2) in overall currency strength (Financial Times Stock Exchange); and number 32 in its infant mortality rate (Save the Children Report).

I haven't the faintest idea why America is in decline, not being a sociologist or even a student of contemporary history. But there can be no question that by the most important standards of measurement we are in a perilous descent. I know it has been inculcated in us that America is the greatest nation in the world, blessed by nature and by

God, and therefore nothing can ever topple us from our pedestal. But just how many areas of moral failure and cultural degeneration can a nation have without losing its preeminence and/or the right to have the appellation of greatness applied to it? Arnold Toynbee, the nineteenth-century British economist and social reformer, said, "An autopsy of history would show that all great nations commit suicide." How far has America already traveled on the road to self-immolation?

Although the evidence of our decline is overwhelming and multifold, one fact alone, all by itself, proves that it has occurred—that we elected George Bush president twice, someone totally unfit for the office, and a virtual embarrassment to this country in every other way. Someone who actually is the object of scorn and hatred throughout the civilized world, almost assuredly the most hated president around the world, by far, in U.S. history. Bush is so reviled, in fact, that when he visits some nations (like Germany) great pains are taken to avoid all contact by Bush with everyday citizens, and to prevent him from even coming close to the thousands of demonstrators out on the street (holding signs calling Bush evil, a terrorist, and a murderer).

What a tremendous difference there is between Bush and past American presidents like FDR, Eisenhower, JFK, and even Bush's father, George H. W. Bush. When Kennedy was assassinated in 1963, with the lone exception of China, the entire world mourned. Indeed, it was said that more people mourned Kennedy's death than that of any other human in history. Hundreds of thousands of people took to the streets in torch-lit marches in the great capitals of the world, and peasants in the dustiest little villages of South and Central America wept as if they had lost a member of their family. Remarkably, despite the fact that it was at the height of the Cold War, even Russia and all its satellite countries behind the Iron Curtain took his death almost as hard as America did. Nobel Prize–winning novelist John Steinbeck was in Warsaw, Poland, on a cultural tour of Iron Curtain countries for the U.S. State Department when news of Kennedy's death reached the Polish capital. He said that the "great sorrow" among the Polish people over Kennedy's death "was the most fantastic thing I ever saw. I've never seen anything like it. The Poles said they'd never seen its like either, *for anyone.*" That was when America was a great nation, and its leaders were men whom one would expect to lead it.

The Iraq war "was a betrayal of world opinion," said German novelist Peter Schneider. "We are much more doubtful of America's high ground." Sabin Will, a recent German high school graduate, said that "we always thought America had high moral standards. We don't anymore."

I maintain that it would have been virtually impossible for someone like Bush to be elected president throughout most of the twentieth century in America, and impossible for him to have been elected in England or any European country. Impossible. But here in America, it happened, twice. Only because we are a nation, as I say, in serious decline.

Einstein once said that there are only two things that are infinite: the universe and the stupidity of man. And he added that he was only unsure of the former. If the majority of people, everywhere, are stupid, are they more stupid and ignorant in America? As the London *Daily Mirror* asked in a large headline after George Bush's 2004 reelection: "How can 59 million people be so stupid?" If people, even those far away, could see that Bush was a very dangerous joke, why couldn't we Americans?

It *is* terribly, terribly, terribly scary that this nation is so abysmally and profoundly stupid that it could easily be talked into going into a deadly war with a nation that wasn't our enemy and as much of a threat to us as you or I.

There *is* little question that we are less intellectually *inclined* than people in European nations. Not only do they read serious books more than we do, and get their news from the best source (newspapers) more than we do, but intellectuals themselves are looked up to more in these countries, even revered as celebrities in France. Who are America's intellectuals? Has anyone even bothered to draw up a list so they can be identified by name?

Other signs that America is not just less intellectual, but at least, for whatever reason, *acts* less intelligently than these other nations is that Americans, more than all other people in the Western world, love to wave the flag and be blindingly patriotic (love America or leave it; my country, right or wrong). This is not a mindset that is conducive to critical thinking.

Another more ominous sign is the increasing religiosity of America. While Europe has for the most part virtually discarded organized religion—increasingly, priests are being utilized, for instance, only in a ceremonial capacity for things like weddings and funerals, and churches are closing throughout Europe because of very low attendance—America is the *only* nation in the Western world (including nations like Canada and the United Kingdom, which are thought to be more similar to the United States) that is becoming *more* religious. Indeed, the biggest-selling books in America for the past several years (with sales figures in the millions of copies) are religious ones dealing with the "rapture," which, I'm told, is the time, coming soon within our lives, when Jesus will return and sweep all born-again followers, from their homes or cars or wherever they are, into his embrace, and he will take them to heaven, leaving behind on earth the heathens who will destroy each other in the Book of Revelation's Armageddon or Apocalypse, their souls burning forevermore in hell. Some estimate that close to 40 percent of Bush's total raw vote in 2004 was provided by self-identified evangelical Christians, a great number of whom subscribe to such beliefs. If all of this isn't evidence of grinding stupidity, what is? Unbelievably, a 2004 national poll found that 71 percent of Americans said they actually "would die [and hence, it would seem, kill] for their God/beliefs." Isn't that big-time scary?

Until a few years ago, I never, even once, had anything but a secure feeling living in America. It was better than that. The thought never even entered my mind, once, of being frightened about living in America. But believe it or not—and others have told me they feel the very same way—I now do not feel 100 percent secure in America. It's beginning to be a scary (however slight) country. You can't have what Ken Starr did to Clinton, and what the Supreme Court did in *Bush v. Gore*, and what the Bush administration did in Iraq happen without its having an alarming effect on you, at least not if you're a sentient person.

Despite all the danger signals, America remains today, fortunately, a civil society. And I feel there are three main things keeping America that way. One is our incredible wealth. It's always easier to be civil when you're economically fat. Two: most Americans are Democrats, Independents, or liberal or moderate Republicans, and none of these groups is dangerous. And three: our wonderful constitution, an exceedingly powerful document, with its amendments, which continues to serve as a judicious guide to all well-intentioned people and, so far, as a severe impediment to those of ill-will. But it has to be noted that the U.S. Constitution is only what those who warm the bench say it is. At present, we have two right-wing zealots on the bench; two right-wingers (we'll know later if they are zealots); one normal, moderate Republican; and four ordinary, sensible people. So we have four justices who are frightening or potentially frightening, and five who are not.

America should realize that if one of the five retires or dies, and Bush (or any conservative successor of his) appoints one more right-winger to take his or her place, America, incrementally, will become a different nation, for the worse, to live in. We are that close, just *one justice*, from waking up in the morning to a new America. Hypothetically—and I'm not saying five right-wing justices would necessarily make such a ruling—if a search and seizure case came before the court in which the police, though having time to get a search warrant, broke into an American home without one, and the court held that this was not an "unreasonable search and seizure" under the Fourth Amendment to the U.S. Constitution, America would change overnight.

The principal enemies I see to a brighter day for America are the right wing, which mostly consists of people who are not only rotten from the top of their heads to the bottom of their feet, but who also successfully appeal to the worst and most base instincts of many outside their group; religious fundamentalism, which is necessarily hostile to a pluralistic society, has always been the source of intolerance and wars through the years, and which can only increase the nation's ignorance and intolerance if it continues to rise as it has here in America; and the entertainment world, mostly Hollywood, which insists on poisoning our culture with the filth it increasingly spews out to the nation's youth and the rest of us.

I have no idea if there is going to be a pendulum effect or if the descent into our oblivion will continue.

Clearly, America is a nation that has lost its way. But although I don't know why, I have a sense that we can one day again be a nation that causes people around the world to look up to (as they always did, and still yearn to), not down on. Maybe I am a victim of the very kind of propaganda I've decried and attacked other people for being duped by in this book. But I just feel that there is still something special about America. That the greatness we once knew and lived by, and the qualities of leadership, fairness, and moral authority that made us the great nation we were, have not died like the rest of the past, but they are still miraculously stored and continue to inhere in the nation's metaphorical soil to be used as protoplasm for its revival.

Because of our heritage, and the unparalleled rich diversity of our people that gives us so much strength, I think it is still within our grasp (though I have no idea how to bring it about, and do not want to resort to platitudinous utterances) to once again be the respected leader of the free world, the land of opportunity like no other, the most generous nation to the world's needy population, number one in everything, whether its heavyweight champions, the tallest buildings, or Nobel Prize winners, a nation whose expansive image will again be embodied by the words written on the Statue of Liberty to other nations across the sea—"Give me your tired, your poor, your huddled masses yearning to breathe free."

NOTES

CHAPTER 1: OPENING UP ONE'S EYES

5 We're talking about the fact that most people see what they expect to see . . . On the pages of this book the reader will see my many references to the stupidity and/or ignorance of the American public. I am obviously only referring to the *majority* of the public, a position I stand firmly behind. But why insult the majority in this book? Because stupidity and ignorance, unfortunately, are not benign, being responsible for much of the misery and injustice in this world. For instance, the tragic war in Iraq has, unlike children, many parents, including the majority of Americans who gave their support to Bush for his war. Without it, Bush may not have gone to war.

Just a few of the many other parents of the Iraq war are the considerable number of spineless congressional Democrats who rolled over and played dead during Bush's rush to war, actually voting to authorize it; the media, which uncritically gave Bush almost a free pass during his propaganda campaign to sell the war; Ralph Nader, since we know the 2000 presidential election came down to a few hundred votes, and he siphoned off more than enough votes from Al Gore to allow Bush to win and take us to war, a war that never would have been fought if Gore had become president; and the endlessly reprehensible and extremely hypocritical Rush Limbaugh, who heavily influences, every day, millions of simple-minded Americans, a great number of whom are ring-around-the-collar types who actually believe that the interests of Limbaugh, who makes around $30 million a year, are coterminous with theirs.

About Limbaugh, although he has an uncontrollable passion for dishing it out, spouting his venom on the Clintons (even, unbelievably, their daughter, Chelsea, whom Limbaugh referred to, when she was growing up in the White House, as "ugly"; and along with Socks, the White House cat, as "the White House dog") and the Democratic Party every single day without letup, he's a yellow coward who can't take it himself. To avoid all opposition or critical comments, he virtually never has any guests on his show (and when he does they are fellow travelers like Dick Cheney) and heavily screens all callers. There's nothing I'd like more to do—and I hereby issue a challenge to him—than to engage Limbaugh in a televised debate for a minimum of two hours on a college campus or elsewhere. And if I am unable to delimb Limbaugh, I promise to turn in my bar card. I have neither the time nor the interest to debate the many Limbaugh wannabes.

6 . . . twelve to fifteen shots were fired at Hussein in an assassination attempt . . . Hussein's prosecutor, Jabbar al-Musawi, made a fool out of himself at the trial on the issue of the assassination attempt. After acknowledging that there was, indeed, such an assassination attempt (from all that I have read, the overwhelming evidence is that there was) in his opening statement on October 19, 2005, to the five judges hearing the case, he began wandering all over the place, at one point saying that the assassination attempt was only "a few bullets by renegade gunmen." (But why isn't even one bullet an assassination attempt?) He later suggested that there was no attempt on Hussein's life, the shots coming from villagers firing their guns in the air to celebrate the president's visit. Finally, on June 19, 2006, when he made his appeal for the death penalty for Hussein to the court, the *Los Angeles Times* (June 20, 2006) quoted him as actually saying, in an embarrassing argument: "The alleged assassination attempt against Saddam involved only 8 to 15 bullets [*only* 8 to 15 bullets?] fired from behind a wall. It was proved there were no heavy weapons. [Heavy weapons are usually used by assassins? Really?] If it had been an attempt it would have been a suicide mission." The prosecutor not only ended his argument on this point with a non sequitur ("it would have been a suicide mission"), but even if the non sequitur were true, what sensible person would be heard to suggest that no Iraqi presidential assassin would be willing to commit suicide to kill Hussein? It should be noted that although the *New York Times* quoted the prosecutor in his appeal for the death penalty as saying that "the assassination attempt was a Machiavellian invention by Hussein" to justify cracking down on Shiites in Dujail (why in the world would an absolute dictator like Hussein feel he had to go through an elaborate charade lasting almost two years to justify what he did?), the *Washington Post* reported it was not the prosecutor but one of the lawyers for the families of the dead who said this.

6 . . . 46 of the 148 had already died from physical torture or execution by their interrogators and guards at Abu Ghraib prison . . . According to Human Rights Watch, which monitored the trial of Hussein and his codefendants, a document produced in court at the trial was an extract of a court verdict from 1986 against an Iraqi interrogator who had worked on the Dujail case and who had been convicted of misconduct. The document stated that 46 persons died during interrogation, and that the interrogators sought to conceal the deaths for fear of reprimand (*Human Rights Watch*, November 2006, vol. 18 no. 9[E] p. 67).

6 The remaining 102 out of the 148 men were eventually convicted and executed for the attempt on Hussein's life. Although Hussein's prosecutor alleged that the 102 men were convicted and sentenced to death without a trial, at Hussein's trial the defense strenuously maintained that there had been a trial of eighteen days' duration. When one of Hussein s codefendants at the trial, Awad al-Bandar (the chief judge of Iraq's Revolutionary Court who presided over the trial of the 102), demanded of the five judges hearing the case that they have the court file on the trial of the 102 turned over to the defense so it could prove the trial took place—a court file that Bandar said had been seized, along with millions of other papers and documents of the Iraqi government, by the American occupying forces following the fall of Baghdad—the judges denied the request, one of them saying that getting the court file "is the work of the defense. Don't ask us to do it." But obviously, the court was in a far better position to get the file from the American authorities than Bandar and his codefendants were.

The prosecutor alleged that at the time of the executions of the 102, "four uninvolved men were swept up" by mistake and executed when the group of 102 condemned men were taken to the gallows.

7 The bottom line is that it appears Hussein did not commit the crime of murder here . . . Even assuming that those who were killed by Hussein had not had a trial and were summarily executed, unless our primary complaint against Hussein was not that he was a murderer, but that he didn't provide American-style "due process" to his victims, and we had him executed because of his due process violations (I'm being facetious), the fact they did not have a trial would be irrelevant. The main issue is whether or not those he killed were guilty or not guilty of having tried to murder him. And it is an unintelligent answer to that question to say that one is only guilty of a crime if a judge or jury says he is. Under that line of reasoning, Adolf Hitler never committed any crimes, Jack the Ripper never committed any crimes, and the only crime Al Capone ever committed was income tax evasion.

Indeed, even if we took the assumption further—that half of those executed were actually innocent (the other half guilty), and directly because of Hussein's due process violations (no trial or an unfair trial) this fact was never allowed to be brought out, it still would only be, at its core, a due process case, nothing more. It would only cease to be a due process case if it were shown that Hussein had criminal intent, that he knowingly executed innocent people. But at least based on what has emerged, the circumstantial evidence seems clear that Hussein believed that those who were executed had conspired to murder him. And if anyone believes that a dictator's killing of those he sincerely believed had tried to kill him is the type of situation contemplated by international tribunals set up—like the International Criminal Court in The Hague, Netherlands, and the Nuremberg trials—to try national leaders for war crimes and crimes against humanity, I do not believe you are correct.

CHAPTER 2: WHY GEORGE BUSH WENT TO WAR

16 . . . the principal reason George Bush gave for invading Iraq in 2003 was that Hussein had weapons of mass destruction . . . In early March of 2003, I was in the midst of working on my book on the assassination of President John F. Kennedy. Far from the political scene in Washington, D.C., I took a good part of around eight or nine days to write from scratch an article arguing against the invasion of Iraq. I submitted it to a national magazine back east for publication, but President George W. Bush preempted me with his so-called preemptive war on Iraq. To summarize my article, I said that *if* we confined ourselves to the *evidence* that had been presented, as well as *common sense*, Saddam Hussein was as much of a threat to this country as you or I.

Before I explain why I said this, let me point out to you the evidence that even those who were vehemently opposed to our going to war nevertheless accepted Bush's premise that Hussein *was* a threat to the security of this country. *The arguments they made in opposition to war all presupposed that Hus-*

sein was a threat. For example, when they made their main argument that "before we go to war, let's give inspections more of a chance," they were necessarily saying that if inspections didn't work (i.e., Hussein failed to comply with UN Security Council Resolution 1441 that he destroy all of his alleged weapons of mass destruction), then we should go to war. Two examples among hundreds: "For now, the inspection process has not been completely explored. The use of force can only be a final recourse," Dominique de Villepin, the French foreign minister, told the UN on February 5, 2003. "We ought not jump to war without giving UN inspectors a chance to work a bit longer," said U.S. senator Christopher J. Dodd on March 7. This position, of course, was conceding that Hussein *was* a threat. Because if he were not a threat to the security of this country, *what difference would it make if he had thousands of weapons of mass destruction?* It would be irrelevant. Russia and China and Great Britain have these thousands of weapons and no one was suggesting we should go to war with them, were they?

And when the opponents of the war made the related argument, "Instead of war, let's pursue a policy of containment of Hussein," they were necessarily saying that Hussein was trying hard to break out of his box so he could start using his weapons of mass destruction on America, but we didn't have to go to war to stop him; we could contain him, keep him harmless in his box.

In a survey of the editorial positions of 43 of the leading newspapers in the country at the time, 18 supported war right then, and 25 wanted to give diplomacy and inspections more of a chance before going to war (*USA Today*, March 17, 2003). In other words, *all* 43 newspapers agreed that Saddam Hussein *was* a threat to the security of this country.

The debate was so askew and distorted that in a lengthy February 16, 2003, article in the *Los Angeles Times* in which two Washington correspondents for the *Times* set forth "some of the most asked questions" about the impending war in Iraq, of the eleven questions asked and discussed, not one of the eleven dealt with the question of whether or not Hussein was an imminent threat to the security of America.

I pointed out in my article that the *only* issue was whether or not Hussein was an imminent threat to this country. This is the issue that should have consumed newspaper editorials and op-ed pieces and magazine articles, as well as radio and TV debates throughout the country. But I assure you that this issue was not being discussed, and the reason was that it was simply assumed that Hussein was a threat. If it had been discussed, I would not have thought there was any reason for me to write the article. Remarkably, Bush's declaration that Hussein *was* an imminent threat to the security of this country served as a tranquilizing dart into the collective psyches not only of millions of everyday people, but virtually every political columnist I know of in America, even the leadership of nations opposed to the war like France, Germany, Russia, and China. No one, but no one, was earnestly discussing the only issue that should have been debated. If you happen to know, for instance, of one column back then, whether it was in the *New York Times, Los Angeles Times, Washington Post, Chicago Tribune, USA Today, Time, Newsweek, U.S. News and World Report*, etc., which said the *only* issue to be debated was whether or not Saddam Hussein was an imminent threat to this country, and proceeded to discuss the issue in depth, what column or article was that?

And, predictably, in a two-hour town hall meeting on ABC with Ted Koppel on March 5, 2003 (just two weeks before the war), not one of the panelists or anyone in the audience, even those who opposed going to war at that time, mentioned the issue. It was apparently considered a truism that since Hussein was believed to have weapons of mass destruction (WMD), he was, indeed, a threat to this country.

Even today, five years later, in ninety-nine out of a hundred articles on the issue, all the writer talks about, if he's attacking Bush, is either that Bush lied to us about Hussein's weapons of mass destruction, or Bush used faulty information in going to war with Iraq because we found out Hussein had no such WMD. In either situation, the inference is inescapable that if, in fact, Hussein had weapons of mass destruction, the war would have been justified. Just a few examples among hundreds. In Alan Dershowitz's fine 2006 book, *Preemption, A Knife That Cuts Both Ways*, he writes that "the invasion of Iraq *was* justified" on the ground "of self-defense against weapons of mass destruction." He goes on to say that this "justification" did not "turn out to be compelling since no WMD were found." A July 16, 2004, *New York Times* editorial said, "If we had known that there were probably no unconventional weapons, we would have argued earlier and harder that invading Iraq made no sense." The *Times* said on August 24, 2005: "We know now that weapons of mass destruction did not exist. If we had all known then what we know now, the invasion would have been stopped by a popular outcry."

In fact, I am almost 100 percent certain that if a large cache of weapons of mass destruction were found in Iraq tomorrow, virtually everyone, including the liberal *New York Times* and *Washington Post*, would say that Bush was right after all, and he would be essentially vindicated. (How many would say, "So what?") Anyone who doesn't believe this is someone who doesn't read the daily newspapers.

What Bush did back in 2003, then, was successfully deflect the debate away from the question it should have been focused on—was Hussein an immediate threat to this country, obviously the only situation that would justify war—to whether or not Hussein was complying with the UN resolution to disarm. As late as Bush's March 6, 2003, televised address to the nation, just two weeks before the war, he said, "The *single* question is—Has Iraq complied with the UN resolution to disarm or has he not?" No, Mr. President. When you are thinking of putting the flower of American youth in harm's way, the single question is whether Saddam Hussein was an imminent threat to this country.

A day earlier (March 5), Colin Powell, in remarks he made to the Center for Strategic and International Studies, said that in making the decision to go to war, "the question is simply this: Has Saddam Hussein made a strategic decision . . . that he will give up these horrible weapons of mass destruction? That's the question. *There is no other question.*" Right, Colin. Even if we assumed for the sake of argument that Saddam Hussein was no threat at all to the people of this country, that's irrelevant. If Saddam has WMD, let's go to war so American soldiers and innocent Iraqis can start getting killed.

Was Saddam an imminent threat to the security of this country? In my article I wrote that if the consequences of Bush's response to this question did not involve the loss of thousands of lives and the hell of war, the question is the type that could understandably evoke close to side-splitting laughter. It's a bad joke. I say that because of two arguments, one of which is powerful in its own right, and the second one conclusive, incontrovertible, and incapable of circumvention.

The first argument in support of the proposition that Hussein was not a threat to this country is that—are you ready?—*Saddam Hussein was not really an enemy of this country*, and no one was pointing this out. Since one goes to war with their enemies, it bears repeating that Saddam Hussein was not an enemy of the United States of America! Although Bush has said that Hussein held "an unrelenting hostility towards the United States," he never offered any credible evidence to support these words.

Some have said that Hussein was our enemy because after the Persian Gulf War he put out a contract on George Bush Sr.'s life when the latter was visiting Kuwait in April of 1993. Well, number one, even if this is true, this was against just one man, the man who ordered the decimating war against him, not an action against the United States itself. And a hatred of one man cannot logically be construed as a hatred of an entire nation. Yet one would never know this listening to the prodigiously egocentric George Bush. "There's no doubt he can't stand *us*," Bush said. "After all, this is a guy who tried to kill my dad at one time." Also, although the Clinton administration concluded, after an investigation, that the plot to kill Bush existed and that it could not have existed without Hussein's approval, a May 13, 1993, classified U.S. intelligence analysis by the CIA's counterterrorism unit concluded that Kuwait's authorities may have "cooked the books" on the alleged plot, deciding to use the discovery of an unrelated Iraqi plot as a plot against Bush in order to remind the Clinton administration of the "continuing Iraqi threat."

Remarkably, many on the right in America claimed that by Hussein having his antiaircraft artillery fire at American and British planes flying over specifically designated Iraqi air space to enforce the "no-fly" zones,* this was proof that Hussein was an "enemy" of the United States. But this is an enormous stretch. America flies airplanes over Iraqi land, and if Hussein has his aircraft fire at the planes that means he hates America?

It should be noted that although the United States has always maintained that American planes flying in the two no-fly zones (covering about 60 percent of Iraq) were doing so pursuant to UN resolution 688 (April 1, 1991), there is no language in 688 that authorized these flights. Therefore, the no-fly zones created by the United States, Britain, and France seemed to be unauthorized, and hence, illegal intrusions on Iraqi airspace. Indeed, Boutros Boutros-Ghali, the secretary general of the United Nations in the early 1990s, said the zones (whose purpose seemed to have ended within a year after the Persian Gulf War and degenerated in later years into being used by the Americans and British to conduct surveillance flights on Iraqi

---

*These were zones established by the United States, Britain, and France after the 1991 Persian Gulf War in which Iraqi aircraft were forbidden to fly. The purpose of the zones was to assist humanitarian efforts by the three countries to counter Hussein's repression of the Kurds in northern Iraq and the Shiites in southern Iraq, who had risen up against Hussein following the war.

military installations, often bombing them) were "illegal." That was always the position of Hussein, who contended the flights were invasions of his nation's sovereignty, and this is why he ordered his aircraft to fire at the planes.

There is one further observation to be made. As of the beginning of the Iraq war in 2003, American and British planes had flown approximately 150,000 flights in the no-fly zones over Iraq during a twelve-year period. Iraqi antiaircraft had fired hundreds upon hundreds of thousands of rounds at the planes and yet not only wasn't one plane ever shot down, but unbelievably, not one single round ever hit an American or British plane. How is this humanly possible? It would seem that either Hussein's air defense personnel were the poorest shooters in history or Hussein—not wanting to actually shoot down a plane for fear of igniting a devastating retaliation against him—was merely venting his anger at the United States and Britain, and the rounds were never intended to hit the planes.

Let's not forget, then, that Hussein was not an enemy of the United States, and never had been. He was an enemy that George Bush, for whatever reason, created out of whole cloth. Not that I would ever accept the uncorroborated word of someone like Saddam Hussein, but when there isn't a speck of evidence to the contrary, I believe what he told Dan Rather in a February 24, 2003, interview. He urged Rather to "convey" to all Americans "that the people of Iraq are not the enemy of the American people." President Bush, flat-out lying, said on July 12, 2004, as well as on other occasions, that "we removed a *declared enemy* of America." But the only one who declared that Hussein was an enemy was Bush himself, yet no member of the media ever called him on the falsehood. Not only hadn't Hussein ever declared that he was an enemy of the United States (my God, we were his biggest oil customer and thereby largely financed his regal lifestyle), but to the contrary, as we have seen, he said the precise opposite. And indeed, on December 20, 1983, Donald Rumsfeld, serving as a special envoy of President Reagan (who gave a pair of cowboy boots to Hussein), traveled to Baghdad and, with a warm smile and handshake (captured by photograph), assured Hussein that the latter could count on America being in his corner in his war with Iran.

But this is all relatively insignificant when compared to the real reason why the notion that Hussein was a threat to this country is too preposterous for words. A few days after Bush gave his first televised speech to the nation (October 7, 2002) asserting that Hussein was an imminent threat to this country, I was having my five strands of hair trimmed at a seven-dollars-a-cut barber I've been going to for years. Joe (not his real name) is a rather bright and very conservative fellow. His weakness, like that of the overwhelming majority of people, is that he doesn't like to give his mind a workout. I asked him, "Joe, if someone gave Saddam Hussein an atomic bomb and gave him the choice of either dropping it on Baghdad or New York City, what would he do?" I already knew, of course, what Joe would say, and he didn't disappoint me. "New York City," he answered quickly. "No, Joe," I said. "You are 100 percent wrong. Obviously, he'd drop it on Baghdad. Hussein, as you know, Joe, is a human monster. Why would he care if thousands of Iraqis were killed? He's been murdering his people for years. If he dropped a bomb on Baghdad, he'd be safely ensconced in a bunker somewhere and he'd be just fine. But, Joe, if he dropped it on New York City, he'd be dead the following day. And guess what, Joe?" "What?" "The last I heard, Hussein wants to live." Joe stared at me for a long moment, then said, "I guess if you put it that way." Whereupon I responded, "Joe, there *is* no other way to put it."

The notion that Hussein would do something that would only serve to ensure his annihilation is too ludicrous to even contemplate. Hussein, obviously (as opposed to the Islamic fundamentalists who crashed into the Twin Towers on 9/11), desperately wanted to live. This incontrovertible reality was confirmed beyond all doubt when, at the time of his capture and arrest on December 13, 2003, in the small town of ad-Dawr in Iraq, near Tikrit, he was found hiding like a rat at the bottom of an eight-foot spider hole near a small mud-walled compound he was living in. "Don't shoot," he said to his military captors. This all makes the notion of his wanting to attack the United States of America all the more insane. I mean, here's someone who had two people, independent of each other, testing every morsel of food that he ate, who slept in a different bed every night; someone who owned forty, yes, forty palaces and loved his life as the supreme dictator of his country. Why would he do anything at all that could only jeopardize his existence? He would have nothing to gain and everything to lose.

It's so downright silly that one could make it the subject of a cartoon. You know, Qusay, one of Hussein's sons, asks his father why he's not eating his eggs, and Hussein responds, "Qusay, Abdul has already tested the food on my plate, but Habib hasn't yet. By the way, is our nuclear bomb still on schedule for the White House at 2:30 this afternoon?"

"Ah," but the war hawks say, "if Hussein wouldn't drop a bomb on us because he'd be afraid of retaliation, he could secretly give the bomb to a group of terrorists like Al Qaeda, who would." But again, Hussein would still be doing something that could cause his annihilation the moment it was discovered, which it almost assuredly would be. Everyone knows that three people can keep a secret, but only if two are dead. Indeed, Hussein would know he'd be destroyed even if it were never proven he was complicit and it was merely *suspected* that he was. As Joseph C. Wilson, chief of mission at the U.S. embassy in Baghdad from 1988 to 1991, said at the time: "Hussein has long known that every terrorist act, and particularly a sophisticated one, raises the question of his involvement and invites blame." (And of course we know that even though Hussein had nothing to do with 9/11, Bush and his people successfully convinced the majority of Americans that he did. See discussion in Chapter 4.)

In any event, what would have been in it for Hussein to provide terrorist groups with his weapons of mass destruction? That they would pay him money for them? Hussein, with these forty palaces and owning the second largest (next to Saudi Arabia) oil reserves in the world, needed some extra spending money? Or would the reason be that he hated us so much that he wanted to kill as many of us as possible? But again, though he undoubtedly hated Bush Sr. and Bush Jr. (Iraqi papers called Bush Jr. "the son of a snake"), where was there any evidence that Hussein hated America or its people? Even if we were to assume, for the sake of argument, that he had this hatred, his instinct for self-preservation, the strongest human instinct, would have easily trumped that hatred. Furnishing nuclear or biological and chemical weapons to groups that truly do hate America, like Al Qaeda, would be something we can feel very confident Hussein would never have even dreamed of doing, even in the most fleeting of his reveries, since he would be taking by far the most life-threatening step he could ever take, with nothing to gain from it.

With respect to the allegation that Hussein would be willing to work in concert with groups like Al Qaeda by furnishing them with WMD, there is evidence that when overtures were made to each of them to work with the other, they both were opposed to it. This was so because Hussein and Al Qaeda went together as well as oil and water. Among other things, Hussein was not only secular, but a dictator who subjugated his people. And the emphasis in his regime was on making money and providing a lavish lifestyle for Iraqi leaders, whereas Bin Laden's lifestyle was that of ascetic Islamic fundamentalism. In Bin Laden's audio-taped message in early February 2003 to his "Muslim brothers in Iraq," in which he urged the Iraqi people to fight in the trenches against America and the "allies of the devil [America]," he clearly distanced himself from Hussein, calling Hussein an "apostate." However, although not agreeing to work with Hussein, he noted that "in the current circumstances" the interests of the Muslim masses in Iraq "coincide" with those of their leader, who, he said, like leaders in Jordan, Morocco, Nigeria, Pakistan, Saudi Arabia, and Yemen, was responsible for the "enslavement" of their people.

Although the Bush administration, before the war and after it commenced, claimed that a Jordanian terrorist fighting U.S. forces in Iraq, Abu Mousab al Zarqawi, was a member of Al Qaeda, later evidence contravened this. In a letter to Bin Laden acquired from a captured courier in 2004, Zarqawi literally beseeched Bin Laden for his support in the terrorist movement against the U.S. in Iraq, saying he needed help. He added, "We do not see ourselves as fit to challenge you." Zarqawi is only asking for an opportunity "to work under your banner, comply with your orders" (*Newsweek*, November 1, 2004). Osama wasn't interested.

Returning to the central point, the fact remains that if we base our conclusion on common sense and the evidence that existed at the time Bush invaded Iraq, Saddam Hussein was not an imminent threat to this country, and therefore, the Bush administration had no justification whatsoever for going to war with Iraq. If the threat of retaliation was enough to deter Hussein's hero, Joseph Stalin—someone whose country was a hundred times more powerful than Iraq, and for a time in the late fifties may have had nuclear superiority over this country (eliminating the presumed "missile gap" was a part of JFK's campaign for election in 1960)—certainly it would be, and was, a deterrent to a small and militarily enfeebled nation like Iraq that was still shattered by, and trying to recuperate from, two recent wars. To believe otherwise is to knowingly thumb one's nose at all conventional notions of logic and common sense, and elevate illogic to stratospheric heights.

But for whatever reason, in all the newspaper and magazine columns and articles as well as editorials I read on the impending war back in 2003, I did not read one that made the obvious argument that Hussein was *not* a threat to this country *because* if he attacked us or helped anyone else do so, he knew he would be destroyed by certain retaliation, and he wanted to live, not die. *Not one.*

Indeed, the mesmerization of America on this issue was so complete that in addition to the right-wing fanatics, even a considerable number of the liberal cognoscenti, three sheets to the wind from imbibing Bush's tommyrot, wanted to go to war. Writing in the *New York Times* (January 8, 2003), Bill Keller said, "The president will take us to war with support from quite a few members of the East Coast liberal cabal. The I-Can't-Believe-I'm-a-Hawk Club includes op-ed regulars at this newspaper [*New York Times*], and *The Washington Post*, the editors of *The New Yorker*, *The New Republic* and *Slate*, and columnists in *Time* and *Newsweek*, because we are hard pressed to see an alternative that is not built on wishful thinking." Right, Bill, it was just wishful thinking that Hussein wouldn't attack America with deadly force the first opportunity he got. Keller's infantile thinking was mirrored by millions of everyday Americans. "I'm all for peace," a subscriber to *Time* magazine wrote the editor, "but are we just going to wait for Saddam to attack first?"

At the end of CBS anchorman Dan Rather's February 26, 2003, one-hour special on his coup interview of Hussein, Rather told his TV audience that the thing that came through about Hussein above all else was that he "judges victory by only one measure: *his own survival*." It would have been nice if the veteran newscaster had added the few words—"And that makes one wonder why he would want to attack the United States or help anyone else to do so?"

Is there any concrete, empirical evidence to support the commonsense deduction that he would not have? Although the proposition is so obvious that it is intellectually sustainable without such evidence, in point of fact there is. On the eve of the Persian Gulf War in 1991, Secretary of State James Baker told Iraqi foreign minister Tarik Aziz that the U.S. would destroy Iraq (as opposed to just removing its forces from Kuwait) if Hussein used chemical and biological weapons on American forces the way he used these weapons in his war with Iran. *And we know that Hussein did not use such weapons* (which at the time he *did* have) *on American soldiers in the Gulf War.*

To conclude, even if, as Bush so fervently claimed, Hussein did have weapons of mass destruction at the time Bush invaded Iraq (which we have learned he did not), the belief that he was an imminent threat to the security of this country, which Bush got the media and the vast majority of Americans to believe, was preposterous on its face.

18 . . . the *real*, unstated reason the Bush administration had for invading Iraq was to overthrow Hussein and establish democracy in Iraq . . . When we trace the genealogy of this purported reason for invading Iraq back to its roots, we find that, at least as early as 1996, three neoconservatives— Richard Perle, Douglas Feith, and David Wurmser, all of whom ended up in the Bush administration—published a paper titled "A Clean Break: A New Strategy for Securing the Realm." The paper recommended invading Iraq and deposing Hussein *not* to remake the Middle East so it would be less of a threat to the United States, but less of a threat to Israel, a declared enemy of Hussein's. Indeed, the paper said that after Hussein was toppled, a leader should be installed to head Iraq who was friendly to Israel. *If* the monstrous Iraq war, with its incalculable losses and suffering, was all about helping our friend Israel (which supported our invasion of Iraq), not the United States, do I have to say how serious the implications of this are?

Ultimately, with Iraqi democracy in flames, we have seen that Bush has been reduced to arguing that Iraq has become the central front in the war on terror, thus necessitating our indefinite engagement there.

19 Apart from the wholly unrealistic and fanciful notion of changing the political culture of the Arab world to our liking . . . The Arab world, with its centuries of very deep religious and secular schisms and rivalries among warring factions, not to mention official intolerance of dissent, is going to give this all up, in Bush's dream, for democracy, which by its nature is pluralistic and tolerant of dissent? And a type of democracy that's friendly to the United States? Under what theory? Nearly all of the Middle East is Arab, and since America supports Israel in its war against the Palestinians, who are Arab, this fact alone makes most of the Arab world not like us.

Also, let me see if I can get this straight. Bush was going to bring democracy to the Arab world, not by overthrowing one of the countries with Islamic rule and no democracy like Saudi Arabia or Iran, but by toppling Hussein, whose governance in Iraq was secular? Say again? Shlomo Avineri, professor of political science at the Hebrew University of Jerusalem, points out the "dangerous illusion" of Bush's plan to democratize the Mideast by the mere means of deposing Hussein and having free elections. "Democracy doesn't mean simply holding elections," he says. "First, you need a democratic culture—a tradition of voluntary associations, a tolerance for nonconformism and pluralism, a shared belief in the dignity of the individual, separation of political power from religious authority and a belief in the legitimacy of dissent." None of which presently exist in the Arab Mideast and which are not easily (if at all) exportable.

Before we even get to the notion of spreading democracy, since the Shiites and Sunnis have been enemies since A.D. 632, and since the Shiites are the majority Muslim sect in Iraq and they've been chafing under Sunni domination for five centuries, wouldn't a democratic election automatically result (as it did) in the Shiites winning power? And as deeply steeped in their religious beliefs as they are, isn't it just a matter of time before they establish a theocracy (to replace the nascent democracy) in Iraq? And aren't Islamic extremists—the type who were involved in 9/11—much more likely to come from the loins of an Islamic nation than from the secular Iraq of Saddam Hussein? And shouldn't Bush's people automatically know such things?

CHAPTER 3:
PROLOGUE TO THE PROSECUTION OF
GEORGE W. BUSH FOR MURDER

39 While young American soldiers were scavenging for their "hillbilly" armor . . . As has been widely reported, of all the contracts awarded to American firms to rebuild Iraq, the largest by far ($2.3 billion) was awarded to Halliburton, the company Cheney headed (and to this day still receives compensation from) before resigning to run with Bush in 2000. As if the aroma of cronyism was not strong enough, Halliburton's contract to repair Iraq's oil infrastructure was secretly awarded to it, without bids (in violation of federal law). Since then, apparently because Halliburton felt it was being underpaid (I'm being sarcastic), it has overbilled the Pentagon well in excess of $100 million. When the overbilling was discovered, instead of Halliburton being prosecuted criminally for the crime of grand theft (obtaining money by false pretenses), Bush merely said that Halliburton would have to pay the money back. Can you imagine a bank robber being told that if he did that he wouldn't be prosecuted?

44 These "men" refused to fight for America when it was their time to fight for this country . . . What is even more unflattering to Bush, Cheney, et al. about their decision not to fight during the Vietnam War is that back then, America and nearly the entire free world deeply feared the global spread of communism, and America had come to the brink of nuclear war with the Soviet Union during the Cuban Missile Crisis in October of 1962. (The *New York Times* said that "historians have called it the most dangerous moment in recorded time.") The fear over Vietnam (which we now know was an erroneous one since North and South Vietnam were only involved in a civil war) was that if communist North Vietnam prevailed, under the so-called domino theory this communist victory might spread throughout Southeast Asia and eventually end at our doorsteps. Secretary of State Dean Rush predicted to President Lyndon Johnson that if America didn't stop the communists in Vietnam it would "almost certainly" end in a "catastrophic war" for America. But even with this fear, which made fighting for this country, many Americans thought, imperative, Bush, Cheney, and Rove decided to bow out, and ran away.

53 . . . how much he suffers over the loss of American lives in Iraq . . . Bush supporters invariably cite his many meetings (usually as an adjunct to his political visit to a city around the country) with what the White House calls the "families of the fallen." But they always fail to point out how such visits are synonymous with his suffering or losing any sleep over what happened to these fallen soldiers. Wouldn't it be a non sequitur to say that they necessarily are?

58 He prefers to run the most important country on earth not by reading up . . . Isn't it just lovely that during his day in the Oval Office, our nation's chief executive apparently is getting his spiritual guidance on how to conduct the affairs of state from his personal conversations with God? Yes, the affairs of state. I mean, when Bush is talking about reading Chambers "on a daily basis to be in the Word," you have to know he's not talking about having God help him decide when and what to eat, whether he should watch the Alabama-Arkansas or Indiana-Ohio State football game on TV, or whether to leave for Camp David for his long weekend at 2:30 or 3:30 p.m. When Bush himself said that in making up his mind on whether to go to war in Iraq "there is a higher father I appeal to" than his biological father, doesn't that eliminate any perceived ambiguity on this matter?

63 ... the blatant cronyism he has practiced in his federal appointments. If any reader is thinking about John F. Kennedy's appointment of his brother Robert F. Kennedy as the nation's attorney general, put that thought out of your mind. Not only did RFK have a passion for civil rights reform and fighting organized crime, two of the biggest problems facing the nation in 1961, but RFK had already served as chief counsel for the Senate's Mc-Clelland Committee (commonly referred to as the "Rackets Committee") and earlier for the Senate's Permanent Sub-Committee on Investigations, both of which went after organized crime in America. So RFK had a lot of experience in going after the mob, and there can be little question that his record against organized crime and his civil rights enforcement as attorney general were the best in the history of the department.

64 Instead, Bush vigorously defended Tenet ... On December 1, 1961, President John F. Kennedy presented the National Security Medal, America's highest award for intelligence work, to Allen Dulles. This was after the disastrous Bay of Pigs invasion that Kennedy, as well as his predecessor, Eisenhower, had been influenced to support by the misinformation of Dulles's CIA. But to put this on the same level as what Bush did for Tenet would be very wrong. Number one, Bush never fired Tenet. Kennedy fired Dulles (that is, accepted his resignation). Also, the award Tenet got was much more prestigious than the one Dulles received. Additionally, not one American soldier was killed in the Bay of Pigs, a three-day affair, whereas if Bush, as he claims, based his invasion of Iraq on CIA intelligence that Iraq had WMD, this resulted in a war already five years long that has claimed thousands of American casualties. And finally, Dulles almost single-handedly founded the modern-day CIA, was its longest-serving director, and was an acknowledged giant in his field. Tenet was none of these things.

79 ... you're not going to have a perfect day. For those right-wing Republicans who say my calling Bush a son of a bitch shows a terrible lack of respect for the office of the presidency, I say this. I only have a total lack of respect for Bush, not the office he occupies. Indeed, one of the many reasons I have an animus for Bush is that I do have a lot of respect for the office of the presidency, and deep contempt for him for what he has done under the august imprimatur of that office.

By the way, although to this very day the hardcore right (about 30 percent of the Republican Party) thinks that Bush had every reason to do what he did in Iraq, and supports him without the slightest qualification, can you imagine, can you just imagine what their position would be if Clinton were in Bush's shoes? If he had done the exact same things Bush did in taking us to war in Iraq under false pretenses, with all the incredibly horrific consequences? I would bet my life, wager every penny I have, that these hypocritical SOBs would be savaging Clinton at the top of their lungs every day and demanding, not his impeachment or even imprisonment, but his scalp. I am absolutely, 100 percent sure of this.

CHAPTER 4:
THE PROSECUTION OF
GEORGE W. BUSH FOR MURDER

82 . . . Bush should have been impeached, convicted, and removed from office. Since Bush is near the end of his term in office, the drawn-out impeachment process would no longer be viable. Moreover, even if there were time and he was impeached, it is fanciful to believe that two-thirds of a Senate that is nearly evenly divided would convict him, as is required by the Constitution.

82 This, for being responsible for over *100,000 horrible deaths?* The 100,000 figure is an extremely conservative estimate. A 2007 national survey in Iraq by a British polling agency, ORB, which asked 1,499 adults, "How many members of your household, if any, have died as a result of the conflict in Iraq since 2003?" found 22 percent of Iraqi households that had suffered at least one death, for a projected 1.2 million deaths. A 2006 analysis by the John Hopkins Bloomberg School of Public Health, which was published in the British medical journal *Lancet,* estimated that 655,000 Iraqi civilians had died in the war. Both of these estimates are considered high by most experts. The lowest estimate of Iraqi civilian war dead comes from the Iraq Body Count, a nongovernmental British group that bases its numbers only on news media accounts, which everyone presumes to be low. From the beginning of the war to December 26, 2007, between 81,026 and 88,466 Iraqi civilians died in the war, the Body Count group said. The most comprehensive study of Iraqi war dead was released in January 2008 and was based on a survey by the Iraqi government supervised by the World Health Organization. The report said that around 150,000 Iraqis died violently in the war between the start of the war in March of 2003 and June of 2006. (Many thousands, of course, have died since then.)

85 . . . one of their options being the imposition of the death penalty . . . Actor Robert Redford, an outspoken foe of Bush and his administration for the Iraq war and an otherwise bright man, has called for a public apology from Bush and his people for "being transparently deceptive about weapons of mass destruction." Bob, apart from the fact that they of course would never, ever do that, if an apology won't even get you off the hook for a traffic ticket, much less a theft, burglary, or even one murder, it might not be quite enough for thousands of murders.

85–86 . . . many have argued that "Bush should be prosecuted for war crimes" (mostly for the torture of prisoners at Abu Ghraib and Guantanamo) at the International Criminal Court in The Hague, Netherlands. But for all intents and purposes this cannot be done. The International Criminal Court (ICC) was created in 2002 in Rome by the United Nations, but although it has a close functional relationship with the UN, it is independent of it. Among the obstacles that would preclude a prosecution of Bush at the ICC for his war in Iraq is the accepted definition of the term "war crimes." War crimes are considered to be large-scale atrocities and crimes against humanity committed during wartime, and thus far have been limited to genocide (the main war crime by far, and which is not involved here), mass torture, and rape. Although torture and rape have been committed by American soldiers in Iraq, certainly Bush never authorized the rapes, which were very few. The torture at the Abu Ghraib prison in Iraq and Guantanamo in Cuba in violation of the Geneva Conventions of

1949 not only was probably on too small a scale for a typical war crimes trial, but it is not clear that Bush himself authorized the torture. A February 7, 2002, executive order of his mandated that all detainees be treated humanely.*

But there are even greater obstacles. One, the ICC only has jurisdiction over nations that are a party to the ICC treaty, which the United States is not.† But even if it were, the ICC is a court of last resort. Article 17(a) of the statute creating the war crimes court expressly provides that it can only exercise its jurisdiction over a matter when the courts of the nation where the prospective defendant lives (here, Bush in the United States) are *"unwilling or unable* to genuinely carry out the investigation or prosecution." Of course, one of the two major purposes of the "Prosecution" chapter is to demonstrate that although it may turn out that no state or federal prosecutor may be *willing* to prosecute Bush for murder, they certainly have the jurisdiction and hence are *able* to.

However, even in situations where the ICC has no original jurisdiction, it can achieve jurisdiction over the citizens of every country in the world irrespective of the above exclusionary conditions if the United Nations Security Council refers a case to the ICC for criminal prosecution. The council consists of five permanent members (United States, China, France, Russia, and Great Britain) and ten countries that serve temporary two-year terms. At least seven of the fifteen Security Council members are needed for any

*Although the possibility of a prosecution of Bush for torture will not be examined in this book, if it could be shown that Bush authorized the torture of Iraq and Afghanistan war detainees and prisoners that we know took place at Abu Ghraib and at Guantanamo respectively, under 18 U.S.C. §2340–2340A (the War Crimes Act of 1996), he could be prosecuted for the torture. If convicted, he could be imprisoned for "not more than 20 years." If death resulted from the torture, he could be punished by "death or imprisoned for any term of years or for life." For a comprehensive discussion of this whole issue of a prosecution of Bush for torture under the War Crimes Act, see Elizabeth Holtzman's article "Torture and Accountability" in the July 18, 2005, issue of the *Nation*.

†Although 105 nations of the world signed the ICC treaty, the United States refused. The only other nations that refused were Israel and distinguished exemplars of freedom and democracy like the Peoples Republic of China, Iraq, Qatar, Libya, and Yemen.

resolution, and each of the five permanent members (except the one that is a party to the dispute; here, the United States) has veto power. It is inconceivable to me that the other four permanent members of the Security Council, one of which is Great Britain (which was complicit with Bush in the Iraq war), would all agree to pass a resolution referring Bush to the ICC for a war crimes prosecution. It's not going to happen. Indeed, even if that happened, and the ICC charged Bush with the war crime of over 100,000 deaths in the Iraq war and issued an arrest warrant to bring him to trial, the ICC is not invested with the power to execute its arrest warrants. Hence, it has to rely on governments to surrender their citizens to them. But the United States would not likely turn Bush over to the ICC for prosecution.

87 In the law, as in its well-known sense, the word "cause" means "to bring about, to bring into existence." *United States v. Leggett,* 269 F. 2d 35 (1959).

88 And as the court said in the 1993 case of *Gallimore v. Commonwealth of Virginia:* "The doctrine of innocent agent. . . ." *Gallimore v. Commonwealth of Virginia,* 436 S.E. 2d 421, 424 (1993). The doctrine of innocent agent is well established in the criminal law, e.g., *Smith v. State,* 17 S.W. 552 (1886); *Aldrich v. People,* 79 N.E. 964, 966 (1907); *State v. Bailey,* 60 S.E. 785 (1908); *United States v. Kenofskey,* 243 U.S. 440 (1916); *United States v. Incisco,* 292 F. 2d 374 (1961); *United States v. Levine,* 457 F. 2d 1186 (1972); see also Section 2.06, 2(a) of the *Model Penal Code and Commentaries,* Part 1, 1985, American Law Institute.

88 The innocent agent "is not an offender" . . . (*People v. Keller,* 79 C.A. 612, 617 [1926]).

88 The defendant "is guilty as if he had done the act himself." (*People v. Whitmer,* 16 N.E.2d 757–758 [1938]).

88 . . . he is criminally responsible for the thousands of American deaths in Iraq. Although the typical situation is where the innocent agent has been tricked or duped by the principal into committing his act, there is no such legal requirement, in the cases or by statute, that this exist before the innocent agent doctrine applies.* With the whole purpose for the doctrine being to prevent someone from escaping criminal responsibility by getting someone else to do his dirty work for him, why would the law care *how* he got the party committing the act to do it?

89 In the law, to instigate is "to stimulate . . . (*Snider v. Wimberly*, 209 S.W. 2d 239, 242 [1948]).

89 So Bush would be criminally responsible for the deaths of the 4,000 American soldiers under both the theories of vicarious liability and aiding and abetting. Under the aiding and abetting theory, the innocent agent, of course, still makes an appearance as the perpetrator of the killing. Under both the vicarious liability of conspiracy and aiding and abetting theories, the innocent agent has no criminal culpability for the killings since, as indicated, he has no criminal intent. So the very same killing by the innocent agent is a legally justifiable homicide as to him, but murder as to Bush.

92 Surely Bush couldn't be heard to argue that a president is incapable of committing a crime under the U.S. Constitution . . . With respect to the issue of whether or not Bush could find any sanctuary in the U.S. Constitution for his criminal conduct, it should be pointed out that by Congress's joint resolution on October 11, 2002, giving its consent for Bush's invasion of Iraq, the normal constitutional question of whether the president, independent of Congress, can go to war with a foreign nation is rendered moot. But as a summary of constitutional law on this point, Article I, §8, cl. 11 of the U.S. Constitution gives Congress the power to declare war. The basis for this power is Article I, §8, cl. 1, which provides that Congress shall "provide for the common defense and general welfare of the United States." Al-

---

*Section 31 of the California Penal Code—which prohibits the encouragement of children under fourteen, and lunatics or idiots, to commit a crime; or bringing about, by fraud [trickery] or force, the drunkenness of another to commit a crime; or threatening or compelling another to commit a crime—cannot be interpreted to read that the innocent agent rule only applies if the agent is tricked into committing a crime. Indeed, in the sole allusion in §31 to trickery, only the use of trickery to get one drunk, not to trick him into committing a crime (which is a separate, though related matter) is mentioned.

though Article II, §2, cl. 1 does provide that "the president shall be Commander-in-Chief of the Army and Navy of the United States," technically this only places the president at the head of this nation's armed forces. It clearly envisions, as a predicate to his conducting war as the head of the nation's armed forces, that war has been declared. And Article I, §8, cl. 11 ("the Congress shall have power . . . to declare war") exclusively and unambiguously gives that power to Congress, not the president. To assume that Art. I, § 8, cl. 11 only gives Congress the power to utter the words, or put in writing "We declare war," not actually initiate war, is to assume that the framers intended to confer upon Congress a totally idle and meaningless power.

So much for the interpretation of words and phrases, and the apparent intent of the framers of the Constitution. The reality is that throughout much of this nation's history, presidents, *without* the approval of Congress, have time and again committed American military forces abroad. Although all presidents, during their inauguration ceremonies, swear to uphold the Constitution, when it comes to arguably the most serious and important (in terms of consequences) part of the Constitution—who has the right to commit the military forces of this nation to an armed conflict with another nation—most presidents, even self-proclaimed "strict constructionists" of the Constitution like Ronald Reagan and the first President George Bush, have cavalierly ignored the explicit constitutional language and their presidential oath. As political commentator Russell Baker has wryly observed: "Presidents now say, sure, the Constitution gives Congress the right to declare war, but it doesn't forbid Presidents to make war, so long as they don't declare it. As a result, the declared war has become obsolete. Its successor is the undeclared war."

In a 1952 U.S. Supreme Court case dealing with a different use of presidential power, the dissent noted that even as of that date, fifty-six years ago, there had been "125 incidents in our history in which presidents, without congressional authorization, and in the absence of a declaration of war, have ordered the armed forces to take action or maintain positions abroad." (In fact, only five times in the nation's history has Congress declared war: the War of 1812, the Mexican War (1846), the Spanish-American War (1898), and World Wars One (1917) and Two (1941).) In the Persian Gulf War, although Congress adopted resolutions authorizing the use of force (not quite the same as a declaration of war), the Bush administration flatly asserted it had the right to commit the nation to war without a congressional declaration of any kind. A 1966 Department of State memorandum states: "Over a very long period in our history, practice and precedent have confirmed the constitutional authority to engage the United States forces in hostility without a declaration of war" ("The Legality of United States Participation in the Defense of Vietnam," 54 *Department of State Bulletin*, 474, 488 [1966]).

So presidents throughout our history (and even since the 1973 War Powers Resolution [50 U.S.C. §'s 1541–1548], which directs, among other things, that the chief executive shall at least "consult with Congress," a law that no president or Congress has taken very seriously) have for the most part not even bothered to seek congressional approval for the employment of military forces abroad. Just a few relatively recent examples include President Bush's invasion of Panama in 1989 and President Clinton's bombing of Kosovo in 1999.

Although, as indicated, the above issue of the dichotomy between presidential as opposed to congressional power in going to war is not an issue in the proposed prosecution of Bush, what is instructive—in fact, almost dispositively so—from all the examples of this nation's use of force in foreign lands, with or without congressional approval, is that every single one of the presidents involved did so (at least there's no credible evidence to the contrary) not only to protect the security and welfare of this country, but they acted in good faith, without criminal intent. That, I believe any historian will find, is the common thread behind all of their actions.

Despite this, we can expect Bush's legal team to trot out, in his defense, the so-called war power of a president, an "inherent" power whose many proponents acknowledge no constitutional language expressly grants, but which, they say, is implied from the aggregate of the president's enumerated powers under the Constitution, particularly Article II, §1, cl. 1 that says: "The executive power shall be vested in [the] President . . ."; Article II, §2, cl. 1 that says: "The President shall be Commander-in-Chief of the Army and Navy of the United States . . ."; and Article II, §3 that says: "He shall take care that the laws be faithfully executed . . ."

The exercise of the "war power" by a president has indeed taken place not only when a president orders this nation's military intervention on foreign soil without congressional authorization, as President Truman did with the Korean War in 1950, but when he takes some action in the *conduct* of any war, e.g., President Lincoln's suspension of the writ of habeas corpus in 1861 during the Civil War.

The position that Bush would *have* to take under the inherent war power argument is that even if he did not take this nation to war lawfully (which he would first maintain he did) and did so, as the prosecution would allege, under false pretenses, his "war power" would protect him from criminal prosecution because the power is absolute, giving him complete discretion. Unfortunately for Bush, there is no authority for this. Two of the principal cases Bush would be expected to rely upon to support his "president as dictator" position are *The Prize Cases* and the *Curtiss-Wright* case. In *The Prize Cases*, the Supreme Court dealt with President Lincoln's declaration in 1861 that the Confederate states were in a state of insurrection against the United States, and the constitutionality of his order, pursuant to this civil war, to blockade and seize foreign ships doing business with Confederate states. The owners of these ships, challenging Lincoln's actions, sued the federal government, but the U.S. Supreme Court upheld the blockade and seizure. In doing so, the court said that the question of how a president should respond to such a state of war is one "to be decided by him."

Though this language has given hope to adherents of expansive presidential war powers, it should not, since the context in which it was used shows it was clearly limited to an *emergency* situation. The court said that for constitutional purposes, an insurrection was no different than repelling a foreign invasion. It is clear that the "to be decided by him" words the court used dealt with the president "suppressing an insurrection" and determining "what degree of force the *crisis* demands" (*The Prize Cases*, 67 U.S. [2 Black] 635–638, 647–649, 668, 670 [1862]). Hence, *The Prize Cases* only stand for the constitutionality of any *defensive* war a president might wage unilaterally.* Obviously, Bush's taking this nation to war when we were neither being invaded by

---

*No one questions, when there is no time to secure congressional authorization, the power and discretion of the president to repel an invasion or suppress an insurrection. "The power need not rest on any specific provision of the Constitution; as a necessary concomitant of sovereignty itself the inherent right of national self-defense gives the President full power to defend the country against sudden attack with whatever means are at his disposal as Commander-in-Chief" (Notes: "Congress, the President and the Power to Commit Forces to Combat," 81 *Harvard Law Review*, pp. 1771, 1778 [1968]). Perhaps the first acknowledgment of this appeared in James Madison's notes at the Constitutional Convention in Philadelphia on August 17, 1787. He wrote: "Mr. M [Madison] and Mr. Gerry moved to insert 'declare,' striking out 'make' war, leaving to the Executive the power to *repel sudden attacks*" (*The Records of the Federal Convention of 1787*, pp. 318–319, edited by Max Farrand, Yale University Press, New Haven, Connecticut, 1911).

Iraq, nor about to be, can find no justification in *The Prize Cases*. Even if the facts had been similar, Bush's great criminality, as opposed to the conduct of Lincoln, would make such a comparison repugnant.

In *Curtiss-Wright*, Congress passed a joint resolution in 1934 providing that *if* the president found that prohibiting "the sale of arms and munitions of war in the United States to those countries [Bolivia and Paraguay] now engaged in armed conflict in the Chaco [a region encompassing parts of Bolivia, Paraguay, and Argentina] may contribute to the reestablishment of peace between those countries," and further, made a proclamation to that effect, then it would be unlawful to sell such arms and munitions. President Roosevelt made such a finding and proclamation, and when the defendant, Curtiss-Wright Corp., violated the president's arms embargo by selling machine guns to Bolivia, it was indicted. The Supreme Court rejected the defendant's appeal that, among other things, the indictment was improper because the president's discretion was "uncontrolled"; that is, unbridled and absolute, and hence, unconstitutional.

The court, in *Curtiss-Wright*, used language in its opinion that has been eagerly seized upon by war power advocates, but criticized by most constitutional scholars as wrong. In dictum, the court spoke of the "exclusive power of the president as the *sole* organ of the federal government in the field of international relations," which these scholars feel suggests that only the executive branch of government, not Congress (legislative branch), has any jurisdiction over foreign affairs. But the court couldn't possibly have meant that since Article I, § 8, cl. 11 of the Constitution reposes in Congress the exclusive authority to "declare war." Moreover, even in the *Curtiss-Wright* case itself, the court spoke of the May 28, 1934, joint resolution of Congress that *delegated* to the president the discretion to make a finding on whether prohibiting sales of arms and munitions would help promote peace in the Chaco. It seems the key words in the language of the court are "international *relations*." And, of course, the executive branch, through the president and the Departments of State and Defense, *is* the only organ of our federal government that officially represents us in foreign affairs. The president and his secretary of state, for instance, meet at summits with their counterparts from other nations like Russia. American ambassadors to foreign nations are in the executive branch of government, etc.

Indeed, the *Curtiss-Wright* court borrowed its "sole organ" language from a March 7, 1800, speech in the House of Representatives by member

John Marshall—which was before he became chief justice of the Supreme Court the following year—in which he coupled his language "the President is the sole organ of the nation in its external *relations*" with the words "and its sole *representative* with foreign nations." Why some scholars feel that the court's saying the president is the sole organ of our government in the field of "international *relations*" is synonymous with saying the *Curtiss* court held that the president can act unilaterally in *making* foreign policy (e.g., Louis Fisher, in his book *Presidential War Power*) is not clear. Even if we make the assumption that this is true, the *Curtiss* court also said that in the president's relations with other nations, Congress should accord the president "a *degree* of discretion and freedom from statutory restriction." The very word "degree" connotes the absence of absolute, unbridled authority, which proponents of broad presidential war powers would want.

In fact, even if we make the further assumption that the much maligned *Curtiss* court meant, by its "sole organ" language, that the president had the next thing to absolute discretion in the conduct of foreign affairs, the court, in the same "sole organ" paragraph, went on to clearly circumscribe that discretion, and in a way that would eviscerate any argument by Bush that the *Curtiss* decision legally authorized whatever his conduct was found to be in taking this nation to war in Iraq. The court said the president's sole organ power in the field of international relations, "like every other governmental power *must* be exercised *in subordination to* the applicable provisions of the Constitution" (*United States v. Curtiss-Wright Export Corp.*, 299 U.S. 304, 307, 311–312, 319–320 [1936]). And Article II, §4 of the Constitution expressly disapproves of the president committing "high crimes and misdemeanors" in the performance of his duties to the extent that, apart from any criminal prosecution, he can be impeached, convicted, and removed from office if he does. Here, with Bush, we're not just talking about high crimes and misdemeanors, we're talking about 4,000 *murders*.*

In any event, no court or serious constitutional scholar would ever say that in an American president's conduct of foreign affairs he has absolute, unqualified discretion and authority to do anything he wants, including

---

*It should be noted parenthetically that perhaps the best definition of "high crimes and misdemeanors" yet was that of Supreme Court justice Story, who wrote in 1833 in his *Commentaries on the Constitution of the United States* that the crime had to be one "in violation of [the president's] public trust and duties."

committing grave criminal offenses, all in the name of national self-defense. This indisputable verity cannot be challenged, and is why any "war power" defense of Bush would be rejected out of hand by the courts. Indeed, can you even *imagine* Bush's lawyer, seeking to quash an indictment for murder against Bush, arguing in front of the U.S. Supreme Court: "Our position is that even if it were proven to be the case that President Bush took this nation to war in Iraq under false pretenses and by lying to the nation, the war power which is inherent in the Constitution is such that he should be immune from criminal prosecution"?

The notion of unbridled and absolute presidential discretion and authority in the name of self-defense is so diametrically in conflict with the antitotalitarian principles upon which this nation was founded that it is rarely even discussed, and when it is, there is the sense that the speaker feels it is almost unworthy of discussion.

In *The Prize Cases* in 1862, the U.S. Supreme Court spoke out against the idea of a president first deciding himself that the nation is in danger, then asserting "the principle of self-defense," and then claiming "all power" like a "dictator" to wage war. "To suppose this court would [even] desire argument against such a notion would be offensive," the court said.

On February 15, 1848, in a letter to a friend, then U.S. House of Representatives member Abraham Lincoln wrote: "Allow the president to invade a neighboring nation whenever *he* shall deem it necessary to repel an invasion, and you allow him to do so, *whenever he may choose to say* he deems it necessary for such a purpose—and you allow him to make war at pleasure . . . If, today, he should choose to say he thinks it necessary to invade Canada to prevent the British from invading us, how could you stop him? You may say to him, 'I see no probability of the British invading us, but he will say to you 'be silent, I see it, if you don't' . . . This, our [Constitutional] Convention understood to be the most oppressive of all Kingly oppressions; and they resolved to so frame the Constitution that *no one man* should hold the power of bringing the oppression upon us" (all emphases in the original) (*The Collected Works of Abraham Lincoln*, 451–452, Roy Basler, ed., vol. 1, Rutgers University Press, New Brunswick, New Jersey, 1953). And Lincoln wasn't even talking about a president taking this nation to war under false pretenses, just to his taking the nation to war at his whim.

Sixteen years after the *Curtiss* case, the U.S. Supreme Court dealt with a much more direct case of a president's war power being exercised to help the United States in an existing war, yet the court, in a six-to-three decision, made it clear that even in this type of situation the president's executive power was far from unlimited. In April of 1952, President Truman, to avert a scheduled work stoppage about to take place in a few hours because of a nationwide strike of steel workers—a strike he believed would jeopardize the defense of this nation during the existing Korean War—issued an executive order directing the secretary of commerce to seize and operate most of this nation's steel mills to maintain production. The steel companies argued that the president's order was not authorized in the Constitution or laws of the United States, and the court agreed. In a concurring opinion, Justice Jackson wrote that the notion of "unlimited executive power" emanating from sources such as Article II, §2, cl. 1 of the Constitution that "the President shall be Commander-in-Chief of the Army and Navy of the United States" was not viable. This constitutional provision, Jackson wrote, "is sometimes advanced as support for any presidential action, internal or external, involving the use of force, the idea being that it vests power to do anything, anywhere, that can be done with an army or navy . . . I cannot foresee all that it might entail if the court should endorse this argument . . . No doctrine that the court could promulgate would seem to me more sinister and alarming . . ." (*Youngstown Sheet and Tube Co. v. Sawyer*, 343 U.S. 579–580, 641–642, 659 [1952]).

If the U.S. Supreme Court held that the president couldn't even take over the steel mills during the Korean War under his "war power," certainly he couldn't take this nation to war on a lie.

If Bush is prosecuted for murder and he seeks protection for his criminal behavior in the "inherent war power" argument, he will find that the container of legal authority for such a proposition is as empty as a bird's nest in winter.

93 The U.S. Supreme Court said in *Morissette v. United States* . . . (342 U.S. 246 [1952]).

93 The *mens rea* for murder is malice aforethought. Since we don't know for sure just what Bush's motive was in taking this nation to war, and since some lay people believe that the prosecution, in a criminal trial, has the burden of proving motive, I want to point out that this is incorrect. Motive is not the same as intent, two terms that are sometimes erroneously used interchangeably by those unfamiliar with the criminal law. In the criminal law, "motive" is the emotional urge that induces someone to commit a crime. It is different from "intent" in that a person can intend to steal property or kill someone and can be found guilty of that theft or homicide irrespective of what his motive was (e.g., need, avarice, revenge, jealousy, etc.). To say it more succinctly, motive is the reason that prompts a person to act (or fail to act). Intent is the state of mind with which the act is done. Motive, of course, may aid you in determining what one's intent or state of mind was. While intent is an element of every serious crime, and a prosecutor has to prove it beyond a reasonable doubt, motive is *never* an element of the *corpus delicti** of any crime. Therefore, the prosecution *never* has to prove motive. All it has to prove is that the defendant (here, prospectively, Bush) did, in fact, commit the crime with the requisite intent, not why. I've put people on death row without knowing for sure what their motive was for the murder. All I knew for sure was that they had put someone in his or her grave and had no legal right (e.g., justifiable homicide) to do it.

93 In this case, the "act" by Bush would be his ordering his military to invade Iraq with American soldiers . . . Even if one were to say that the "act" would be the actual act of an Iraqi killing an American soldier, such as by shooting him, Bush would still be guilty of this act under the vicarious liability and aiding and abetting theories discussed in the text. But in a war situation where thousands have been killed, no court would expect a prosecution of Bush to examine 4,000 separate acts of killing in Iraq. The real criminal act here is Bush's invading Iraq, an act that is synonymous with the act of killing, since Bush knew the invasion would automatically cause the deaths of American soldiers.

94 . . . that is, the self-defense argument—he reasonably believed that Iraq constituted an imminent threat to the security of this country, so Bush

---

**Corpus delicti* is not, as many lay people believe, the dead body in a homicide case, but rather the body or elements of the crime.

struck first . . . Is there any way that Bush could argue that credibly after the Second World War the charter of the United Nations was ratified on August 8, 1945, as a treaty by the U.S. Senate, and the U.S. Constitution (Article VI, cl. 2) provides that "this Constitution and the Laws of the United States which shall be made in pursuance thereof and *all treaties made*, or which shall be made, under the authority of the United States, *shall be the supreme law of the land*"? And that Article 51 of the treaty (UN charter) *authorizes* unilateral self-defense? Actually, Bush would be worse off making this argument of self-defense than utilizing the traditional law of self-defense, which allows one to use deadly force if in reasonable fear of imminent death or great bodily harm. Article 51 provides that "nothing in the present Charter shall impair the inherent right of individual . . . self-defense if an *armed attack occurs* against a Member of the United Nations . . ." Under this incorrectly crafted language, a nation could only unilaterally act in self-defense *after* it was already attacked, which makes no sense at all. Also, by definition, such an attacked nation wouldn't even have time, under these circumstances, to first get the UN Security Council's approval to respond in self-defense. And Security Council approval for anything short of what is provided in Article 51 is made clear in Article 51 when it goes on to say that what a member does while acting unilaterally in self-defense "shall be immediately reported to the Security Council and shall not in any way affect the authority and responsibility of the Security Council under the present Charter to take at any time such action as it deems necessary in order to maintain or restore international peace and security."

As is clearly shown in the main text, Bush's conduct neither qualified as self-defense under Article 51, since Iraq never invaded the United States, nor under the traditional law of self-defense, since the evidence is overwhelming that Bush had no reasonable fear of an imminent attack by Hussein or anyone he was aiding and abetting.

In any event, Bush can find no comfort in the treaty–U.S. Constitution–UN argument. All he can find is that in addition to his having violated the murder statutes of America, he violated international law when he invaded Iraq. Article 2 (4) of the UN charter expressly provides that "all members *shall refrain* in their international relations from the threat or *use of force* against the territorial integrity or political independence of any state . . ." Only a UN Security Council resolution could have authorized such an invasion.* Bush, of course, knew this, and this is why he sought such a resolution (the so-called second resolution, since the UN Security Council, in its first resolution, authorized Bush's father to use force against Iraq in the 1991 Gulf War, but only to achieve the limited objective of removing Hussein's forces from Kuwait, not to invade Iraq itself or remove Hussein from power). And we all know that the UN Security Council refused to make such a resolution; that is, refused to authorize Bush's invasion of Iraq. Indeed, on March 17, 2003, two days before the war, UN secretary-general Kofi Annan said that any attack by the United States on Iraq without a further resolution would be a violation of the UN charter. Despite this, Bush, in a rogue fashion, invaded Iraq anyway.

Bush apologists can be expected to argue that UN Resolution 1441, made in November of 2002, sought to "ensure full and immediate compliance" by Iraq with UN Resolution 687 (made in April of 1991 after the Persian Gulf War), which required Iraq to "unconditionally accept the destruction, removal or rendering harmless under international supervision of all chemical and biological weapons." Resolution 1441 said that if Iraq did not comply with its "disarmament obligations," it would face "serious consequences." What those serious consequences were was not set forth in 1441. In any event, since this was a UN resolution, even if the consequences included an invasion and war, the invasion would have to be by a coalition of UN forces operating with UN Security Council approval, which is not what occurred.

Bush defenders would sound terribly foolish arguing that the legal justi-

---

*And even this authorization would have been vitiated if obtained by false representations made to the United Nations by the Bush administration, which occurred in this case (e.g., in Secretary of State Colin Powell's address to the UN Security Council on February 5, 2003). Moreover, an American court prosecuting Bush for murder where he *had* gotten a UN resolution authorizing war could be expected to say, in effect, "Although the United Nations can authorize war, it cannot authorize murder. There is no statutory defense to murder in the criminal codes of this state (e.g., Arizona, Vermont, California) called 'the United Nation's defense.'" So even UN approval would not, per se, insulate Bush from criminal responsibility. But as indicated, this discussion is moot since the United Nations never gave its approval for Bush to go to war.

fication for Bush's war lies in Iraq's failure to comply with UN Resolutions 687 and 1441. In other words, they would be *relying completely* on the UN resolutions that Iraq disarm, but at the same time presuming that it wasn't necessary to get UN approval for a war based on a violation of the UN's own resolutions—that the United States, not the UN, should decide how to deal with a violation of UN resolutions.* That argument is legally embarrassing.

By way of footnote, it also isn't a legal defense for Bush to argue: "Well, the U.S. bombed the Kosovo province of Yugoslavia in 1999 without UN approval, only that of NATO." That would be like a driver of a car saying to a police officer about to give him a speeding ticket: "Why are you giving me one when cars on my left and right were traveling just as fast as I?" So, maybe the U.S. (in the Clinton administration) was also in violation of Article 2. But by the way, there is no evidence that President Clinton and his people engaged in lies, deliberate distortions, and hence, criminality leading up to our bombing of Kosovo to stop the genocide of the ethnic Albanians by the Serbs there. Indeed, even if Clinton had lied to the American people in the Kosovo intervention, since not one American soldier lost his life, this would, by definition, preclude any *murder* prosecution of Clinton.

95 There are cases where a period of time as short as several seconds sufficed. (For example, *People v. Wells*, 10 C. 2d 610, 625 [1938]).

95 Even a killing where there was only implied malice *and no specific intent to kill* can not only result in a conviction of murder (which it could in any state), but a sentence of death . . . It shouldn't be assumed that since Bush never intended to kill any of the specific American soldiers who died in his war that no express malice could be shown against him. To be guilty of murder it is not necessary that you intend to kill a specific *identifiable* person, which is the usual situation. Defendants have been convicted of murder, even sentenced to death, for shooting into a house or car or train or

---

*It should be noted that when Bush went to war, the United Nations had *not* declared that Iraq was in violation of the new round of inspections commencing in November of 2002 and continuing right up to almost the eve of war.

room and killing someone even though they did not know who was inside, and did not intend to kill any specific person. So a specific intent to kill the actual victim need not be shown to constitute murder. Therefore, the fact that Bush did not specifically intend to kill a *particular* soldier or soldiers would not, by itself, be a defense to murder.

96 "... it follows that if one willfully does an act, *the natural tendency of which* is to destroy another's life, the irresistible conclusion ... is that the destruction of such other person's life *was intended.*"(*People v. Coolidge*, 26 Ill. 2d 533, 537 [1963]; see also, *People v. Fitzgerald*, 524 NE 2d 1190, 1193 [1988].

97 The main underlying felonies that are usually mentioned in statutes throughout the land ... (For example, §189 of the California Penal Code; Title 18 of the United States Code, §1111.)

98 In the 1983 case of *United States v. Shaw*, the premeditation was in the form of "lying in wait," ... (701 F. 2d 367, 374–376, 392–394 [1983]).

98 ... the defendant thereby doing an act exceedingly dangerous with reckless and wanton disregard for the consequences, though no specific intent to kill was shown. The conviction of first degree murder in the Shaw case was affirmed on appeal and the U.S. Supreme Court denied *certiorari*; that is, denied the defendant's attempt to have the highest court review the case.

99 Ironically, the case relied on in the federal courts for the best definition of implied malice in a second degree murder prosecution is *United States of America v. Bush* ... (416 F. 2d 823, 826 [1969]).

101 One of the strongest pieces of evidence that Bush lied to Congress and the American people about Hussein being an imminent threat to the security of this country so he could get their support for the war ... Conservatives, in response to this book, can be expected to counter that the so-called Gulf of Tonkin incident in August of 1964 was staged by the administration of President Johnson and used by LBJ to get

Congress's and the nation's support for the Gulf of Tonkin Resolution, enabling LBJ to take America to the war he wanted with Vietnam. But there is no merit to this argument and no comparison between Bush's and LBJ's conduct.

With respect to the Gulf of Tonkin incident, briefly, at 3:40 a.m. (EST) on August 2, 1964, a U.S. destroyer, the USS *Maddox*, on reconnaissance patrol in the Gulf of Tonkin (an arm of the South China sea off North Vietnam), was fired on by three North Vietnamese torpedo boats, though none of the torpedoes struck the *Maddox*. Aircraft from the nearby U.S. aircraft carrier *Ticonderoga* destroyed one of the three torpedo boats and damaged the other two. The *Maddox* and *Ticonderoga* were in international waters about 28 nautical miles (31.2 statute miles) off the North Vietnam coast conducting covert operations at the time. This attack on the *Maddox* is not in dispute and North Vietnam never denied the attack, although in 1997, General Nguyen Dinh Uoc, the director of the Institute of Military History in Hanoi, said that the assault was instituted by a local North Vietnamese commander, not the North Vietnamese government. In any event, it was an unprovoked attack, but the Johnson administration did nothing to retaliate beyond the actions of the aircraft from the *Ticonderoga*. So at least up to this point no one could possibly claim that the Gulf of Tonkin incident reflected any desire by LBJ to go to war.

Where the "LBJ wanted to go to war" proponents make their argument is with a second alleged attack, again by three torpedo boats, on the *Maddox* in the late morning of August 4, 1964. One has to say "alleged" because such an attack was never confirmed to anyone's complete satisfaction. Indeed, later, at 1:25 p.m. that day, Captain John J. Herrick, commander of the two destroyer patrol of the *Maddox* and the *C. Turner Joy*, cabled Honolulu (headquarters of the Pacific Fleet) and Washington: "Review of action makes many recorded contacts and torpedoes fired appear doubtful. Freak weather effects and over eager sonarman may have accounted for many reports. No actual sightings by *Maddox*. Suggest complete evaluation before any further action." Pursuant to this, Secretary of Defense Robert McNamara telephoned Admiral Ulysses S. Grant Sharp, the commander-in-chief, Pacific Fleet, in Hawaii and told him they had to "be damned sure that no retaliatory action was taken until any doubts as to what went on were eliminated." At 2:48 p.m., Herrrick sent another and different message which now stated,

"Certain that original ambush was bonafide."* Sharp continued to investigate and at 5:23 p.m. called Air Force lieutenant general David A. Burchinal of the Joint Chiefs of Staff and stated he had no doubt that a second attack on the *Maddox* had, indeed, taken place.

On LBJ's authorization, at 10:43 p.m., U.S. aircraft from the *Ticonderoga* and *Constellation* started flying sixty-four sorties against North Vietnamese

---

*In October of 2005, the *New York Times* learned the contents of a then classified 2001 report by a historian for the National Security Agency (NSA), the nation's top-secret eavesdropping and code-breaking agency. The historian, Robert J. Hanyok, wrote in his report that during this second incident, NSA officers had misinterpreted North Vietnamese intercepts, making an apparently honest mistake in concluding that there had been an attack. However, after months studying documents in the NSA archives, Hanyok further concluded that midlevel agency officials at NSA discovered the errors very shortly thereafter but covered the errors up and doctored documents so as to provide evidence of an actual attack. Hanyok's report also concluded that neither President Johnson and his advisers nor even top NSA and defense department officials knew of the deception.

If Hanyok is correct, this inexcusable deception played a part in Congress ultimately signing the Gulf of Tonkin Resolution, which authorized war with North Vietnam. Indeed, the first paragraph of the Resolution reads: "Whereas naval units of the Communist regime in Vietnam, in violation of the United Nations and of international law, have deliberately and *repeatedly* attacked United States naval vessels lawfully present in international waters . . ." So the deception could not have been more serious, although, as indicated, no one disputes the first attack on the *Maddox*, which alone could have contributed substantially to the resolution. Edwin E. Moise of Clemson University, a longtime student of the Gulf of Tonkin incident, said he was "surprised at the notion of deliberate deception at NSA. But I get surprised a lot."

On November 30, 2005, the NSA released the classified report, and it confirmed the accuracy of the October *New York Times* article. In the report, Hanyok says the NSA's intelligence officers "deliberately skewed" the evidence passed on to policy makers to lead them to believe that North Vietnamese ships had attacked American destroyers on August 4, 1964. Hanyok said that 90 percent of the NSA's intercepts of North Vietnamese communications regarding the alleged August 4 attack were never passed on to policy makers. "The overwhelming body of reports, if used, would have told the story that no attack had happened. So a conscious effort ensued to demonstrate that an attack occurred."

patrol boat bases and a nearby oil complex supporting the boats. It was the first U.S. bombing of North Vietnam in what was to become the Vietnam War. It was estimated that twenty-five patrol boats were damaged or destroyed and 90 percent of the oil complex was destroyed. At 11:36 p.m., President Johnson told the nation, in a televised address from the White House, of the North Vietnamese attack and our retaliation, saying, "We seek no wider war."

On August 7, just a few days after the above incidents, Congress passed the Gulf of Tonkin Resolution sought by the Johnson administration by an overwhelming vote of 88–2 in the Senate and 416–0 in the House of Representatives. The resolution authorized the president "to take all necessary steps, including the use of armed force, to assist any member" of SEATO (Southeast Asia Treaty Organization, which included South Vietnam) "in defense of its freedom." In other words, Congress gave President Johnson the authority to go to war in Vietnam if he so chose.

Many have alleged, almost from the very beginning, that the whole Gulf of Tonkin incident was a pretext for war provoked or staged by the Johnson administration to help him during his campaign for reelection against Senator Barry Goldwater. The corollary argument, shorn of its political allegation, has also been made that the incident was provoked or staged, as indicated, to enable Johnson to get a congressional resolution authorizing war. But William P. Bundy, assistant secretary of state for Far Eastern affairs, told the Senate Foreign Relations Committee on September 20, 1966, that he was in the process of drafting a similar resolution for the Johnson administration *before* the Gulf of Tonkin incident occurred, explaining this was routine and normal contingency planning to prepare for the reality that "things might take a more drastic turn" for the worse in Vietnam. One of those who began to strongly suggest the pretext argument was Senator J. William Fulbright, who had helped gather support for the passage of the Tonkin Resolution but later came to believe he had been misled by the Johnson administration. And a February 1968 Senate Foreign Relations Committee hearing that reexamined the evidence was unable to categorically resolve precisely what happened.

But in addition to the very important fact that no credible evidence has surfaced in almost forty-five years that the Gulf of Tonkin incident was provoked or staged, there is one reality that I believe clearly demonstrates everything was on the up-and-up, at least as far as Johnson and his advisers were concerned. And that comes from the book *Taking Charge*, edited with commentary by presidential historian Michael Beschloss, which was published in 1997 and contains transcripts of taped telephone conversations between LBJ and his advisers, primarily Secretary of Defense Robert McNamara, during the Tonkin incident. As the transcripts reflect, from the moment LBJ first discusses the incident all the way through his working out how to resolve it, he clearly is dealing with new information and an evolving situation not of his making. One example is August 4, 1964, 11:06 a.m. (around the time of the alleged second attack):

MCNAMARA: Mr. President, we just had word by telephone from Admiral Sharp that the destroyer is under torpedo attack.

LBJ: [almost inaudible sound]

MCNAMARA: I think I might get Dean Rusk and Mac Bundy and have them come over here and we'll go over these retaliatory actions and then we ought to —

LBJ : I sure think you ought to agree to that. Yeah . . . Now where are these torpedoes coming from?

MCNAMARA: We don't know. Presumably from these unidentified craft that I mentioned to you a moment ago. We thought that the unidentified craft might include one PT boat, which has torpedo capability, and two Savatow boats, which we don't credit with torpedo capability, although they may have it.

LBJ : What are these planes of ours doing around while they're being attacked?

MCNAMARA: Presumably the planes are attacking the ships. We don't have any word from Sharp on that. The planes would be in the area at the present time. All eight of them.

LBJ : Okay, you get them over there and then you come over here.

Are we to believe that LBJ and McNamara (who, if the Tonkin incident were not legitimate, *would have had* to be the main architects of the charade, as indeed some claim them to be) not only manufactured the whole incident, but when they thereafter discussed it on the phone with each other were following a fabricated script, right down to the interruptions and un-grammatical utterances? Though one would have to say that this was *theoretically* possible, how many people would actually believe this, particularly in view of the context—the clear weight of the evidence showing that Johnson was searching for a way to avoid war, not precipitate it?

By way of footnote on this issue, in November of 1995, McNamara, on a visit to Hanoi, spoke to General Vo Nguyen Giap. Giap was the North Vietnamese vice premier for defense during the Gulf of Tonkin period, and Mc-Namara reported that Giap had convinced him that no second attack on the *Maddox* had ever happened. "I am absolutely positive," McNamara said, that the second attack never took place. (Giap did confirm to McNamara that a Vietnamese ship did carry out the first attack on the USS *Maddox*.) If McNamara had been a part of a deliberately provoked or staged Gulf of Tonkin incident (which again, if the incident were provoked or staged, he would have had to be), he hardly would have made any concession suggesting that the Tonkin incident never happened.

If the Gulf of Tonkin incident that led to the resolution had been pro-voked or staged by the Johnson administration to get the resolution, it would seem that with the nation and the whole of Congress behind John-son, *that* would have been the opportune time, politically, for him to have sent combat troops to Vietnam. But as we know, it wasn't until March 8, 1965, *seven months after the resolution*, that LBJ finally sent U.S. combat troops to Vietnam, and July 27, 1965, that he decided to embark on a major ground war in Vietnam. A few hours of sorties against the North Vietnamese patrol boats and their supporting oil complex was the only and very limited extent of LBJ's response to the Tonkin incident at the time it allegedly occurred. So no comparison can be made at all to LBJ's conduct regarding the Gulf of Tonkin incident and Bush's egregiously criminal conduct in taking America to war in Iraq on a lie.

Bush apologists, always denying all malfeasance on Bush's part, like to say that even if what the Democrats claim about Bush were true, President Franklin Delano Roosevelt was even worse during Pearl Harbor, yet Democrats have no desire to attack him for this. As with Johnson, there is no parallel between Bush's conduct vis-à-vis Roosevelt's in the Second World War. Though some have claimed that Roosevelt knew the attack on Pearl Harbor was coming and did nothing about it because he wanted to go to war with Japan, most historians do not believe this. No one has ever accused Roosevelt of being an evil person, and if he knew the attack was coming, he'd have had to be evil to not alert the navy that an attack was expected. With an alert, the sailors could have left their ships and the battleships would have been separated, instead of their being lined up next to each other, as they were, enabling the greatest harm to be done. In other words, if Roosevelt wanted the Japanese to attack Pearl Harbor to justify going to war, he could have still had the same justification for war because of the Japanese attack without knowingly sacrificing the twenty-four hundred American lives that were lost. Again, no one has ever suggested Roosevelt was an evil man, and there's simply no way to compare Roosevelt's conduct to what Bush did in Iraq.

But here's the clincher with respect to Johnson and Roosevelt. If, in fact, they did do what many Bush supporters and conservatives say they did, then they should have been prosecuted for murder, too. And if they had, the punkish college cheerleader from Crawford, Texas, may have thought twice before lying to the nation to take us to war in Iraq.

105 Bush framed the threat as being imminent when he said this could happen "on any given day." Bush added that if Hussein could acquire the necessary components (which Bush said Hussein was actively seeking to do), Iraq "could have a nuclear weapon in *less than a year*." But Bush was lying to the American people. His own CIA's 2002 National Intelligence Estimate report, published on October 1, 2002, six days *before* Bush's speech, said, "*If left unchecked*, it [Iraq] probably will have a nuclear weapon during *this decade*." But obviously, Iraq was not being "left unchecked." It was swarming with United Nations inspectors. And on September 24, 2002, just two weeks before Bush's speech, British intelligence released a report saying that Iraq "would not be able to produce a nuclear weapon" while UN inspections continued in Iraq, and added that even without UN inspections and sanctions, Iraq would need "at least five years" to build a nuclear bomb. Of course, Bush and his people knew that while millions of Americans would hear the lie in his televised speech, none would read the classified NIE report, and few would read published excerpts from the British report. There oughta be a law against presidents telling bald-faced lies to the American people like this.

109 Democratic senator Tom Daschle, the senate majority leader, said, "Bush was telling me that Iraq had WMD and we had to move." Writing about Democratic senator John Edwards saying at the time, "Saddam Hussein's regime represents a grave threat to America and our allies," the *Los Angeles Times*'s Jacob Heilbrunn wrote that in television interviews of Edwards it was very clear that he was completely unaware what the true situation was, being politically opportunistic in saying what he did, and intellectually slovenly in making no effort to research the accuracy of what he was saying. "Like most of his colleagues on the [Senate intelligence] committee," Heilbrunn wrote, "Edwards acquiesced easily to the administration's bogus claims about Iraqi weapons."

111 It is inconceivable that without the intercession of Rice or some other Bush administration representative, the CIA would decide, on its own . . . That the Bush administration contacted the CIA on this and asked for the lie that was the White Paper cannot be seriously questioned. Enterprising reporters Michael Isikoff and David Corn, coauthors of the well-researched book, *Hubris, the Inside Story of Spin, Scandal, and the Selling of the Iraq War,* found and interviewed the CIA intelligence officer who was in charge of preparing the White Paper, Paul Pillar. Although he didn't say (if he even knew) precisely who was behind the decision to mislead Congress and the American people by way of the White Paper, the authors write: "Pillar was embarrassed by the White Paper. 'In retrospect, we shouldn't have done that White Paper at all,' he said . . . He wished he had mustered the courage to tell the CIA leadership *and the White House* [obviously, the White House would have had to first tell the CIA what it wanted—no one would believe the CIA contacted the White House and asked permission to prepare a fraudulent document, and one that contradicted the classified NIE report it had just issued three days earlier] that he wouldn't put out such a document. 'One of the biggest regrets of my career is, I didn't find a way to say no,' he said. 'If I had to do it all over again, I would say, hell no, I'm not going to do that.'"

Senator Graham, a good man who wisely and, with political courage, voted against giving Bush authority to go to war, has a different view about the provenance of the White Paper which, in all deference to him, seems lacking in logic. He believes the White paper was not a "tinkered with" version of the classified NIE report, but a report on Iraq's weapons of mass destruction the CIA had already prepared, per a White House request, for the Bush administration "in the early summer of 2002" (May) that "the White House had put on the shelf" and not released. Graham believes that when he made his request on October 1, 2002, for a declassified version of the classified NIE report, "the White House and CIA took the report off the shelf" and sent it to his committee. But Isikoff and Corn wrote that "Pillar was told to redo" the old CIA report "and to keep it in sync with the [new, classified] NIE."

Assuming, however, that Pillar's credibility is not the best (given his knowing participation in the formulation of the White Paper, a document that was meant to mislead Congress and the American people), I don't believe Graham's reasons for his belief are sound. One reason he gives is that he doesn't see how the CIA could come out with a new version of the NIE report in only three days. But all that had to be done is delete blocks of pages, the qualifying words (e.g., "We assess that"), and the dissents, which takes very little time. Graham also argues that if the White Paper was a new version of the classified NIE, it would be expected to have "redactions" (words blacked out) in it. But the Bush administration (who Graham himself concedes was pushing for war) would never in a million years present a document to the American public replete with blacked-out words. That would only serve to create a suspicion in the minds of millions of Americans that the administration was concealing important information from them that they had a right to know. So redactions were not an option. Graham's own words that the new document he was given was "propaganda" and a "cry for war" defeat his redaction argument, since redactions would have been completely counterproductive.

But there is an even stronger reason why Senator Graham's belief is, respectfully, almost assuredly wrong. I asked him: "Senator Graham, since we know the Bush administration wanted war, and they were doing everything possible to convince the public that Hussein had weapons of mass destruction he could use against us, why would they keep this CIA document [the White Paper], a document they would have every reason to believe would help them make a case for war, on the shelf and not show it to the American public? Why would they wait for you to request, just ten days before the vote in Congress on the war resolution, an unclassified version of the NIE report—which they would have had no way of knowing you would even do—before they released the White Paper to the public?" Graham could only say that if he hadn't made his request, "they would have found some other way to release it to the public." "Why would they have to 'find' some other way?" I said. "They'd simply automatically release this CIA document that supported their case for war."

Senator Graham's belief, which he acknowledges he has no proof of, is at best speculation. But it is not speculation that if the White House had a CIA document that supported their rush to war, they would not have suppressed it from the American public. We don't know what the May 2000 CIA report said. It may have been weak. But we do know what the October 4, 2002, White Paper said, and it was not weak.

It should be added that the Senate Intelligence Committee report in 2004 does not agree with Senator Graham's interpretation of events. The committee's report said, "The intelligence community's *elimination* of the caveats from the unclassified White Paper misrepresented their judgments to the public, which did not have access to the classified National Intelligence Estimate containing the more carefully worded assessments." Though not dispositive of the issue, the CIA, with a full opportunity to say the unclassified White Paper was an earlier document, didn't do so. A Senate Intelligence Committee aide told the media (*Los Angeles Times*, July 10, 2004) that when the committee asked CIA director Tenet and Stu Cohen (the acting chairman of the National Intelligence Council, which oversaw production of the classified NIE), who was responsible for *inserting* the words "potentially against the U.S. homeland" *into* the White Paper, both (without correcting the questioner by saying the words were not inserted, they were already there) claimed they did not know. Moreover, I later read Graham's article in the *St. Petersburg Times* on June 17, 2007, in which he set forth the chronology of events mentioned above. In this article he did seem to suggest that the White Paper was a document that had been previously prepared by the CIA. Indeed, though he did not expressly say so, he implied that the classified NIE had been "doctored" to produce the White Paper. In referring to the White Paper, he wrote: "Gone was the debate over the aluminum tubes and any other dissents or reservations. Gone was the unanimous conclusion that Saddam would only use weapons of mass destruction if Iraq were first attacked. That was the last straw. The Bush administration was clearly scheming to manipulate [public] opinion in favor of war."

It has to be noted that even if the position that former senator Graham is now taking (that the White Paper had *already* been prepared) is correct, which it is possible it is, what we do know for sure is that the Bush administration and CIA gave Graham and his Senate Intelligence Committee a document (White Paper) on October 4 that did not contain what he asked for—the dissents and qualifications in the classified NIE report, and the conclusion of the NIE that Hussein was not an imminent threat to the security of this country. In Graham's *St. Petersburg Times* article, he wrote: "I was livid" about this. He told me that because of this omission, that very same day, October 4, he wrote to Tenet demanding that he send Graham a letter resolving the ambiguity between the October 1 and 4 documents by clearly setting forth the CIA's belief that Hussein was not an imminent threat. After several requests, Tenet finally did this on October 7 by the letter his deputy, John McLaughlin, signed on his behalf. (See main text.)

112 "*We judge that* Iraq has continued its weapons of mass destruction (WMD) programs in defiance of UN resolutions . . ." We know in hindsight that this was 100 percent wrong. But *even at the time*, the CIA had *no evidence* except from discredited informants like "Curveball" (see discussion in main text) that Hussein had continued his WMD programs. Indeed, the last U.S. intelligence assessment was that of the Defense Intelligence Agency in September 2002 that "there is no reliable information on whether Iraq is producing and stockpiling chemical weapons."

114 . . . they believed the tubes were "not intended" for and "not part of" any alleged Iraqi nuclear program. The State Department said that "the very large quantities [of the tubes] being sought, the way the tubes were tested by the Iraqis, and the atypical lack of attention to operational security in the procurement efforts [which would be in serious violation of UN resolutions] are among the factors" that led it to its conclusion. An earlier, August 17, 2001, Department of Energy report concluded that the tubes were more likely purchased for "rocket production," not nuclear weapons. In his statement to the UN Security Council on March 7, 2003, Mohammed ElBaradei, the chief nuclear inspector in Iraq who was the director general of the International Atomic Energy Agency, said his agency had come to the same conclusion.

118 (. . . whom the Bush administration at one time was grooming to re-place Hussein when he fell, and whose "information" was sometimes flat-out fabricated.) The Senate Select Committee on Intelligence report in September of 2006 said that the Iraqi National Congress (INC) "attempted to influence United States policy on Iraq by providing false information through defectors directed at convincing the United States that Iraq pos-sessed weapons of mass destruction and had links to terrorists." Despite re-peatedly being warned by U.S. intelligence agencies that Chalabi and his group were unreliable, the Bush administration continued to use INC infor-mation to help build its case for war.

The determination of Bush and his aspiring oligarchs to twist reality in a way to support the march to war was such that, in January of 2002, Deputy Defense Secretary Paul Wolfowitz actually directed the under secretary of Defense for Policy, Douglas Feith, to set up an operation within his office that would serve as a de facto intelligence unit, independent of the CIA and other U.S. intelligence agencies, to prove an Iraq–Al Qaeda relationship. The fact that this new operation, a small unit that came to be known as the "Iraqi intelligence cell," was beyond the legislative scope of Feith's office, and in-telligence analysis was being made by people like Feith, a neoconservative ideologue, who had no intelligence training at all, was apparently irrelevant to Wolfowitz. What Wolfowitz (and Bush, Cheney, Rice, etc.) was getting was a literally rogue gang of war hawks who—as opposed to agencies like the CIA and the Defense Department's own Defense Intelligence Agency whose conclusions were sometimes not quite strong enough for an adminis-tration hell-bent on war—could always be counted upon to manipulate the evidence in a light most supportive of an invasion of Iraq.

A February 9, 2007, report of the inspector general of the Department of Defense ("Review of the Pre-Iraqi War Activities of the Office of the Under Secretary of Defense for Policy") said that Feith's office "expanded its role and mission from formulating defense policy to analyzing and disseminating alternative intelligence," which was "inappropriate," and that the group fur-nished the Bush administration with "some conclusions that were inconsis-tent with the consensus of the Intelligence Community" (e.g., that Mohamed Atta, the head hijacker on 9/11, had met with an Iraqi intelli-gence official on April 9, 2001, in Prague).

So although there were already sixteen authorized federal U.S. intelligence agencies, led by the CIA, to evaluate and disseminate intelligence relative to the issues of whether Iraq was involved with Al Qaeda in 9/11 and whether Iraq constituted an imminent threat to the security of this country justifying our invading Iraq, these sixteen intelligence agencies just weren't quite enough for Bush and his criminal gang. They wanted their own bought-and-paid-for intelligence unit.

121 . . . the CIA itself never even personally interviewed Curveball, a Baghdad-born chemical engineer who sought political asylum in Germany . . . The *Los Angeles Times* on November 20, 2005, reported that the CIA did attempt to interrogate Curveball, but the BND (German intelligence service) declined to let them do it. Noting the "rocky" relationship between the BND and CIA since the Cold War, during which the BND thought the CIA treated it like a second-class citizen, the *Times* article said, "Spy services jealously guard their sources, and the BND was not obligated to share access to Curveball. 'We would never let them see one of ours,' said a former CIA operations officer."

123 "CIA officials," the *Times* wrote, "now concede that the Iraqi [Curveball] fused fact, . . . into a nightmarish fantasy that played on U.S. fears after the September 11 attacks." Curveball's motive, CIA officials said, was not to start a war. He simply was seeking a German visa. Or was his reason much more sinister? In James Bamford's 2004 book, *A Pretext for War*, he writes that it was later discovered that Curveball was the brother of a top aide to Ahmed Chalabi, the Iraqi exile leader who was a bitter enemy of Hussein and headed the Iraqi National Congress, the group established to find a way to remove Hussein from power. Throughout this entire period, Chalabi had been the favorite of the Bush administration to replace Hussein as Iraq's leader, and they were priming him for this position before he became radioactive with U.S. intelligence because of his corruption and the demonstrably false information about Hussein he was providing. In fact, the *New York Times*'s Judith Miller, who by her reportage on Hussein in the lead-up to war clearly was a supporter of the invasion, acknowledged in a 2003 e-mail to the *New York Times* Baghdad office that Chalabi had provided her with "most of the front page exclusives on [Iraq's] WMD [*what* weapons of mass destruction?] to our paper."

130 The UN inspectors were making substantial progress and Hussein was giving them unlimited access. Although Hussein was giving UN inspectors unlimited access, his compliance was not complete, which apparently was intentional on his part. The documentation he submitted on December 7, 2002, in a 12,200-page declaration to the United Nations Security Council covering what illicit weapons he had once possessed, and how and when he had disposed of them, had gaps. And Hussein would not allow his weapons scientists to leave the country, where UN officials could interview them without their feeling the pressure of still living under Hussein's rule. This caused a great many thinking people to say that if Hussein did not have any weapons of mass destruction, why did he keep acting like he did? They therefore concluded he did, indeed, have WMD.

The question of why Hussein acted guilty by holding back a little has been explained by the American military in an effort overseen by the Joint Forces Command whose 2005 report was titled "Iraqi Perspectives on Operation Iraqi Freedom, Major Combat Operations." Based on interviews with over 110 former Iraqi officials and military officers, some conducted after sumptuous dinners and wine to open up their vocal chords, U.S. military intelligence concluded that although Hussein wanted to give United Nations inspectors total access to Iraq, and eventually did, he also wanted to create some ambiguity about whether he, in fact, still possessed unconventional weapons, a technique one of his former generals, General Hamdani, called "deterrence by doubt." Why? Not, as everyone would assume, because Hussein wanted to deter the United States from invading Iraq. Hussein, military intelligence found, never thought America would invade Iraq, and this was not an irrational thought on his part. After all, Bush's father hadn't. Hussein believed that Bush would only heavily bomb Iraq, but wouldn't be willing to actually put soldiers on the ground and risk many casualties. (He had also seen what we had just done in Afghanistan. Before the fall of the Taliban, the Northern Alliance fought the real war there. Our "invasion" of Afghanistan was almost exclusively by air. See main text.)

No. It wasn't America he feared and was seeking to deter, but Iran, Iraq's neighbor to the east with whom Iraq had not too long ago fought an eight-year war (1980–1988) with hundreds of thousands of casualties. Hussein had the same fear of Iran that the Bush administration said it had—that Iran might be close to having nuclear weapons—and every year the Iraqi military conducted a military exercise called "Golden Falcon" that dealt with the defense of the Iraqi-Iran border. The U.S. military report said that Hussein also wanted to preserve an element of ambiguity to deter the Shiites in Iraq from rising up against him after the American bombing, as they did at the conclusion of the Persian Gulf War. So, in a classic irony, Hussein ended up hiding the fact he had no WMD.

An earlier CIA report from the CIA's Iraq Survey Group (called the "Duelfer Report" after Charles A. Duelfer, the head of the group and, following David Kay, the CIA's chief weapons-hunting sleuth in Iraq) was released on October 6, 2004, and reached the same conclusion. Indeed, the report pointed out, this strategy of bluffing was one that Hussein himself had acknowledged to his FBI interrogators while in custody after his capture on December 13, 2003. "The Iranian threat," Duelfer told members of the Senate Armed Services Committee on October 6, "was very, very palpable to him, and . . . he felt he had to deter them. So he wanted to create the impression" that he had weapons of mass destruction, weapons, Duelfer's report said, that were "essentially destroyed" by Hussein after the Persian Gulf War in 1991 and never rebuilt. The 960-page report, based on fifteen months of work and interviews in Iraq, also concluded that Hussein ended his program to build a nuclear weapon in 1991 and never tried to restart it. However, according to the report, former Iraqi officials said they "heard [Hussein] say" or they "inferred" that Hussein "intended to resume" developing his chemical and nuclear weapon (but not biological weapon) capabilities once the UN sanctions were lifted. He felt such weapons were a sign of strength, and any country with the ability to develop them had an intrinsic right to do so, adding that it was chemical weapons that had saved his regime against Iran's human-wave attacks on Iraq during their 1980–1988 war.

Very interestingly, the report, which concluded that Hussein never felt the United States would actually invade Iraq, said that Hussein believed (quite rationally) that his country was a natural friend and ally of the United States against a mutual enemy, Iran. He also believed, before the war, that the United States would eventually decide it was clearly in its interest to align itself with his country against Iran (as the United States did before, during Iraq's war with Iran), particularly since Iraq was secular and had enormous oil resources. Hussein said he believed he could become America's "best friend in the region, bar none," and he could have been if the small man from Crawford wanted peace, not war.

131 He said that since Hussein, in a letter to Blix, had invited UN weapons instructors back into his country in late November of 2002 . . . The inspection staff numbered over 250 from 60 countries, including 100 UNMOVIC (United Nations Monitoring, Verification and Inspection Commission) inspectors and 50 from the International Atomic Energy Agency.

137 It may be made either expressly, or by implication. (*People v. Mace*, 71 C.A. 10, 21 [1925]).

140 Note that Bush knew he couldn't ever say straight out that Hussein *was* involved in 9/11 . . . Although Bush never flat-out declared *to the American people* that Hussein was involved in 9/11, in a jumble of words he did do this in a letter from him to the speaker of the House of Representatives and the president pro tempore of the Senate on March 18, 2003, the day before he invaded Iraq. Bush said that "consistent with section 3(b) of the Authorization for Use of Military Force Against Iraq Resolution of 2002 (Public Law 107–243), I determine that . . . acting pursuant to the Constitution and Public Law 107–243 is consistent with the United States and other countries continuing to take the necessary actions against international terrorists and terrorist organizations, including those nations, organizations, or persons who planned, authorized, committed, or aided the terrorist attacks that occurred on September 11, 2001."

147 The report also said the committee learned that at one point before the war Hussein was warned by his intelligence chief "that U.S. intelligence was attempting to fabricate connections . . . Perhaps the most fascinating entry in the 356-page Senate report is their reference to a CIA report that said Hussein was surprised by the aggressiveness of UN weapons inspectors in Iraq following the Gulf War and ordered not only the secret destruction of undeclared weapons, but all records and documents pertaining to them. In the process, Hussein destroyed the very records UN inspectors sought before the Iraq War to account for what happened to certain illicit weapons of his. The Senate report, citing the CIA analysis, said, "The result was that Iraq was unable to provide proof when it tried at a later time to establish compliance" with UN resolutions.

This analysis, of course, is not conclusive, particularly since it conflicts with an earlier U.S. military intelligence report and a CIA report (see previous note) that Hussein wasn't accounting to UN inspectors for all of the weapons he had destroyed because he wanted to create the impression—in order to ward off an attack by the enemy he *really* feared, Iran—that he still had the illicit weapons.

148 . . . an astonishing 64 percent of Americans believed that Hussein had had a strong connection with Al Qaeda prior to 9/11. One of the documents seized from the Iraqi government by U.S. forces after the invasion is dated August 17, 2002. The internal document, from Iraq's intelligence service to its agents, says that an informant had said that two members of Al Qaeda were presently somewhere in Iraq. The agents are told they should "search the tourist sites [hotels, residential apartments and rental houses]" for them. Some relationship between Iraq and Al Qaeda.

148 It couldn't be any clearer that although Bush may have believed (like nearly all Americans did) that Hussein had at least some WMD . . . I say "may have" believed because it is possible that Bush already knew there were no weapons of mass destruction in Iraq. Certainly, his and Blair's belief, as set forth in the Manning memo (see main text), that no WMD would ever be found in Iraq goes in that direction, although not finding them and none being present to find are two different things. But in addition to Hussein's not cooperating completely with UN inspectors for a period of time, which suggested he had WMD, there is something else that arguably militates against the conclusion that Bush actually knew there were no WMD in Iraq. Bush is intelligent enough to know (even if he is not, more intelligent people around him would inform him) that if he were lying about Hussein having WMD, postwar inspections (as was the case) would undoubtedly be conducted and show that no WMD were present in Iraq.

However, this realization by Bush would not necessarily deter him from telling his grand lie. This is so because such a finding would not foreclose his administration's arguing (as it in fact did when no WMD were found in Iraq) that Hussein did have WMD throughout the period Bush said he did, and either destroyed all of them just before the war, or moved them to another country. Moreover, whatever Bush's crime was in taking the nation to war on such a lie, he probably felt extremely confident that there would be no consequences for him to pay. And after all, not only hasn't he been impeached for taking this nation to war on a lie, he hasn't even been investigated.

152 As indicated, Bush's expected main defense to the murder charge would be that he acted in self-defense. Technically, it might be argued that Bush was not acting in *self*-defense, which implies he was only trying to defend himself, but that he was acting in defense of America. In this case, Bush's defense would be termed "defense of others." In this well-recognized legal defense, "others" typically, as under California law, are "a wife or husband, parent, child, master, mistress or servant." In this case of first impression, I have no doubt that a court would extend this list to the people of America whom Bush had an obligation to protect, thereby allowing Bush to utilize this defense. In any event, in "defense of others," the same conditions would have to be shown as with self-defense—that Bush had reasonable grounds for believing that the citizens of American were in imminent danger of death or great bodily harm from Saddam Hussein, and it was pursuant to this fear that he conducted his preemptive strike by invading Iraq.

152 The burden of proof in a criminal trial always remains with the prosecution, and therefore, Bush's prosecutor would have the burden of proving that Bush did *not* act in self-defense. The legal justification of self-defense requires *not only* that the defendant himself believed that he was in imminent danger of death or great bodily harm, but that the conduct of the other party was such that it would have produced that fear *in a reasonable person*. To meet the requirement of imminence for an individual (as opposed to a country), it must be shown that to the defendant the peril appeared to exist *at the very time* he used deadly force on the other party. As an appellate court said, "In other words, the peril must appear to be immediate and present and not prospective or even in the near future. An imminent peril is one that, from appearances, must be instantly dealt with."

Obviously, what would be imminent for a private person would not apply to a nation. Indeed, since there is no legal precedent, it is not certain that a court would retain the "imminent" term with respect to a nation, perhaps substituting words like "soon" or "clear and present danger" for it. (However, the U.S. Supreme Court, speaking theoretically in a 1952 case, spoke about an American president's constitutional power to defend the nation if it were "*imminently* threatened with total war. (*Youngstown Sheet and Tube Co. v. Sawyer*, 343 U.S. 579, 659). In fact, the U.S. Constitution itself, in prohibiting states from engaging in war without the consent of Congress, says that an exception is where the state is in *"imminent* danger" of an attack (Article 1, §10, cl. 3). In any event, we can be confident that the judge presiding over the prosecution of Bush would require the prosecutor to prove *either* that Bush himself did not believe that Hussein was about to attack America imminently or soon, *or* that a reasonable leader of America would not have believed it. If he proved either proposition beyond a reasonable doubt, Bush's defense of self-defense would fall. In other words, only going after real enemies who were poised to attack soon would justify what Bush did. Going after hypothetical enemies would not.

As to what would constitute "imminent" or "soon" with nations, it would be impossible to quantify this into specific minutes, hours, days, weeks, or months. It would be like trying to measure the immeasurable with a rubber ruler. But just as a U.S. Supreme Court justice said that "I can't define obscenity, but I know it when I see it," any reasonable leader of a nation would know, in the context of varying situations, what would qualify as "imminent" or "soon." And it is virtually impossible to believe that any *reasonable* leader of America would have thought that Hussein intended to attack America imminently or soon. The killer for Bush is that the prosecutor would have a ton of evidence to show that irrespective of the reasonable man test, *Bush himself* did not believe that Hussein was about to attack the United States.

152 Although self-defense would be the heart of Bush's defense . . . There is another defense to the charge of murder that Bush could possibly raise, the defense of necessity, also known as the "choice of evils" or "lesser evil" defense. But in doing so, Bush would be jumping from the fire into the furnace, and hence would be extremely unlikely to do so. The heart of the necessity defense is that yes, I committed a crime, but I did so to avert a greater harm. Although the genesis of the necessity defense has been lost in the mists of time, it has been recognized as a legitimate defense to a crime* for centuries, and over half of American jurisdictions accept it. When a court accepts this defense, it balances the evils and rules that conduct otherwise

---

*Courts normally hold it is a defense to all crimes except homicide. However, where, if true, the lives of millions of Americans were at stake, if other requirements were met I imagine a court would say that committing a homicide was justifiable.

criminal was legitimized by the dire circumstances in which the defendant found himself. The necessity defense fails when the harm to be avoided is no greater than, or is outweighed by, that which resulted from the defendant's crime.

When one invokes the necessity defense (successfully or unsuccessfully), *he admits committing the crime*; for example, stealing food to avoid starvation; escaping prison to avoid forced sexual assaults and threats of death; killing an abortion doctor to prevent the deaths of an unknown number of fetuses; possessing a firearm without a license to protect oneself against a threat to one's life; using marijuana to reduce the nausea and pain of AIDS or cancer; and so on.

But if Bush were to admit that he took this nation to war on a lie and 4,000 U.S. soldiers lost their lives because of it—and hence, he committed the crime of murder—what justification could he have for doing so? That if he didn't lie the American people and Congress wouldn't have backed him in his war—a war he would claim was a necessity because if he did not invade Iraq, Iraq would have either used WMD on us or given them to a terrorist organization to do so? But since the *only* issue is whether or not Hussein was an imminent threat to the security of this country, if Bush were to admit that he lied when he said Hussein *was* such a threat, what could the truth possibly have been other than that Hussein was *not* an imminent threat? But if that is so, then what greater harm did Bush prevent by committing his crime of murder?

Apart from the fact that Bush would never voluntarily admit that he committed murder, and hence, the necessity defense would almost assuredly never be raised by Bush, even if he were to do so there would be another very significant problem for him. The majority of jurisdictions that allow the defense of necessity either by case law (e.g., California) or statute (e.g., Texas Penal Code Ann. §9.22 (1), Vernon, 1974) require that the greater harm sought to be prevented was "imminent" or "immediate," the very same requirement of self-defense that we know Bush could not meet with respect to Hussein and Iraq. As the court said in a California case, all of the necessity defense cases in the state that the court reviewed required "immediacy and imminency of the threatened action: each represents the situation of a present and active aggressor threatening immediate danger; none depict a phantasmagoria of future harm" (*People v. Otis*, 174 C.A. 2d 119, 125 [1969]).

The biggest booster of the notion that imminence should not be a required element of the choice of evils defense is the American Law Institute (ALI). Its Model Penal Code, Section 3.02, does not set forth imminence as one of the requirements of the defense. But the Model Penal Code, though very influential because of the prestigious ALI (consisting of prominent judges, lawyers, and law professors) that produced it, is not the law and very few cases (e.g., *People v. Unger*, 362 N.E. 2d 319 [1977]) and jurisdictions have jettisoned the "imminence" requirement.* Indeed, even in a jurisdiction that has statutorily adopted §3.02 of the Model Penal Code verbation (Pa. Cons. Stat. Ann. Tit. 18, §503), later case law was still requiring imminence in a necessity defense (*Com. v. Merriwether*, 555 A. 2d 906 [1989]).

In any event, Bush would only be weakening his defense to the murder charge against him by, in effect, abandoning self-defense and admitting he committed murder, but under necessity.

153 On its face, it makes no sense that people of this enormous stature in our society would have done the horrendous things that Mr. [prosecutor's last name] is claiming they did." Because some prospective jurors might, indeed, be susceptible to this argument (see my reference to this precise matter near the end of the opening chapter of this book), during *voir dire* (jury selection), I would ask each juror, "Are you of such a frame of mind that because Mr. Bush occupied the highest position in the land, the presidency of the United States, he simply would not be capable of committing a crime such as the murders alleged in the indictment in this case?" If the juror said yes or was even hesitant or ambiguous in his answer, he or she could be challenged for cause and removed from the jury panel. If he said no, I would get a commitment from him, under oath, that he would take that state of mind into the jury room during the jury's deliberations, a commitment I would remind him (and the other eleven jurors) of during my final summation.

*The hypothetical the ALI presents as a justification for saying it would be "a mistake to erect imminence as an *absolute* requirement" is the following: "If A and B have driven in A's car to a remote mountain location for a month's stay and B learns that A plans to kill him near the end of the stay, B would be justified in escaping with A's car although the threatened harm will not occur for three weeks."

154 . . . attorney general of the United States through his Department of Justice. For those readers who may believe that since, under the U.S. Constitution (Article II, Section 2), the President is the "Commander in Chief of the Army and Navy of the United States," he is, by definition, a member of the military, and hence could only be prosecuted in a military tribunal by the office of the Judge Advocate General, the President is not a member of the American military, and therefore, the military has no jurisdiction over him. He is a civilian elected by the citizens of this country, and one of his civilian functions as President is to be the commander in Chief of our armed forces.

As an adjunct to this, author and historian Gary Wills notes that when modern presidents return salutes given to them by the military upon getting off Air Force One or the presidential helicopter, there is no basis for this. He writes: "That is an innovation that was begun by Ronald Reagan. Dwight Eisenhower, a real general, knew that the salute is for the uniform, and as president he was not wearing one. An exchange of salutes was out of order."

154 The statutory authority for prosecuting Bush for conspiracy to commit murder and for first (or second) degree murder would be 18 U.S.C. §§'s1117 (Conspiracy) and 1111 (Murder). In any prosecution of Bush for murder in this case, the important question of jurisdiction (the legal right by which a court has the power to exercise its authority) arises. And although, as with virtually all cases where the criminal conduct is not confined to the United States (or one individual state), the resolution of jurisdiction is predictably murky, it is definitely present. The other reality one has to keep in mind on this matter of jurisdiction is that although the legal framework *is* present to provide jurisdiction for the prosecution of Bush for murder and conspiracy to commit murder, the factual situation obviously is a case of first impression and hence, by definition, there can be no appellate court cases to cite that are directly in point.

In the federal courts, the murder statute is 18 U.S.C. §1111(a). It provides for first and second degree murder with a standard definition of first degree murder, adding that "any other murder is murder in the second degree." However, section (b) provides that no federal court has jurisdiction to prosecute such a murder unless it was committed "within the . . . territorial jurisdiction of the United States." Indeed, such a limitation exists for all federal crimes, not just murder. So a federal prosecution of Bush under §1111(a) would immediately be objected to by his legal counsel, who would argue that under §1111(b), the federal court had no jurisdiction to try the case since even if we assume for the sake of argument that the killings of the American soldiers constituted murder, the murders were committed in Iraq, outside the territorial jurisdiction of the United States.

But their objection, I believe, would be denied. Under what has come to be known as the "protective principle," the "law of nations" (international law) confers jurisdiction to American courts for criminal conduct engaged in *outside* the United States (and hence, under §1111(b), otherwise outside the jurisdiction of the federal court) where the crime committed injures the nation. For instance, in *U.S. v. Benitez*, the defendant Benitez was prosecuted for conspiring, in Colombia, to murder U.S. DEA agents, for assaulting the agents, and for robbing them. Although Colombia is otherwise outside the territorial jurisdiction of the United States, Benitez's argument that the federal district court for the Southern District of Florida had no jurisdiction was rejected, the court ruling that "under the protective principle," the crimes committed in Colombia "certainly had a potentially adverse effect upon the security or governmental functions of the nation." If a case in Colombia resulting in only an assault on federal DEA agents and the robbery of their passports and DEA credentials was held to have a potentially adverse effect upon the United States, as lawyers like to say, "a fortiori" (all the more so), a case where 4,000 American soldiers have been killed in Iraq in a war that has cost America thus far over one trillion dollars would certainly be deemed by any federal court to have had an extremely deleterious effect upon this country.

Additionally, the jurisdictional basis for a prosecution of Bush in a U.S. federal court would be much more robust than in *Benitez* since no part of Benitez's crimes were committed here in the United States. With Bush, the *conspiracy* to commit the murders in Iraq was committed entirely in the United States.

The *Benitez* court found another separate and independent basis under the law of nations for conferring jurisdiction on the Florida District Court, "the nationality or national character of the victim" principle, the court saying that "the nationality of the victims, who are also United States government agents, clearly supports jurisdiction" (*United States v. Benitez*, 741 F. 2d 1312, 1316 [1984]). (Obviously, the 4,000 American soldiers who have died in Iraq fighting Bush's war were all U.S. citizens.) Many other federal cases have stood for the same law of nations' exceptions to the territorial jurisdiction limitation (e.g., *United States v. Pizzarusso*, 388 F. 2d 8–11 [1968]; *Rocha v. United States*, 288 F. 2d 545–549 [1961]; *Rivard v. United States*, 375 F. 2d 882, 885–887 [1967]; *Ford v. United States*, 273 U.S. 593 [1927]; *Marin v. United States*, 352 F. 2d 174 [1965]).

It should be noted that the entire law of nations' exception to territorial jurisdiction is arguably rooted in Article 1, §8, cl. 10 of the U.S. Constitution, which provides that "Congress shall have the power . . . to define and punish . . . offenses against the Law of Nations," and in the "necessary and proper" clause of the Constitution (Article 1, §8, cl. 18).

However, I feel the more natural way to provide federal jurisdiction to prosecute Bush under the federal murder statute, §1111, is the federal conspiracy to commit murder statute, 18 U.S.C. §1117. Although §1117 does not contain the express requirement that the conspiracy have taken place within the territorial jurisdiction of the United States, this requirement would be picked up under the general section for federal jurisdiction, 18 U.S.C. §7. Here, the conspiracy obviously took place between Bush and people like Cheney and Rice in the White House, which of course *is* within the territorial jurisdiction of the United States (Article 1, §8, cl. 17 of the U.S. Constitution).* So Bush could very definitely be prosecuted by the *federal* authorities for conspiracy to commit murder. And if we went no further, if he was convicted, under §1117 he could be sentenced to a maximum punishment of life imprisonment. (If he were convicted under §1111, the federal murder statute, he could be sentenced to either life imprisonment or death.)

With respect to prosecuting Bush in the federal courts for murder on the

---

*Could it be "read into" §1117 that for Bush to even be guilty of conspiracy to commit murder, he had to conspire to commit murders that were to take place "within the territorial jurisdiction of the United States," on the rationale that such language is a part of the murder statute, §1111? No. That language, in §1111(b), is not a part of the definition of murder under §1111(a). Indeed, it is in a separate paragraph following the definition of murder. Moreover, that language does not deal with the issue of whether there was a murder, but whether the federal authorities have the jurisdiction to prosecute it. As the court said in *United States v. Young*, the federal definition of murder "is found *exclusively* in section 1111(a) . . . Section 1111(b), by contrast, is not a definitional section at all. Instead it sets forth penalties for murder under §18 U.S.C. §1111 and *creates a jurisdictional requirement* for such [murder] count" (248 F. 3d 274–275 [2001]; see also, *U.S. v. Tuck. Chong*, 123 F.Supp. 2d 563, 566 [1999]).

foundation of the conspiracy statute, §1117, it is standard, boilerplate state and federal law that all coconspirators are criminally responsible for all crimes committed by their coconspirators (as well as here, innocent agents) to further the object of the conspiracy. In this case, the object was a war, and since the nation was taken to war by Bush and his people under false pretenses, the killings of American soldiers in the war constitute murder. And Bush is guilty of these murders even though he did not, of course, personally commit any of them. By analogy, as set forth in the main text, Charles Manson, a member of the conspiracy to murder the seven Tate–La Bianca victims, was guilty of these murders even though he himself (like Bush) did not commit any of the seven murders. Although I prosecuted him for the murders under §187 of the California Penal Code, I also prosecuted him and his codefendants for the crime of conspiracy to commit murder under §182 of the California Penal Code, and it was *that* statute, the conspiracy statute, that allowed me to prosecute Manson for the murders under §187.

155 . . . any state attorney general in the fifty states . . . could bring a murder charge against Bush for any soldiers in that state who lost their lives fighting Bush's war. Bush would not achieve anything by arguing that the subject state had no jurisdiction to prosecute him because in going to war in Iraq he was carrying out his duties as a federal constitutional officer (i.e., president), and hence, under the supremacy clause of the U.S. Constitution (Article VI, cl. 2), he could *only* be prosecuted, if at all, in a federal court under federal law. But the supremacy clause as well as the facts of this case would offer no legal shelter for Bush. If Bush committed an act that constituted murder under both state and federal law, there would be concurrent jurisdiction to prosecute him, and, in the absence of a federal prosecution, the supremacy clause would not preclude any state court prosecution. The clause would only be applicable if both state and federal authorities wanted to prosecute him at the same time, in which case federal law would prevail and the state court would be without jurisdiction to proceed at that time. Here, if there was a federal prosecution and conviction of Bush for murder under federal law, there would be no pressing need for a state prosecution anyway, though the state could prosecute him after the federal prosecution concluded under the principle of dual sovereignty, which recognizes that the federal government as well as the individual states are separate sovereigns. As the court said in *United States v. Davis*, "Under this well-established principle, a federal prosecution does not bar [under the double jeopardy clause of the Fifth Amendment to the U.S. Constitution] a subsequent state prosecution of the same person for the same acts, and a state prosecution does not bar a federal one . . . When a single act violates the laws of two sovereigns, the wrongdoer has committed two distinct offenses" (906 F. 2d 829, 832 [1990]; see also, *Bartkus v. Illinois*, 359 U.S. 121 [1959], and *Abbate v. United States*, 359 U.S. 187 [1959]).

Let's take the hypothetical situation where the federal government did not want to prosecute Bush, and without a supremacy clause issue, state court proceedings were instituted against him. Could he seek a writ of habeas corpus in a federal court to bar the state prosecution on the ground that he could not be found guilty in a state court for any act of his that took place in the performance of his official duties as a federal officer? Yes. But the writ would be denied unless he could prove in the federal habeas corpus proceeding that as president, he had a "duty to do" the act (i.e., take this nation to war), and that his conduct was "necessary and proper" (*In re Neagle*, 135 U.S. 1, 75–76 [1890]; see also *In re McShane's Petition*, 235 F. Supp. 262 271–272 [1964]; *In re Waite*, 81 F. 359, 365 [1897]; *Clifton v. Superior Court*, 35 C.A. 3d 654, 658, [1973]; 28 U.S.C. §§'s 2241, 2251). If the facts are as I believe them to be, this he could not possibly do, and the federal court would not issue the writ.

Bush could be expected to make one or more other challenges to the jurisdiction of any state court to prosecute him for murder, including citing the language of Article III, §2, cl. 3 of the U.S. Constitution (and 18 U.S.C. §3238) that when a crime is "not committed within any state" (the killing of American soldiers took place in Iraq), the trial shall take place in a *federal* court. But here, as indicated in the main text, the crime of conspiracy to commit murder *was* committed in the states by the overt acts of Bush, Cheney and Rice—on their misrepresentations on TV, radio, and in print reaching all fifty states, and in the recruitment of soldiers in the states—taking the nation to war under false pretenses. Once jurisdiction has fastened on the state court to prosecute Bush et al. for the crime of conspiracy to commit murder, killings that were the direct result of that conspiracy would also fall under the jurisdiction of the subject state court. In this regard, state courts can avail themselves, as the federal courts, of the law of nations' principles of jurisdiction (e.g., the "protective" or "effects" principles) to give them extraterritorial jurisdiction.

The leading case for this proposition is the U.S. Supreme Court case of

Strassheim v. Daily, 221 U.S. 280, 285 (1910), in which Justice Oliver Wendell Holmes said, "Acts outside a [state's] jurisdiction, but intended to produce and producing detrimental effects within it [which would certainly include the deaths in Iraq of the citizens of a state], justify a state in punishing the cause of the harm as if he had been present at the effect, if the state should succeed in getting him within its power." (Any state could do the latter with its prosecution of Bush for conspiracy to commit murder.) See also, *Skiriotes v. Florida*, 313 U.S. 69, 73, 76 (1941), where the conduct of a citizen of Florida on the high seas (outside the territorial jurisdiction of the state of Florida) was held to be within the jurisdiction of Florida's courts where a state interest was involved. But it's not necessary to a state's jurisdiction that the defendant be a citizen of the state. See *State v. Bundrant*, 546 P. 2d 530, 534–535, 554–556 (1976). Indeed, the state can extend jurisdiction under the effects doctrine even where the conduct adversely affecting the state takes place within the territorial jurisdiction of another country. See *State v. Jack*, 125 P. 3d 311, 318–322 (2005), where the state was Alaska, and the country Canada. For a discussion of this issue, see Robinson, Paul H., *Criminal Law*, pp. 102–103, Aspen Publishers, New York, 1997).

It has to be noted that efforts by Bush to have state proceedings against him terminated on the ground that only a federal court would have jurisdiction would only serve to publicize the fact to the nation that a federal prosecutor should step forward to prosecute Bush under federal law, which, as I've indicated, would be the most natural and best venue to bring Bush to justice.

155 But a *necessary element* of the corpus delicti of the federal crime of conspiracy is that at least one overt act be committed by one or more members of the conspiracy to further the object of the conspiracy. (*Hyde v. United States*, 225 U.S. 347, 361–365 [1911]; Federal Judicial Center, Pattern Criminal Jury Instructions, 5.06A).

156 To repeat, the attorney general in each of these fifty states would have jurisdiction to prosecute Bush for conspiracy to commit murder and murder. There is even a statutory basis for a prosecution of Bush by the states for conspiracy to commit murder. It is found in the well-accepted rule of law that if any part of a crime is committed in a state, that state has jurisdiction to prosecute. A typical state statute would be that in California. Section 778a of the California Penal Code (enacted way back in 1872) reads:

"Whenever a person, with intent to commit a crime, *does any act* within this state in execution or *part* execution of that intent, which culminates in the commission of a crime, either within *or without* [outside] this state, the person is punishable for that crime *in* this state in the same manner as if the crime had been committed entirely within this state."

Although some states (e.g., California: see *People v. Buffum*, 40 C. 2d 709, 716 [1953]) hold that the "act" within the state not be "any act," but one that is the legal equivalent of a criminal attempt, it has been noted that only "a small group of states retain" the requirement of an attempt. "The larger group of [state] provisions based on the Model Penal Code [§1.03 (1) (a)] require only that 'an element of the offense' occurs within the state. Conduct can meet this standard without coming so close to substantial completion as a state might require for an attempt" (La Fave, Wayne R; Israel, Jerold H; King, Nancy J., *Criminal Procedure*, 2d edition, Vol. 4, p. 583, West Group, St. Paul, 1999).

A classic example of this already well-established rule in case law is where the premeditation to commit murder (premeditation being an essential *element* of first degree murder) is formed in one state, but the murder itself takes place in another. In *Lane v. State of Florida*, the defendant formed the premeditation in Florida for a murder committed in Alabama. The court held that Florida had jurisdiction to prosecute the defendant for first degree murder in Florida for the Alabama murder (388 So. 2d 1022 [1980]; see also, *State v. Harrington*, 260 A. 2d 692, 697 [1969]; *Conrad v. Alabama*, 317 N.E. 789 [1974]; *State v. Willoughby*, 892 P. 2d 1319; and *Commonwealth v. Thomas*, 189 A. 2d 255, 258–259 [1963]).

Since an overt act is a *necessary element* of the crime of conspiracy, this fact alone would give the majority of American states jurisdiction to prosecute Bush for the crime of conspiracy to commit murder. Even in the minority states that require that the act committed within the state amount to an attempt (not an attempt to commit the murders in Iraq), there are several reasons why an overt act is a special act that cannot be put in the "any act" category that the California Supreme Court, in the *Buffum* case, said should really be like an attempt. "A criminal attempt is a step towards a criminal offense [like robbery, burglary, murder, etc.] with specific intent to commit that particular crime," one eminent legal scholar wrote. Virtually all courts demand that the step come reasonably close to the actual commission of the crime. Hence, mere preparation to commit the crime will not suffice. Certainly, if A fires at B to kill him, and misses, this is attempted murder.

How far away from the successful completion of the offense can one go and still be held, by his actions, to have attempted to commit the crime? "It is not practical to prescribe guiding rules for determining this," the court said in *People v. Gibson*, 94 C.A. 2d 468, 471 (1949). But an example or two will be instructive. In *People v. Lanzit*, the defendant, intending to kill his wife by dynamiting her place of business, procured someone to make the bomb, went with him to his wife's business, and while getting ready there, was arrested. This was held to be attempted murder (70 C.A. 498, 504, 506, [1925]). Two men, having agreed to rob a payroll clerk, went to the bank where the clerk was scheduled to receive his payroll and stationed themselves to rob him but were arrested before the clerk appeared on the scene. The court, in *People v. Gormley*, 225 N.Y.5. 653 (1927), held this was attempted robbery.

One can be guilty of an attempt without his act having constituted an element of the crime he sought to commit. For instance, robbery is the taking of personal property from the possession of another, by force or fear, with the intent to steal. Note that none of these elements of robbery were present in the *Gormley* case (not even an intent to steal, since said intent has to be *contemporaneous* with the act of taking, and there was no taking), yet Gormley was guilty of attempted robbery. But the crime of conspiracy cannot even be committed without an overt act, since the overt act is an element of the crime of conspiracy, thereby elevating it to a special act status.

So *any* overt act will give jurisdiction in a conspiracy case, whereas that same overt act might not be nearly enough to constitute an attempt to commit a crime such as robbery, arson, or burglary. For example, if A and B conspired to rob C when he arrived home from work, B's making a phone call to C's factory to learn when C's shift ended would definitely constitute an overt act under the law of conspiracy, but would just as definitely not constitute, at that point, an attempted robbery. So an overt act isn't just "any" act.*

---

*In a sense, comparing an overt act in a conspiracy with an act constituting a criminal attempt is like comparing apples with oranges. The two don't lend themselves to comparison if for no other reason than that although there can be acts constituting a criminal attempt to commit every other crime on the books (such as attempted arson, or rape, burglary, murder, extortion, theft, etc.), I've never even heard of an attempted conspiracy, and am under the impression that no such crime exists.

As the court said in a federal case, "A conspiracy may be prosecuted in the district where it was formed, *or in any district in which an overt act was committed* in furtherance of its objects. The place where the conspiracy was formed is immaterial if at least one of the overt acts alleged and proved took place within the district where the defendant is tried. It is not essential that the defendant ever enter the state or district of trial" (*Downing v. United States*, 348 F. 2d 594, 598 [1965]; see also, *Hyde v. United States*, 225 U.S. 347, 361–365 [1911]; 18 U.S.C. §3237[a]).

And we can't forget that just as overt acts aren't "any" acts, the two overt acts in this case giving every state in the Union jurisdiction to prosecute Bush for conspiracy to commit murder weren't "any overt acts" either. Telling lies to the American people to get their support to go to war and recruiting soldiers to fight this war couldn't possibly be more important to Bush and his coconspirators in achieving the object of their conspiracy.

157 And the existence of the conspiracy "can be inferred if the evidence reveals that the alleged participants shared 'a common aim or purpose' and 'mutual dependence and assistance existed'" (*United States v. De Luna*, 763 F. 2d 897, 918 [1985], quoting from *United States v. Jackson*, 696 F. 2d 578, 582–583 [1982]).

157 Two who definitely should be are Cheney and Rice, coconspirators and aiders and abettors in the murders. It should be noted that an automatic additional count against Bush and his coconspirators in any federal indictment against them would be the federal felony of "conspiracy to defraud the United States" under 18 USC §371, which provides: "If two or more persons conspire . . . to defraud the United States, or any agency thereof [certainly Congress would be such an agency] in any manner or for any purpose, and one or more of such persons do any act to effect the object of the conspiracy, each shall be fined under this title or imprisoned not more than five years, or both." But obviously, given the enormity of what these people did, they deserve much worse. Only a conviction of murder would be adequate here.

By the way, a felony-murder prosecution against Bush and his coconspirators under 18 U.S.C. §1111 could not take place since the §371 felony is not one of the enumerated felonies set forth in §1111.

161 He, of course, couldn't come up with any such agency (or member thereof) . . . If Bush answered that he received this information from Douglas Feith's rogue unit at the Department of Defense (which already had its own *authorized* intelligence agency, the DIA), his position would not stand up on cross-examination. As alluded to in an earlier note, unlike any of the sixteen U.S. intelligence agencies authorized by federal law, Feith's unit was only authorized by a key Iraqi war architect, Paul Wolfowitz (Secretary of Defense Donald Rumsfeld's chief deputy), who himself, along with Feith, in my opinion, were likely coconspirators with Bush in taking this nation to war on a lie. Moreover, neither Feith nor any member of his staff had any training or background in intelligence. Additionally, Bush has never even said, in the previous six years, that Feith's group provided him with any document or report that concluded Hussein was an imminent threat to the security of this country.

Apart from the fact that Feith would be the type of lower-level conspirator the prosecutor might grant immunity from prosecution to testify against Bush, for Bush to assert he relied on the conclusions of Feith's motley, amateur group (assuming for the sake of argument they even told Bush that Hussein was an imminent threat) over the conclusions of sixteen well-established federal intelligence agencies led by the CIA would make Bush not only look ridiculous and implausible to the jury, but worse, it would look like he was relying on his own coconspirators to go to war.

CHAPTER 5: BUSH "COULDN'T POSSIBLY" HAVE BEEN ANY WORSE IN HANDLING THE WAR ON TERRORISM

174 It was widely accepted that killing Bin Laden in the process of attempting to capture him was not to be discouraged. Clinton's national security advisers told the 9/11 Commission that Clinton wanted Bin Laden dead and his legal advisers said that killing Bin Laden would be lawful because the killing of anyone who posed a threat to the country would not constitute an "assassination," the latter being prohibited by earlier presidential executive orders of Presidents Ford and Reagan. In 1976, President Ford issued Executive Order 11905, which provided that "no employee of the United States Government shall engage in, or conspire to engage in, political assassination." On December 4, 1981, in his Executive Order 12333, President Reagan even tightened the ban, dropping the word "political" and adding that nobody "acting on behalf of" the United States could assassinate anyone. The 9/11 Commission said that every CIA official whom they interviewed on the matter, including CIA director George J. Tenet, told the commission that Bin Laden could only be *lawfully* killed if he died in an operation whose objective was to *capture* him.

175 On August 20, 1998, Clinton's CIA did launch sixty Tomahawk cruise missiles on an Afghan camp where Bin Laden was believed to be . . . A missile strike in 1999 against a desert camp in Afghanistan where Bin Laden was supposed to be was called off at the last moment because predator cameras seemed to show the presence of officials from the United Arab Emirates (considered to be an ally of America) visiting the camp. Another strike in Kandahar in 1999 was called off because of the fear of civilian casualties and the lack of confidence in the accuracy of intelligence.

In 2000, Clinton visited Pakistan and urged its government to use its influence with the neighboring Afghanistan government of the Taliban to expel Bin Laden from their country, but the 9/11 Commission said, "The Pakistani position was that their government had to support the Taliban [most of whose members received their religious training at schools in Pakistan], and that the only way forward was to engage them and try to moderate their behavior."

179 Although Ms. Rice spoke very vaguely about the Bush administration having worked prior to 9/11 on a "comprehensive strategy" to destroy the Al Qaeda network . . . There is no evidence that the Bush administration did anything other than disregard the findings of an earlier report on February 15, 2001, from a federal commission headed up by former U.S. senators Gary Hart (Democrat) and Warren Rudman (Republican) concluding that "mass-casualty terrorism directed against the U.S. homeland was of serious and growing concern." The commission, formed during the presidency of Bill Clinton, recommended that a national homeland security agency be created. But it was Democrats in Congress who later urged the creation of such an agency (the cosponsors of the proposed legislation were Senators Joe Lieberman and Max Cleland), with the Bush administration *opposing* it for months until it reversed itself and backed the Homeland Security Act of 2002 with a cabinet-level director in charge of the new department.

180 "In this time period, I'm not talking to him, no." It has to be added that despite Tenet's testimony before the 9/11 Commission in 2004, later, in his 2007 book, *At the Center of the Storm*, Tenet said that "a few weeks after the August 6" memo was delivered to Bush he flew to Texas to "make sure the President stayed current on events"—presumably referring to the terrorist threats, although he curiously makes no mention at all of what he told the president in this regard.

It is difficult to reconcile the fact that in 2004 Tenet *testified under oath* that he did not see or talk to Bush during the month of August of 2001, yet in his book three years later (when one would expect his memory to be worse, not better) he said he did meet with Bush in August. Some time after Tenet's embarrassing (to Bush and himself) testimony before the 9/11 Commission, the CIA said that their records showed that Tenet met with Bush twice in August of 2001: once at Bush's ranch on August 17 (about two weeks after the August 6 memo) and once in Washington, D.C., on August 31, but did not say that the meetings concerned the August 6 memo.

181 . . . Bush told *Washington Post* reporter Bob Woodward that before 9/11, "I didn't feel that sense of urgency . . . I was not on point." Secretary of State Powell, the ever-loyal public servant, tried to help Bush by telling the 9/11 Commission: "We wanted to move beyond the rollback policy of containment, criminal prosecution, and limited retaliation for specific terrorist attacks. We wanted to destroy Al Qaeda." But Secretary Powell, if you all felt Al Qaeda was that serious a threat, why did all of you move at such an elephantine pace? If the type of fear of Al Qaeda that you suggest existed, shouldn't the pace have been more reminiscent of that of Jesse Owens at the Berlin Olympics of 1936? Doesn't the pace you took betray your true state of mind of being largely oblivious to the threat?

191 Moore asked, "Was he thinking, 'I've been hanging out with the wrong crowd. Which one of them screwed me?'" But wait. There perhaps is another good reason for Bush staying in that classroom as long as the second-graders kept reading. We know that Bush has been incredibly audacious and impervious to reason as he has destroyed everything in his path. The story the children were reading was about a young girl's pet goat that eats everything in its path. How can we blame Bush for not wanting to know how this story ended? He may have identified with this goat.

197 You don't give anyone any credit for something he had no choice but to do. This phenomenon of people failing to grasp that credit requires a choice has rarely been exemplified more than in the godlike glorification and deafening praise heaped upon Rudy Giuliani for his performance on 9/11. Over and over he was called *"the* hero of 9/11." Encomiums such as he was "Babe Ruth, John Wayne, and the Beatles all rolled into one" and was "America's Winston Churchill" were common. No one, obviously, could be expected to be more fair to Giuliani than Giuliani himself, a notorious self-promoter. But when I read Giuliani's own testimony before the 9/11 Commission and his own book, *Leadership,* to find out *just what he did* on 9/11 other than what any other competent mayor would have done that singled him out, I found absolutely nothing at all. And if anyone can read what Giuliani himself said he did after the two planes crashed into the Twin Towers that was special in any way at all, they are much better linguistic archaeologists than I.

Another example out of literally thousands of this phenomenon, this one from a few years back. Mills Lane was the referee in the June 28, 1997, Mike Tyson–Evander Holyfield heavyweight championship fight. After Tyson, who gave new meaning to the term "hungry fighter," bit Holyfield's *left* ear in the third round, causing Holyfield to leap in pain across the ring, a minute later he actually bit off a chunk of Holyfield's *right* ear, Lane naturally disqualified Tyson. But overnight, Lane became a media sensation. "He's a hero," the sports editor of the *Los Angeles Times* gushed. Tributes to Lane came in from around the country; he was the cover story in *USA Today*; and Jay Leno, *Larry King Live*, and *Good Morning America*, among many others, wanted him on their show. But what had Lane done that was so "heroic" that any other rational referee would not have done? Are we to believe that other referees would have waited until Tyson approached Holyfield with a jar of mustard and ketchup before finally stepping in?

Indeed, people are so crazy that one doesn't even have to do *anything* to be denominated a hero. After fifty-two Americans were captured in 1979 at the U.S. embassy in Tehran by a group of militant Iranian university students, held hostage for 444 days, and released on January 20, 1981, these American hostages were treated like heroes everywhere in America, actually being given a ticker-tape parade through the Canyon of Heroes on Broadway in lower Manhattan. But for what? No one ever said.

198 Not giving a speech saying he was going to go after the terrorists? Actually, Bush *did* fail in one not insignificant way. With the nation in shock and mourning from the tremendous tragedy and the first foreign attack ever on our soil, obviously Bush should have addressed the nation in depth within no more than a few days of 9/11. His speaking on television for around one minute outside the Sarasota classroom certainly didn't qualify. Neither did the two- or three-minute "speech" he gave to the nation on the evening of 9/11. It was so short that the *Los Angeles Times* properly felt it didn't even rise to the dignity of a speech or an address, calling it only a "brief statement." While the nation waited to hear a formal and substantive address from its commander-in-chief about 9/11, Bush, for all intents and purposes, hid out. There was no major speech from him to the nation on September the 12th, or 13th, or 14th. Nor on the 15th, or even the 16th, or 17th. September 18th came and went and Bush was a no-show. Same for the 19th. Finally, finally, on the evening of September 20th, almost ten days after the tragedy (*a third of a month later*), Bush addressed the nation. President Franklin Delano Roosevelt, acting as a normal president would, addressed the nation by radio (no TV then) on the evening of December 9, 1941, two days after Pearl Harbor. (Roosevelt's famous description of December 7, 1941, as "a date which will live in infamy" was delivered by him in a brief statement to Congress the previous day.)

201 So *saying* that Gore and the Democrats wouldn't have responded to 9/11 . . . This, of course, is ridiculous. Although Clinton, after the car bombings of American embassies in Kenya and Tanzania in August of 1998 that killed 224 people, 12 of whom were Americans, didn't invade Afghanistan (where the leadership of Al Qaeda, who were believed to be behind the bombings, were), that's because you don't invade a foreign country when terrorists from that country kill Americans in foreign capitals. The 9/11 Commission said that "both civilian and military officials of the Defense Department state flatly that neither Congress or the American public would have supported large-scale military operations in Afghanistan before the shock of 9/11." Condoleezza Rice told the 9/11 Commission that prior to 9/11 "no one counseled an all-out war against Afghanistan of the kind that we did after 9/11 . . . [It] was not recommended."

210 Relatives of the victims in the room applauded Clarke. Even though it is not subject to dispute that 9/11 happened because, by definition, Bush's

FBI and CIA did not detect the Al Qaeda conspiracy to attack the World Trade Center Towers on 9/11, *Bush not only failed to apologize to the nation or the victims' survivors,* he demonstrated his total lack of leadership by refusing to fire or even criticize those in these agencies who, like Bush, let this nation down. As in private life, to stimulate excellence, good performances have to be rewarded and gross negligence and incompetence punished. How did President John F. Kennedy respond to the CIA's botched handling of the Bay of Pigs invasion in Cuba in 1961? He called the director of the CIA, Allen W. Dulles, and two of his chief assistants—Lieutenant General Charles Cabell, the deputy director of the CIA, and Richard Bissell, the CIA deputy director of Plans who was the chief architect behind the invasion—each of whom Kennedy was friendly with and respected, into his office and told them: "Under the British system I would have to go. But under our system, I'm afraid it's got to be you." After allowing a decent passage of time, Kennedy accepted the resignations of Dulles and Bissell, and Cabell retired. But you see, Kennedy was a leader and real president. Bush is neither. CIA director George Tenet did resign (on June 3, 2004, nearly three years after 9/11, due to mounting criticism of his performance), but there wasn't the slightest intimation from anyone that Bush asked or even wanted him to.

211 ... although the 9/11 bipartisan commission consisted of distinguished people, they were all political insiders and seemed reluctant or incapable of asking the necessary, tough questions. People like Democrat Richard Ben-Veniste, a lawyer, give the impression that their main goal is to make sure they don't do anything that will prevent their appointment to the next commission. They growl just loud enough (you know, things like, "Just answer the question") to be acceptable to the Democrats. I shouldn't be too harsh on Ben-Veniste. If he's a typical lawyer, he simply is incapable of asking penetrating, cross-examination questions.

225 We also all know that Iraq had no terrorists before Bush invaded it. The only one ... Abu Nidal (real name, Sabri al-Banna) was a Palestinian terrorist who, in the 1970s through the 1990s, headed up a small terrorist group that floated throughout the Mideast, including Syria, Libya, and Iraq, although Iraq after harboring and supporting Nidal, expelled him in 1983. Nidal is believed to have been behind the deaths of three hundred people in twenty countries. Before his death in Baghdad in August of 2002 he was reported to be in poor health, and the circumstances surrounding his death have been questioned by some. Iraqi authorities claim that Nidal had entered Iraq illegally, and when he was discovered by Iraqi officials he committed suicide by shooting himself.

226 They were free to pursue any lifestyle or religion they wanted—Muslim, Christian, gay . . . As a representative sample of the stark difference between prewar Iraq and now, under Hussein Baghdad was a city where sexual freedom flourished. No more. In fact, in 2005 the grand ayatollah Ali al-Sistani, the most revered Shiite religious figure in Iraq, issued a decree (since lifted) calling for all gay men and lesbians to be killed in the "worst, most severe way." A Baghdad gay told the *New York Times* in December of 2007: "The way things were before was so much better than where we are now." Gays in today's Iraq are forced to hide their sexual orientation and practice their lifestyle in great secrecy.

228 Slightly more than that do not even want us in their country, viewing us not as liberators but as invaders and occupiers. If Bush had any sense, he would have taken the advice of his father, who in his 1998 book, *A World Transformed*, coauthored with Brent Scowcroft, explained why he didn't seek to oust Saddam Hussein from power after his anti-Iraq coalition forced Hussein's military forces out of Kuwait. "Trying to eliminate Saddam [by] extending the ground war into an occupation of Iraq," he wrote, "would have incurred incalculable human and political costs . . . Had we gone the invasion route, the United States could conceivably still be an occupying power in a bitterly hostile land."

It wasn't just his father. On May 25, 2007, the U.S. Senate Intelligence Committee issued a report in which it cited previously classified documents showing that two months before Bush invaded Iraq, U.S. intelligence agencies twice presciently warned the Bush administration of the extreme difficulty of establishing a democracy in Iraq after removing Hussein from power. They predicted that Al Qaeda would exploit the inevitable instability in Iraq to increase its operations and influence. But when you're hell-bent on going to war, as Bush was, you don't take anyone's advice, including that of your own father.

Although all but the flag-waving right wing agree that the situation in Iraq has disintegrated to the point where the war has become hopeless, and our role has essentially been reduced to trying to protect Iraqi people from the Sunni insurgents and Shiite militia, and trying to protect each of these groups from each other, Bush desperately clings to the "stay the course" plan. Why? Can it be that Bush knows if he leaves Iraq now, this will be an open admission that the war that completely defined his presidency was an abysmal failure, one that will consign him to the trash heap of history for all time? Indeed, this might happen whatever he does. But if he leaves now, he knows it is certain to happen.

He also knows that if he keeps us in Iraq to the bitter end of his presidency (which he has said he will do, telling author Bob Woodward that he would continue the war even if the only ones supporting him were "my wife and Barney," his dog), maybe, just maybe, he can salvage something, anything at all, for his ignominious legacy. Or that maybe his successor, burdened with the disaster Bush left him or her with, will, like Nixon in Vietnam, start to share the blame.*

In the meantime, young American soldiers continue to die violent deaths in Iraq in a senseless war that has already been lost. And although arguments can be made for our gradual, as opposed to immediate, withdrawal, this very slow withdrawal, resulting in a continuation of the war, *may* be an intentional sacrifice of American lives and blood by Bush for no other reason than to help him, in his mind, diminish the blame directed toward him. Although I obviously do not know this to be true, I believe it to be a real possibility only because I believe this man is, or is close to being, a human monster.

228 Out of the blood and debris of the Iraq war, how many young Bin Ladens will we eventually have to deal with down the line, whom Bush created . . . What I've said here is just common sense, but indeed, there's an interesting historical precedent for this phenomenon. Bin Laden himself was one of many young Muslim volunteers to go to Afghanistan in the

---

*Remarkably, Hollywood director Oliver Stone, whose specialty is distorting history in his cinematic reveries (e.g., in his film, *JFK*, on the assassination of President John F. Kennedy, other than having the city, date, and victim of the assassination correct, his movie was one continuous lie), actually went further when he suggested in his movie *Born on the Fourth of July* that Nixon, not LBJ, was the one most responsible for the Vietnam War.

1980s to join in a jihad (holy war or struggle) against the Soviet Union invaders of Afghanistan (supported, as it happens, by the United States). After the Afghan-Soviet War in the late 1980s, Bin Laden formed his Al Qaeda network to start jihads elsewhere, culminating in 9/11.

229 The report said, "We judge that the United States currently is in a heightened threat environment." Against this incontrovertible evidence of gross, shamefully reckless incompetence, what is the favorite argument that Bush and his people trumpet to convince nonbelievers that they have been effective in combating terrorism? That Al Qaeda hasn't struck again on our shores since 2001. But doesn't that presuppose that they have tried since then and have been successfully repelled? If so, where is the evidence? And it certainly can't be that they haven't tried because of the high state of our homeland security, which virtually everyone agrees is alarmingly poor. Remarkably, right-wing columnists like Charles Krauthammer started making the argument of "no further attacks" since 9/11 *just two years later!* Indeed, Karl Rove, in early May of 2003, just over a year and a half after 9/11, was crowing to the public: "The country has not been hit since 9/11." But under that flabby reasoning, inasmuch as prior to September 11, 2001, Al Qaeda hadn't struck in America since the World Trade Center bombing in 1993, which would include seven years of the Clinton presidency, I guess we should give Clinton credit for repelling them for seven years.

229 They've called Democrats "quitters" and people who want to "cut and run" because they want to end our disastrous war in Iraq . . . The essence of Bush's current *main* argument for continuing his war in Iraq is captured in this statement of his on September 11, 2006: "Whatever mistakes have been made in Iraq, the worst mistake would be to think that if we pulled out, the terrorists would leave us alone. They will not leave us alone. They will follow us. The safety of America *depends* on the outcome of the battle in the streets of Baghdad." But this is pure claptrap. Our terrorist enemy, everyone knows, is Osama Bin Laden's Al Qaeda. No one questions the fact that not just Bin Laden, but the strength and heart of his organization is presently residing in the tribal and lawless badlands of northwestern Pakistan, a rugged and dense mountain range with jagged peaks hard by the Afghanistan border. So even if we succeeded in routing a group called Al Qaeda in Iraq (a very small part of the insurgency, but an effective one that was led by Zarqawi before his death in 2006, and which, although it has sworn allegiance to Bin Laden and he has spoken in support of the group, is not believed to be an official part of Bin Laden's terrorist network), this obviously would have little, if any, effect on Bin Laden's plans nor his ability to conduct further terrorist attacks on American soil from his safe haven in Pakistan—a haven that Pakistani president General Pervez Musharraf either doesn't want to, or can't by himself end.

CHAPTER 6: AMERICA, UP OR DOWN?

244 I know it has been inculcated in us that America is the greatest nation in the world. One of the clichés that Americans unconsciously embrace is that Americans are free, that we have freedom in America. We utter it without thinking. But when you stop and think about it for a moment, the cliché lacks merit, not because it is untrue, but because of what it implies—that the people of other nations are not free. After all, if we're just one of a hundred nations that are free, what is there to brag about or even mention? Aren't the people of Great Britain as free as we are? What about Italy, Germany, France, Spain, Norway, Sweden, Finland, Australia, New Zealand, and a great number of other nations? Aren't they also as free as we are? Maybe I'm wrong, but I think they are. And I doubt very much that these nations try to distinguish themselves from other nations with this cliché. There *are* some nations in the world (e.g., Saudi Arabia, Iran, China, Cuba, North Korea, etc.) where the people are not free, but aren't they in the decided minority?

INDEX

ABOUT
THE AUTHOR

Vincent Bugliosi received his law degree in 1964. In his career at the L.A. County District Attorney's office, he successfully prosecuted 105 out of 106 felony jury trials, including 21 murder convictions without a single loss. His most famous trial, the Charles Manson case, became the basis of his classic, *Helter Skelter*, the biggest selling true-crime book in publishing history. Two of Bugliosi's other books, *And the Sea Will Tell* and *Outrage*, also reached #1 on the *New York Times* hardcover bestseller list. No other American true-crime writer has ever had more than one book that achieved this ranking. His latest book, *Reclaiming History: The Assassination of President John F. Kennedy*, has been heralded as "epic" and "a book for the ages." HBO, in association with Tom Hanks' PlayTone Productions, will be producing this as a ten hour mini-series.

Bugliosi has uncommonly attained success in two separate and distinct fields, as an author and a lawyer. His excellence as a trial lawyer is best captured in the judgment of his peers. "Bugliosi is as good a prosecutor as there ever was," Alan Dershowitz says.

F. Lee Bailey calls Bugliosi "the quintessential prosecutor." "There is only one Vince Bugliosi. He's the best," says Robert Tanenbaum, for years the top homicide prosecutor in the Manhattan D.A.'s office. Most telling is the comment by Gerry Spence, who squared off against Bugliosi in a twenty-one-hour televised, scriptless "docu-trial" of Lee Harvey Oswald, in which the original key witnesses to the

Kennedy assassination testified and were cross-examined. After the Dallas jury returned a guilty verdict in Bugliosi's favor, Spence said, "No other lawyer in America could have done what Vince did in this case."

Bugliosi lives with his wife, Gail, in Los Angeles.

Acevedo Aponte, Ramon A., 51, Watertown, N.Y.

 Adams, Brent A. , 40, West View, Pa.

 Adcock, Shane T., 27, Mechanicsville, Va.

 Adkins, Dustin M., 22, Finger, Tenn.

 Aguilar, Andres Jr., 21, Victoria, Tex.

 Aguirre, Nathaniel A., 21, Carrollton, Tex.

 Akers, Spencer C., 35, Traverse City, Mich.

 Alarcon, Ivan V., 23, Jerome, Idaho

 Algrim, Wilson A., 21, Howell, Mich.

 Allcott, Jacob H., 21, Caldwell, Idaho

 Allen, Lonnie C. Jr., 26, Bellevue, Neb.

 Allman, Daniel J. II, 20, Canon, Ga.

 Almazan, David J., 27, Van Nuys, Calif.

 Alonzo, Joshua C., 21, Moore, Tex.

 Anderson, Andy D., 24, Falls Church, Va.

 Anderson, Christopher A., 24, Longmont, Colo.

 Andrews, Harley D., 22, Weimar, Calif.

 Angus, Brett E., 40, St. Paul, Minn.

 Arechaga, Julian M., 23, Oceanside, N.Y.

 Arellano, James J., 19, Cheyenne, Wyo.

 Armijo, Santos R., 22, Phoenix, Ariz.

 Arellano, Carlos, 22, Rosemead, Calif.

 Arvanitis, Nicholas A., 22, Salem, N.H.

 Asbury, Brandon S., 21, Tazewell, Va.

 Babb, Brock A., 40, Evansville, Ind.

 Babcock, Howard E. IV, 33, Houston, Tex.

 Babineau, David J., 25, Springfield, Mass.

 Bachar, Salem, 20, Chula Vista, Calif.

 Baines, Joe L., 19, Newark, N.J.

 Baker, Riley E., 22, Pacific, Mo.

 Balint, Paul Jr., 22, Park, Tex.

  Banaszak, Debra A., 35, Bloomington, Il

 Barbosa, Felipe C., 21, High Point, N.C.

 Barlow, Patrick O., 42, Greensboro, N.C.

 Barnes, Matthew R., 20, West Monroe, La.

 Baroncini, Lester D. Jr., 33, Bakersfield, Calif.

 Barraza, Ricardo, 24, Shafter, Calif.

 Barta, John P., 25, Corpus Christi, Tex.

 Bass, Aram J., 25, Niagara Falls, N.Y.

Bass, David A., 20, Nashville, Tenn

 Beery, Brock A., 30, White House, Tenn.

 Beisel, Jacob W., 21, Lackawaxen, Pa.

 Bennett, Keith A., 32, Holtwood, Pa.

 Bennett, Richard A., 25, Girard, Kan.

 Benson, Darry, 46, Greenville, N.C.

 Benson, Johnathan L., 21, North Branch, Minn.

 Beste, Bradley H., 22, Naperville, Ill.

 Bevington, Allan R., 22, Beaver Falls, P

 Bievre, Mario J., 34, Glendale Heights, Ill.

 Bishop, Jason L., 31, Williamstown, Ky.

 Bixler, Evan A., 21, Racine, Wis.

 Bixler, Stephen R., 20, Suffield, Conn.

 Blair, Jonathan F., 21, Fort Wayne, Ind.

 Blair, Robert E., 22, Ocala, Fla.

 Blakley, Richard A., 34, Plainfield, Ind.

 Blanco, Joseph A., 25, Bloomington, Calif.